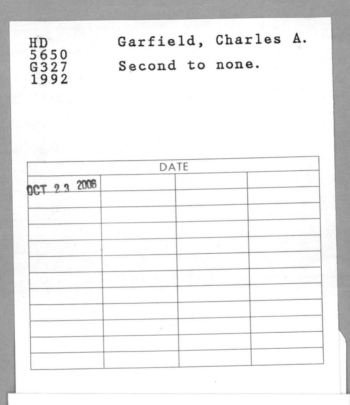

SECOND TO NONE
How Our
Smartest Companies
Put People First

CHARLES GARFIELD

BUSINESS ONE IRWIN
Homewood, Illinois 60430

Sponsoring editor: Jeffrey A. Krames
Project editor: Jane Lightell
Production manager: Ann Cassady
Compositor: Eastern Graphics
Typeface: 11/13 Palatino
Printer: Arcata Graphics/Kingsport

Library of Congress Cataloging-in-Publication Data

Garfield, Charles A.
    Second to none : how our smartest companies put people first /
Charles Garfield.
        p.   cm.
    ISBN 1-55623-360-4
    1. Management—Employee participation.   2. Organizational change.
3. Personnel management.   4. Customer service.   I. Title.
HD5650.G327   1992
658.3—dc20   91–20224

Printed in the United States of America

1 2 3 4 5 6 7 8 9 0   K   8 7 6 5 4 3 2 1

Great ideas, it has been said, come into the world
as gently as doves. Perhaps then, if we listen
attentively, we shall hear, amid the uproar of
empires and nations, a faint flutter of wings,
the gentle stirring of life and hope.

Some will say that this hope lies in a nation;
others, in a man. I believe rather that it is
awakened, revived, nourished by millions of
solitary individuals whose deeds and works every
day negate frontiers and the crudest implications
of history. As a result there shines forth
fleetingly the ever threatened truth that each
and every one of us, on the foundation of our
own sufferings and joys, builds for all.

> — *Albert Camus*
> *from a lecture entitled, "Create Dangerously"*

"The dogmas of the quiet past . . .
. . . are inadequate to the stormy present."

—*Abraham Lincoln*

"Great economic and social forces flow with a tidal sweep
over communities that are only half conscious of that
which is befalling them."

—*John, Viscount Morley*, LIFE OF RICHARD COBDEN

". . . executives cannot count on the presence of markets;
the availability of technologies; the likely actions
of competitors, foreign and domestic; and of legislators
and regulatory bodies; or the actions of employees, of
their families, and, indeed, of their own bodies and minds
to the kinds of actions they are contemplating. . . . In a
destabilized context, you cannot know exactly what your
problems are! . . . [It's] permanent white water."

—*Peter B. Vaill*, MANAGING AS A PERFORMING ART

CONTENTS

10. Learning Tales   353

Conclusion: Giving Voice to the Vision   377

INTRODUCTION

We live and work in a time of transformation, marked by regional conflicts, national struggles for freedom and democracy, global crises, and a dizzying rate of technological and social change. The corporation, no less than any other social organism, is undergoing an extraordinary transformation in attempting to meet the complex challenges of operating in a global market place, in an era of uncertainty.

What happens to organizations and their employees when society, indeed when the entire world transforms itself into something new and unexpected? The past offers guidance, but it cannot adequately inform us of the possibilities or pitfalls that lie ahead.

The challenges the corporation faces today are dramatic, complex, sweeping—and to a large extent unfamiliar. No refinement of isolated business strategies will be adequate to meet them. All of our fascinations of recent years—excellence, product quality, customer service, intrapreneuring, peak performance, and the rest—are but fragmented and, ultimately, futile attempts to deal with the endless stream of changes coming at us with lightning speed. No silver bullets will save us now.

Second to None starts from the premise that the high-speed changes bombarding the modern corporation, while seemingly random and chaotic, are in fact part of a larger pattern whose shape we are just beginning to discern. The more we strive to understand the forces that are giving rise to this new pattern, this "new story" of business, the more likely it is that we will deal with them holistically rather than react to them haphazardly, one by one, in a panic.

Each of the new story exemplars profiled in *Second to None* provides unique insights into the transformation of the modern corporation. Each offers us a "developed alternative" (philosopher of science Thomas Kuhn's phrase), a new way of thinking about or-

ganizations and the men and women who work in them. Each
exemplar serves as a model to help us make sense of the changes
swirling around us so we can thrive in their midst. From their
collective experiences we can begin to piece together the shape of
the new story of business.

The business leaders profiled in these pages vary widely, but
they all share a single characteristic: a heartfelt commitment to
reconciling the welfare of their people with their need for profits.
It is not that they are unconcerned about the bottom line. They
are astute businesspeople whose humanism is pragmatic and
results-oriented. They understand that profits are far more likely
to be generated by employees who are treated with dignity and
respect, in an environment that is a true community and not just a
place to work.

Our interviewees ranged from the most powerful to the recently empowered. Contributions came from the executive suite
and the factory floor. I have learned from men and women at
corporate and association conferences, board meetings and executive retreats, panel discussions and brainstorming sessions.
Each context was an observation post and each group a source of
new and useful perspectives.

Some of our exemplars talked with excitement of their ongoing
attempts to throw off the constraints of the past, of "the way
things are done around here." Others spoke boldly about the new
concepts of work and new organizational structures they had developed from scratch, and their mood was positive and contagious. Overall, their messages were filled with a cautious optimism that more than balanced their inevitable anxiety about the
unknown.

I make no apologies for the optimistic tone of *Second to None*.
For years I have been impatient with the fashionable pessimism of
the business intelligentsia. It bewilders me that any quasi-hopeful
analysis of the state of the modern corporation is viewed in some
quarters as suspect, while pessimistic prognostication is somehow viewed as more trustworthy (and the graver the demeanor of
the speaker, the more trustworthy the analysis is deemed).

In no way do I minimize the formidable challenges the corporation faces. But optimism and pessimism are attitudes we adopt, as
important to our success or failure as the circumstances, however
troubling, in which we find ourselves. They condition our percep-

tion, color our interpretation of data and events, and influence our choice of outcomes for better or worse. In these challenging times, it seems more productive to focus on what we can do to survive and thrive than to engage in endless laments over the fact of our condition.

The reader can get the maximum benefit from the experiences of our exemplars by approaching their stories with the fewest possible preconceptions. Their comments are valuable not only for the facts they contain but, more important, for the song of possibility that rings through their words. Their ultimate value to the reader is not merely in their findings, but also in their ways of looking.

Hundreds of employees in dozens of organizations generously contributed their time and energy in helping to define the shape of the corporation in a radically altered world. *Second to None* is my story of the tales they so kindly shared with me.

Chapter One

Piecing Together the New Story of Business

There is an ancient Hindu parable about three blind men and an elephant. None of the men had encountered an elephant before, and each was asked to touch the animal and describe it to the others. The first exclaimed: "It is much like a tree, round and solid." The second disagreed, saying: "No, it is more like a python, thick and flexible." The third asserted: "You are both wrong. An elephant is like a piece of cord, long and sturdy."

Something akin to what happened in the Hindu parable is happening in the world of business as we move toward the new millennium. Companies across the country and across the sea are struggling to come to grips with a rapidly shrinking world that is changing continually and erratically, a world in which the old rules of doing business are becoming obsolete. The leaders of these companies are being forced to rethink their philosophies and restructure their organizations, to develop entirely new management approaches in order to remain competitive—in many cases, in order to survive. None has developed a full-blown philosophy for success in these turbulent times, but each can describe a partial approach.

Steelcase, Preston Corporation, and Semco S/A are three companies that aptly represent the universal struggle of business to redefine itself in the 1990s. Steelcase, headquartered in Grand Rapids, Michigan, is the world's leading manufacturer of office furniture, with revenues of $1.9 billion in 1990 and 21,000 employees worldwide. Preston Corporation, based in Preston, Maryland, is a heavily unionized trucking company with 6,000 employees and 1990 revenues of $495 million. Semco S/A is located in São Paulo, Brazil. With 800 employees and 1990 revenues totaling $35 million, Semco is Brazil's largest manufacturer of marine and food processing machinery.

1

While widely separated by barriers of geography and industry, each of these companies has been forced by a convergence of internal and external forces to reorder its priorities and institute major changes in order to remain viable in the coming decade. Steelcase completely restructured its operations to strengthen its position in an increasingly competitive world market. Preston transformed its hostile union-management relations in the face of imminent deregulation. The management of Semco S/A radically reordered the business in a last-ditch effort to remain solvent.

I spoke at length with the leaders of these three companies: Will Potter, chairman of Preston Corporation; Frank Merlotti, CEO of Steelcase; and Ricardo Semler, president of Semco S/A. From these interviews and others, it became clear to me that, like the blind men in the parable, each leader has grasped a "piece of the elephant." It also became clear to me that none of them has yet been able to assemble a coherent whole, a new philosophy and model of doing business that will allow companies around the country and around the globe to thrive in an era of uncertainty. Each of these leaders spoke to me about the serious challenges his company is facing—and overcoming—as it moves toward the new millennium:

WILL POTTER, Chairman, Preston Corporation

In 1978, we were concerned about deregulation of the trucking industry. It was on the horizon, and we knew it was going to change everything. Small companies with no unions and less overhead were going to underbid all the established lines.

The relations between Preston management and the Teamsters and Longshoremen's unions were rough in some of the terminals. There were grievances every day. One day, in the summer of 1978, a driver delivering in Detroit stayed in a customer's yard for several hours. He wanted to prove who ran the company. We seriously considered shutting the terminal in Detroit down and never reopening it again.

So we were faced with deregulation and a lot of labor difficulties. We knew, I think, that Preston would never survive unless we did something different.

We said: "Let's assume deregulation is going to happen. What do we do then?" We decided that even though we felt we were doing relatively well, we had to improve service and become even more productive.

I kept saying: "Let's not look at what we've done historically. Let's think about what other models are out there. They may be different from what we've seen in this industry, but that may be the way for the future. The world's going to be a lot different in 10 years.

So we decided to do a survey of some of our employees to see how they felt about the company. We decided on two terminals—the bad one in Detroit and a really good one in York, Pennsylvania. The survey contained over 100 questions, and it was given to everybody in both facilities.

We got the results back, and to our horror they were actually worse in York than those in Detroit. The common complaint was: "Nobody tells me what my job is. Nobody tells me when I do a good job." For every positive comment in that work environment, there were 40 negative comments.

We said: "Gee, now that we recognize the extent of the problem, what do we do?" It was clear that we had a lot of homework to do toward improving the relationships of the people on the job at Preston. And we knew it was key to our survival.

What we needed most was to build trust. When we started, we figured it would take at least two years just to begin to establish it. We often say that people don't give you their trust, they lend it to you. You have to earn it every day.

Part of trust building was giving power to people. Now over 50 of our 87 terminals are opened at 4 or 5 o'clock in the morning by the drivers and dockworkers. There's nobody there from management.

We also established the Performance Improvement Process, which all the associates—we don't use the term *employee* anymore—are accountable for. The process consists of pinpoints, or certain behaviors, measurement, feedback, and the use of consequences— primarily positive reinforcement—to get associates to perform better. And it's working. I said that there were 40 negative comments to every positive one in 1978; today there are about 3.75 positives to one negative.

When we started out making changes, we didn't have any specific philosophy, but we've learned that it's very important for people to internalize the values of the company. They include respect for the individual and concern about the needs of the other associates and the needs of the customers. People want to feel they're part of a team, a family. They want to have freedom on the job. They want to be able to learn, and to contribute.

We discovered that one of the biggest motivators is a real sense of having contributed to the company. It used to be that if someone on a loading dock said: "Hey, I got this great idea," the boss would say: "Great. I'll get back to you." Twenty years might go by. Now if someone says "I got a way we can save time" or "We could make this job easier," they have the ability to try it. In 1990 the 6,000 associates generated a total of 9,209 quality-related suggestions—and 96 percent of them were actually implemented.

Another way we've unlocked a lot of the talent that was present but unused at Preston was to spend a lot more time training people. That includes giving the drivers training in sales. It makes sense, since they're the ones who interact face-to-face with the customer. And it's been an eye-opener for them. We've had examples of where business is down and we've said to the driver: "We'll give you a car to use, or use your own. Put on a coat and tie and start making sales calls. See if you can get more business." When he comes back, he says: "I thought all the salesmen did was go to lunch and play golf. That's hard work!" So the guy doesn't look at himself as only a driver. And he has made another vital link to the organization.

We make sure all our people have access to the information they need to do their jobs. I remember a shop steward saying: "This is amazing. I can go to a terminal manager's office, open the desk drawer, and pull out the profit report. I know exactly how much this terminal is making or losing at any point in time."

All of this has added up to a new way of doing business. Our initial goal of improving relations has been way surpassed. Now we do things like hold truck driving schools in cooperation with the locals, such as Local 89 in Louisville or 641 in New Jersey.

But the real proof of our success is in the way the associates operate every day. You can see the pride in working for Preston; you can feel the commitment as those suggestions roll in. And that shows up in improvements in quality, improvements in productivity, and improvements in service. And the proof is in the fact that in 1980 there were 61 of the largest trucking companies in our category. Only 14 are left today.

I'd say the biggest change we've made is our focus on people. Our motto on every truck is: "Preston People: We Make the Difference." And we all live by it.

FRANK MERLOTTI, President and CEO, Steelcase Inc.

In the early 1980s, Steelcase was doing fine; we were number one in our industry. But as time went on and competition got a little tougher, our market started slowing down. We'd have a management dinner once a year and stand up there and tell our people what a great job they did. It was true; the company was on top—but not far. It seemed to me that it was time to let our people know that nothing is forever. You can point to companies that were leaders before you were, and today they're gone.

We kept saying we were the best. We started thinking that maybe the best time to start making some changes and try something different is when you're on top rather than waiting until you're in trouble and then trying to claw your way back up. We talked about the old wild frog syndrome: If you throw a frog in a pot of boiling water he jumps out; but if you put a frog in a pot of cold water and heat it slowly, he'll sit in there and boil to death. We didn't want to get boiled.

We talked to a lot of our customers and did some surveys. Most of the results were positive, but some people said: "Hey, you guys are good, but in some cases those guys over at Brand X do a little better than you." That was a sobering thought.

We kept talking about that frog getting boiled. We even had one small team which came to be called "Frankie's Froggies."

The message was clear: We can't just keep relying on a small group of people to make all the decisions, to decide what's best for the company. We need to involve everybody. We've got a huge knowledge base here, and we've got to end the idea that the bosses do all the thinking and the workers are just workers. Our industry is about innovation, and we need all the brainpower we can get.

The biggest symbol of the changes at Steelcase is our new Corporate Development Center—the CDC. We started to build the CDC in 1986, when we were just beginning to think about making some major changes. When it opened in 1989, it captured our new thinking. It's a flattened pyramid with lots of open space—over 500,000 square feet of space on seven levels—and it's designed for people to work in multidiscipline teams, everything to encourage people to interface. We put in an escalator so people would talk. We tried to remove anything that got in the way of people communicating, discussing ideas. We wanted to get rid of this top-down thing.

There are no separate departments for different functions anymore. There are areas for teams to work and other spaces where people can do special projects. And the executives are clustered around the center of the building, where everybody has easy access to them.

It's taken several years for this new mode to take hold. But now we're using the team process in other parts of the country, not just at the CDC. We have over 400 teams now.

It's changed our whole environment. People are very caught up in the team concept, in having a say in every aspect of a product. We're seeing new programs develop and hearing people doing strategizing at levels that didn't exist a few years ago. People who had never stood up before a group are now talking with a dozen other employees and using a flip chart. Now we've got everybody thinking. Our delivery cycles have been cut in half, and our inventory has been cut dramatically. Now we go by the theory that you don't make it till you need it.

I think companies that don't free up the creativity in their people are going to be sitting around wondering what happened to their business.

RICARDO SEMLER, President, Semco S/A

When I joined Semco in 1980, the company my father founded, we were on the brink of going out of business. We manufactured hydraulic pumps for ships back then. The company had been run in a very informal way. Contracts were privately made and then forgotten. When I took over, we spent days sorting through old filing cabinets trying to put all the pieces together and figure out where we stood. It became clear that in order to survive we had to diversify our products and get a professional level of management.

I spent two years and came up with about a half-dozen more licensing agreements so we could get into manufacturing food processing equipment in addition to marine equipment. That helped to stabilize the company, so we could focus on internal matters.

When I joined the company, we only had about 100 employees, and now we have more than 1,000. As soon as we started growing, people would say, "Well, now you have to stop. Now you can't organize yourself the way you used to. Things can't be informal in any way. Now you have to check what time people are coming in, you have to set salary structures, you have to develop organization charts, you have to have separate offices."

We started thinking about that and we said, "Is that the only way to operate?" And we decided it was not. It became clear that we wanted something else, something different. We wanted a company that prospered because we could count on the people, not because we controlled every move they made.

It's true that if you have thousands of people in a given place, you cannot possibly treat them individually, as human beings. You have to treat them in a mass way. Everything has to be quantified. You have to control them by building systems and having large policy manuals.

So we said, "What if we do something else? What if we break up a group every time it grows? Our divisions only have about 150 people in them. When they hit 200–250 people we break them up into two units. That helps keep the focus on people rather than numbers.

We knew when we set out to change Semco that there was no comparison between a workforce that dreads coming to work and gives minimum effort and one that is fully involved. To get employees to participate more in the business, we tried a lot of different things. First, we cut down the number of management layers from 11 to 3. When I say three layers, I mean that from the lathe operator or office clerk to the general manager, there is only one layer in between.

Every Monday morning we hold a meeting. The "partner," which is what we call the person known as the "division general manager" in other places, meets with the 12 or 14 people who report to him, who have leadership positions in marketing, production, sales, human resources, and so on. They decide strategy, pricing, salary increases, investments, any kind of operational decisions they need to make.

It's a system that puts a lot of weight on leaders because they can no longer simply protect themselves with symbols of power like closed offices or special parking places. They have to rely exclusively on their ability to generate respect.

It's tough to be a manager in a company that's based on constant change. We are always adding new product lines or entering new joint ventures. And then we have to deal with the fact that Brazil goes through such tremendous upheavals in the economy, which adds to the changes we have to make.

We insist that people rotate leadership positions every two or three years. That reduces departmental conflicts tremendously. Say a guy who was a salesperson exchanges jobs with a guy who was a financial controller who had been pushing the sales guy all the time to sell shorter terms. When they're in each other's shoes, they end up laughing at each other, because the guy who was the financial controller goes out to sell and learns how hard it is to get better terms, and the former sales guy now understands how hard it is to cover payroll when everybody is selling at long terms.

We got rid of all the nit-picking regulations at Semco and just started using common sense. We don't have a dress code, no security room padlocks, no audits of petty cash. All the associates [*Semco, like Preston, adopted the term associate to reflect a partnership relationship with employees*] set their own work hours and set the factory schedules.

Some people were worried that associates would take advantage of flexible hours. So when we started flextime, we decided to hold regular meetings to handle abuses and problems with production. That was years ago, and we haven't held the first meeting yet.

Every Semco division has a separate profit-sharing program. Twice a year, we calculate 23 percent of after-tax profit and give a check to the associates. They meet and decide by majority vote how they want to spend the money. Most of the time, they divide it equally—the floor sweeper gets the same amount as the partner. One division decided to use the money as a fund for housing construction. On the other hand, when they know the division is facing a downturn, they get together and draw up a plan that may include reducing salaries for everyone and taking over some jobs that are usually done by outside vendors, like cooking in the cafeteria and cleaning up. That way they can avoid layoffs.

I don't know if our democratic management style is transferable to other situations. But I think the experiment at Semco points at a way to do things differently. I spend much of my time traveling around the world and finding ways to preserve the Brazilian rain forest, and it makes me realize that we need a sense of preservation. We are doing things at a tremendous speed, things that are all very short-term decisions. Tremendous companies and tremendous efforts are reduced to dust, sometimes in a decade or two or three.

I think the lesson from the rain forest is that it is not worth it for mankind to be constantly tearing away things that were the root of its existence, just to generate short-term results. I think we end up using short-term decision making as a substitute for understanding much more complex issues, which includes our place in the world as a whole.

Probably the greatest challenge we face is in developing roots, letting roots grow, and building things which are going to last for a very long time. It's the capacity to adapt—that's the impression I get of what we are doing at Semco.

I guess the real roots that are growing underneath are the roots of living in a more cooperative, less aggressive environment. That includes having satisfaction in your work and doing something that seems worthwhile. Those roots are getting sturdier. But how that will evolve—which way the branches go, what color the leaves are, how much sun has to be filtered out, how much rain brought in—those are questions that can only be answered day to day, season to season.

———————————

The three men profiled in our opening tales, and the organizations they represent, are in the midst of a grand experiment. It is clear from their stories that these corporate leaders are involved in something deeper than a few incremental reforms. They and their counterparts around the world are turning their organizations inside out, developing a radically new notion of "how things work," rethinking the very concept of the corporation—its purpose, its structure, its operation, and its internal and external relationships.

An upheaval is taking place at every level and in every department of the corporation, as businesses like Steelcase, Preston, and Semco transform themselves to cope with changing economic and social realities. Information technology is shifting the balance of power from the executive suite to the factory floor. Rigid, authoritarian styles of management are being discarded in favor of greater employee participation in decision making. Less hierarchical, more fluid organizational forms are being tried. Unions and management are being transformed from adversaries into allies. Command-and-control managers are becoming coaches and counselors. The central theme of the these changes is partnership.

To many of those caught up in the whirlwind, the changes sweeping the corporation today are bewildering, frightening—and seemingly random. But out of the whirlwind, out of what appear to be isolated, piecemeal attempts by corporations to cope with an unfamiliar and unpredictable world, a coherent pattern is gradually emerging. A whole "elephant" is being pieced together, a new paradigm of business is being born. Defining and refining that new paradigm is the major task of leaders like Frank Merlotti, Ricardo Semler, Will Potter, and others you will meet in this book.

The Greek word *paradigma* means "pattern." In *The Structure of Scientific Revolutions*, Thomas Kuhn defines this word in the sense that we use it, as "a constellation of concepts, values, perceptions, and practices shared by a community which forms a particular vision of reality that is the basis of the way a community organizes itself."

More simply put, a paradigm is a story, or a set of stories, that we invent in order to make sense of the world around us. These stories provide us with a framework by which we create order out of chaos, a practical road map for making our way in the world. They enable us to sort out complexity, to comprehend, evaluate, and categorize the information rapidly and incessantly coming at us from all sides. Most of us are not conscious of the stories by which we operate, but they dictate our behavior nevertheless. In the business sphere, our stories—what we hold to be "true" about the world and its workings—dictate, among many other things, which ethical standards we accept, how we organize the corporation, how we conduct ourselves as managers, how we treat employees, which people we promote, how much of our resources we devote to training, how we treat customers, and how involved we are with the community outside the corporation.

The move toward partnership is gradually transforming the stories that guided us to success in the industrial era, the stories by which we have organized and operated our businesses throughout most of the 20th century. What are those stories?

There are many, but four central stories stand out: the story of the organization as a finely tuned machine; the story of progress as unlimited economic growth; the story of the pyramid as the primary structure of the organization; and the story of the lone pioneer, the rugged individualist, as the hero of the business world.

As we will see, each of these stories was relevant to the time in which it was part of the lore. But they have all outlived their usefulness and are gradually being subsumed by a story that has greater explanatory and functional power in the current economic and social environment. This is what Kuhn termed "a paradigm shift."

Stories come and go over time, as new data render a particular story less useful or completely obsolete. For example, it was useful and appropriate to believe that the earth was flat until the development of astronomy and navigation proved otherwise. Once a story becomes obsolete, it must be replaced by a newer story, with greater explanatory powers, one that incorporates the data that the old story cannot explain.

It is easiest to understand how stories shift by turning to the world of science. For decades, such men as Copernicus, Galileo, and Kepler struggled to formulate a model of astronomy that would accommodate new data not explained by the existing paradigm, which held that the sun revolves around the earth.

Tycho Brahe, a little-known scientist of the 16th century, was the first astronomer to systematically record the movements of the stars across the night sky. Johannes Kepler was a theoretician and a protégé of Brahe's. According to Carl Sagan, "Tycho was the greatest observational genius of the age, and Kepler the greatest theoretician. Each knew that alone he would be unable to achieve a synthesis of an accurate and coherent world system, which they both felt to be imminent."

Finally, after laboring over Brahe's figures, Kepler formulated laws describing how the planets move around the sun. This conclusion was the culmination of more than a century of research by some of the best scientific minds of the time. All at once, the paradigm shifted. A whole new story of how the universe works gained ascendancy.

Business leaders today find themselves in a position similar to that of Brahe, Kepler, and their colleagues, poised at the brink of a major shift in stories. Just as Kepler and his contemporaries were faced with data that didn't fit the current theory of astronomy, businesses are struggling, each with incomplete data, to develop a new story of business that will explain and accommodate the myriad changes taking place in the world. For our old stories no longer make sense.

"It is no wonder, then, that we manage our way to economic decline," says management consultant Stan Davis. "Our managerial models, the 'context' in which we manage, don't suit the 'content' of today's business." That content includes increasing global competition, a frighteningly rapid pace of change, growing instability and unpredictability, an explosion of information, and quantum leaps in technology.

In this radically altered world, the management methods and organizational structures of the past have lost much of their meaning and effectiveness. Yet many of us cling to stories that were developed for a predictable world, one that no longer exists. In fact, rather than abandoning our old ways of conducting business, we are all too often applying them with a renewed vigor.

But pushing our old stories to the limit is not the solution to our predicament, any more than defiantly proclaiming that the world is flat would make it so. As Richard Pascale of the Stanford Graduate School of Business points out, "The trouble is, 99 percent of managerial attention today is devoted to the techniques that squeeze more out of the existing paradigm—and it's killing us. Tools, techniques, and 'how-to' recipes won't do the job without a higher order . . . concept of management."

We witnessed the failure of many such how-to recipes in the 1980s. During that decade, most of our efforts to deal with a changing business landscape were, unfortunately, partial ones. We hopscotched from campaign to campaign—from organizational excellence to quality improvement, to customer service, to employee participation—in attempts to find the silver bullet, the "one right way," the secret that would spark a "management revolution" and make us more competitive in the new global economy.

By and large, those attempts represented, not a paradigm shift, not a fundamentally changed view of the world and the corporation, but a revival of tired old strategies or the application of new strategies in an unchanged environment that rendered them ineffective. Employee participation campaigns were thwarted by rigid hierarchies and threatened managers accustomed to command and control. Quality improvement campaigns were undermined by conflicting emphases on short-term deadlines and maximizing profits. Campaigns to "achieve excellence" fell flat in organizations whose workforces had been systematically demoralized by failed management promises, massive layoffs, and generally poor treatment.

These attempts represented not so much creative responses to change as predictable reactions to it, desperate endeavors to *stave off change*. They failed because they were based on stories that made sense in the industrial era but are ill suited to today's realities.

THE URGE TO MERGE: THE GLOBAL MOVE TOWARD PARTNERSHIP

What we need is not a resurrection of tried but no longer true strategies, or even the sincere application of new strategies within old structures and cultures. What we need is an entirely new context for doing business, a more powerful, more appropriate story to guide us into the next millennium. We see glimpses of just such a new story emerging in the tales of Steelcase, Preston, and Semco.

While the details remain to be explored, one thing is clear: The focus is on cooperation, on group accomplishments that integrate individual efforts.

The new story acknowledges our interdependence and emphasizes the role of partnership in achieving shared goals. In this new story, the corporation is seen, not as an isolated, independent entity, but in its *context* as part of a complex, interconnected world.

The new story recognizes the needs, not just of shareholders, but of the much broader population of "stakeholders" in the business—employees, customers, the community, the environment, and any other constituents on which the firm has an effect and on which it depends for its continued existence. Acknowledging these needs has important implications for how we conduct our business. No longer do we view the corporation as simply a moneymaking instrument. In the new story, we view profits as one goal alongside many, a goal that must be reconciled with a host of competing responsibilities, from employee welfare to environmental imperatives.

To understand the shift toward partnership, it is instructive to examine the global forces that are shaping change at the corporate level. The last decade has witnessed, for good reason, a growing global trend toward collaboration and joint effort. As we proceed toward the millennium, it is becoming increasingly apparent that the major problems of our time cannot be understood, or solved, in isolation. Partnership will be required to deal with the myriad challenges of a world linked by technology, economics, and the threat of environmental disaster.

In this precarious environment, partnership has emerged as a driving force in business at the macro level. By 1992, the countries of Europe will have begun the process of forming a single economic community in order to strengthen their competitive position. Plans for a similar consortium of Pacific nations are already under discussion, and Latin America is expected to initiate yet another venture of this kind in the near future.

The focus on cooperation at the global level is reflected at the micro level of business, as corporations come to grips with a fundamental paradox of business life in a world without borders: To compete, we must cooperate. Not only are businesses joining forces with one another to produce economic synergy, they are also entering into unlikely alliances with former adversaries to address issues of urgent common importance. This explains, for example, the increasingly frequent linkage of corporations with environmentalists, once bitter enemies, in order to avert ecological disaster. Adversarial relationships are giving way to partnerships at every level of the organization, and to partnerships with customers, suppliers, distributors, and other key outsiders as well.

The theme of partnership is clearly visible in the stories of Preston, Steelcase, and Semco. Preston, which was once torn apart by labor-management strife, now makes the statement: "Preston People must be regarded as partners." The company extends that partnership approach to its customers, who play an integral role in defining corporate expectations, measuring corporate improvements, and celebrating corporate achievements.

The commitment of Steelcase to partnership is most readily apparent in the Corporate Development Center, whose physical structure maximizes opportunities for close collaboration among Steelcase employees. In addition, Steelcase has strengthened its linkages outside the corporation, in part by forming the Steelcase Design Partnership, a consortium of design-oriented companies with important ties to selected markets. Both the consortium companies and Steelcase are benefiting from the joint arrangement. The consortium companies have gained access to the deep pockets of Steelcase for product development, and Steelcase has gained access to hard-to-reach customers.

Semco, too, has gone to great lengths to promote close connections with its employees. The company's democratic structure effectively makes all employees true partners in the business, responsible for its major decisions and sharing in its rewards.

THE CHANGING STORIES OF BUSINESS

The machine is a central metaphor for life in the 20th century. Our mechanical view of the world is reflected not only in the way we run our businesses but in the way we conduct our everyday lives. Machines tell us when to wake up, drive us to work, fly us across the country. We communicate more often than not through the intermediary of a machine—a telephone, a television screen, a fax machine. Our language reflects our propensity toward the mechanical—even in our personal relationships. "We think of people's lives as either 'running smoothly' or 'breaking down.' If the latter, then we expect that, in short order, they will be put back together or 'readjusted.'" We value the speed of the machine over the slower rhythms of nature. In our mechanical view of the world, we see nature as simply a resource to fuel the machines of industry and society.

Scientific theories eventually trickle down to our daily lives, including our business lives. So it was no coincidence that the machine model of the corporation evolved in a world dominated by the physics of Isaac Newton, who theorized a machinelike, "clockwork" universe composed of individual particles whose movements could be predicted and controlled.

For most of this century, our economic situation seemed to parallel Newton's theory. The world *was* reasonably predictable. Change came infrequently and relatively slowly. American markets were isolated from the rest of the world, affording domestic companies a large measure of control over them. Mass production was the rule, and in this environment companies could be, and were, run like machines. Work was divided into small, discrete units and parceled out to relatively unskilled laborers—the cogs in the wheel—whose function was not to think, but to perform simple, repetitive tasks.

But the assumptions of classical physics, which provided a theoretical basis for the conduct of our economic life, were largely refuted by Albert Einstein, who postulated that the universe, far from being static and predictable, is in constant flux.

Ironically, the world of business, too, came to resemble Einstein's theory more than Newton's. Market isolation, and the control and predictability it implied, gave way to global competition. A host of foreign competitors emerged in American markets. Remember when Volkswagens and Sony transistor radios became commonplace? "Made in Japan," a phrase that once elicited snickers of derision, came to replace the Good Housekeeping Seal of Approval as the primary indicator of product quality. From autos and appliances to computers and car phones, overseas products commanded a gradually increasing share of U.S. dollars. Now upwards of 80 percent of American products are subject to foreign competition, and the percentage is still climbing.

The very concept of mass markets began to disintegrate in a world that was being subdivided into ever smaller niches. Mass production, which allowed work to be divided into discrete tasks, has given way to mass customization, which puts a premium on speed, flexibility, and responsiveness. Rapid advances in technology added a growing measure of unpredictability to the marketplace.

The Breakdown of the Machine Story

The machine was ill equipped to respond to these dramatic changes. In the midst of upheaval, it became clear that the mechanical model of the corporation, which we upheld for so long as the "right way," was in fact no more than a temporary solution, a product of historical circumstances. Under the very different circumstances that we face today, the limitations of the model have become painfully obvious.

Competing in a world of minimarkets requires innovation at a dizzying rate. Keeping up with fast-paced global competition requires continuous improvement of products and services. Staying ahead requires the transformation of organizational structures so as to liberate human ingenuity for across-the-board innovation.

But the machine, far from liberating human ingenuity, was designed to suppress it. In the machine model of the corporation, employees were viewed as no more than factors of production, reduced to fractions of their potential. The fixed systems of the machine story were never meant to accommodate living, dynamic, complex human beings. In order to make the machinery run, workers had to be systematically dehumanized, transformed into simple automatons.

Alvin Toffler describes the human devastation wrought by this misguided view:

> During years spent working as factory and foundry workers, we put in time on an auto assembly line. Even now, more than a third of a century later, it is impossible to forget what it felt like—especially the harrowing impact of the speedup. Every day, from the moment the bell started our shift, we workers raced to do our repetitive jobs while desperately trying to keep pace with the car bodies moving past us on the clanking, fast-jerking conveyor. The company was forever trying to accelerate the line.
>
> Suppressed rage so filled the plant that every once in a while, for no apparent reason, an eerie wordless wail would issue from the throats of hundreds of workers, swell into a keening,

ear-knifing sound as it was picked up and passed from department to department, then fade away into the clatter and roar of the machines.

This dehumanization of workers was not limited to factories at the height of the industrial era. Author Robert Levering recalls the poor treatment of workers at Preston in 1978, before the company instituted major changes. According to Levering, "One worker said supervisors occasionally referred to workers as 'scum, garbage, idiots, and so forth.'" And a worker at the York terminal reported: "In all my years on this job, I have never known of anyone in management even asking any one of the workers how he felt about how things are done."

Charles Hampden-Turner, a professor at the London Business School, points out, "It's not just wrong to exploit workers, it's stupid. Workers among our major competitors now supervise themselves, maintain quality through their own efforts, solve problems before management ever sees them, and in the case of Matsushita, produce 20,000 usable suggestions per year. The trouble with crushing workers is that you then have to try and make high-quality products with crushed people." There is a tragic irony in the recognition that the workforce we have subjected to decades of maltreatment, the employees whose initiative, drive, and creativity we have systematically stifled in the service of the machine, now hold the key to our world-class competitiveness—even to our very survival. The suppression of human potential is the most serious negative consequence of our devotion to the machine view of the organization.

The Organization as Ecosystem

The philosopher Lewis Mumford wrote, "If you are enamored with a machine, there is something wrong with your love life. If you worship a machine, there is something wrong with your religion." Even if the mechanical model of the corporation and the economy had usefulness in its time, that time has clearly passed. Rather than continue to worship the machine, we must develop a new story that better explains the dynamics of living systems.

Such a story is gradually emerging. Companies like Steelcase, Preston, and Semco are beginning to view the corporation, not in mechanical terms, but, in the words of Alvin Toffler, "as a living creature." Collectively, they are piecing together a new story in which the organization is viewed, not as a static, predictable machine, but as a living, dynamic ecosystem, a community constantly evolving in response to its environment.

Roger Harrison writes:

> Seen from a global viewpoint, the organization exists only as part of a larger reality, supported and nurtured by the larger system on which it depends: the nation, its culture, and many interest groups, the world economic and political system, and the psychical and biological planet itself. . . . From such a viewpoint, organizational purpose is not simply decided by its members, but is in large part "given" by its membership in the larger system. . . .
>
> According to this point of view, it should not be difficult for an organization to survive and thrive, any more than an organ in the healthy body has to work especially hard to survive. When it plays its part, it receives the nourishment it needs.

Viewing the organization as an ecosystem, dependent on a larger ecosystem of which it is a part, puts it into context—something that it lacks when it is viewed as a simple machine, operating independently from its environment. The view of the corporation as an isolated entity is essentially flawed. Nothing that resides in nature can ever be completely independent—including organizations and economies. Every being or entity is part of some larger system of which it is a part and on which its existence depends.

For this reason, living systems cannot be understood by reducing them to parts and analyzing each part individually. For it is not merely the sum of their parts, but also the *interaction* of the parts with one another, and with the external environment, that determines their character.

We are witnessing the gradual emergence of *systems thinking* in the corporation as we move into the 1990s. Systems thinking is a discipline for viewing things as wholes, in their context, rather than as independent objects, operating in isolation. Systems thinking enables corporate managers to view the organization as a dynamic pattern of relationships rather than as a simple collection of people and machinery.

Philosopher Arthur Koestler has coined the term *holon* to describe the subsystems of nature that are both wholes and parts of a greater whole. For example, a tree is a holon, a whole that is dependent on a larger system, the environment, for its existence.

Each holon, says Koestler, has two opposite tendencies: an *integrative* tendency to function as part of the greater whole and a *self-assertive* tendency to preserve its autonomy. In a healthy system—whether biological, social, or economic—a balance is maintained between self-assertion and integration, between opposing needs for autonomy and community. This balance is not static; rather, there is a dynamic interplay between the two opposing tendencies, which together make the entire system flexible and open to change.

Scientist Elisabet Sahtouris expands on Koestler's idea by coining the word *holarchy* to describe a "whole of wholes," the larger environment in which holons are embedded. A corporation is a holarchy in which holons such as teams function. It is also a holon, embedded in the society/holarchy in which it operates. An individual is also a holon. But in the old story of business, he or she often felt like an outsider looking in *at* the organization, rather than as a participant embedded *within* a living system.

Charles Darwin theorized that every natural creature looks out for its own interests by feeding and protecting itself as best it can. But what Darwin (and the social Darwinists who embraced his views) failed to comprehend is that organisms do not evolve in isolation. Rather, as scientists have discovered in recent years, they *coevolve*—they evolve in relation to one another. A butterfly, a tree, a person, a team, a business organization—these are all organisms, and living systems.

The same is true in the economic sphere. As we enter a global era of business, it is becoming increasingly clear that organizations and economies are dependent on one another, and the environment, for their success or failure, for their continued survival or their ultimate demise. We cannot operate in isolation—even if we delude ourselves into believing otherwise.

Once we embrace the new story of the organization as an ecosystem, as both a holarchy composed of holons and as a holon nested within a larger holarchy—society, the global economy, the environment—our behavior, decision making, and the structure of our organizations change profoundly. We no longer view employees as machine parts, cogs in the wheel, or factors of production that are to be used, manipulated, and discarded, but as vital organs, holons whose full commitment and contribution determine the overall health of the corporate organism. We make all corporate decisions with full consideration of their social and environmental impact. And we structure the corporation, not according to a rigid mandate, but so that it will best contribute to the health and optimal functioning of the larger holarchy.

The new view of the organization as an ecosystem changes the definition of corporate ethics. In the old story world of business,* a corporation that created heavy pollution could nevertheless be considered ethical, since business was viewed as separate from the environment. The new story ethics, on the other hand, makes corporations responsible for everyone and everything on which they have an impact—including the earth. No longer separate from the ecological system that supports it, business in the new story takes its rightful place as a partner with the earth, an advocate for the environment rather than its adversary.

REWRITING THE PROGRESS MYTH

Until the recent past, we believed in a story that equated "progress" with the accumulation of material wealth. We believed that pursuing a strategy of continuous economic growth would satisfy all of our basic needs and enable us to advance toward ever higher levels of civilization. The environment was the major resource for accomplishing these aims, and technology was the primary tool.

In this story, anything that promoted economic growth was considered, by definition, a positive. No self-respecting economist entertained the idea that growth could be obstructive, unhealthy, even pathological. The vast majority of economists—whether capitalist or Marxist, Keynesian or monetarist—lacked an ecological perspective. Economics was dissociated from the ecological fabric in which it is embedded. It stood high above the earth, in the airy realm of theoretics.

---

*From now on, I will be using "old story" as an umbrella phrase that designates the entire collection of stories under which we operated in a mass market economy.

The great fallacy inherent in the story of progress, and at the basis of our economic system, is the implicit belief that the earth's capacity, like the frontier of old, is unlimited. So vast were our natural resources for centuries that we were able to sustain this belief. Technology also helped us maintain the delusion that we were divorced from nature, capable of reordering the world according to our whims and desires. The machine held out the promise of conquering even death. We no longer needed to abide by nature's rhythms. Time lost its connection with the natural cycles of birth and death. Our technology allowed us to control time, create energy, and assure ever greater levels of material goods and the happiness we believed they would bring. If "progress" produced a few tragedies along the way, such as Three Mile Island; the poisoning death of thousands in Bhopal, India; and the Exxon Valdez oil spill, this was viewed as an inevitable by-product. It did little to alter our view that technology would ultimately improve our future and solve all our woes.

The serious environmental problems we struggle with today fly in the face of the story of progress. It has become ever more obvious that what environmentalists call a "sustainable society" is not compatible with unchecked growth. At some point, one too many rivers is polluted, one too many forests is destroyed, the globe warms, soil is depleted, and human life itself is threatened with extinction. Resources, we now understand, can indeed be exhausted, and our environment destroyed in the process.

Paradoxically, the "healthy" economy that continued to grow without limit has led to steady ecological decline. It is interesting to note that the words *whole* and *health* come from the same root (the Old English *hal*, as in "hale and hearty"). The unhealthiness of our world today is in large part due to our inability to perceive the world as a whole. The technology that was to lead us to a higher plane of living has also impaired the quality of our lives, creating a physically unhealthy and psychologically stressful environment. Polluted air, irritating noise, traffic congestion, chemical contaminants, radiation hazards, hazardous wastes, poisoned groundwater—these are the legacy of the story of progress, the environmental and social costs that rarely figure into the calculations of economists.

There is an additional negative effect of the progress story. When the goal is solely to increase profits, corporations seek to become as large as possible in order to maximize the wealth of their shareholders. As corporations grow larger, adding layers of bureaucracy or swallowing other corporations whole, they inevitably become more impersonal—"bureaucratic machines." Employees become demoralized and alienated in direct proportion to the growth of these machines.

A New View of Growth

As we move through the 1990s, harsh environmental and social realities, the by-products of our belief in growth without end, are challenging the validity of our old story of progress. The average citizen today has a visceral understanding that something is amiss, a sense that, in the words of writer Joe Harvey, "by the time his kids are his age, Tucson will look like Phoenix, Phoenix like Los Angeles, Los Angeles like Mexico City, Mexico City like two of itself, and so on; that life is not getting any easier, cheaper, or more fun; that the economic 'miracle' is starting to look like an environmental and social disaster."

As a nation and as a global society, we are beginning to question whether more is truly better. Even some Western economists are cautiously challenging the wisdom of unbridled growth as it becomes increasingly difficult to find a correlation between additional wealth and additional well-being.

To replace our traditional view of progress, a new story is emerging. In this story, progress is redefined as health and growth is considered in a broader context that incorporates the needs, not just of shareholders, but of all "stakeholders" who are affected by the organization and on whom the organization relies. In this story, the unlimited economic growth that characterized the old story is regarded, not as healthy, but as cancerous. The focus in the new story is on *sustainable*, rather than *maximal*, growth.

The human quest for maximal growth, which is at the heart of the old story of progress, is in striking contrast to the way in which growth proceeds in the rest of the natural world. Virtually all natural systems grow at an *optimal* rate, rather than growing as fast as possible. In fact, when growth in nature becomes excessive—as it does in cancer—the survival of the system itself is put in jeopardy.

This shift in thinking inherent in the new story of progress will affect the organization's dealings with the environment, its pursuit of technology, and its form. Economic decisions will be made with full consideration of their environmental consequences. The "hard" technologies that produced pollution and toxic waste will be integrated with the "soft" technologies of recycling, redistribution of resources, cooperation, and conflict resolution—"technology with a human face." (Already three companies whose service is "cleaning up the environment" have made it into the Fortune 500—Wellman Industries, Zura Industries, and Safety-Kleen.) And the shape and size of our organizations will be determined with human as well as economic imperatives in mind. This could be characterized as a shift from "getting bigger" to "getting smarter."

This does not necessarily mean that we will no longer have large organizations. As Ricardo Semler has shown, a large company restructured into smaller, "human scale" groupings can be run humanely. It *does* mean that in the new story institutional growth will be balanced by a consideration of human costs.

THE DISAPPEARANCE OF THE CORPORATION AS WE KNOW IT

Throughout most of the 20th century, the corporation was organized as a pyramid structure, with a single leader at the top, successively lower levels of management below, and the bulk of workers at the base. The primary responsibilities, and rewards, of the organization were reserved for the upper levels of the pyramid. The pyramid is still the predominant corporate structure as we move into the 1990s.

The pyramid structure seemed a natural way of organizing in the industrial era. This hierarchical structure paralleled the class structure of the society at large. So accustomed were we to organizing people into vertical hierarchies, in business and society, that we came to view the pyramid as the only "natural" arrangement.

Indeed, the pyramid structure was suited to a mass-production environment in which highly complicated tasks could be divided into discrete, repetitive functions requiring simple skills. It was efficient in an economy in which a handful of people at the top of

the organization could think up major innovations. It offered predictability in the industrial age, when functions changed relatively slowly, and people could be assigned to predetermined
"boxes."

The durability of the pyramid structure depended to a large
extent on controlling information at the top of the organization,
parceling it out as needed to those below. Knowledge is power,
and the structure of an organization is frequently determined by
the distribution of information. During the industrial era, the top
of the organization hoarded information, controlling the masses
below largely by withholding information from them.

Recent advances in information technology have radically altered the power structure of organizations. Personal computers,
linked to or substituted for mainframes, now make it possible to
disseminate information quickly and cheaply to all levels of the
organization. Power in the organization is now to be found at
every keyboard as well as in the executive suite. Even when withholding information wasn't manipulative, it was assumed that
most employees didn't need to see the larger picture in order to
do their jobs.

But technological capability alone has not been sufficient to alter the balance of corporate power. At the same time that advances in computers were making it possible for clerks to act as
mini-CEOs, technology was shrinking and linking the world. Foreign competitors, aided by technology, were gaining ever greater
access to U.S. markets. American firms could still choose to hoard
power and information at the top—but they could no longer expect to be competitive if they did so.

Another factor entered into the equation: Technological advances allowed for mass markets to be divided up into numerous
minimarkets. Mass specialization came to replace mass production as the primary mode of business activity. Success in business
could no longer be achieved by churning out huge quantities of
products for homogeneous markets. Continuous incremental innovation became the new avenue to success, and speed and flexibility became the prerequisites for achieving it.

The Crumbling of the Pyramid

With ongoing innovation as the source of success, the pyramid
structure increasingly lost its purpose and effectiveness. Deci-

sions now had to be made both at the front line and in the executive suite. To keep pace with the competition, information had to move quickly and people had to be given the freedom to function in flexible configurations. In the new story, employees at all levels must be equipped and empowered to make what amount to strategic decisions concerning customers and suppliers on a daily basis. This requires flexibility and the rapid flow of information.

But pyramids are inherently rigid and inflexible, bound in time-consuming bureaucracy. Information needed by frontline managers and employees cannot move quickly through the official channels of the pyramid. The flexibility required to produce ongoing innovation cannot be achieved within the confines of the pyramid. This rigid structure, with its preassigned departments and predetermined functions, cannot easily accommodate a world in which continuous flux is the norm. The pyramid may be adequate for producing known goods and services. It is hopelessly *inadequate* for dealing with today's environment of continuous innovation.

Innovation requires, above all, the liberation of creativity within the organization. But the pyramid, with its emphasis on rules and regulations, divisions and power struggles, stifles creativity and eliminates the spontaneity that gives birth to innovation. Alvin Toffler writes: "Bureaucracies, with all their cubbyholes and channels prespecified, suppress spontaneous discovery and innovation. In contrast, the new systems, by permitting intuitive as well as systematic searching, open the door to precisely the *serendipity needed for innovation.*" (Steelcase's Corporate Development Center was designed specifically to encourage serendipitous encounters.)

The Shape of the New Story Organization

Many business leaders have come to understand that the bulky and cumbersome bureaucracies of the industrial era cannot deal effectively with the rapid changes that are now a fact of economic life. But many have thus far failed to recognize that the root of the problem is not simply the size of the bureaucracy but the fundamental structure of the organization.

Thus we witnessed a massive wave of layoffs in the 1980s. In an attempt to increase the speed, reduce costs, and improve the efficiency of the organization, layer after layer of bureaucracy was slashed and huge cuts were made in middle management.

This collective attempt by corporate America to become "lean and mean" did not achieve the desired results. Despite all the slashing, productivity in the manufacturing sector declined steadily from 1984 to 1988.

The reason for the decline is still unclear to many executives, who argue for even greater cuts in the 1990s. But this argument arises from a fundamental misunderstanding of the underlying problem. Until the structure of the organization is significantly altered, no dramatic improvements in speed or flexibility can be achieved. A pyramid, however small, is still rigid and slow. What is needed is an entirely new arrangement that overcomes the drawbacks of the pyramid structure and accommodates the need for ongoing innovation and full employee participation. A growing number of corporations, including those profiled in our opening tales, are experimenting with new organizational forms.

One approach to restructuring that has been widely publicized and heavily promoted in recent years is to flatten the pyramid. The Steelcase Corporate Development Center, whose physical structure resembles a flattened pyramid (though the company's network of relationships is looser), is perhaps the most striking visual example of this approach.

Another approach is to turn the pyramid upside down. In order to become more customer-responsive, such companies as Nordstrom and Scandanavian Airlines are standing the pyramid on its head, with customers at the top and senior management at the base—supporting middle managers who, in turn, support frontline employees who are serving the customers.

But such attempts to reshape the pyramid as though it were so much Silly Putty are no more than interim steps on the path to structural transformation, which can be achieved only by breaking out of the pyramid structure and experimenting with entirely new forms.

Semco, for example, has a circular structure—three "rings" of management. The counselors, the "highest" level of management, are in the inner ring. They are surrounded by a ring consisting of the partners who head Semco's eight units. Finally, the outer ring encompasses the rest of the company's associates and coordinators (supervisors).

This circular structure allows people to move easily and fluidly within the company. People are also rotated from function to function every two to three years, to maximize flexibility and encourage fresh thinking.

This form evolved as a consequence of adhering to what Ricardo Semler calls Semco's core value: democracy. In Chapter 2, we'll examine in more detail how democratic forms of organization can emerge as organizational pyramids crumble.

It is doubtful that a single model will emerge from the efforts of Semco and other companies to develop more flexible and functional organizational structures. Companies will probably continue to develop structures that suit their unique requirements, and those structures will be dynamic, changing over time in response to changes in the external environment.

Speaking of GE's future, Jack Welch, its CEO, stated: "To move toward a winning culture, we've got to create what we call a 'boundaryless' company. We no longer have the time to climb over barriers between functions like engineering and marketing, or between people—hourly, salaried, management, and the like."

In addition to removing their internal barriers, companies must redraw their external boundaries. Technology has made it possible to link people anywhere in the world, and this can alter traditional work structures dramatically. Through computers, companies are now linking directly to their suppliers, distributors, and customers. Technology has also made it possible for more employees to work at home. Of Semco's 40 or so leaders, 32 work two or three half days at home, according to Ricardo Semler, who adds: "They have a fax, they have a microcomputer, and they can communicate with the office whenever they want and however they want."

Such advances call into question the need for formal organizational structure. Increasingly, organizational chart structure is being replaced by relationships—as reflected in terms such as *partners* (Semco) and *associates* (Preston). In the new story, structure will no longer dictate (or inhibit) strategy. Instead, structure will evolve to meet the organization's needs at any given time.

THE DEATH OF THE LONE PIONEER AND THE BIRTH OF THE FULLY PARTICIPATING PARTNER

The story of the lone pioneer is firmly rooted in American culture. It was the pioneer spirit that conquered the frontier, that built the corporate dynasties of the industrial era, that transformed penniless immigrants into captains of industry.

The essence of the pioneer myth, still deeply ingrained in our collective psyche, is this: With enough luck, spunk, talent, and competitive drive, anybody can make it in America. The rugged, competitive, occasionally ruthless individual who rises to the top of the organization, or starts a new one, is still the archetypal American hero.

Few leaders capture the essence—and the limitations—of the lone pioneer style better than Frank Lorenzo, former head of Texas Air, who used bankruptcy to break the Continental Airlines unions. Business writer Aaron Bernstein compares Lorenzo to Captain Ahab, the protagonist of *Moby Dick*. In this American classic, Captain Ahab, the master of a commercial whaling ship, encounters Moby Dick, a great white whale who roams the sea peacefully until he is hit by Ahab's harpoons. The whale responds by lashing out in self-defense and causes the loss of Ahab's leg. Ahab takes this personally without seeing his role in precipitating the whale's attack. He becomes obsessed with hunting down and killing Moby Dick.

Fueled by his obsession, Ahab pursues his mission with a vengeance, forcing his crew to join him in his irrational quest, putting aside all considerations of human compassion. For example, when the son of another whaler is swept overboard, Ahab refuses to join in the search.

When Ahab's whaling ship finally encounters the great white whale, Ahab goes overboard to his death, tangled in the ropes of the harpoon that was meant to destroy his prey. The whaling ship sinks, and all but one crew member are lost.

Like Captain Ahab, Frank Lorenzo risked everything in his obsessive, single-minded quest to destroy his nemesis, the airline unions. And also like Ahab, he destroyed himself and his "shipmates" in the process. He was absolutely unyielding in his quest. Bernstein points out that in 1986, when Texas Air and Lorenzo bought Eastern, the unions wanted to meet him halfway. The toughest Eastern union boss, Charles Bryan of the Machinists, sent Lorenzo a telegram the day after the sale, pledging to work with him and asking for a meeting. Lorenzo never replied, and shortly thereafter began dismembering Eastern.

Lorenzo sincerely believed that dramatically lowering labor costs was the only road to survival, the "One Right Way." "Frank's a confrontational individual and very much a numbers guy," said John Pincavage, a partner at the New York City–based Transportation Group. "If the numbers say X, be damned with what it means to employees. Just do it."

Lorenzo, not surprisingly, objected to such unflattering portrayals. But those close to Continental remember regular fights between Lorenzo and his managers. And in his nine years at the airline, he went through six presidents.

Frank Lorenzo is a haunting symbol of an old story ethic that admires individualism, however narrow its scope, and refuses to acknowledge interdependence. Lorenzo was unable to see that he was a part of the system he was attacking. By ignoring and destroying the context in which he was operating, he assured his own downfall.

While Frank Lorenzo represents an extreme example of the lone pioneer model, America still applauds more benign versions of the model as business heroes. Lee Iacocca is the most prominent recent example. Inspired by the words of his immigrant father, who told him, "You can be anything you want to be if you want it badly enough and are willing to work for it," Iacocca rose through the ranks to become president of Ford Motor Company and then was fired by Henry Ford II. Presumably as much out of revenge as out of concern for Chrysler, he resurrected Chrysler Corporation—single-handedly, or so the media would have us believe.

Peter Ueberroth, son of a traveling salesman, built a $300 million business empire, organized the 1984 Olympics, and became *Time* magazine's Man of the Year, and commissioner of baseball. Steven Jobs spawned an entire new industry in his garage and became a multimillionaire before his 30th birthday.

Iacocca, Ueberroth, Jobs, and other rugged individualists like them are still the model to which most ambitious Americans aspire. To a large extent, we view these intelligent and resourceful people as the engines of the economy. They stand apart from and above the masses of workers who populate the corporations and depend on the creativity, courage, and benevolence of the pioneer heroes for their livelihoods.

Stories are vehicles for communicating the dominant perception of reality—of "The Way Things Work." The problem with the story of the lone pioneer is not that it is right or wrong, but that it has outlived its usefulness. When *Fortune* surveyed the reputations of 306 major U.S. corporations in early 1991 as to quality of management, companies headed by "rugged individualists" did not fare well. Chrysler, led by Lee Iacocca, came in 269th. American Express, run by James D. Robinson III, was 209th, and Occidental Petroleum, then headed by Armand Hammer, ranked 276th among the 306 companies. Along with the tales of unlimited progress and the pyramid structure of the organization, the myth of the pioneer individualist is a product of historical circumstances. And those circumstances have changed markedly. The most dramatic change is in the nature of innovation. In the heyday of the business pioneer, the height of the industrial era, innovation consisted primarily of grand inventions that could be made in America, sold in America, and hoarded in America. Because the United States was relatively isolated from the rest of the world, there was little threat that other countries would steal or improve on the ideas of the pioneer.

But as Robert Reich so eloquently outlines in *Tales of a New America*, it is no longer possible to hoard "big ideas" at home. Rapid advances in technology and transportation have made it possible for ideas to be turned into products quickly and efficiently, anywhere in the world.

The innovation of today's economy is no longer primarily the big idea, born of the ingenuity of a lone pioneer. Today the bulk of innovation is *collective*, consisting of incremental improvements in products and processes more often than grand inventions.

Furthermore, the primary resource in today's age of information is knowledge, which cannot be hoarded or used up. Success in today's economic environment requires, not the solitary ingenuity and leadership of a lone pioneer, but the innovation, creativity, and full participation of every member of the organization. In this environment, the distinction between pioneers and all others in the organization breaks down. The peak performer of the new story—whether senior manager or junior clerk—is the collaborator, the team player, the partner, the associate.

Redefining the Peak Performer

I first saw peak performance unleashed on a grand scale when I worked as a computer scientist on the *Apollo 11* space project. During a period of heightened commitment, the bumbling NASA bureaucracy was transformed into an efficient network of highly motivated workers who rose to John Kennedy's challenge of sending a man to the moon by the end of the 60s. In 1986, less than two decades later, the same organization that had served as a model of partnership and full participation—the organization that had engineered one of the greatest technological feats of the 20th century—produced the *Challenger* disaster.

The *Challenger* tragedy rocked the nation. For those of us who had worked closely together in the happier days of the space program, the news was particularly devastating. It shook me badly.

The *Challenger* project was the embodiment of everything that *Apollo 11* was not. The work environment I knew during the *Apollo 11* days was an environment of openness and partnership, of putting aside petty differences and pulling together to realize a great and compelling mission. Questioning and experimenting weren't risky in that environment; they were expected.

By the time 1986 rolled around, the space program had long since regressed into a slow, lumbering giant, riddled with red tape and steeped in politics. The NASA environment that produced the *Challenger* tragedy was quite the opposite of the one I knew. From an organization that demanded the best of us, NASA had been reduced to a politicized bureaucracy that ignored, and later reprimanded, the capable engineers who warned that the now-infamous O-rings on the shuttle booster might fail. In the end, lives were lost so that faces could be saved.

The *Challenger* trauma motivated me to rethink my notion of what it takes to generate peak performance. After that tragic moment in 1986, I came to understand more fully the tremendous power of the organizational context to elicit or inhibit peak performance.

I realized that my ongoing research into peak performance, launched during *Apollo 11*, had overemphasized the role of the individual and minimized the *context* in which he or she worked. Where I had acknowledged the influence of environment in my research, it was usually to note how well top performers succeeded in *overcoming* it. Many of the corporate superachievers I profiled in *Peak Performers* produced great accomplishments *in spite of* their organizations. The peak performer was the manager who doubled the productivity of his team by isolating it from the petty politics of the larger organization; the engineer who ignored protocol and produced his designs twice as fast, at half the cost, by building "illegal" alliances outside the corporation; the department head who launched a major project over the objections of her superiors, and got away with it.

Initially, I viewed the ability of these peak performers to rise above the environment as a positive characteristic, a skill that could be taught to others who wanted to perform at their highest levels in any environment, including a hostile one. But *Challenger* jolted me into the realization that there was something slightly pathological about a model of peak performance that required battling the organization in order to achieve.

Furthermore, the failure of *Challenger*, contrasted with the success of *Apollo 11*, reinforced the idea that peak performance need not be limited to a few hardy individuals. It can be achieved—or inhibited—*on a grand scale*, depending on the culture of the organization. I knew that the employees of NASA during the time of *Challenger* were no less competent or qualified than those of us who worked on *Apollo 11*. But the highly political environment at NASA suppressed their talent, and produced an underutilized and risk-averse group of men and women.

I took a closer look at the peak performers of my research. They appeared at first glance to be cut from the mold of the lone pioneer, the rugged individualist, especially since they had to expend a great deal of energy in fighting the organizations that stood in the way of their achievements. Upon closer scrutiny, though, a more complex profile emerged.

Many of the peak performers of my research were managers whose team-building skills enabled them to reach levels of performance that they would not have reached on their own. Far from being radical individualists, they were collaborators who valued relationships and understood the importance of connection. Their tendency toward partnership, though, was frustrated by an organizational context that forced them to forge their own path.

They should not be confused with the lone pioneers of old. The person who bucks the system, without considering the impact on others, is not my peak performer. I have nothing against iconoclastic innovation, but some management theorists admire and praise these Lone Rangers as much for their *noncollaborative* styles as for their achievements, for their ability to win through intimidation rather than collaboration.

Flamboyant individualism may be a popular stereotype, but it is neither necessary nor desirable in the new story world of collective innovation. Macho types and gameplaying corporate politicians alienate more people than they attract to their side—something we can no longer afford in an era that requires the full commitment and participation of *all* employees.

The Fully Participating Partner: The Newest Hero of Business

In an era that demands partnership, a time when our emphasis must shift toward cooperative efforts, the individual paradoxically takes on far greater importance. We can no longer afford to operate companies in which masses of "hired hands" are chronically underutilized while a few "heads" at the top do all the thinking and reap all the rewards. Competing in an era that demands continuous innovation requires us to harness the brainpower of *every* individual in the organization.

The new story requires a radical redefinition of the role of the corporate employee. We can no longer look to the rugged individualist as an effective model for the corporate manager. Neither can we tolerate the organization man, who obediently adheres to rules and regulations imposed from above. The model employee in the new story of business, whether managing or managed, must be the *fully participating partner*.

We can see in the peak performers of my research prototypes for the fully participating partner. While they were the hardiest of old story employees, they provided a hint of the high performance levels that *every employee* can achieve, if supported rather than inhibited by the organization.

The peak performer of the new story will be the fully participating partner, a lifelong learner, well trained and well rewarded. Unlike the peak performer of old, the high achiever in the new story will thrive *because of*, not *in spite of*, the organization. And because of the organization's support, the fully participating partner, the peak performer of the new story, will be the rule rather than the exception.

THE ROLE OF PARADOX IN THE NEW STORY WORLD

A coherent story, one that works in the reality of the 1990s, will have to look at familiar things in an unfamiliar light. We will have to embrace ways of doing business that will seem contradictory by the standards of the old story but are consistent with the new environment of business. Our new story will have to accommodate a variety of paradoxes that are central facts of business life in the 1990s.

We've already introduced the central paradox: In order to compete more effectively, we must cooperate. Another important paradox of the new story is the paradox of individualism: The more we become linked as partners, the more important our role as individuals becomes. In the old story of business in the industrial era, the individual employee was regarded as relatively unimportant, except for the few rugged individualists who made it to the top of the corporate pyramid. In an assembly line world, employees were viewed and used as interchangeable parts. If an employee "broke down," you could exchange him or her for another employee without gumming up the works. The controllers at the top of the organization, those who did the thinking, were regarded as the only "irreplaceable" parts in the corporate machinery.

In the current environment in which incremental innovation is crucial, each individual is a holon, a creative contributor and an essential, interconnected partner in the group. Paradoxically, as the group becomes more important, the individual becomes more important.

Another paradox of the new story is that dealing with an accelerating pace of external change requires fostering greater internal stability. The more unstable and unpredictable the world becomes, the more we require stability in order to deal with it—a stability derived, not from the external situation, but from close internal relationships. Such stability is what enables us to process continual change and proceed innovatively in an environment of increasing complexity.

Paradox plays an integral role in all creative activities. One study of the milestone contributions of 58 scientists and artists, including Einstein, Picasso, and Mozart, found that their creative breakthroughs shared a common pattern: all occurred when "two or more opposites were conceived simultaneously, existing side-by-side—as equally valid, operative, and true."

"In an apparent defiance of logic," the investigation continues, "the creative person consciously embraced antithetical elements and developed these into integrated entities and creations." A similar challenge, of reconciling opposites through paradox, is at the heart of the paradigm shift to the new story of business.

A company that is still operating out of an old story framework will run into trouble when it encounters paradoxes. It is likely to interpret them as the contradictions they were under the old story. It may recognize, for example, that continuous innovation is essential to success (new story thinking) while clinging to the view that success is achieved by being prudent and not tampering with the status quo (old story thinking). As a result, the company might say—and mean—that it is dedicated to continuous innovation (new story thinking) while frowning on the errors that make such innovation possible (old story thinking).

By not understanding that success requires failure, the company, instead of creating a meaningful story, unwittingly creates an impossible contradiction for its workers. They are told to innovate, but they are punished for doing the very things that lead to innovation. They're damned if they do and damned if they don't.

It will not be easy for us to develop a mindset that accommodates paradox. We've been trained since childhood to think in absolute categories: good-bad, either-or, black-white. We are taught to argue positions "for or against"; the middle ground is suspect. Acknowledging the value of both sides of a situation is considered wishy-washy, especially by the pioneer of old.

By adulthood, these intellectual habits are deeply ingrained, and we carry them into our business lives. In the mass-market world, things were viewed as black or white, as either-or. The assumption under the old story was that opposites could not be integrated. In the old story, either the company's interests *or* the interests of the environment prevailed. An employee often won *or* lost by taking risks. Rigid vertical hierarchies dictated that only one *or* the other employee could be promoted.

In the new story, either-or thinking gives way to both/and thinking. The interests of the organization are reconciled with those of the environment. An employee can "win" by taking a risk, even if he "loses"—that is, if an innovation fails—since failure is accepted as necessary for learning and continuous innovation. And rigid vertical hierarchies are replaced by more fluid organizational forms that allow all employees to contribute fully; one employee need not "get ahead" at the expense of another.

To demonstrate how opposites can be integrated, Stan Davis tells the story of a king without heirs who was fond of food and intellect. This king offered to leave his domain to the person who could create the best dish of food that was both hot and cold at the same time. The winner, not stumped by the apparent contradiction, created the hot fudge sundae.

Integrating opposites, even if the result seems paradoxical, is central to the new story of business. We must tolerate both internal order and external chaos. We must cooperate in order to compete. We must replace either-or thinking with both-and thinking. To understand the wisdom of the new story of business in the 1990s, we must learn to hold opposites in our vision, to embrace paradox, to create hot fudge sundaes.

THE BIRTH OF THE NEW STORY FIRM

The individuals and organizations you will meet in this book are among the first to define—and live—the new story of business. A story in which the organization is viewed as a living, dynamic organism, a story in which "progress" means sustainable growth, in which partnership and collaboration subsume competition and rugged individualism, in which traditional structure gives way to new organizational forms. Born into the age of the machine but evolving into the age of the ecosystem, these individuals and organizations may sometimes take tentative or misguided steps. They are living systems in process, and their stories, and the track record of their successes, make it clear that they are headed in a healthy direction.

No one struggling to define the new shape of business dismisses the difficulties. Says Will Potter of Preston Trucking: "We had no idea where we were going when we started. We had no concepts about some of the things that we have a better understanding of today. It's not easy. It's a lot of hard work. People have to understand that it's a team process."

The challenges can be formidable. Steelcase, for example, encountered considerable resistance to the team concept, according to Frank Merlotti, who told me:

> We made it mandatory that everybody in the factories had to be on a team, if they liked it or not. We have a lot of piecework in our factories. A lot of employees out there just said, "I don't want to take an hour to sit with the team. I am losing piecework. Just leave me alone. I just want to come in and do my job, run my machine, and go home." We said, "No, you don't have to take part, but you have to go to the meeting. If you want to sit in the back of the room and sleep, fine." Some did just that. They would come to the meeting and go to the back. They didn't take part. But that only lasted until the team completed a successful project that was publicized.

And Ricardo Semler reports that while employees may embrace the newfound autonomy at Semco, they are also frightened by the new sense of responsibility that accompanies it: "There is no [longer any] system on which you can hang your doubts and your responsibilities. So you are left pretty much on your own, which then gives you an added responsibility. For example, pay situations, vacations, latitude of work time, the ability to work at home, or wherever you want, whenever you want, and setting your own salary—it's an interesting experience, certainly, but it is also a more demanding situation."

Thomas Kuhn points out that some scientists continue to defend theories to which they have become emotionally attached long after the theories have been disproved: "Even when confronted with overwhelming evidence, they will go to their graves with their faith unshaken, stubbornly clinging to the limited but familiar points of view."

Brahe was like that, says Kuhn: "While Brahe amassed facts, he totally missed the point of their meaning. An analyst of great discipline, he clung to the prevailing theory of his day that the planets, sun, and stars circled the earth, which his own observations increasingly showed to be wrong. It took 30 years of accumulated frustration with these inconsistencies before Kepler, Brahe's protégé, reexamined the evidence and confirmed Copernicus's radical view of the universe that the planets orbited the sun." Although Brahe had all of the information that Kepler needed to draw this conclusion, he could not bring himself to draw it.

Many people in business, like Brahe, are so hypnotized by the power of the old story that they are unable or unwilling to see the emerging new story. For the new story of business, while exhilarating, is also threatening. It undermines many of the things on which our businesses are based (including the traditional power structure). It replaces stability and certainty with change and uncertainty. It challenges us, but it does not comfort us.

Some people are simply unable to make the break from the old story to the new. About 25 percent of Preston's managers left after the company radically altered its management philosophy. Among those who left were managers who had been with the company for 10, 15, 20 years or more.

But this is the price of transformation, according to Will Potter: "The guys that we need in the future, the number one competence is people competence, not technical competence. Sure, you lost some technical competence, but you had some people who were incompetent when it came to really communicating, leading, and giving people an environment which they would find to be motivating. That's a big issue."

Despite the defections, Preston's altered philosophy appears to have made a tremendous positive difference for the company. As Robert Levering points out in *The 100 Best Companies to Work for in America*, "The only sure way to judge the quality of a workplace is to talk to employees. I have interviewed a variety of Preston employees in several different locations, . . . [and] I have found no dissenters, only boosters."

Frank Merlotti believes that the move toward teamwork and a flexible organization has also had a positive impact on Steelcase: "I think the employees are thrilled with the building [the Corporate Development Center]. It is a great place to work. I think for the most part they like the process, they like openness. They like the teamwork now that they are doing it. They got rid of some of their fears about 'you guys are saying all this stuff, but do you really mean it?' It has been three years now. I think it is obvious that it [teams] isn't going to die."

Merlotti adds: "Some of the guys that were the most adamant about this all being BS and it will blow over and who needs it are now team leaders. These were some of the same guys that everybody else in the company that knew them would have said, 'These guys are never going to go with it.' But they are running good teams."

Despite the understandable trepidation we feel in the midst of the dramatic changes that are altering the face of business, I sense in my travels through corporate America an underlying excitement. As I speak on the deep transformations that are taking place in business, I sense that they satisfy a widespread secret yearning for fuller participation and deeper partnership.

What shape will the new story of business take as it unfolds over the coming decade? Where may we be headed as we move swiftly toward the next millennium? What potential lies waiting to be unlocked within our organizations and our employees?

I asked Ricardo Semler to predict the future of Semco. What, I asked, would the company look like 10 years from now? Semler responded:

> About three months ago, we took all of our people who are in leadership positions off to a faraway hotel. For three days, we did a program, a whole procedure which in the United States is known as "visioning."
>
> We went through the procedure, saying what we imagined Semco to look like in the year 2010. We chose 2010 because we thought that the year 2000 was already too close for them to really use their imaginations.
>
> What came out of that [exercise] was a very coherent, very cohesive image of a company that is not much larger than the company is today. A company that has less machinery. A company that relies on people, relies on minds, relies on engineering, relies on the software part of the world—not in the computer sense, but in the sense of creating ideas and taking them forward through the organization. A very fluid organiza-

tion, where there is a high quality of life, and relatively little growth, and a low amount of institutional stress. Where people work in a time period that they allot as they want, which includes a lot of people working at home and almost never coming to the company itself. . . . A very fluid organization with products that are changing rapidly and with new businesses constantly being formed.

In the chapters that follow we will strive to articulate the new story of business as it is evolving in organizations throughout the country and around the world. A new story of business that puts people first, and links us in relationship in a living system of organization characterized by democracy, fully participating partnerships, and sustainable growth. In Chapter 2, we will begin to fill in the details of the new story, focusing on its emergence at Steelcase during the past decade.

Chapter Two

Transforming the Corporation from Machine to Living System

Steelcase, introduced in Chapter 1, was organized along old story lines, with a traditional vertical hierarchy, until the mid-1980s, when senior executives realized that the company needed a major restructuring if it was to keep pace in an environment of intense global competition. So Steelcase set out to revamp its product development process, reorganizing into multifunctional teams and investing $111 million in a Corporate Development Center (CDC). This 575,000-square-foot, seven-story glass and granite structure unites design, engineering, and marketing staffs that were previously scattered in several locations. The CDC was established to spur the creation of innovative products and shorten the product development cycle.

Al Lehnerd, vice president of product development, arrived at Steelcase in the spring of 1987, not long after the company had begun the process of transforming itself. He brought with him a strong sense of the organization as a system in which all parts must function interdependently. With this orientation, he served as a catalyst for the transformation of Steelcase.

Lehnerd told me about his involvement in the effort to establish a team-based structure:

My tenure here at Steelcase is just three years as of April 1 [1990]. I started in the R&D, Product Development, and Industrial Design sector and had a conversation with Bob Pew, the chairman of the board, at the first NEOCON meeting—that's a big office meeting we have in Chicago every June. We were standing in the showroom, and he sidled up to me and asked, "Well, you've been here a couple of months. What do you think?" I said, "Well, in 25 words or less, I find that it's a tremendous company, tremendous people, tremendous product line. But as far as the product line is concerned, nobody has any ownership of it. We have a 9000 series furniture line with $600 million in sales, but I have yet to find anyone who gets up every morning thinking about that product line."

Pew asked what I would do about it. I responded, "I would try to structure an organization that is treating every product as though it were a business—where has it been? where do you want to take it? And that doesn't mean just a single function has to do it—not just Product Development, not just Marketing or Sales. You have to get *everybody* to take ownership of products and product development."

So what we decided to do is form what we call Business Management Groups (BMGs) that are focused around product groupings. We said, "These products are yours. You are to treat them as though they were your own business. You grow the business." That requires a core team of someone from Marketing, mostly to take care of the chairing of the BMGs; people from Product Development and Industrial Design, who have a lot to say about how our products look; and from Manufacturing and Accounting.

This is all well and good, but the problem was that we didn't have the facilities to accommodate multidiscipline teams. We had a tech center, where all the engineers and designers sat. We had a manufacturing operation and a marketing group in another building. So the Corporate Development Center, the CDC, which was already in construction, took a new form in that we decided to place people in the CDC around the BMGs rather than by functions. The building was originally designed to have the functions all there, but they would interrelate.

Now when you go to the CDC, you will not find an Industrial Design Department. You will not find a Marketing Department. Nor will you find a Product Engineering Department. What you will find are BMGs. So we actually put these people in immediate proximity of one another. A Marketing fellow is in one office, the Engineering fellow is next, and next is the Industrial Design office. All their people are out in this immediate area adjacent to their offices. They have their own dedicated project rooms, conference rooms, and so forth.

Now what that has done is that all of the members, be they Manufacturing members or Engineering members, can get up and make a presentation about their projects and nobody can tell what function they are from. This has happened because they work together, they think of things as businesses, and they can all articulate the programs, and they do take ownership of the projects.

We provided the physical neighborhoods for them to work in, and we gave them a structure for these cross-functional teams. One of the big problems we had was that all the members wondered how they were going to get measured and wanted to see the organization chart. I said, "This is not an organization chart, this is an *activity chart.*" My personal philosophy was, "Let the task measure you." If the task could talk, how well would it measure you on how you have done it? Forget about your pay raises and your proposals, and let the task be the boss. If the task is good, everyone will know that and will be your cheering section, and you will all get your rewards appropriately.

When the teams first started getting together, they had problems with the functional managers not wanting to release decision making to their subordinates who were representing their function in the group. We had some bad starts. We had people make a decision in a BMG that got reversed by the functional manager. Then they went back to the team [the BMG] and said, "My boss says we can't do it that way, it has to be done this way." The process started to crumble.

Teams must have ownership. It took a little orientation of the functional managers to allow these people in the BMGs to take ownership of their decisions and make business decisions. One example: There was a big conflict in a Business Management Group in which a Marketing person wanted to have 21 different colors in some plastic amenities. The Manufacturing people said, "That is a disaster"; the Engineering people said, "That's too many parts"; the Logistics people said, "We'll never be able to keep inventory," etc. But the Marketing person said they wanted those 21 colors, and tried to bring that decision out of the team. So the team went back to discussion and worked with the Marketing person and ended up with two colors. When the BMGs finally realized they could make decisions without permission from their functional boss, they could take responsibility, they started to get a better grasp on things.

Another obstacle was group facilitation. When you've brought people together who are coming from different points of view, who teaches the group how to facilitate itself? How does it run itself?

So what we did was develop a guidebook, a product development guidebook, a policy guide which took several years to put together. It could have been done faster by saying, "This is how Eastman Kodak does it," "Here's the way Digital does it," etc. But we didn't want to have it be someone else's with our colors on it.

So we put together a team of people, a multidiscipline team, to take these guides and say, "How should we be running this business?" We had a facilitator who made sure that all the stuff got published and adopted. We also developed a glossary of terms that became common language.

For instance, one of the big problems we had was that certain projects didn't have any identity as to where they were in the development cycle. Until people understood where things were in the cycle, they asked the wrong questions at the wrong time. So we developed a concept of project types. We don't know yet whether it will work.

What we have done is broken the work up into Type 0, Type 1, and Type 2. We developed the rules and regulations as to what happened in Type 0 work, which is all the design and planning. Simultaneously, while you're doing the Type 0 work in Engineering, you do Type 0 work in the Marketing group. How will it sell, *will* it sell, what should it look like? And then when Type 0 work was done, it would be moved from Type 0 to Type 1 work, which was implementation—who does what and how often you have to come back for review, budgets, etc. Type 2 work is life-cycle management—keeping the line hot, new colors, model numbers, price lists.

There are tollgates which have to be met by the BMG and the Product Development Committee and the Product Management Committee, depending on where the product is in the development cycle. When a product moved from Type 0 to Type 1, it usually went to the top committee because it meant they were really going to start spending some money and a lot more people were committed to it. So we spent a lot of time defining Type 0 work.

If you don't organize things in these three areas, what you find is that too much effort is being spent on Type 2 work—keeping price lists, colors, etc. You don't have enough people doing Type 0 work, looking over the horizon.

So breaking it up this way, we've got these teams speaking the same language, whether a case goods team, a systems team, or any other team. Everybody now has a language and a guidebook.

Publishing the guidebook was one thing, but then we actually ended up having everyone go through a training course. Every functional team went through a training course of what the policy guide was about and also took training courses on multiteam responsibilities, what you do in teams, and so forth. So the education side of getting this new form up and running was really quite significant. We had to bring in some special programs. We brought in facilitators, and we've introduced some other activities which we felt would help us be competitive.

It's all based on a team approach. It takes a lot of work to do product development in teams. Although it may add six weeks to the development cycle, we've found that doing a better job at the front end actually shortens the development cycle by a year, because we weren't always second-guessing ourselves as we went through the evolutionary steps.

And now, I'd say, after three years of experimentation and getting out the kinks, we have the Corporate Development Center, an organization based on teams, and individuals who are excited and committed. At first it seemed real awkward, but now we don't have to think about it—it's just the way we do business.

———————————

Unlike many companies that embrace the new story of partnership and participation only when a crisis threatens their continued viability, Steelcase wisely began to transform itself while it was functioning effectively. An increase in global and domestic competition provided an impetus to change, but Steelcase was still in a solid leadership position when it began to restructure along new story lines. The foresight of its management is especially noteworthy because the company was firmly rooted in traditions dating back to its founding in the early part of the 20th century.

The reorganization along team lines and the building of the Corporate Development Center are two recent and dramatic examples of Steelcase's transformation to the new story. But before making such visible moves, the company had taken other steps to create a working environment that fostered partnership and encouraged participation. At Steelcase, flexible schedules, a cafeteria-style menu of benefits, and a pay-for-performance system all help build employee loyalty and involvement.

Roughly 400 of the company's 2,000 office workers are on flextime, and 40 of them share 20 jobs. Employees praise the flex schedules, which allow them to juggle the demands of home and work more easily. Steelcase is now starting a job-sharing program for factory workers, by popular demand.

Under the Steelcase benefits plan, workers are allotted "benefit dollars," which they use to select from a menu of choices that include eight medical plans, three dental options, and various forms of disability and life insurance. Employees with benefit dollars left over at year-end can put the money into tax-free accounts to pay for health care or off-site day-care costs, invest it in a retirement fund, or pocket the cash.

Basic pay for the 6,000 factory workers at Steelcase averages $8 to $9 an hour. But they can more than double that hourly wage with piecework and profit sharing bonuses, which bring the average annual income of a factory worker to $35,000.

The flexible policies of Steelcase have boosted morale and resulted in substantial cost savings. Flexible hours have reduced absenteeism. Incentive bonuses ensure payment only for productivity. And some job sharers eventually become full-time employees, reducing the cost of recruiting and training new hires.

One measure of employee satisfaction with the new Steelcase is annual turnover among its 8,000 Grand Rapids-based workers, which stands at just 3 percent. Workers say that the flexible policies go a long way toward explaining their satisfaction and the company's success.

PUTTING PEOPLE FIRST

At the heart of the new story of business are organizations and employees thriving together as fully participating partners. No longer can companies afford to devalue and demoralize their workers, to succeed at the expense of those who help make success possible. Steelcase and other companies are coming face-to-face with a fundamental truth: Today the success of businesses is directly linked to the development, commitment, and full participation of all employees.

In a world in which information, raw materials, and technology move freely across corporate and national borders, the bulk of an organization's assets are interchangeable with those of any other organization. The same basic tools are available to the firm, whether it is in Toledo or in Taiwan. Only one asset holds the power to differentiate it in this environment: a dedicated, productive, innovative workforce.

The challenge for business in the 1990s will be to liberate the creativity and win the full commitment of all employees. The challenge is particularly daunting in light of the fact that American companies are facing a shortage of highly qualified, well-educated workers. Because of this, the competition for the most competent workers will be keen during the next decade. Employees in high demand will increasingly be viewed as volunteers who have many other options and will stay with an organization only as long as it meets their personal and professional needs for responsibility, fulfillment, and equitable rewards. Only organizations that gain the trust, respect, and commitment of these employee/volunteers can hope to keep pace with their competitors.

William Wiggenhorn, a senior vice president of Motorola (whose transformation we'll be exploring in Chapter 7), comments on the challenge of winning the hearts and minds of workers:

I believe that [in the past] many companies viewed individuals as being expendable. If you didn't have the right skill mix, you could always buy it. And I think we are now realizing that, one, you can't always do that because of demographics; there simply aren't going to be enough people with certain skills. Two, loyalty has a value. Just putting people out on the street and hiring new ones is not good for the long haul. If you are asking people to accept change and deal with constant change, then it has to be a longer term commitment.

For decades, business leaders have proclaimed the importance of employees to the success of the firm while suppressing their creativity, reinforcing systems that devalued their efforts, and withholding their just rewards. Until recently, few corporations "walked their talk" about embracing partnership, encouraging participation, or welcoming gender and ethnic diversity. The most serious failure of American business in world-class competition has been the chronic underutilization of the creative talents of the vast majority of its workers. The sad truth is that the majority of American firms, including some lauded as industry leaders, are operating at a fraction of their potential.

THE AWAKENING

Throughout the industrial era, business—especially American business—was lulled into a deep sleep, unconsciously going through the mechanical motions of churning out products for a mass market, secure in its isolation, "rich and confident in a world that was poor and pessimistic," oblivious to the human and environmental consequences of its actions.

While business was sleeping, however, the world outside was changing dramatically. Technology began breaking up mass markets into smaller units and eliminating competitive barriers of geography and company size. Accelerated environmental destruction made the search for ways to avert ecological disaster a global quest. Democracy began to emerge as a social force in unexpected places around the world.

This convergence of forces startled business into a collective, abrupt awakening. After decades of blissful slumber, corporations were shocked back into waking consciousness and compelled to restructure their operations, rethink their philosophies, and redesign their strategies to cope with a vastly different reality.

James F. Moore, president of GEO Partners Research, compares this phenomenon to the periodic upheavals that occur in nature:

> Evolutionary biologists argue that periods of stability are "punctuated" by dramatic events that can overturn ecological orders. A fire, a volcano or a flood can wipe out a large area. Afterward, species compete to become parts of the new ecological order. . . .
>
> Savvy executives see the business parallel. New technologies, deregulation and changes in customer behavior provide the metaphorical equivalent of floods and fires, opening up new competitive landscapes. On such fertile grounds, new or transformed industries can grow.

This captures the experiences of our three exemplars (Preston Trucking, Steelcase, and Semco) as outlined in Chapter 1. Each of these new story leaders responded creatively to chaotic conditions by turning them into fertile ground for future growth and innovation.

A *Fortune* magazine article captured the chaos in stark statistics: "In general, the 1980s proved a far more tumultuous decade than the 1970s. In 1980, roughly three-quarters of the companies that had been on the 500 10 years earlier still remained on the list. But by 1990, nearly *half* those on the 500 in 1980 had fallen off. Mergers were a major reason. Other causes: an occasional change of stripe from manufacturer to service company and poor performance."

In looking at a list of the top 10 discounters in 1962, the year that Kmart, Wal-Mart, and Target started operating, Wal-Mart CEO David Glass noted that *not one of the 10 exists today*. In 1988, Glass rocked the industry by predicting that 50 percent of all retailers would not be around in the year 2000. More recently, Glass commented that his 50 percent prediction may have been an underestimation.

Although several common forces are nudging and sometimes shoving companies toward transformation, each organization begins the process of change for a different reason, often because of a specific threat or challenge to its long-term viability.

Global competition can trigger the transformation. The incursion of Japanese products into the American marketplace spurred Ford Motor, under the leadership of Don Petersen, to adopt a teamwork strategy and radically restructure the way it designs and builds cars.

Deregulation can sound the alarm. Preston Trucking had to forge a partnership between management and union members if it was to survive in a deregulated climate. (Many of its former competitors, which slept through the alarm, disappeared in the newly deregulated environment of the 1980s.)

Environmental threats can provide the impetus for change. Even companies as well grounded in the old story as Du Pont have been compelled to revamp their operations and refocus their businesses in the face of community pressure to address environmental problems.

The impact of social problems on the workplace can pressure companies to transform themselves. When, in the early 1980s, Motorola equipped a factory in Illinois with the latest computer technology, the factory's dedicated workforce suddenly became unproductive. It turned out that most of the workers had trouble reading the instructions for operating the computerized machines. This sparked a revolution within the company that led to the establishment of Motorola University, an unprecedented corporate system of ongoing education.

Sometimes the pressure to change is more subtle, involving nothing more than an uneasy recognition that old ways of doing business no longer work. An industry leader is forced to acknowledge that the smaller competitor it once dismissed has surpassed it in innovation and profits. A company is perplexed when no noticeable improvement results from a traditional strategy for cost cutting, such as laying off frontline workers and paring the ranks of middle management. Or, like Steelcase, an industry leader foresees a threat to its position and takes advance action to avert that threat.

Sometimes the transformation of the organization is forced by employees. With America facing a shortage of workers in the 1990s, qualified employees have the clout to insist on shared responsibility and profits, meaningful work, and environments that allow them to integrate their work lives with their personal lives. Their influence is profoundly changing the nature and structure of the workplace.

THE PROCESS OF TRANSFORMATION

Once a company is awakened, by whatever alarm, it may try old story piecemeal measures or it can begin the process of transformation toward the new story. By "transformation," I mean *fundamental change* that cuts to the core of the company's values, culture, and operating methods. I am not talking here of reforms, of one-shot programs that leave the organization basically unchanged, but of a radically new way of approaching the business. Allan Gilmour, head of Ford's automotive operations and a leading candidate to become its next CEO, admits: "I have been in this business 30 years, and much of what I have learned is wrong." That admission captures the depth of the challenge.

The process of transformation is ongoing, permeates the entire organization, and represents a sharp break with the past. This break is a major difference between transformation and simple reform. While reform is an attempt to go down the same path more efficiently, transformation involves the development or discovery of entirely new paths. A familiar example will demonstrate the difference: When lagging sales and poor productivity threatened a General Motors plant in Fremont, California, with closure in the early 1980s, GM teamed up with arch-rival Toyota rather than close the plant. In a joint venture called NUMMI (New United Motors), the two automakers totally restructured the design of the plant, reorganized workers into teams, and *transformed* the plant into one of GM's most productive facilities, despite the fact that the plant's level of automation was below average for GM.

Transformation involves viewing the organization and its people in an entirely new way, one that opens up possibilities unavailable to those who choose to follow the "tried and true" strategies. Because of this, as the NUMMI example demonstrates, transformation, unlike reform, can produce major leaps in productivity even in situations that would be considered highly unpromising by old story standards.

ELEMENTS OF TRANSFORMATION

A few organizations embrace a new story philosophy from the start. Herman Miller, the furniture manufacturer, was founded on new story ideals of partnership and participation. So was The Body Shop, our featured company in Chapter 9. Far more common, though, are the old story organizations that must undergo a fundamental transformation in order to thrive in a new story world—companies like Motorola, Steelcase, Ford, and GE.

Old story organizations begin the process of transformation by addressing some basic questions:

- What is our company's *vision* of the future? What values guide our actions as we move toward achieving our vision? An organization's values might include loyalty, democracy, integrity, equal opportunity, and so on. What kind of organization do we want to create?

- What is the purpose of our organization? What is our *mission*? Our new story organizations have in common a mission that transcends the goal of making profits. They seek to contribute to society in some unique way, to add their own distinct source of value to the world in which they operate.

When taken together, the answers to these questions determine the direction the organization will take as it begins the process of transformation. Although the specifics differ from organization to organization, certain elements appear to be common to the organization that is moving in the direction of transformation:

- Everyone within the organization shares the same core values.

- The organization balances its legitimate needs for profit and growth with concern for the environment, for human welfare and fulfillment, and for the health and well-being of *all* its stakeholders.

- The organization adopts a fluid, flexible structure that accommodates rapid change and generates continuous innovation.

- A new thinking is evident within the organization, a mindset that eschews the "one right way" of doing things, and that embraces paradox and reconciles opposites.

A final common element, which is so central to the transformation of the organization that we will devote the next chapter to it, is the emergence of the fully participating partner.

Shared Values

If a company hopes to thrive in an era that demands the full participation and partnership of all workers, it must be committed to an explicit set of values. Values are the overarching principles to which an organization and its members dedicate themselves. They are the foundation on which the organization is built, the underlying philosophy that guides such things as how employees are treated; how "outsiders" such as suppliers, customers, and distributors are viewed; whether and how environmental and other societal issues are addressed; how much of the budget is devoted to education and training; how profits are shared; how growth will take place; how quality is defined; and what benefits employees receive. Values shape the corporate culture and determine the environment in which employees will operate and how the organization will interact with outsiders.

Shared values are a critical prerequisite for making the transformation to the new story. Transformation involves periods of tremendous upheaval and the frightening prospect of a journey into the unknown. Undertaking the journey requires a level of trust and commitment that can be achieved only if employees believe in the values of the organization and if the organization believes in the potential of its employees.

A company's value system can often be discerned from its mission statement. In fact, the development of a mission statement is often the first concrete step in an organization's transformation to the new story. The mission statement, if well thought out and sincere, can be an effective tool for aligning all employees around the same vision.

Upon radically restructuring itself, Preston Trucking adopted a mission statement that calls on the company "to provide its cus-

tomers with superior services at a reasonable price through efficient operations and innovative thinking to the ultimate benefit of
its associates and stockholders." The mission statement cuts to
the core of Preston's transformation, focusing on the company's
newfound emphasis on people in partnership and on its need to
provide superior service in a newly deregulated environment.

Sometimes a company's mission is captured in a brief slogan.
IBM has been known for its commitment to providing the "best
customer service in the world." Ford Motor Co.'s mission is
summed up in its motto, "Quality Is Job One."

A mission statement makes concrete a purpose around which
employees can rally—if it incorporates values worthy of their best
efforts. Mission statements are never about bottom-line goals
(though they directly affect the bottom line). Profit is not a value
around which employees are likely to rally. Author Jeff Hallet argues that "profit will not motivate the vast majority of workers.
Return on investment and price-earnings ratios cannot mobilize a
work force. The goal is abstract and has little connection to individual employee efforts. But they will be inspired by values that
can be concretely demonstrated in their everyday work lives."

A fine example of values that can inspire is the Levi Strauss
Aspiration Statement which was developed by employees.

> We all want a company that our people are proud of and com-
> mitted to, where all employees have an opportunity to contrib-
> ute, learn, grow, and advance based on merit, not politics or
> background. We want our people to feel respected, treated
> fairly, listened to, and involved. Above all, we want satisfaction
> from accomplishments and friendships, balanced personal and
> professional lives, and to have fun in our endeavors.
>
> When we describe the kind of L S & Co. we want in the fu-
> ture, what we are talking about is building on the foundation
> we have inherited: affirming the best of our company's tradi-
> tions, closing gaps that may exist between principles and prac-
> tices, and updating some of our values to reflect contemporary
> circumstances.

Of course, a statement, however noble its contents, is no guarantee of transformation. Everyone knows of companies whose
laminated and beautifully printed values, vision, and mission

statements are buried in the desk drawers or wallets of employees, never to be seen again. There may be little connection between the words under plastic and the everyday life of the organization.

Despite the abuses of these concepts, they are potentially powerful guides. When sincere, mission or vision statements can provide a major impetus toward transforming the organization.

For example, a telling sign of a transformed organization is that it strives to live by its stated mission. This does not mean that it adheres to its mission completely and perfectly but that it makes a sincere attempt to do so, and corrects course when it veers away from the values embodied in the mission statement.

Will Potter, chairman of Preston, tells how the company's mission statement translates into the everyday behavior of employees:

> We say in our mission statement that we provide superior service through innovative thinking. Here is an example of both those things: When we are loading these pup trailers, you have to be careful because sometimes they will go down on their nose if you put too much weight in front of them. To prevent this, you have to back a tractor underneath the front of them, and that costs time and money. Somebody came up with this bright idea: "Let's take a couple of those drums you see around at all trucking companies, and we will fill them full of cement. We'll put some slots in there for the forklift blades to go through, and we will put two of those drums on the back of a pup, and that's the counterweight." That suggestion came from one of the associates, and you will see those drums, those weights, in almost every terminal. And when we bring customers in, we'll say, "Hey, Charlie came up with that idea. That's an example of how our associates live the mission."

Sustainable Growth

In Chapter 1, we introduced a new story definition of progress that integrates the quest for growth with concern for the environment and employee well-being. The new story organization understands that true progress is measured in terms of *health*—the health of the environment and the health of all the organization's stakeholders—and not simply in terms of the organization's size, market share, or profits. This shift in focus from growth to health, from quantity to quality, does not mean that size doesn't count in the new story organization. The new story notion of progress does not represent a shift from growth to health but rather an integration of the two.

Old story economists have been oblivious to sustainable growth. They have left out of their equations the health costs of a blind devotion to unlimited growth, which they call "externalities." Externalities are unwanted by-products that are produced by individuals or corporations but paid for by the public at large. Air pollution is an obvious example of an externality, produced by a company's smokestacks or a driver's automobile but paid for by the community as a whole. Another example is the toxic waste from manufacturers of computer components, which seeps into the local groundwater. Less obvious are the "human externalities" produced by corporations that ignore or minimize the needs of employees—the emotional costs of massive layoffs, the demoralization caused by bureaucracy, the anguish of employees who are engaged in uninteresting or meaningless work.

In the old story of business, these externalities were largely ignored. Forests could be felled in the name of progress, with little concern for the effect on the health of the planet. Layoffs and downsizings could be initiated in the name of "efficiency," with little thought of the human costs. Workers' requests to address the needs of their families—illness, day care, the death of a family member—were often ignored.

Until recently, we were able to maintain our collective illusion of "progress" by excluding from our definition and measurements the overwhelming costs of such externalities. But in recent years we have begun to dispel our illusion. In the words of economist Hazel Henderson: "We began to smell the dirty air, hear the rising noise levels, taste the adulterated food and water, see the growing piles of garbage, experience the dislocation of our families and communities, feel the pain of unemployment and meaninglessness, and sense the ungovernability (now confirmed by many studies) of our anonymous cities, giant bureaucracies, corporations, and institutions." In short, we began to grasp that there was something pathological about a "healthy" economy that produced such devastating environmental and human consequences.

Ironically, IBM communicates its passion for unlimited growth by referring to employees who resist moves or other organizational changes as "tree huggers." Language is a powerful conditioner of attitudes and behavior, and IBM's reference is clear. Although the company has become more environmentally aware in recent years, it still chooses to condemn anyone who opposes unlimited growth as "antiprogress," and uses a graphic ecological image to do so.

The new story organization, far from ignoring the externalities of doing business, strives to address and reduce them. The focus is on *sustainable* growth rather than unlimited, unhealthy growth.

The World Commission on the Environment and Development, in a 1987 report, describes the requirements for sustainable growth at the global level and the major structural reform it entails: "The pursuit of sustainability requires major change in international economic relations. . . . Two conditions must be satisfied. . . . The sustainability of ecosystems on which the global economy depends must be guaranteed. And the economic partners must be satisfied that the basis of exchange is equitable; relationships that are unequal and based on dominance of one kind or another are not a sound and durable basis for interdependence."

Lester Brown of the Worldwatch Institute captures the essence of the concept of "sustainability": "A sustainable society is one that satisfies its needs without jeopardizing the prospects of future generations. Inherent in this definition is the responsibility of each generation to ensure that the next one inherits an undiminished natural and economic endowment."

The gradual corporate shift in orientation toward sustainable growth is most obvious in the growing trend toward corporate environmental responsibility. It is now difficult to find a corporation that does not give at least lip service to environmental issues. Household names like Wal-Mart and McDonald's are pitching environmentally friendly products, preaching conservation, and advocating recycling. Companies are being formed for the sole purpose of addressing environmental issues. It is hardly possible to pick up a newspaper or make a trip to the supermarket without becoming aware of the "greening" of the corporation.

Many of the new story companies profiled in this book have incorporated environmental concerns into their operations. Manco, Inc. (highlighted in Chapter 6), a manufacturer of tapes, weather stripping, and mailing supplies, recently formed a "green team" dedicated to recycling, environmentally sound packaging, and other environmental efforts. PC Connection (profiled in Chapter 4), a direct mail supplier of personal computer accessories, was cofounded by an anthropologist (and avid backpacker) who translates environmental concern into company policy. The Body Shop, our featured company in Chapter 9, has gained international recognition as much for its activist involvement in environmental causes as for its line of natural cosmetics.

In addition to supporting the health of the environment, new story organizations are taking pains to avoid or reduce the human externalities that plagued old story organizations. They recognize the need to create internal environments that address employees' needs for community, fulfillment, meaningful work, and balanced lives. They are concerned as much for the physical and emotional health of their employees as for the health of their bottom lines.

We see this human orientation in the new story exemplars profiled in this book. Steelcase, for example, in addition to providing a healthy, creative work environment, offers flextime and job sharing to help its employees integrate family and career. Levi Strauss's commitment to creating a workplace designed for human fulfillment is clear from its Aspiration Statement. America West, currently struggling for survival in the brutally competitive airline industry, still offers its employees round-the-clock care for their children, a share in its stock for virtually all employees, and an environment that allows new people to learn a variety of jobs and take on significant responsibility from the start.

A Concern for Remote Consequences.   Lewis Mumford wrote: "The ecological investigations of Darwin and the later biologists established a concept of the web of life, of that complex interplay of geological formation, climate, soil, plants, animals, protozoa, and bacteria which maintains a harmonious adjustment of species to habitat. To cut down a forest, or to introduce a new species of tree or insect, might be to set in motion a whole chain of remote consequences."

In their health-conscious approach to the environment and to employees, new story organizations show sincere concern for both the short- and long-term ramifications of their actions. By contrast, the failure to consider long-term consequences was a central problem in the old story organization.

Nowhere was this failure more evident than in the wave of cost-cutting that swept through corporate America in the 1980s. In the interest of becoming lean and mean, many corporations severely slashed their workforces, with little concern for the impact of their actions on the health and welfare of their employees.

Wells Fargo Bank provides a typical example. During the 1980s, the banking industry was shaken by deregulation and the variety of new competition it created. Profit margins were squeezed, and many institutions scrambled to find ways of increasing productivity. Laying off workers became a primary strategy for achieving this aim.

Wells Fargo, one of California's leading banks, attempted this quick fix. In 1983, Wells Fargo said its costs were skyrocketing out of control, and it was feeling the pressure of increased competition. Carl Reichardt was brought in as new CEO to return it to profitability. Within four years, Reichardt turned Wells Fargo into the most profitable bank in California. During that period, the price of Wells Fargo stock rose by a factor of five and the bank's rate of return on assets was significantly above the industry norm.

Wells Fargo accomplished the turnaround by also acquiring Crocker Bank in 1986. With the merger, it absorbed an institution of equal size and increased its share of the California market by two thirds, without increasing its full-time paid positions. In other words, there were massive layoffs.

The Crocker merger was a rousing success, according to the numbers, and Reichardt was widely praised in the business press for his pragmatic moves. But if you look behind the numbers, you can read quite a different story.

In November 1987, after massive layoffs in the wake of the Crocker merger, an internal poll of 12,000 Wells Fargo employees showed that nearly half were worried about their jobs, no matter what performance they turned in. In the four years after Reichardt became CEO, basic turnover at Wells Fargo jumped by a third, to 28 percent in 1987. In many departments, those who remained after the restructuring saw their workloads doubled or worse. John McGuinn, a lawyer representing 12 former branch managers who sued the bank after the merger, commented that Wells Fargo was run on the "burnout theory": "They figure they can get five good years before somebody says, 'I can't take it anymore'."

While the cost-cutting efforts have succeeded in padding the Wells Fargo bottom line in the short run, they have also created an environment in which it will be difficult for Wells Fargo to generate the sustained productivity and employee commitment needed to compete in the long run. Overwork is bound to result in declining levels of customer service (and, ultimately, customers). Poor working conditions inevitably lead to loss of employees, especially the highly skilled employees with the greatest number of options. And what sort of commitment can be expected in an organization in which half of the employees are in fear of losing their jobs? How can the company hope to maintain a competitive, innovative culture if it crushes its workers?

High turnover, loss of continuity, and a growing fund of customer ill will are just some of the hidden costs, the remote consequences that are bound to impair Wells Fargo's performance in the long run unless it adopts a partnership style. And Wells Fargo is far from alone. Variations on its story could be found in organizations and industries throughout the country in the last decade.

Safeway is another example. This Oakland, California, based grocery chain fended off a threatened hostile takeover in 1986 with a leveraged buyout. During the process, 63,000 Safeway employees were let go through store sales or layoffs, regardless of seniority or their contribution to the company. Even CEO Peter Magowan, who presided over the layoffs, admitted that many of the people fired at the corporate headquarters were "very good" employees. In a court deposition, Magowan said that the cuts were made in a hurry, so as "to put this whole unpleasant matter behind us as soon as possible."

Both Wells Fargo and Safeway, in their short-term approaches to cost-cutting, may be jeopardizing the long-term health and vitality of their organizations. Both companies boasted improved profits and productivity after major layoffs. But such short-term gains are deceptive. Wells Fargo and Safeway are in industries with tight profit margins, industries in which service will be a major factor in sustaining success in the 1990s.

There are indications that service has suffered since the layoffs at each company—due partly to overburdened workers and partly to morale problems. In the 1990s, Safeway, Wells Fargo, and companies like them will begin to confront the long-term consequences of their shortsighted actions.

But the issue goes far beyond the question of long-term profitability. Even if Wells Fargo and Safeway are financial successes in the long run, the price of that success in human terms will be dear if the companies continue to pursue policies that reduce people to mere cost items on an income statement. We must ask the question—to paraphrase the New Testament—"What does it profit a company if it gains the whole world but loses its soul?"

New story organizations take a more humane approach to layoffs, and one which incorporates a concern for maintaining the overall health of the organization and ensuring its future. In the new story, there will still be workforce reductions. But instead of engaging in indiscriminate downsizing, simply chopping 10 percent across the board, new story organizations focus on "right sizing." They consider the potential consequences of any layoffs, including loss of collective wisdom and disruptions in important relationships that hold the corporate ecosystem together. They often involve employees in the decision process, thus reducing the impact on morale.

In some cases, employees find creative solutions that reconcile the need to reduce costs with the need to maintain jobs—reducing the workweek, carrying out tasks more efficiently, recycling materials, and so on. This maintains or even improves the overall integrity and vitality of the organization, and strengthens the partnership between the organization and its employees. (See the Levi Strauss Learning Tale in Chapter 10.)

For many businesspeople, substituting the word *health* for *growth* in reference to their organization has led to the Aha! of the paradigm shift to the new story. *Health* is a positive state of living systems. *Growth* can have negative implications, as in cancerous growth. New story organizations are finding ways to reconcile growth with health to create *sustainable growth*, a term that is gaining currency in business circles worldwide.

The Shape of the New Story Organization

The Rise of Democracy.   If hierarchy was central to the old story of business, a lack of hierarchy is central to the new story. This shift away from hierarchy does not, despite the fears of many corporate managers, spell the death of order. The opposite of hierarchy is not anarchy. What is emerging in place of the rigid structure of the old story organization are a variety of flexible new forms with a single feature in common: all value and practice more democratic decision making.

Philip Slater and Warren Bennis, writing in the *Harvard Business Review*, argue that democracy is inevitable in environments that must accommodate rapid and endless change. They propose that "democracy in industry is not an idealistic conception but a hard necessity in those areas where change is ever present and creative scientific enterprise must be nourished. For democracy is the only system of organization that is compatible with perpetual change."

Change is certainly "ever present" for all corporations in the 1990s, and "creative scientific enterprise" in the form of continuous innovation is certainly basic to survival. In this environment, corporate democracy is indeed a hard necessity.

Slater and Bennis describe democracy as a system that includes full and free communication, reliance on harmony, the idea that influence is based on knowledge and competence rather than domination, an atmosphere that permits the expression of emotion, and an environment that accepts conflict as inevitable and is willing to cope with it—in short, the central characteristics of the new story organization.

Democracy is essential in organizations that rely on the creativity of all workers to produce continuous innovation. Innovation requires democratic processes: the sharing of information across departments, functions, and organizational levels; team decision making; conflict resolution; and deference to the person with the best idea rather than the most senior title.

Slater and Bennis first made the astute observation that corporate democracy is inevitable in 1964. It has taken nearly three decades for companies to begin restructuring themselves along more democratic lines. For while corporations may have paid lip service to democracy, most of them could avoid it until recently.

Quantum leaps in technology, particularly in microcomputer capabilities, over the past three decades have made the inevitability of corporate democracy clearer now than it was in the 1960s. With a PC linked to a mainframe or minicomputer, employees on the factory floor, in the office, or on a customer call have much of the organization's knowledge at their fingertips. With information more accessible to every employee, the process of democratization is encouraged.

As SAS chairman Jan Carlzon puts it: "An individual without information cannot take responsibility; an individual who is given information cannot help but take responsibility." Without the technology barriers that allowed senior management to control information, responsibility and power cannot be hoarded at the top of the organization.

Alvin Toffler points out: "By definition, both force and wealth are the property of the strong and the rich. It is the truly revolutionary characteristic of knowledge that it can be grasped by the weak and the poor as well. . . . Knowledge is the most democratic source of power."

The new story organizations profiled in these pages clearly recognize the need for democratic structures. Ricardo Semler cites democracy as one of the three values by which Semco S/A is run. The other two—profit distribution and information sharing—are hallmarks of corporate democracy. The reorganization of Steelcase, with its heavy reliance on eliminating barriers and sharing information and profits, is a significant step toward democracy in action.

The Fluid Firm.   Many people are struggling to identify the shape of the new story organization. A variety of new forms are emerging. Whatever their shape, all are loose, *organic* arrangements of people and technology—flexible, adaptive, capable of reconfiguration to meet the requirements of the moment.

Within these fluid structures, employees work in self-managing teams, functioning with great autonomy as long as their work is compatible with the mission, values, and objectives of the organization. Some teams are more or less fixed, working together over long spans of time. Others form spontaneously—across functions and levels, even across organizational boundaries—to solve problems and produce innovations, then disband once they have achieved their goals.

These new story teams frequently elect or rotate leaders, set their own schedules, jointly resolve problems, and set production goals. At Semco, work teams even use a democratic process—simple majority vote—to determine how bonuses will be distributed among team members.

One advantage of these democratic teams is that they waste little time or energy on finding scapegoats for problems, bad decisions, or failed projects. The group takes responsibility; there is no one left to blame. This frees up its collective energies to focus on the more important matters of steadily improving decision making and developing more effective work procedures.

Alvin Toffler refers to the emerging new story corporation as the "flexfirm," a fluid organization that can metamorphose into a variety of different forms to suit its context. A variation on Toffler's flexfirm is the "hollow corporation," which contracts as much work as possible to outsiders. Subcontracting (sometimes dubbed "outsourcing") allows companies to remain lean, flexible, and fast, while securing the best experts available to carry out a particular function. The hollow structure can be a boon to big firms especially, since their size can spawn lethargy and inefficiency.

Many management theorists see the organizational structure of the future as some form of network in which employees who are free to move outward in any direction, across boundaries of function and level, can easily link up with others to accomplish a task. The network structure effectively eliminates the barriers that inhibit involvement and prevent the cross-fertilization of ideas.

That includes barriers between companies. More and more organizations are extending their networks outside the corporate walls, linking up electronically with suppliers, distributors, customers, and others to form a boundaryless organization. Raymond Miles, former dean of the UC-Berkeley Business School, refers to this new way of doing business as the "dynamic network model." In this model, a number of companies, each with a specific competence, join forces; each of these companies is a link in the design-manufacture-distribution chain.

To describe how the network functions, Miles uses the example of a piece of ice hockey equipment that was designed in Scandinavia, engineered in the United States to meet the requirements of the large U.S. and Canadian market, manufactured in Korea, and distributed through a multinational market network with initial distribution from Japan. Instead of one company being responsible for the entire cycle from design to distribution, several companies join forces to create a single product "event."

The operations are linked through "brokers" whose role is to bring people and resources together. The broker's role, says Miles, can be taken by the players who put part or all of the network together. The brokering, connecting, networking role is becoming increasingly important in a rapidly changing environment. Miles observes: "Whether locating materials, putting designers in contact with available plant space, or arranging temporary workforces, the ability to bring people and things together quickly and efficiently (often through computer technology) is a key factor in organizational flexibility."

Network is the term most commonly used by corporate executives and management theorists to describe the shape of the new story organization. But as I pointed out in Chapter 1, we must take care not to fall into the trap of thinking that the new story organization will assume one predictable form. At the heart of the new story is the reality of constant flux; no predictable structure can accommodate continuous change. The same organization may adopt many different forms over time, and different structures may emerge within a single organization. It is more accurate to say that *networking* will be the glue that holds the organization together than to suggest that a *network structure* will be the primary form of organization.

Embracing Diversity.   Jamie Houghton, president of Corning Glass Works, asserts: "Companies simply can't prosper in a diverse and multicultural world unless they reflect that diversity to some degree. It's like the Darwinian idea that diversity in the gene pool creates strengths and survivability in any species. A corporation that successfully draws on the talents and abilities of all of its employees as individuals will be best positioned for success."

In the new story organization, we will see a shift to more encompassing styles of leadership that draw on the talents of women and minorities, and reflect the diversity within the larger society. Because so many new leaders will be drawn from the ranks of minorities, managers in the new story will be in a better position to promote intercultural contacts within the workplace, to encourage the expression and acceptance of diversity, and to help reconcile multiple working styles and opposing points of view.

We cannot yet predict the shape of the new style of leadership, for it is still in its embryonic stages. While more women are gradually appearing in upper management positions, their numbers are still minuscule in relative terms. And minority leadership is even less common in mainstream corporate America. Even Xerox, a recognized leader in promoting workforce diversity, concedes that no one yet knows what changes a diverse leadership will bring. Theodore Payne, a manager in the Xerox corporate affirmative action and equal opportunity department, admits: "We set goals for each group and try to make managers accountable, but we haven't begun to manage differently. It's still white males telling white males how to manage women and minorities."

As Payne's comment implies, old story ways of relating to one another will gradually give way to new, far more egalitarian styles of relating. As more women enter companies that value flexibility and democracy, they will speed the process of transformation.

An Architecture for Learning. The physical space of the new story organization reflects the shift from hierarchy and control to democracy, flexibility, and greater workforce participation. The cubicles of the vertical hierarchy are being replaced by flexible arrangements that accommodate continuous change and facilitate learning and innovation. Structure in the new story resembles the architecture of atoms, held together not by rigid links but by the energy of relationship. Modular furniture is making it possible for workers to regroup easily and quickly into new configurations as the need arises.

The Corporate Development Center at Steelcase is a premier example of the new story approach to designing the organization's physical space. One objective of the CDC design is to foster increased interaction—both spontaneous and planned—among designers, engineers, and others involved in the product development process, and thus to enhance the possibilities for innovation and learning.

To that end, the CDC design centralizes traffic patterns. All employees must come to the central atrium, called the Town Square, when entering or exiting the building. Loftlike floors offer visual access to all levels of the building's interior. Sloped exterior walls visually reinforce the central clustering of employees. The company's own modular furniture systems permit easy reconfiguration of work spaces.

The 14 "think tanks" on the sixth floor of the CDC are another stimulus to innovative thinking. These glass-enclosed offices are specifically designed to limit access to only one person. They are equipped with computers but no telephones. Occupants get an inspirational view of the 80 acres of restored prairie on which the headquarters building stands.

In addition to fostering innovation, the CDC is designed to be a pleasing, inviting work environment. For example, it boasts an outside office of nearly 60,000 square feet on four floors, designed so that on nice Michigan days office workers can conduct their business outdoors.

Manco is another organization that carefully designed its headquarters building outside Cleveland to reflect company values. All of Manco's activities—product development, strategy sessions, customer meetings—are conducted in a large room in the center of the building. This room is the focus of company energy, a "junk room, in a constant state of change and flux," according to CEO Jack Kahl, who adds: "Most companies would get that room out of sight, put it downstairs next to a sample room. I want that room right smack in the center, in the heart of the building, because that's where all the news, all the innovation, and all the creativity happen."

A hallway that Kahl refers to as "Action Alley" connects this central room to the offices of Manco's vice presidents. As for Kahl's office: "They stuck me a little bit to one corner because I'm not supposed to be always in the center of things. I'm close enough to it, but I'm a little bit further away than most."

The End of the One Right Way

Jan Carlzon, CEO of Scandinavian Airlines, reflects: "I didn't learn much at business school. To be frank, I simply learned that if you had a problem, there were only two strategies that could be used to extricate yourself from it—increase revenues or decrease costs." He continues: "I made that apparently simplistic comment in front of a large [Swedish] group recently. One of my former economics professors, to my surprise, happened to be in the audience. He stood up and said, 'Mr. Carlzon, as I suspected, you weren't listening. We didn't provide you with two tools, but only with one—reduce costs.'"

This anecdote nicely illustrates the narrow-mindedness of the old story, which severely restricted the choices of business, sometimes to the point of absurdity. Is it any wonder that businesses find themselves struggling frantically to cope with a complex reality?

A key aspect of the old story was the "one right way" mentality. This mentality still abounds. During the 80s, we were treated to a procession of new remedies for the ills of the corporation. Throughout the decade, the business literature was filled with news of the latest prescription, the magical cure for all our business woes. Strategic planning was "the" solution for a time. Quality was the potion of choice for a while. At one point, customer service was the recommended cure. Massive cost cutting was also a prescribed palliative for much of the 80s.

Each remedy was to be the silver bullet. Each prescription held out the promise of unlocking the secret to success in a chaotic world. In our lemming-like rush to embrace the latest management technique, the "one right way" to become more competitive, *the* formula for thriving in a hostile world of continuous change, we failed to stop and notice that, for the most part, the remedies weren't working.

It was not because the remedies were wrongheaded. Each had its place, its value for the corporation. Applied diligently and monitored over time, *in companies committed to transformation*, all produced effective results. What *was* wrongheaded was the expectation that any single solution could address the complex bundle of challenges facing the corporation today—or that corporations, each facing its unique mix of problems, could all obtain the same results from the same techniques. What was wrongheaded was the notion of the "one right way."

In the new story organization, there is no such thing as the One Right Way. These new story firms have arrived at their successes by very different paths. Furthermore, while they may emphasize one theme in generating their successes—an obsession with quality, a dedication to service, a devotion to employee participation—none has thrived by pursuing only one theme, technique, or strategy.

One of our exemplar companies, America West Airlines, has discovered that even an extraordinary commitment to employee empowerment cannot always provide protection from the vicissitudes of the marketplace. AWA enjoyed seven years of unparalleled success. It was the only air carrier founded after deregulation that survived; more than 100 of its competitors failed. Then, in the summer of 1991, AWA found itself struggling with bankruptcy, due to a combination of increasing oil prices and a general recession.

We are living in a turbulent environment. As Peter Vaill of the George Washington University School of Government and Administration puts it: "We can no longer assume that the basic structure of the context surrounding a situation will hold still long enough to make a planned course of action feasible." This certainly is true of the American West struggle.

Vaill adds that in such a situation of "permanent white water," it is not even possible for a company to know the exact nature of its problems. Furthermore, he points out that "at the same time our culture is rapidly evolving a turbulent new society and collection of organizations, old ways of talking about these new forms hang on and cloud our thinking, depress our energies, and cause us to view with alarm and prepare for the worst."

Reconciling Opposites

As Sigmund Freud observed: "Insight is not equivalent to cure." The transformation from a machine mentality to that of an ecosystem involves reconciling a host of competing demands, values, and viewpoints. Simple either-or choices will not suffice.

In our new story organizations, we see examples of major reconciliations. Preston Trucking survived only because it was able to reconcile the viewpoints of two diametrically opposed groups: union members and management. Steelcase strengthened its competitive position by integrating all of its product development functions. Semco S/A has had to reconcile its need for profit with a wildly fluctuating Brazilian economy.

Charles Hampden-Turner describes how reconciling seemingly incompatible opposites can result in the development of superior products, rich in "value added." He offers the automobile as an example.

We are accustomed to thinking of certain attributes of automobiles as opposites. You have either a high-performance car or an inexpensive one, a sports car or a "safe" one, a high-priced luxury car with custom components or a less costly one with standard features. Hampden-Turner argues that a superior car can be produced by combining these opposites. He describes such a car:

> It would perform outstandingly and yet be priced below other offerings that were not even its equivalent. It could be sporty and dashing, and yet engineered to withstand collisions and protect its occupants, thereby commanding lower insurance premiums. It would represent the finest aspirations of those who designed and produced it and would arouse the enthusiasm of customers. Although highly reliable and fetching a premium price on the used car market, it would be traded in for a newer model because constant innovations and improvements made recent models more attractive. Great economies of scale could be realized through the standardization of components, yet the finished car, thanks to the techniques of flexible manufacturing, could appear in many varieties with customized special features.

The greater the number of reconciliations in the finished product, Hampden-Turner notes, the broader its appeal. (The reconciliation of a host of opposites in Japanese cars is a significant factor in their popularity.) From the example above, we can begin to grasp the power of reconciliation. Whether a reconciliation involves products or people, it can produce quantum leaps in productivity and competitive strength that simply cannot be matched by strategies based on either-or choices.

NUMMI, the GM-Toyota venture described earlier, succeeded by reconciling and integrating the cultures and resources of the American and Japanese automakers. As a result of this reconciliation, the productivity of the NUMMI plant matched and even exceeded the stringent Japanese standards.

Without the reconciliation, this result could not have been achieved. This became clear a decade after NUMMI, when General Motors introduced its Saturn model. Production of the model began in the summer of 1990. More than six months later, the Saturn plant was still operating at just one third of its capacity of more than 1,000 cars a day. Furthermore, sales were slow—fewer than 4,000 Saturns were sold during the first six months that the car was on the market. (By contrast, it took Toyota's new Lexus division just five months to outsell BMW and Mercedes in the U.S. marketplace.)

Saturn failed to produce the expected results because it represented, not a successful integration of new techniques or cultures, but an attempt at reform, an attempt to utilize new story concepts of teamwork within a culture that remained rigidly hierarchical. It inevitably ran into serious problems because there was a contradiction between its stated philosophy of partnership and teamwork and the command-and-control GM culture in which it was embedded.

This became obvious when Saturn recalled 1,210 cars in February 1991 to correct faulty seat-back recliners. Senior management blamed the recall on Saturn's employees and on one of its suppliers. The supplier had failed to notify Saturn of a slight change in the process it was using to build the recliners, and this led to trouble farther down the production line. And according to Saturn senior managers, Saturn employees were at fault for not spotting the defects before the cars left the factory. A second recall in May 1991 involved having to replace over 1,800 cars because of a corrosive coolant in the engine. This was blamed on the supplier, Texaco Refining and Marketing Company.

Conspicuously absent from these public explanations was the responsibility of management. Clearly, Saturn has not been able to reconcile the old story culture of GM with the new story partnership approach needed to make the Saturn experiment a success.

Reconciling "Hard" and "Soft"

Among the key tasks of the new story organization will be integrating the values that were systematically suppressed in the old story. One of the most basic challenges will be the reconciliation of "hard" and "soft."

The old story machine culture overemphasized "hard" values—a focus on facts and figures, quantifiable gains, domination and control. It de-emphasized anything that was considered "soft"—relationships, environmental sensitivity, consensus, balance, a service orientation, and whatever smacked of "fun." Even the word *soft* carried strong negative overtones.

In the old story world, with its either-or approach, hard and soft were thought to be incompatible. You were either "tough-minded," "rational," and goal-oriented, or you were relationship-oriented, cooperative, emotional—and suspect. At best, your human "weaknesses" of compassion and sensitivity were overlooked if you were regarded as a "creative type." At worst, you were dismissed as ineffectual.

The challenge in the new story is to reconcile the hard values associated with the male-dominated culture of the machine with the soft values commonly associated with the feminine perspective. For example, Scandinavian Airlines has to reconcile the hard values of safety and engineering/technical excellence with the soft value of customer service.

I am not suggesting, by the way, that hard values are solely the province of men or that soft values are associated exclusively with women. However, it is not an overstatement to say that the soft values of caring, empathy, and relationship were conspicuously absent from the old story organization—and no one would deny that the old story organization was fashioned by men.

This does not mean that we must now substitute the soft for the hard; "masculine" characteristics will not be absent from the new story organization. Rather, they will be *integrated* with their opposites to form organizations that are healthier, more flexible, and more adaptable.

One reason for the critical importance of "feminine" values in the new story is that reconciliation is central to innovation. Reconciliation requires, above all, close, cooperative relationships among people.

The old story devalued cooperation and close relationships and favored a competitive style. The new story reconciles competition with cooperation. Competition—within and among species, individuals, businesses, and ideas—keeps unhealthy overgrowth at bay and fosters innovation. Cooperation is the glue that holds systems together.

A word of caution: We must not confuse new story attempts at reconciling hard and soft with the old story behavioral approach to integrating the two. "Soft" gained a modicum of respect in the last decade, as old story corporations took a new interest in the potential of employees as "productive assets." This utilitarian view of employees could accommodate the "soft" attributes of caring and concern, on the theory that happy employees would produce more profits. Thus the focus shifted to determining what rewards, benefits, and organizational structures would most effectively motivate people to produce profits. The practitioners of this utilitarian approach were no more committed to putting people first than the old story boss who sincerely viewed his subordinates as mere cogs in the wheel. New story managers, by contrast, truly value cooperation and are sincere in their concern for the welfare of employees.

Reconciling opposing values and viewpoints, by definition, involves managing conflict. To be successful at reconciliation, we must become more comfortable with conflict. Unfortunately, most people are decidedly *uncomfortable* with conflict. This is partly because the old story associated conflict with emotional violence, with domination. In the old story, the outcome of conflict was a winner and a loser.

But conflict is essential to growth. In the natural world, dynamic tension among species promotes evolutionary advances. Disequilibrium is necessary to keep unilateral growth in check.

What the business world requires is not the elimination of conflict but a new view of conflict as a catalyst for the creation of new products or approaches, an impetus to the synthesis of ideas. Conflict among people who view one another as partners rather than adversaries does not result in winners or losers, because the concept of sides has been eliminated.

Reconciling opposites, a central task of the new story participant, can be carried out best in the context of a democratic organization. If we are to resolve conflicts constructively, we must share common values. More than that, we must trust, or at least respect, one another enough to take the considerable risks involved in the new story approach. As Charles Hampden-Turner observes: "You are not going to combine high engine performance with low costs, unless the cost accountants and the performance engineers establish harmony between them."

Reconciling the views of accountants and engineers is an example of embracing the diversity required for success in the new story of business. Ethnic and gender diversity bring more complexity and richness to the workplace. The "One Right Way," based on the perspective of a powerful minority of stakeholders, devolves into "one possible approach" we can try.

STUCK IN THE OLD STORY: REFUSING, REFORMING, AND REVERTING

While many companies will make the transformation to the new story of business, others are likely to remain stuck in the old story. Some will simply refuse to acknowledge the need for transformation. Others will confuse transformation with reform, and attempt to apply new story approaches within fundamentally unchanged organizations. Still others will begin the transformation, only to revert to the old story during a period of crisis.

Refusing the Call

The Moby Dick story in Chapter 1 is a superb parable of the old story leader who refuses to recognize new possibilities. Frank Lorenzo was not alone in following the misguided course of Captain Ahab, stubbornly clinging to a version of reality that had little to do with the real world. Lee Iacocca is another example of a CEO whose success is firmly grounded in the old story now refusing the call to transformation.

Iacocca continues to decry foreign competition and to cry for protectionism, rather than focusing on fundamentally restructuring an ailing Chrysler. There have been attempts within Chrysler to make the transformation, but those attempts were initiated by younger staff members and resisted by Iacocca. In response to pressure, Iacocca did make some changes in the company's management structure and methods, but the changes fell far short of transformation. In late 1987, Chrysler's Youth Committee recommended a Chrysler study of Honda's collegial environment. After conducting the study for a year, the committee recommended that Chrysler emulate Honda's egalitarian style. "The word *teamwork* was used about 5,000 times" in its report, according to Chrysler vice president Tom Denomme.

But Iacocca is no great fan of true teamwork and partnership. He was seemingly oblivious to union complaints when his salary rose to an astronomical $23.6 million in 1986. And he clung tenaciously to his executive perks. The Youth Committee "got carried away" with Honda, he insisted. "They wanted us to eat in the cafeteria and go through the rain in the parking lot like everybody else. We don't go for that."

Time will reveal Chrysler's fate. But it doesn't seem likely that the company will undergo the process of transformation desperately needed to compete among the world's automakers in the 1990s unless Iacocca undergoes a transformation himself, or is replaced by a leader more oriented to the new story. What is true for Chrysler is true for the other old story organizations, in the auto industry and elsewhere. It will be increasingly difficult to maintain a competitive posture in the 1990s by refusing the call to transformation. On the whole, as I pointed out in Chapter 1, our attempts to improve productivity by summarily chopping the workforce have not succeeded. Our only recourse now is to undertake the fundamental change required to make our organizations, not lean and mean, but healthy.

Reforming

There is an important distinction between transformation and reform. Reform is an attempt to preserve the old form; transformation involves developing and discovering new forms. Going from metal coins to paper dollars is a reform in money transactions. Going from paper dollars to credit cards is a transformation.

The decade of the 1980s was filled with examples of reform. Organizations pursued quality, automated the factory, installed just-in-time inventory systems, streamlined bureaucracy, laid off workers—and in many cases failed to generate significant improvements by doing so. While many of these strategies represented sincere, if partial, attempts at transformation, far more were initiated to regain control over the organization, to perpetuate the status quo.

Many organizations that tout the need for transformation in fact do their best to squelch any attempts at true transformative change. This is not surprising. Change is unsettling to human beings; few people—especially people in power—welcome the upheaval and seeming loss of power that accompanies transformation.

Chuck House, a senior manager at Hewlett-Packard who has headed up several pockets of transformation within the company, turning around ailing divisions and successfully launching new products, laments the obstacles faced by those who try to implement fundamental change within HP. "People don't like to sign up for revolutions," he told me. "People with power especially don't like to. That's just not big on their list. They want to perpetuate the existing system as long as they can."

Jim Stryker, whose story we'll be telling in Chapters 4 and 5, led an Ingersoll-Rand team that developed a new power tool in one quarter the usual time. But it was a tough struggle, with the larger organization strongly resisting the process. Stryker says that there were "lots of efforts by the organization to eat the team alive." The project succeeded, and other groups within Ingersoll-Rand have adopted the teamwork strategy that led to the success of the "Strykeforce." Whether Ingersoll-Rand as a whole will make the transformation to the new story remains to be seen.

It is not always easy to differentiate reform from transformation. Sometimes the beginnings of a true transformation look a lot like simple reform. And sometimes reform triggers transformation. A sincere attempt at reform can lead an organization in the direction of the new story. See Chapter 7 for an excellent example. Motorola's strong commitment to its Six Sigma program—originally an attempt at reform—led the company down the path of transformation, prompting management to adopt a new paradigm for viewing its employees.

One sign that reform rather than transformation is at work is the presence of what I call "crazymakers," discrepancies between what management says the company stands for and the reality that employees experience.

Crazymakers are contradictory demands that result from conflicts of values. For example, telling employees to innovate while punishing them for taking risks is a crazymaker. So are stressing the importance of cooperation while rewarding employees for competing with one another, promoting the concept of "investing in people" while cutting the training budget, and preaching partnership while awarding bonuses only to executives.

Like the parent who expresses love of a child while clearly demonstrating resentment, the company that conveys such mixed messages leaves employees bewildered and frustrated. Crazymakers put workers in a double bind: they feel that they're "damned if they do and damned if they don't."

Transformation is not possible in an organization that conveys mixed messages. Shared values are a critical prerequisite for transformation. The presence of crazymakers is a clear sign that an organization is experiencing conflicts of values.

Crazymakers are often the expression of a company in transition, caught between two stories, wanting to implement the new while still clinging fearfully to the old. Once the company is able to realign around new story values, the process of transformation can begin in earnest.

If the presence of crazymakers is a sign of attempted reform, a high level of employee participation—especially in the form of spontaneous innovation—is an indication that a company is moving toward transformation. The more an organization exhibits new story approaches to work (democracy, information sharing, flexibility), the more likely it is that the organization is transforming itself.

Reverting

Some organizations refuse the call to transformation. Others pursue reform strategies. Then there are the organizations that attempt transformative change, with some apparent success, but fall back on old story coping styles when the going gets rough—reinstituting command-and-control strategies, reimposing rigid hierarchies, undermining democratic processes, and restoring a tough-minded, simplistic, either-or approach to managing.

James O'Toole describes how ARCO fell prey to reverting. For years, it had been a premier advocate of new story values. But then came a crisis. O'Toole writes:

> When the price of oil plummeted, ARCO's immediate reaction was to abandon the very characteristics that had led to their distinction. Formerly, ARCO had been statesmanlike leaders of their industry, masters at flexible, long-term planning, gloriously entrepreneurial, and always careful to assess the impact of their activities on host communities. But, almost overnight, the company reverted to the "tough-minded" practices of their least imaginative competitors (and, in so doing, they not only added to the depth of their fall, but may have destroyed corporate morale to the extent that a full recovery is problematic). . . .
> In corporation after corporation the same pattern repeats itself. When times get rough, the guys in the black hats gain credibility because they offer this clear, unambiguous response to any crisis: "Cut out all the gooey malarkey, and get tough!" In the absence of confident leadership, such calls for expedient behavior carry the day because they promise immediate results.

ARCO had been made particularly vulnerable to such expedience because the architect of their old culture, Thorton Bradshaw, had recently left the company (and was off saving RCA when the price of oil collapsed). Fortunately, after taking two steps backwards, ARCO now has a new CEO dedicated to restoring the levels of performance and moral leadership enjoyed under the tutelage of Bradshaw.

Not surprisingly, when anxiety builds in an organization undergoing transformation, there is an increasing temptation to fall back on more familiar old story practices. A downturn in the economy, a decline in stock prices, the rise in short-term costs that results from implementing transformative change are just a few of the variables that can trigger a setback.

O'Toole applauds Motorola for staying true to its vision, no matter what the circumstances:

Motorola plans ahead and is often—but not always—able to utilize reduced workweeks in lieu of morale-destroying layoffs. Most important, when recessions hit Motorola, they respond in a fashion alien to the inhabitants of Silicon Valley: They do *nothing* fundamentally different than in good times. Of course, they respond by making appropriate strategic, tactical, and product changes; but the company's fundamental principles—including employee participation in decision making, sharing of productivity gains, "open and complete argument on controversial issues," honesty, integrity, and the goal of "zero product defects"—are never compromised.

It remains to be seen whether America West Airlines' commitment to fully participating partners is strong enough to see it through its current financial crisis. All of the exemplars profiled in this book will no doubt face periods when their commitment to new story values is tested.

THE COMMITMENT TO CHANGE

The commitment of Motorola's management to transformation is a primary reason why the company is succeeding. Earlier I pointed out that there is no "right way" to go about transformation. Let me add now that technique is the least of the challenges involved.

The essential catalyst for transformation can best be described as an "aha!" experience, the sudden recognition by senior management that the organization is a *living system*, an organism that interacts with other organisms, rather than a *mechanical entity* whose primary function is to generate widgets, or services, or profits to shareholders. While this concept may be easily grasped in a moment of insight, incorporating the new understanding into the everyday life of the corporation is challenging, and by no means instantaneous, as our new story leaders will testify. (To get a better understanding of the "aha!" experience, and the challenges involved in transformation, read any of the stories that begin each chapter.)

The commitment to transformation involves significant risk for employees. Transformation is a difficult process for workers at all levels of the organization. Employees who have spent decades responding to orders are now being asked to think, innovate, and make strategic decisions. Workers accustomed to being commanded from above must now assume a high level of autonomy and responsibility.

By the same token, managers accustomed to giving orders must learn to adapt to a participative environment. Executives who have spent years getting ahead by dominating and controlling others now have to change the very modes of thinking and behavior that made them successful.

Robert Swiggett, retired CEO of the Kollmorgen Corporation, points out that transformation will not be easy: "In moving from the traditional authoritarian, hierarchical organization to a locally controlled organization, the single greatest issue is control. Beyond money, beyond fame, what drives most executives of traditional organizations is power, the desire to be in control. Most would rather give up anything than control."

Transforming an organization is likely to arouse deep-seated fears, to foster short-term confusion, and to generate intense struggles at both the personal and organizational level. Employees of all kinds may experience anxiety or outright panic when confronted with the necessity of adjusting their roles, which, for many, are tied closely to their basic self-concept.

Recall Peter Vaill's reference to business during transformation as a world of "permanent white water." Transformation is indeed like roaring down a wild river, unable to understand and less able to control the turmoil and with no end of the turmoil in sight.

For an organization undertaking the process of transformation, the turmoil gradually becomes the norm; relentless change becomes the accepted context in which the organization operates. As employees learn the skills required to manage change, they become more comfortable with being in continuous flux. At some point, they begin to welcome change, to focus on the growth opportunities that change affords rather than the struggle that it entails.

At Preston Trucking, employees are growing accustomed to an environment that encourages them to incorporate continuous innovation into their jobs. Some Preston employees have been eager for the opportunity to innovate, and reluctant employees are learning from them. Says Will Potter: "There are some people out there who have been yearning for this [the opportunity to innovate]. The ones who have been yearning for it, when they are given the opportunity, they click. The guy who is skeptical, when he sees that his peers are beginning to do this for real, he begins to get interested. And there are always going to be some people who say, 'Hey, this is not for me; I am just doing this, and that's it.' But that's a very small percentage."

For a major corporation, transformation can take many years, and even then, maintaining the culture of transformation is an ongoing challenge. Al Lehnerd says that it took three years for Steelcase to get its major changes accepted as "just the way we do business." And William Wiggenhorn, who spearheaded an effort that is accelerating Motorola's transformation, culminating in the establishment of Motorola University, reflects:

I remember one of the senior vice presidents, who has since retired, told me early on, "Bill, we are all going to try and reject this because it does require major change, and change in an institution of this size is difficult. If you can last four years, we will probably embrace it [Motorola University] and institutionalize it. It will then be very difficult to ever change back to not having training." When I look back, I realize it was about four years before the institution went from fighting us to accepting us and then beginning to capitalize on it.

Leading Transformation: The Role of the CEO

Despite formidable obstacles, transformation not only can happen but *is* happening—even in longtime old story corporations. There is no doubt that it requires time, patience, and, above all, committed leadership. William Wiggenhorn credits former Motorola chairman Bob Galvin with providing the encouragement to keep going when the odds against success seemed overwhelming. Says Wiggenhorn: "In years two and three, we could have easily folded, gone away, and no one would have known the difference. What happened during that time that helped was that Bob Galvin kept giving us the support we needed."

If transformation is to occur, top management must be fully committed to it. This means, among other things, that senior managers must sincerely believe in the ability of workers at all levels to accept responsibility and contribute fully, as partners, in a participatory environment.

At Motorola, commitment to transformation involved a major shift in the thinking of upper management. Wiggenhorn comments:

> Our view of how productive people can really be if they are freed to do it has changed dramatically. I think in the past we have made some very bad assumptions, especially about the employees at the operator level—that they didn't want to work, that you had to drive them, that they wouldn't work past a certain time period, that they didn't have ideals. All those things have blown up in our face during the 80s, and we found out that if you give employees the right environment and the right set of tools, they are as committed as anyone else.

Management in the new story partnership organization is primarily a matter of encouraging others to develop and use their capacities, of empowering them rather than controlling them. In the same way that a gifted teacher draws out the innate capacities of the student, the gifted new story leader helps workers to discover and harness their creative, innovative capacities. Managers in the new story act as facilitators, as catalysts of change.

This new style of leadership is exemplified by Don Petersen, who led the transformation of Ford Motor Company. Petersen believed wholeheartedly in employee participation and sincerely supported the concept of transformation. The highly successful Ford Taurus was evidence of the considerable power of committed leadership to begin transforming an old story organization. Taurus marked the start of Ford's climb to the top of the U.S. auto industry and remains a shining symbol of the company's move toward transformation to the new story.

Contrast Petersen with Lee Iacocca. No doubt, Iacocca played a major role in bringing Chrysler back from the brink of bankruptcy in the 1980s. But, to paraphrase Mark Twain, the news of Chrysler's resurrection was greatly exaggerated. Today the company continues to struggle, in part because its structure never changed. It still has a rigid hierarchy. Its manufacturing and engineering operations have undergone relatively minor changes. It is still fighting with the union. And its future viability remains in doubt.

The contrast between Don Petersen and Lee Iacocca helps explain the difference in the outlooks for Ford and Chrysler. It is true that Ford is struggling at the moment. Ford's U.S. and European market shares are shrinking, and the company is further burdened by an industry-wide slump in auto sales. Nevertheless, Ford's long-term prospects appear to be far brighter than Chrysler's. Ford plans to unveil two dozen new models by 1995. And Executive Vice President Alex Trotman, head of its North American operations, is taking up the banner of teamwork, finding ways to learn from and improve on the cross-functional team process that led to the success of Taurus and Mercury Sable. Ford's newest teams have already succeeded in squeezing a full year out of the development cycle.

How Chrysler and Ford will fare in the coming decade remains to be seen. It is clear, however, that if an organization is to transform itself, in most cases it must have a committed leader at the top who is willing to change, learn, and grow.

Will Potter, chairman of Preston Trucking; Frank Merlotti, CEO of Steelcase; and Ricardo Semler, president of Semco, are three executives, deeply committed to transformation, who "walk their talk" about participation and partnership. As a result, all three of their companies are making the move to the new story.

This is not to say that an enlightened CEO can mandate corporate transformation. However, a CEO committed to transformation can go a long way toward ensuring that it proceeds.

THE EMERGING PATTERN

It is all too easy to focus on the chaos caused by the transformation of the corporation and thus to miss the overall pattern that is emerging from the chaos.

We find a common thread in the companies that are undergoing the process of transformation. For many of them, the process began as a series of seemingly independent initiatives carried out in various parts of the organization. Over time, these initiatives flowed together and became mutually reinforcing. Only in hindsight could the pattern of "systematic change efforts" that led to the transformation be discerned. While the process was taking place, it seemed anything but systematic.

Ford Motor is a good example. Executive Education Director Nancy Badore described the beginnings of Ford's transformation under Don Petersen:

> There was no single node of intelligence at Ford. Top management certainly wasn't on top of all that was going on. In the formative stages, their role was largely one of policy support. What happened instead is that you had a number of change efforts tackling things that were central to the business. These efforts were not coordinated in any way; in fact, there was a kind of jealousy between the various internal change efforts—gossip about whose program was the best "grounded." But we shared two common goals—crisis and a drive for quality. Crisis heightened our "consciousness." "Quality" was a wonderful unifying objective because it tied everyone from the chairman to the hourly workers together. These shared values were so compelling that the false starts weren't fatal. They overcame the politics, sloppy training, and mistakes.

As we move into the 1990s, our corporations can choose to follow the customary path—cutting costs, reducing management layers, competing for scarce employees and resources, adopting any fad that promises to improve productivity, and keeping the organization essentially unchanged.

Or they can take the lessons of our emerging new story organizations to heart and reexamine their relationships with employees, suppliers, customers, and other stakeholders; dismantle their rigid vertical hierarchies; and embrace partnership and participation—in short, begin the process of creating an organization where people are second to none.

New story organizations will emerge with greater frequency in the 1990s and beyond, as business continues to be pummeled by the forces of change.

A critical minority of new story organizations will lead the way and provide lessons, learned through experimentation, for other organizations. We will examine some of these organizations in subsequent chapters. Taken together, their experiences provide a glimpse into the new story as it is evolving both in America and abroad.

Chapter 3, highlighting America West Airlines, explores the new story ideal of the fully participating partner and lays out the steps involved in creating an environment for participation.

Chapter 4, featuring PC Connection, examines the process of innovation central to the new story.

Chapter 5 focuses on the challenges of building a team-based organization. Semco S/A is the featured organization.

Chapter 6 shows how involving the customer as "one of us" is central to the firm of the new story. Manco, Inc. provides the lessons.

Chapter 7, focusing on Motorola, looks at the learning organization and how it transforms hiring, training, rewarding, and career development.

Chapter 8, which highlights Digital Equipment Corporation, explores diversity in the workforce, offering a variety of perspectives from those who deal with the challenges of diversity every day.

Chapter 9, featuring The Body Shop, looks at the organization in its larger context, focusing on environmental and social issues.

Chapter 10 consists of Learning Tales that provide additional guides for organizations searching for their own path to transformation.

The prospect of embracing the new story of participation and partnership is exhilarating and liberating, but it is also frightening—even for the growing number of managers who recognize the necessity of transformation. Most people prefer a dangerous or destructive *known* to a benign or even beneficial *unknown*.

Steelcase CEO Frank Merlotti reflects on the internal struggle of many corporate leaders to begin the process of transformation: "When you really stop to think about it, what is there really to be afraid of? You still have managers. You are still running the company. You still say no to things. You aren't going to let people do stupid stuff. Why isn't it better to have 100 people in the department all looking for somewhere to improve your company than have two?"

While moving toward the new story may seem risky, *not* moving is riskier still. The simple fact is that sustained success in the new story world of the 1990s and beyond will not be possible without the full participation and partnership of employees working in a democratic environment.

Chapter Three

The New Peak Performer: The Fully Participating Partner

In 1989, the U.S. Department of Transportation designated America West Airlines a "major" carrier after it achieved $1 billion in annual revenues. That ranked the fledgling Phoenix-based company, founded just six years earlier, among the nation's largest airlines.

Founder, chairman, and CEO Ed Beauvais was an airline economist before he launched America West with three planes that made nine flights a day to five southwestern cities. Until recently, AWA's growth was dramatic. In early 1991, it had 14,000 employees and 115 planes flying 330 times a day to 55 cities across the country and carrying more than a million passengers each month. Then the airline was overcome by the "permanent whitewater" conditions of the global marketplace. In the wake of a general recession, terrorist threats, and the escalation of oil prices due to the Persian Gulf war, AWA filed for Chapter 11 bankruptcy protection in the summer of 1991.

Mike Conway left Continental Airlines in 1983 to help Ed Beauvais form AWA; Conway became its president. He talked to me in the summer of 1990 about his commitment to the founding values of the company and the challenges of succeeding in the deregulated airline industry:

There have been 104 airlines formed since 1978. Some got to fly and others didn't, but of the 104, there are only 2 left—ourselves and Midway.*

---

*In March 1991, Midway filed for Chapter 11 bankruptcy protection. In June of the same year, AWA sought similar protection.

And that doesn't include all the ones that were around *before* 1978 that are not around any more. How come we have made it and so many others have failed?

The people who are just interested in the financial side would say that we are the most fuel-efficient airline in the United States. That was a conscious strategy; we have an all-Boeing, modern, fuel-efficient fleet.

But there's much more to it. Our people have a productivity rate that is higher than anybody in the industry. And the reason is, we spend an inordinate amount of time screening people on the front end.

The people who are the fully cross-utilized CSRs [customer service representatives] are the ones who are trained at all the airport jobs. We are the only airline that does that. We maybe pick 1 out of every 70 people that we interview for that job.

We spend the money and time to train them—18 weeks versus 3 to 4 weeks at any other airline, for any one function, such as a flight attendant or a reservation agent. We do that to give the employees a better job, to give them more job variety. It's more challenging, and for those who are interested in upward mobility, it exposes them to about 16 different areas of the company versus the one they would be exposed to if we specialized.

It is not unusual for the America West flight crew—if they are running a little bit late and we need to make up time and turn the aircraft at one of the spokes—for a pilot to go back into the cabin and start helping clean up the airplane. Or for pilots, after they do their check of the airplane, to help unload baggage. It's not unusual for one of our CSRs who might be working as a flight attendant, if the airplane gets to a field station and things are backed up, to jump behind the boarding gate counter and start processing people. They are all trained to do that; it is really a team concept. This is an everyday occurrence.

We are a company that is in one of the most heavily unionized industries, and we don't have one union. Not even Delta can say that; they've had a pilots' union for a good number of years. And we are not antiunion at all; we are just propeople. We think that we offer people a better choice than paying their after-tax money to somebody who is adversarial, by definition, with the management. God knows, the unions try. We've had formal votes, and they have gone down to defeat by significant margins.

We are not the highest payers in the industry, and we are not the lowest, but we are closer to the top than we are to the bottom. And for what we are paying, we get more productivity.

One reason is that virtually all of our employees are stockholders in the company. It's a condition of employment in all but a couple of places where they have state laws that prohibit mandatory stock participation—California is one of them—but most of those employees are taking the program on a voluntary basis. So you've got people in the company controlling 30 percent of the voting interest. It's a piece of the rock that they have.

In addition to that, we have a very simple but significant profit sharing program where 15 percent of the company's pretax profits on an annual basis are distributed back, *in cash*, to the workforce. It's not something you vest in a hundred years from now; they get immediate, tangible benefits and feedback in the form of cash. What finer feedback is there?

So you've got the ownership, you've got the profit sharing, but there is something else that we have that no other public company in the United States, to my knowledge, has: We are the only company that annually gives all employees incentive stock options that they vest in at the rate of 20 percent a year. They are good for a 10-year period. These are the same incentive stock options that public companies only give to the highest executives. We think it makes sense for everybody.

Our people are really incentive-driven; the better the company does, the better they do. That's part of why they do some of the things they do. There is a tremendous amount of peer pressure that I think keeps the teamwork going. Our people are aggressive, they really are enthusiastic, and they really have this "eye of the tiger" that we look for. They're just not going to tolerate you not doing your share at the expense of everybody else on the team. When you have people who are owners, who really buy into the fact that they work for a caring company that they want to make a career with, they are insulted if someone isn't pulling his own weight, and it disturbs them.

We have an open-door policy which is truly just that; it's not just words. Anybody can go see anybody. You've got to let them in if they want to see you, no matter what they want to talk to you about. If they have an issue, we encourage people to use the chain of command, but they don't have to. Maybe they have problems with somebody in the chain of command. What do you do then?

We have a hotline that anyone can use, with an 800 number. They can call in and yell at the umpire, but also they use it for constructive suggestions and sometimes just for rumor control—you name it. And that hotline goes directly to myself and the chairman, and we respond to all of the calls. So they know there is a forum in which they can be heard. That doesn't mean that they will always get their way, but they've got access to the top decision makers in the company, and that is very important.

We're a company that's not yet seven years in operation, and yet we have probably the foremost child care program in the entire United States. We have more than 500 children of our employees in a quality child care program, both in centers and in homes. We go out and recruit responsible adults who are interested in taking children into their homes, mainly where there aren't many centers that will take infants. We interview them. We put them through FBI background checks, we fingerprint them, and we monitor the home to ensure that it is a proper place for children. We monitor the ratios of the number of children they are taking care of. Our child care program is available to people in Phoenix and Las Vegas, and several other cities in our system. Eventually, it'll be available in every city we serve. Now that's one thing we do for employees.

We've very proud of that one, and we've received national recognition for it, but that's not why we do it. We do it because it's the right thing to do. It makes good business sense.

We also have an employee assistance program that is staffed by professionals who deal with issues such as alcohol dependency, other forms of chemical abuse, codependency, stress, and so on. These people are there on a totally confidential basis to help, not just the employees, but also dependents of the employees, to deal with the problems that we all deal with today in a complex society.

It is not unusual for an employee to come forward who has a chemical dependency problem, for us to send that employee to a Betty Ford or a Cottonwood clinic for as much as a couple of months, and we pay virtually all of the cost.

We have people, just like any company, who run into financial problems, and most of the time they're not of their own doing. But they are just wiped out financially. Well, they know that while we are not a bank, if the traditional sources turn them down for financial assistance, they can come here.

It is not unusual for somebody to be in my office, for example, with a shoe box full of bills. We will just pay all of the bills. We put the employees on a program that they can handle, paying the company back over an extended period of time at a very nominal interest rate, far better than they could get at any bank.

Now why do we do these things? There isn't a book that tells us to do it, but we actually care about the individual employee. What we are trying to be is just one additional component in an overall support system that people need in this complex society. We are not trying to be captain of the world. We are not a bank. We are not trying to be surrogate parents. We are certainly not a hospital. But we are one place that has both the time and resources available if you need help. And that's why we do it. People know that, and we go out of our way to demonstrate it all the time.

We care, truly care, and I think that people see that. I think there is a loyalty that builds up. People don't mind doing the extraordinary if it's going to make the company better. The betterment of the company is synonymous with their own individual economic and emotional welfare.

The story of America West Airlines gives us some insight into the values, attitudes, and style of operation that motivates employees to participate fully in the organization. The company empowers its workers by providing the tools, training, and autonomy that they need to participate, by offering them an ownership stake in the business, and by providing a climate of caring and trust. It is not surprising that in such an environment, in which human needs are acknowledged and talent and creativity are allowed to flourish, employees give their all, particularly in difficult times.

When Mike Conway left Continental Airlines to become president of America West, he made clear his intention to keep rules and regulations to a minimum. He was determined to avoid building a mindless bureaucracy that would stifle initiative and inhibit employee involvement.

Conway focused on tools rather than rules, providing employees with intensive training so they would be well equipped to do, in his words, "whatever it takes" to make America West succeed. Training for the airline's 3,000 customer service representatives (CSRs) is rigorous—an 18-week program that covers all of the functions required to get passengers ticketed, onto, and off the planes safely and efficiently.

Such thorough training allows employees to act with autonomy and authority to solve problems as they arise, without having to ask for the blessing of supervisors. Unlike senior managers at most organizations, President Mike Conway and Chairman Ed Beauvais take for granted that the 14,000 plus employees of America West will manage themselves. Risk-taking and responsibility are basic requirements of every job.

Communication is open and frequent at America West—and it is two-way. Directives flow from the executive suite, but criticisms, suggestions, and concerns flow back as well, through such vehicles as the employee hotline.

Trust is a hallmark of America West operations. For example, Mike Conway started a program of rewarding employees with "guest passes," heavily discounted plane tickets, for perfect attendance records. A few managers wanted to know what to do about solid employees who legitimately missed some work time, making their records slightly less than perfect. Without hesitating, Conway told them: "Bend the rules!"

Another America West program, an anniversary prepayment plan, rewards employees with up to a quarter of their annual salary in advance, beginning on their third anniversary with the company. Some nervous managers worried that unscrupulous employees might take the money and run. Conway's response? "Forget the 1 percent who might take advantage of the program. Focus on the 99 percent who will be motivated by it."

The culture of caring and trust that we find at America West is a vital prerequisite for full participation. But while the company's leaders may be softhearted, they are hardheaded when it comes to performance standards. Conway and Beauvais reconcile the needs to be both hard and soft. They are, in the words of Charles Hampden-Turner, "tough on the problem, tender on the person."

Mike Conway explains:

> It's almost like you can be very hard on your family members, but God forbid anyone outside your family takes a shot—that's the only thing that I can think of that's analogous. We live in a fiercely competitive business, day after day, in our company, but we've lived through it, and our competitors have not. All along the way, people did not try to compete with America West for market share like United competes with American and Delta; they tried to put us out of business.
>
> When people are going for your very lifeline, you need to be tough to deal with that. But as tough as you need to be to your competitors, you need to be as compassionate, with the same amount of energy, to the people who are going to have to take shot after shot from the outside world. I think the combination works.

While the typical American company focuses on short-term profits, both Beauvais and Conway are committed to the future of America West—in business for the long haul, not the fast buck. They are equally committed to partnership with their employees, and they've taken concrete steps to prove it. Fully half of the America West stock is in the hands of executives (12 percent), employees (18 percent), and a friendly investor, Australia's Ansett Airlines (20 percent). And to discourage a hostile takeover, the company has provided a poison pill for employees, to the tune of a whopping 250 percent of their annual salaries. This makes AWA an expensive and thus unlikely takeover target.

How do the employee/owners respond to the partnership style of America West? Do they really participate more fully in the business than employees at other airlines? The answer is a resounding yes.

PROFILE OF THE FULLY PARTICIPATING PARTNER

Ruth Thomson has been a CSR at America West for more than four years. I asked her whether AWA employees really had the autonomy and authority to do "whatever it takes" to keep customers happy and make the airline a success. In response, she launched into this example of peak performance, from her own recent experience:

> We were on a flight to San Jose, and a man got on our plane and sat down. We made our announcement that we were going to San Jose, and he jumped up; he was pretty upset. He started grabbing his stuff, and ran off the plane.
>
> I followed him up the jetway, and it turns out that he was supposed to go to San Francisco, and it was the gate right next door. One of us [CSRs] had taken him to our gate instead. I guess she had gotten confused.
>
> Right next door, we saw his San Francisco plane backing away, and it was too late to get it. The man was trying to open the jetway door. He was pretty upset.
>
> Our plane was going to leave in 5 or 10 minutes, but I took him over to one of our counters and calmed him down. Because I know reservations and the computer, we were able to look up his reservation. I made the decision—America West encourages us to make decisions on our own, and they will back us up—to take him with us to San Jose. Once we got to San Jose, I knew that we could arrange ground transportation for him to San Francisco. We have the facilities to do that.
>
> So I changed his reservation and put a note in his record. His uncle was meeting him in San Francisco, and he was really worried that he would be waiting for him and he wouldn't have any idea what was happening. So I put a note in his record, for his uncle in San Francisco. I sent a message to San Jose, to the supervisor there, through the computer, so that

he could have ground transportation arranged ahead of time, so we wouldn't waste any time when we landed.

This seemed to calm him down a lot. We took him back on the plane, and when we got to San Jose, I took him to the thoroughfare and made sure everything was ready, and made sure his uncle had been notified of that in San Francisco.

I felt really responsible because it was one of us that had made the mistake. But not just that. He didn't fly a whole lot, and this was a real interesting experience for him, to be flying across country (I think he was from the Midwest). I wanted it to be a good experience.

So when I got back to Phoenix from my flight a day later, I looked up the reservation again and found out when he was coming back to town. It was about three days later. I went to the airport and met his incoming flight, and he remembered me. I took him to his connecting flight, just so there would be no problems and we were sure that he was on the right flight. I brought him 10 chocolate chip cookies for his trip back. And I went to a supervisor and got him to write up a travel voucher so that he could have another free round trip on us—just to kind of make up for whatever inconvenience he had had.

Ruth Thomson is not an isolated example of a stellar employee. Her initiative is repeated throughout America West Airlines, where going above and beyond the call of duty has been "business as usual."

Derryl Cox, another CSR, explains how extensive cross-training allows America West employees to switch positions at a moment's notice and affords the airline a high degree of flexibility. He cites an example:

I recently had a gate supervisor come up to me and ask, "Hey, Derryl, would you mind taking this flight to Los Angeles?" I happened to be at a slow gate; I wasn't very busy that night, and there was somebody who could cover for me. My supervisor took me off the gate position and took two other individuals, one was at a passenger assistance counter, the other one was working at another gate position, and reassigned us on the plane to LA.

It's very common to have a delayed flight or a late flight where you don't get a crew inbound, and the operation requires somebody to take an aircraft to Los Angeles, or somewhere else, to get it back to Phoenix [AWA's hub], where the original crew can get back on the aircraft. I have only done that once, but it happens relatively often.

He adds:

Because they were able to use people right on the premises rather than calling in CSRs from another area, or calling in reserves, we avoided a flight delay. Without the cross-training, we certainly wouldn't have been able to ever consider doing that. The aircraft certainly would have been on a minimum of an hour delay, if not a two-hour delay.

Mike Conway compares the full participation of America West employees with the rigidity of other airlines, whose employees stick to their specialized functions:

If you want to put a United Airlines flight attendant into shock, show her a four-part ticket and ask her a question about pricing. She doesn't have a clue. She doesn't know what capacity control or yield management is or any of those things that are critical to this business today. If there is a flight delayed and there is chaos in the airline terminal and flights are running behind, grab a flight attendant from US Air and say, "Hey, can you help check me in here?" They don't know what a CRT console is. Or ask them about the equipment outside. . . . Not only do our people know about it, they operate the equipment. They can back airplanes up, they can marshal airplanes in. They know about commissary operations because they have worked in Provisioning, putting food in those carts. They are more in tune with what is going on. They are much more responsive to the passengers because of the body of knowledge that they have.

To reinforce his point, Conway recalls an incident a while back, when an America West plane made an emergency landing at a remote airport in the southwest. There was no ground crew available to help out. No matter. Without so much as making a phone call, the in-flight crew changed into jeans, unloaded baggage, and booked hotels for the stranded customers. In the morning, they changed back into their uniforms, loaded the baggage, and started preparing breakfast. The passengers were duly impressed, but according to Mike Conway this was simply "routine operating procedure."

(For another outstanding profile of a fully participating partner see Goran Carstedt in Learning Tales, Chapter 10.)

THE EMERGENCE OF THE FULLY PARTICIPATING PARTNER

As I pointed out in Chapter 1, throughout most of the 20th century the "pioneer" was the hero of American business, the model to which ambitious workers aspired. Rugged individualists like Lee Iacocca and strong-willed entrepreneurs like Steven Jobs are the epitome of the lone pioneer archetype.

We viewed such Lone Rangers as the source of the organization's power and the reason for its success. They stood above and apart from the worshipful masses of employees, who toiled from 9 to 5, seldom took initiative, and considered themselves "hired hands" whose primary role was to carry out orders from on high.

But even if the story of the lone pioneer had some validity at one time, it is woefully obsolete in today's world. Success in the current economic environment, with its freewheeling competition, its proliferation of information, and its emphasis on "mass customization" rather than mass marketing, requires the innovation and involvement of every person in the organization.

The model employee of the new story organization is the fully participating partner, the empowered employee—whether manager, secretary, technician, or CEO—who is well trained and well rewarded, who takes initiative, works autonomously as well as on teams, and has the authority to make strategic decisions.

Fully participating partners, whether senior executives or senior clerks, have a monetary and emotional stake in the business. These new story employees think and respond like owners, continually searching for ways to please the customer and ensure the success of the organization. They are highly motivated to act in the best interest of the organization since there is no split between the organization's interest and their own.

Ruth Thomson expressed this spirit of partnership when she told me: "I feel like part of the company. When someone is talking about America West, when I see a commercial on TV, it makes me feel proud, because I know it's *me*, a part of me. It's not just my employer."

In companies such as America West Airlines, Preston Trucking, Steelcase, and Semco, the *typical* employee is like Ruth Thomson—fully involved as a partner in the business. Such widespread commitment to participation cannot be mandated from above. Rather, it occurs spontaneously, emerging naturally in a particular kind of corporate environment.

CREATING A CULTURE OF PARTICIPATION

An organization in which fully participating partners are the rule rather than the exception meets the following conditions:

- It provides a compelling *mission* and/or a set of worthy *values* with which employees can identify.

- It provides a *structure* that encourages maximum participation by emphasizing flexibility and autonomy.

- It provides *rewards* for employee participation, and it does not punish employees for taking risks.

- It has *ongoing involvement programs* in place to ensure that full participation remains standard operating procedure.

- It recognizes and supports every employee's need to *integrate work with family life.*

Shared Mission and Values

Ruth Thomson recalls: "When I showed up that third day with this tin of chocolate chip cookies for the gentleman who missed his flight, even the supervisor at the airport said, 'Wow, this is your day off. What are you doing here?' And I said, 'I feel responsible for this man, and I feel like this is his impression of America West. This is his impression of me, this is my company.' "

She adds: "I am not just doing this for my employers, to impress them. I am doing it because I feel part of it, because I want the company to do well. I want the company to be a success."

Thomson went out of her way to serve her stranded customer, not because of a mandate from above, but because she *wanted* to do so. And she wanted to do so, as she explained, because she was "proud" of her company. Because she respects what America West stands for, she *voluntarily* contributes her best efforts in return. Because she believes in America West, she makes the organization's mission her own.

In speaking with Thomson, I was reminded of another fine example of an employee who "personalized" an organizational mission, at IBM. In 1984, I gave a series of lectures at IBM facilities for their high achievers from around the world. Wherever I traveled, I asked IBM employees whether they were aware of their organization's mission. Everyone I asked gave me the same reply, usually without hesitation: "Best customer service in the world." I was impressed at how well IBM had communicated its service mission to such a diverse group of employees (a third of a million people).

I was even more impressed when I spoke with an IBM maintenance man after one of my lectures. As I left a meeting room in Austin, Texas, late one evening, I observed the man sweeping his heart out. Here at last, I figured, was one employee who would tell me he didn't know the company's mission

So I asked my usual question. The man looked puzzled by the term *mission*, so I rephrased my question, asking him: "Why do you work so hard? Is your boss around here?" "No," he replied. I continued, "He's not going to come in here tomorrow morning to see how well you swept up?" "No," he replied. So I asked: "Then why are you working so hard?" The man, who looked perplexed and a little annoyed at what he obviously considered a stupid question, gave me this answer: "Why, because our customers, they come here" (he looked me up and down as he said this), "and you might be one of them." Like Ruth Thomson at America West, this man had taken the mission of the organization, service to the customer, and made it his own.

Since my experience with that maintenance man in 1984, IBM's service star has become slightly tarnished. Struggling to maintain International Business Machines in an era of paradigm shift has been fatiguing. An IBM client who was quoted in a *Fortune* article captured the dilemma well. Commenting on the fact that three different sets of IBM managers had called on him in the past year, the client noted: "They never asked about our needs. They don't listen. All they do is talk and show you the charts they've brought along."

Worthy Purposes.   An employee is far more likely to embrace the company's mission, and act on it, if he or she considers it a worthy one, such as providing the "best customer service in the world." The mission need not relate directly to the success of the organization. Some companies elicit full participation by pursuing an "external" mission of social activism.

Ben & Jerry's Ice Cream has the mission of supporting peace projects. The company sets aside 7.5 percent of its pre-tax profits for that purpose. The Body Shop is a strong activist on behalf of environmental causes. And Levi Strauss is known as much for its community involvement as for the blue jeans it manufactures.

When the attitude of concern exists internally as well, employees can more easily align their energies with these companies. They are naturally inclined, even inspired, to participate fully because they view the companies' social missions as worthy. Aligning with their companies makes the employees feel more worthy.

But an organization may not be socially active yet still inspire employees to full participation. If it demonstrates the values of caring, trust, and respect, if its mission is putting people first, workers are likely to want to give it their best efforts in return. Will Potter, chairman of Preston Trucking, came to understand that employees must accept and internalize the values of the company if they are to act as fully participating partners. He told me: "When we started, we didn't have any specific philosophy or values, and we have learned that it's very important that people are able to internalize the values of the company."

He cited an example:

> Today we conduct what we call product knowledge classes, and we will bring in 30 associates from the field, and in that group will be a service center leader, and coordinators, some dockworkers, some clerical people, and some of those people may be stewards.
>
> I remember getting up in the class and talking for about two hours about our values. . . . At the end of the session, a guy by the name of Roger Wad stood up, and Roger was a steward from Baltimore. He said, "You know, Will, I haven't been too supportive over the years." (This is in front of the entire class.) And I said, "Yeah, Roger, I understand that." He said, "Well, I want to tell you something. You got me now."

I said, "Roger, I really appreciate that. Tell me a little bit more what you are really saying." He said, "I have read about these things, I have heard you all speak about them, but I really didn't understand them, and I didn't know what the words meant. Now I understand completely, and it makes sense, and I agree with it." Then he added: "There's a more important reason. Now I know that it comes from the heart."

And I guess that pretty well sums up everything we have learned since we started in 1978. We have gotten to the point where if it doesn't come from the heart, it's not going to be internalized, and people are not going to be guided by those values.

Potter related another incident that shows how Preston's sincerity has helped employees to internalize company values—in this case, a commitment to safety.

We put together a kind of workbook with examples and exercises. The service center leader will conduct a meeting with everybody on the shift, once or twice a month. I was in Peoria not too long ago, and I saw a copy of the pages of one of these workbooks, and I asked the service center leader: "Hey, what's this?" and he said, "Oh, that's for our meeting."

I said, "What do you mean it's for your meeting?" He said, "Well, I xerox the page we are going to be using, and I distribute the page to each one of the men to discuss."

I said, "Yeah, and they just hoot and holler and laugh" [at the exercises]. And he said, "Yeah, that happens a little bit, but let me tell you something. I find a couple of days later when I'm walking around on the dock, these guys are kidding with each other, saying, 'Hey, how many of those were you able to do when you went home?' So sure, everybody has got a good sense of humor, and everybody makes fun of some things, but it gets through. There's not nearly the rolling of the eyes that there used to be, because they recognize that this is a sincere thing."

While employees must identify with the organization's mission or values if they are to be motivated to participate fully, they can each be motivated for very different reasons. IAMS Pet Foods is a

$150 million company based in Dayton, Ohio, with a high level of employee participation and commitment. But as CEO Clay Mathile explained to me, this does not mean that everyone is committed to the success of IAMS for the same reason. Said Mathile:

> We each care in different ways. Some people care because it is intellectually stimulating—Bill Wirch, for example. He cares because I gave him the freedom to be the best in his field, which happens to be information systems. Les cares because he never worked for an honest company before, so he saw IAMS and saw how honest it was, and how sincere we are, and now you can't pry him away from this place. Bob Meyer cares because he wants to see more dogs and cats eat IAMS; he's a cat lover. He just saw what it did to his cats, and he said, "God, we've got to sell more of this stuff." He's not so wrapped up in the people aspects of it.

The point is that employees will participate fully in the organization if, and only if, they have a compelling *personal* reason to do so. A worthy mission and a worthwhile set of corporate values can provide the personal motivation and inspiration that lead to involvement. When America West announced its filing for bankruptcy in June 1991, 2,000 of the 9,000 employees based in the Phoenix area showed up for a pep rally at the Sky Harbor Airport. They raised $6,000 to buy an advertisement that ran in the *Arizona Republic* newspaper that month.

The ad read in part: "The Employee Owners of America West Airlines have our own secret ingredient—and ours cannot be duplicated. With this ingredient comes motivation, an on-time departure and arrival [record], and an exemplary safety record, all of which are second to none. . . . We ask you now to show your support and confidence in our abilities and our company."

Structuring for Participation: Creating Flexibility

While a commitment to the organization, based on a shared mission and shared values, is a necessary first step toward full participation, it is not sufficient. For employees to act as fully participating partners, the structure of the organization must be highly flexible, so that it facilitates rather than impedes participation.

Mike Conway came to America West with a stated agenda of eliminating needless bureaucracy. Ricardo Semler, president of Semco, whose story we'll be covering in Chapter 5, encourages employees to use the rule of "common sense" in making decisions; there are no corporate policy manuals to consult. In part because of their commitment to eliminating cumbersome rules and regulations, these leaders have created two of the most participative working environments I have encountered in my research.

A growing number of organizations are learning that to elicit the full involvement of workers, they must loosen the corporate structure by tackling the "sludge"—the endless rules and regulations—that bog it down. NCR, the data processing giant, is one of them. NCR reduced its corporate policy manual in 1989, from 341 to 125 pages, by "eliminating all the can'ts, don'ts and mustn'ts," according to Jim McElwain, vice president of personnel resources. "People want to do the right things," explains McElwain. "They want overall direction; then they can figure out what to do."

PayLess, a discount store chain, also took a stab at shrinking its policy manual, in an effort to free up employees to work more swiftly and effectively. Over the years, the manual had grown to more than 2,000 pages. Now a three-part value statement that focuses on serving customers, treating people well, and using common sense has replaced most policies (though the manual still contains a hefty 900 pages).

Steven Schiff, who was responsible for taming the PayLess manual, plans to continue carving policies away until only procedural guidelines are left. "Until we're done, I tell our people, if a policy doesn't allow you to do something, but it makes common sense, go ahead and break the rule."

To generate greater employee participation, many organizations, like America West, are eliminating or reducing the number of fixed positions and cross-training employees in a variety of functions. Cross-functional training can greatly increase the flexibility and competitive strength of the organization, as the America West examples earlier in the chapter demonstrate.

Preston Trucking is another company that cross-trains its employees. Will Potter recounts an incident that demonstrates the competitive power of cross-utilization:

For years, we haven't referred to the local drivers as "drivers." We always refer to them as "driver/salesmen." They've all been exposed to training videos as to how to conduct themselves when they are in front of the customer.

I will never forget several years ago, when one of our driver/salesmen was trying to get some freight to California. Basically, we are a short-haul company, but we have a partner in California. We can put the freight on the Santa Fe, our partner gets it in California, and we deliver it. The customers don't look at this as the freight we are normally going after, but we have the capability to handle it, and we can be competitive.

The driver/salesman who is at this location wanted some of that business, and he hadn't been getting any. One of our competitors who had that business was in there one day, and the competitor's driver went up and bumped into a pallet that had these boxes on it.

The boxes went all over the floor, and the competing driver went up and started to get the paperwork and so forth, and the customer says, "Gee, before you leave, will you pick up those boxes?" And the driver says, "I don't have time to pick up those boxes. Give me my freight; I have to get out of here."

Our guy saw this. Nobody asked him to do anything, but he went ahead and piled all the boxes back up on the pallet, and thanked the customer for the business that he got that day. Then he said, "Gee, I sure would like that business to California." The customer said, "I understand." The next day he went back in there, and he had all the business to California.

In addition to increasing the organization's competitive strength, cross-training can improve customer service by preventing boredom and burnout. Derryl Cox of America West explains:

Being able to have the flexibility to move from job to job with this company is certainly a morale booster. It has definitely kept my ability to maintain a positive attitude in my job function. With cross-utilization, if I don't feel like I want to work ramp, that's fine. We bid for positions on a monthly basis. For myself, I prefer to work ground functions about half of the time and in-flight half of the time. It keeps my morale and my sanity. I am able to smile when I am on an aircraft, because I have a choice in job functions and know that I am going to be back in town in a few days, and then I get to work on the ground. It keeps me very happy because I get to be at home for whatever reason I may need to.

Ruth Thomson agrees that the flexibility of cross-training is a morale and productivity booster: "I have a family, and I can arrange my schedule to accommodate my family. And if I am tired for any reason, like after the holidays, and it takes a little too much out of me to go down and work on the ramp, to throw bags, or to work in-flight, which is tiring, I can go sit in reservations. I'm not tied down to one job. I am never going to get bored with my job; its like four, five, or six jobs in one. I can change it each month, each week, whenever I want."

Cross-functional, self-managed teams, such as those we see at Steelcase, Semco, and other new story organizations, are fast becoming one of the most popular, and most effective, vehicles for generating greater employee participation. We will examine the development of these new story "smart" teams in depth in Chapter 5.

One final word about structuring for participation: As I pointed out in Chapter 2, the organization must design its physical space to facilitate involvement rather than inhibit it. To foster employee interaction and teamwork, Steelcase, Manco, and other highly participative companies are experimenting with a variety of office arrangements, many with movable walls and flexible furniture systems.

Rewarding for Participation

Wherever I have seen employees fully involved in the operations of a company, some form of ownership or profit sharing plan was in place. This is simply common sense. It is naive to expect employees to contribute their best efforts to an organization that does not allow them to share in the rewards of those efforts.

At companies where employee participation is high, such as America West, Steelcase, and Semco, rewards are shared. America West employees own 12 percent of the company's stock. Semco divides 23 percent of its annual after-tax profits among its employees. And at Steelcase, profit and productivity bonuses average 60 percent of base pay.

If workers are to be fully involved partners, they must share the downside as well as the upside of the business. One reason for the high level of participation at America West is that executives suffer along with the other employees when the business turns sour. For example, when the airline began experiencing a downturn in the first quarter of 1991, top executives took a 25 percent pay cut, while salaries of other managers were reduced by just 10 percent. This sent a powerful message of partnership to all employees.

While equitable rewards are a necessary prerequisite for full participation, money is not the only compensation firms can offer. Increasingly, employees are becoming as interested in the quality of work life as in its economic benefits. In addition to money, employees now look for compensation in the form of recognition, respect, open communication, flexible work schedules, lifelong training and education, family-oriented benefits, and the opportunity to make an impact on the business.

Finally, if it is important to reward workers for their participation, it is equally important not to punish them for making decisions and taking risks. Ruth Thomson of America West comments:

> I have been here for three years. We hear over and over in our classes, from our supervisors, that at some point in time you have to make a decision. They make me feel like I can take responsibility and make some decisions on my own, and that the company will support me. That's very important, knowing that no one is going to jump on my case, nobody is going to chew me out for doing something.

Thomson recalled her decision to arrange ground transportation for her San Francisco–bound passenger:

> My plane was leaving in five minutes. They were waiting for me and this other passenger. It was either leave this guy in Phoenix, and the next flight wasn't leaving until the next morning, so we would have to put him up in a hotel. Sure, we would take care of him, but what good was that going to do, with his uncle sitting in San Francisco?
>
> I had been told that I would be backed up, and this was the only alternative. I could have gone and found a supervisor

somewhere, but it just would have taken so much time that we wouldn't have been able to accommodate him in this way. This was the quickest, easiest way to do it. I made a decision; I made the passenger happy; I made it all work out; and I knew that I would not have any backlash from that, that they would support me.

Will Potter of Preston Trucking agrees that if you want to increase the participation of employees and improve the quality of their work, they must not be afraid to take action. Says Potter: "We are going to be surveying—I don't know yet with what frequency—but there will be a survey at every service center, so we will know exactly how the leadership is doing in that terminal with respect to communications. We will also understand whether any fear exists in that terminal. That's a big factor. You can't have quality if there is one little iota of fear."

Ongoing Involvement Programs

Wal-Mart, the discount store giant, holds regular "grassroots research" meetings to make sure that communication lines between management and employees remain wide open. It has an ongoing program that encourages employee suggestions—and acts on them. For example, the presence of a "people greeter" in every Wal-Mart store is the result of an hourly employee's suggestion. Sam Walton, chairman and founder of Wal-Mart, liked the idea and turned it into store policy.

Furthermore, to inspire employees and make sure senior management stays in touch with what is happening in the stores, each of Wal-Mart's top executives sponsors a store item. The executives choose these items at the beginning of the year and sponsor them throughout the year. They are responsible for tracking the progress of their chosen items and for pushing store managers to market them aggressively. The choices are announced publicly, and regular progress reports—good or bad—are made to the entire company.

Another ongoing feature of Wal-Mart's effort to keep employee involvement alive is a weekly sales pep rally for store managers. Sam Walton used to attend these rallies every Saturday morning.

For total employee involvement to become a self-sustaining way of life, it must be *continually reinforced* through ongoing company programs, as it is at Wal-Mart. Such programs are a vital force that keeps the firm alive, healthy, and fully functioning.

Companies making the transition to an organization of fully participating partners frequently implement a suggestion system of some kind as an early step along the path of transformation. If designed and implemented properly, such a system can increase employee involvement by showing immediate results.

The most effective suggestion systems, sometimes dubbed "total improvement systems," focus on generating a steady stream of small, inexpensive, incremental improvements throughout the organization. These systems encourage only suggestions that the authors can readily implement in their own work areas. This places responsibility squarely on the shoulders of each participant. Because the focus is on making small, inexpensive improvements, a high percentage of suggestions are implemented, and this provides an additional incentive to participate.

Preston Trucking has an excellent suggestion system in place, as a part of its overall Performance Improvement Process. As noted in the Chapter 1 tale, in 1990 the roughly 6,000 Preston "associates" turned in 9,209 suggestions, 96 percent of which were implemented.

The results of the Preston system are in striking contrast to the results of the old story organization's "suggestion box" programs. One reason is that these programs often focused on generating suggestions for major improvements, so only a handful of suggestions could be implemented. Worse still, few of the programs were taken seriously by management, or by anyone else in the organization. As a result, few employees bothered to participate.

The Preston system is quite different from the old story model. For one thing, it gives all ideas serious consideration. "The greatest motivation for making suggestions is to very quickly see your suggestion put in place, to be utilized, or to get an answer very quickly on why it cannot be utilized," says Will Potter.

He continues: "We set up a suggestion process so that a coordinator can't turn it down. In other words, he can either implement it or pass it on to a higher level. . . . If he says, 'Gee, I can't approve it because it costs too much money,' it goes up to a higher level, or if he says, 'I can't approve it because it involves people outside our area,' then it goes up to a higher committee in the terminal, and then as quickly as possible, an answer gets back to that associate who made the suggestion."

Because all suggestions receive serious consideration, the volume of suggestions has steadily increased since the program was implemented in 1984. Says Potter: "I think what happened over time was people saw that their suggestions were being put in place. They said, 'Wait a minute, this thing really works.' The *Quality Communicator* [an internal newsletter] came out, and there were names of people who had made suggestions, and there were people sitting around saying, 'Gee, if Charlie can do it, I can do it. Hey, I got a suggestion.'"

Here is a sampling of the suggestions offered by Preston associates and of the annual savings that such suggestions generated: replacing a cleaning service with a part-time associate ($3,900), reusing brown envelopes for in-house correspondence ($7,500), and having users of company cars purchase self-service rather than full-service gasoline ($40,000).

Many ongoing involvement programs are designed to elicit employee participation *directly*. This category includes training programs such as that of America West, suggestion systems such as that of Preston Trucking, and periodic grassroots meetings such as those held at Wal-Mart.

Other ongoing programs can generate employee participation *indirectly* by addressing employee needs and concerns and thus creating a favorable *climate* for participation. Child care, educational assistance programs, financial aid programs, drug counseling and treatment, and other employee assistance programs fall into this category.

America West provides round-the-clock child care for its employees, because, as Mike Conway asserts: "Work and family are no longer separate. When a parent feels good about how his or her child is being taken care of, his or her disposition at work is better. If we have a 'leave your personal life at home' attitude, we're going to pay for it."

As I pointed out in this chapter's opening tale, America West offers a wide assortment of employee assistance programs. Conway believes that this is one reason why its employees develop a strong loyalty to the company.

RECONCILING WORK WITH FAMILY LIFE

In a 1990 *Fortune* magazine cover story entitled "Why Grade-A Executives Get an F as Parents," Brian O'Reilly reported that children of successful executives are more likely to evidence a host of health problems than are children of "less successful" parents. O'Reilly noted that one Ann Arbor, Michigan, study showed that 36 percent of the children of executives are treated for psychiatric or drug-abuse problems each year, compared with 15 percent of children of nonexecutives in the same companies. The chief causes were long work hours and personal habits such as perfectionism, impatience, and efficiency. The executives were told that they needed to learn how to enhance their children's self-esteem.

Peter Senge of M.I.T. found it interesting that the article said nothing about the contributions of the executives' organizations to their problems as parents. And no ideas were offered about how the companies might help improve family life. The bottom line seemed to be: work inevitably conflicts with family life, and the company has no role or responsibility in reconciling the two.

Traditional old story organizations, with their either-or approaches, inevitably foster conflict between work and family. It is all too common, Senge notes, for employees to hear the message, "If you want to get ahead here, you must be willing to make sacrifices"—that is, to give up much of your family and personal life. Inevitably, the organization fosters conflict by creating demands and pressures on the individual that clash with family and personal time. These demands include company travel, trade association meetings, breakfast and dinner meetings, weekend retreats, and workdays seemingly without limit.

This conflict between work and family is a natural outgrowth of the old story mentality that puts the organization's goals and objectives ahead of, and in opposition to, the personal goals and aspirations of employees. There is simply no room in the old story organization for reconciling the needs of individuals with those of the organization. The company always comes first.

In the new story organization, on the other hand, the focus is on *reconciling* competing goals and objectives. Levi Strauss and Steelcase, for example, understand that work and family life are all of a piece, holons in the holarchy of life. They understand that employees cannot share the company's mission unless it meshes with their personal missions—missions that involve deeply felt beliefs, dreams, and goals. They approach the organization as a living, interdependent system, realizing that the boundary between work and family life is arbitrary and increasingly dysfunctional, a product of old story thinking that reduced wholes into isolated parts.

These new story leaders see the natural connection that exists between an individual's working life and all other aspects of his or her life. As a result, their policies and operations are geared toward integrating organizational and individual needs, rather than forcing employees to choose between the family and the job.

Corporations are gradually realizing that distress about a child's day care, schooling, or health can directly affect mom's or dad's productivity and absenteeism rates. The sheer numbers of employees struggling mightily to reconcile work and family are moving companies in the direction of change. For example, in 1991 there were some 10 million mothers of preschool children pursuing careers in this country.

Wendy Hoerner is a Steelcase product engineer who has been working part-time since 1985, when she was pregnant with her first child. She was able to handle substantial projects during this time and to keep moving her career forward. In 1988, when pregnant with her second child and still typically working 7:30–11:30 A.M. each day, she was promoted to senior product engineer. Hoerner managed to lead design teams, meet with outside vendors, and turn in a first-class performance while maintaining a strong commitment to her family.

Jerry Jasinowski, president of the National Association of Manufacturers, predicts that flexible family-oriented benefits will become a "major competitive strategy" for corporations. And the Child Care Action Campaign reports that some 4,000 employers now offer some form of child care aid, a 400 percent increase over the past decade. This includes support for day care that adds an educational component, now referred to as "educare."

A growing number of companies are beginning to recognize the core truth of Mike Conway's assertion, that in order to participate, employees must be able to reconcile their personal lives with their working lives—and are instituting policies to help them do so. Du Pont lengthened maternity leaves, instituted flexible work schedules, and boosted funding for community child care centers to more than $1 million after it learned from a survey that one fourth of its male employees and half of its female employees had considered looking elsewhere for jobs that offered them more flexibility to deal with family needs. Merck & Co. now provides six weeks of paid maternity leave and six months of unpaid leave to both parents. IBM joined Corning Glass Works, Marriott, Pepsi Co, Honeywell, and other major corporations in providing day care for the children of employees. Some companies have even begun their own on-site schools for children of employees (see Chapter 9). And AT&T offers one year of unpaid leave to new parents and to those who must care for aging parents, with guaranteed reinstatement to similar jobs when they return.

Levi Strauss is well known for its commitment to balancing work and family life. The company's most recent demonstration of this commitment is a Family Task Force. According to Sue Thompson, director of human resources, the task force was formed

> . . . in order to examine the changing needs of our employee population, in terms of flex time, part-time jobs, or job share, different kinds of benefits and leaves, and a multitude of other issues. And that task force is being chaired by Bob Haas, who is our CEO. And he attends every meeting. He is intimately involved in working with a cross-section of line and staff managers in terms of what kind of policies and programs we need to put in place to make this attractive and viable for the talented people we want to work here.

Jenny Crowe-Innes, director of employment, employee relations, and EEO, is co-chair of the Family Task Force. She comments:

> We've got a very diverse group whose varied perspectives allow us to get a pretty accurate picture of the company when we meet. Our diversity involves more than just home office, other U.S. facilities, and sales force. We have the whole range—from hourly workers to managers, single parents, single people, do-

mestic partners, widows, divorcees—we are trying to cover everyone.

Such programs demonstrate concretely that the company is sincere when it claims to "put people first." They increase the *ability* of employees to participate. More importantly, they increase the *desire* of employees to contribute their best efforts to the organization when their commitment is reciprocated by the company.

OVERCOMING OBSTACLES TO FULL PARTICIPATION

CEO Jack Welch talks about the challenges GE faces as it struggles to transform itself into an organization of fully participating partners:

> We want 300,000 people with different career objectives, different family aspirations, different financial goals, to share directly in this company's vision, the information, the decision-making process, and the rewards. We want to build a more stimulating environment, a more creative environment, a freer work atmosphere, with incentives tied directly to what people do.
>
> The practical objective is to get rid of thousands of bad habits accumulated since the creation of General Electric. How would you like to move from a house after 112 years? Think of what would be in the closets and the attic. We have got 112 . . . years of closets and attics in the company. I want to flush them out, to start with a brand-new house with empty closets, to begin the whole game again.
>
> Ultimately, we're talking about redefining the relationship between boss and subordinate. I want to get to a point where people challenge their bosses every day: "Why do you require me to do these wasteful things? Why don't you let me do the things you shouldn't be doing so you can move on and create? That's the job of a leader—to create, not to control. Trust me to do my job, and don't make me waste all my time trying to deal with you on the control issue.

The move to an environment of fully participating partners is a massive physical and psychological undertaking. It requires the transformation of the organizational structure and philosophy

"It's always 'Sit,' 'Stay,' 'Heel'—never
'Think,' 'Innovate,' 'Be yourself.'"

Drawing by P. Steiner; © 1991 The New Yorker Magazine, Inc.

and of the people who must make the leap to participation. That leap is often met with resistance, particularly from people well grounded in old story management approaches—which includes most of us.

While such resistance can be found among employees throughout the organization, it is strongest, and most critical, among supervisors and managers, who tend to view transformation as more a threat than an opportunity.

The Reluctant Manager

David Rhodes, of the consulting firm Towers Perrin, predicts that by the year 2000 the typical large corporation will have half of the management levels and one third of the managers that it had in 1990. The transformation of organizations to an environment of fully participating partners will inevitably reduce the ranks of middle managers and will dramatically alter the role of managers. In light of these prospects, many managers are understandably reluctant to embrace the concept of full participation.

Janice Klein of the Harvard Business School has done extensive research on supervisor attitudes toward worker participation. In a study of eight plants, she found considerable supervisor resistance to their employee involvement programs. The reasons boiled down to essentially one: a substantial majority of the supervisors didn't think full employee participation was a good thing.

The supervisors' reluctance to embrace participation had four root causes: worries over job security, lack of role clarification, the extra supervisory work needed to implement employee involvement programs, and personality type. Some personality types, Klein argues, are especially unlikely to welcome empowerment of the workforce. These include "skeptics," who don't believe people can change; "status seekers," who put personal ambition ahead of company goals; and "deal makers," who like the power of controlling subordinates.

Whatever the reasons for managers' resistance to full participation, they often constitute a talented group whose continued commitment is essential to the organization's growth and development. Furthermore, they are the employees who are best equipped to train other employees in the management skills that *all* employees must develop in the newly participatory environment. No company can easily afford to ignore their legitimate worries.

Overcoming Management Resistance

Companies that are making the transformation to fully participating partnerships, such as Preston and Steelcase, have developed methods for overcoming management resistance. Will Potter admits that Preston did not pay enough attention to the worries of managers when it shifted to a participatory environment. Eventually, though, Preston's senior managers took steps to correct this mistake. Potter recalls:

> We made a mistake in the beginning. At some point in the early history, we bypassed middle management. We said, "Gee, we have to get down to the front line." And so middle managers became uncomfortable. They didn't understand. They became very nervous, and I guess that some of them felt that their legs were being cut out from under them.
>
> So we corrected that in terms of understanding, so they could come to the realization that if they gave out more responsibility to their people, it would make their life that much easier. And that's what has been evolving, so that the good ones see that by getting the job performers involved in the solutions to some of these problems, they can come up with better solutions. Then they don't find their desk piling up because they don't have time to make the decisions that have to be made.

Potter cites two examples of once-reluctant managers who became advocates of full participation:

> Floyd Genshaw, our present vice president of maintenance, had just received a promotion to eastern fleet manager in 1978 when we started our Performance Management process. Floyd readily admits that he did not accept for almost a year the tenets of our philosophy statement. He says that it was easy enough to accept the portions that pertained to treating people fairly, etc., but he had an extremely hard time accepting the proposition that "the person doing the job knows most about the job" and thereby should be empowered to perform.
>
> However, after Floyd began to hold regular shift meetings where he could answer each mechanic's questions, he began experimenting with self-managed work teams. Floyd quickly learned that the men themselves solved many of the problems that before had been handled by the supervisors, so that the managers could now take on greater responsibilities and help remove any impediments that prevented the teams from having superior results. The outcome has been that the mechanics now view themselves as a profit center rather than a cost center. And Preston Trucking Company is now doing maintenance work for many of our competitors.

Warren Fraise is a tire supervisor in the Preston maintenance department. He had been in his position for about five years when Preston made the shift to participative management. When his title was changed from supervisor to coordinator, he recalls, "I did not feel too good about it. I felt like I lost some of my so-called power."

Fraise continues: "As we went further and further into it, I got quite upset, because we were taking information and giving it to the men and letting them help me make the decisions. At first, I couldn't accept that, . . . but I found it made my job easier." He acknowledges, however, that "it took a little while to realize that."

Steelcase CEO Frank Merlotti stressed the importance of training and of taking one step at a time in overcoming the resistance of plant supervisors to self-management and teamwork. Merlotti reflects:

We thought we did an inordinate amount of training and explaining, but we found out that we hadn't done half enough. The minute we got into those plants and started creating teams—and we always made the supervisor the first team leader—as they got into it more, and the teams started selecting their own leaders, . . . the message got interpreted as "We won't need as many supervisors," and that came across as a big threat. One guy said, "I've been in this department for 18 years. I've been the boss, and now you are telling me—what are you telling me? You don't need foremen anymore." But that's not true. We are always going to need foremen.

Merlotti continues:

I think the line supervisors . . . were the most reluctant, the most concerned, and the most threatened, and took the most amount of convincing, even today. We've got maybe 50 percent of the work force on these teams, and the other 50 percent are still coming. We are taking it a piece at a time.

Bob North, a Steelcase supervisor, is one of many rotating team leaders in a plant that stamps out parts and assemblies for desks, files, and cabinets. Involved early on in training employees in the teamwork process, he harbored doubts about the move to participation, but over time he has become more comfortable with the idea.

North recalls:

> We had a seminar here in the company for supervisors to introduce the [participative management] program. They said, "This is what we'd like to do in the plant. What are your reactions?"
>
> Well, this involved a lot of changes, and I thought, "Boy, I don't know if I can change like that. This is completely different." But I thought if we're going to move ahead and stay number one, we would have to change.
>
> We [supervisors] said we would be team leaders and would train employees to work in teams. This was a whole new idea for me. I never did teaching before, just instructed workers on how to use the machines. This was a complete turnaround.
>
> It was a struggle at first—but I'm now learning to live with it. It's been about two years now. I can see the improvements that we've made. Fantastic—a lot of good things, a lot of cost-saving ideas.
>
> I've had a lot of the responsibility for decision making taken away from me. I think it's good. The people are happier. If they're happier, I'm happier. They put out the small fires and give me extra time to work on cost-saving projects and do the things I really should be doing.

North adds that while not everyone at Steelcase has accepted the teamwork process, there are fewer and fewer holdouts:

> We have some people who are still a little bit doubtful. But we're working toward 100 percent, and we've won some people over, and they're going to change. It will take some time. It's a radical change. To go from saying "This is the way I want this done" to "What are your ideas?" is quite a turnaround.

The Reluctant CEO

While managers throughout the organization must be committed to full participation if the organization is to be transformed, an initial commitment of the chief executive is vital. In some organizations, the greatest obstacle to full participation is a reluctant CEO.

Even the strong commitment of a well-meaning CEO to full participation can be undermined by the CEO's deep-seated, unconscious belief in the more familiar command-and-control style of management. Keith Dunn, a CEO who started out with a strong conscious commitment to employee involvement, discovered this the hard way.

When Dunn, along with two partners, started McGuffey's Restaurants, Inc. in 1983, he was determined to treat their employees well. He had suffered considerable abuse as an employee of several restaurant chains, and he intended to give his own employees the kind of top-notch treatment he had never experienced.

He succeeded—at first. Among other benefits, McGuffey's employees were given a free drink and a meal at the end of every shift. The owners allowed them to give away appetizers and desserts, and provided them a week of paid vacation each year. Soon a special camaraderie developed among them, and turnover in the early days was low.

But as McGuffey's expanded to two more locations, sales at its original restaurant, in Asheville, North Carolina, started to decline. And without realizing it, Keith Dunn began drifting away from his employees. They said that around 1985 he had "his nose in the air," was "all dressed up for the bankers," and "never said hello." Dunn himself later admitted, "Success breeds ego, and ego breeds contempt."

Employees at the original restaurant complained that the owners didn't seem to care about it anymore. And employees at the nearby Hendersonville restaurant, the second in the chain, were also disgruntled. "The magic was gone," says Sharon Morales, a bartender.

Dunn would return from trade shows or real estate meetings all pumped up. "Isn't this exciting?" he'd ask an employee. "We're going to open a new restaurant next year." When his enthusiasm was met with blank stares, he felt resentful. He didn't see that while his world was expanding, his employees were still busing tables or cooking burgers.

Or leaving. Sales and service deteriorated, and many employees quit. When Tom Valdez, the Asheville kitchen manager, left, he told Dunn bitterly, "Keith, you are turning out to be like all the other companies." Dunn shrugged. "We're a big company, and we've got to do big company things." Later he said, "I was allowing the company to become like the companies we hated, because I thought it was inevitable."

By the end of 1986, Sneakers, the third restaurant in the ailing chain, was spun off to David Lynn, one of the original partners.

But the sudden infusion of cash did little to help the company's long-term prospects. Sales and service at the two remaining restaurants continued to deteriorate.

The owners, wrapped up in themselves, could not understand why their business was in trouble. So Dunn sent out an anonymous questionnaire to employees, in an attempt to pinpoint the problem. Among other things, they were asked to rate the owners' performance on a scale of 1 to 10. The responses were mostly zeros and twos. "Plenty of people seemed to hate my guts," Dunn remembers.

He was irate at first, then shattered by the results, and, finally, perplexed. "All you do is sit and wonder, 'What could I have done to make them hate me so much?'"

Dunn hired a consultant to help him find ways to generate more commitment from his staff. With the consultant's help, he instituted a bonus program and launched a contest offering a $1,000 prize to the employee team that did the best job of keeping the restaurants clean, talking to customers, and in other ways improving the quality of service. He even embarked on a campaign to "bring the magic back," requiring all bartenders to perform magic tricks along with mixing drinks.

Nothing worked. The bonus requirements were almost impossible to meet, and most employees simply quit trying. A handful of employees worked hard to win the contest, but most of them were demoralized by the prospect of improving their performance and still losing. And few of the bartenders wanted any part of the magic tricks. "When somebody is hollering for a drink," said Bruce Ladd, a bartender in the Asheville restaurant, "they do not want to see a magic trick."

Finally, Dunn asked his managers whether they had any clues about why things weren't working at McGuffey's. Once he started listening, it quickly became clear to him that everything he had done to generate a higher level of employee participation had been done, ironically, *without the employees' involvement*.

Now that he realized what the problem was, Dunn began to truly listen to his employees. He set up an associate board, composed of workers from each restaurant, that would meet with the owners once a month. He formed employee focus groups to ensure that every employee would meet with one of the owners at least every six months.

To increase employee participation even further, Dunn turned the Asheville restaurant into a "self-managing store" for a three-month trial, giving employees incentives to meet financial goals and responsibility for hiring and menu planning.

The new system has changed employees "in motivational terms, in feeling like they are more involved," says Dunn. He continues: "It's not earth-shattering. But it's the next step, so that someday—three to five years out—McGuffey's will be a truly employee-involved company."

The saga of McGuffey's Restaurants illustrates how insidious and tenacious old story ways of thinking are, and how destructive they are to employee participation. How could Keith Dunn have fallen into the trap of treating employees in the same manner that had caused him to leave several restaurant chains and strike out on his own?

The answer is that Dunn never gave up the command-and-control style of management that had victimized him as a restaurant worker. Now, however, he was the victimizer rather than the victim, the controller rather than the controlled. Because he hadn't achieved the *personal transformation* necessary to become a fully participating partner, because at a "gut level" he hadn't truly accepted the concept of full participation, he ended up mistreating his own employees, despite his conscious commitment to doing just the opposite.

Keith Dunn's story is not unusual. The grip of the old story, top-down philosophy of management is powerful, and a deep and abiding belief in fully participating partners cannot be acquired without a profound personal transformation.

Many of the corporate leaders who have been schooled in the philosophy of command and control are silently skeptical or openly indignant over the notion of giving employees more authority and responsibility. In 1986, Frank Borman, then the chairman of Eastern Airlines, vowed, "I'm not going to have the monkeys running the zoo." His attitude may have been extreme, but in a less virulent form it is still all too common.

More common still is the attitude of the "ambiguous executive" who embraces full participation in theory but shies away from it in practice. In the words of Peter Kizills, this person is attracted by "a fantasy version of empowerment and simultaneously repelled by the reality."

Kizills captures the ambivalence of the reluctant CEO as well as the *crazymakers* at its core:

How lovely to have energetic, dedicated workers who always seize the initiative (but only when "appropriate"), who enjoy taking risks (but never *risky* ones), who volunteer their ideas (but only brilliant ones), who solve problems on their own (but make no mistakes), who aren't afraid to speak their minds (but never ruffle any feathers), who always give their very best to the company (but ask no unpleasant question about what the company is giving them back). How nice it would be, in short, to empower workers without actually giving them any power.

THE CEO AS FULLY PARTICIPATING PARTNER

In organizations making a successful transformation to full participation, you'll find a CEO who has overcome whatever ambivalence he or she might have had about the power of an involved and committed workforce. A CEO who has embraced wholeheartedly the concept of fully participating partners. By their words and their actions, such CEOs set the tone for their organizations and ensure that the organizational climate remains favorable for participation. They are visionaries who keep the mission of achieving full participation alive even when the pace seems agonizingly slow and even when disheartening setbacks have occurred.

The CEOs of this kind that I have observed seem to have one essential characteristic in common: empathy for their employees. This empathy often stems from their own past work experiences, as managers who encountered the lure of power and the frustrations of supervision and/or as workers who, like Keith Dunn, underwent mistreatment and haven't forgotten how it felt.

Ed Beauvais is such a CEO. Looking back to the formation of America West, Mike Conway recalls:

We [Conway and CEO Ed Beauvais] had an opportunity that was really the opportunity of a lifetime, to create a company from a blank sheet of paper. How many people get that chance? So that anything that you put into place, it's your nickel. You are not inheriting anything.

By definition, what we wanted to do was start a company together that we would have liked to start our careers with. The things that we saw out there that really created an environment of loyalty, that made people want to come to work every day and made them feel good about themselves and created high self-esteem—those are the things we wanted.

Frank Merlotti can empathize with Steelcase supervisors who are reluctant to embrace participation, because he's been in their shoes. And because he's been there, he can also more easily communicate to them the benefits of participation. Says Merlotti:

We try to have a foreman or forewoman control about 27–30 people. The foremen are running around like chickens with their heads cut off all day, trying to keep those 27 people active, busy, supplied, talking about their personal problems, who did something wrong today. What we had to do was convince these guys that if you have 6 teams that you are responsible for, instead of 27 people, you may have 60–70 people that you have control over.

But they [the team members] are doing all the running around, not you. They are solving their own problems. And you are sitting back and doing some planning, and doing what all the books always said the manager *should* do, and what not 1 out of 100 do, because they are always running around, always putting out fires.

I used to be one of those, buddy. Worked in plants all my life. I know exactly what the supervisors do. Wouldn't it be better to come in the morning and have the teams in place, and have them decide their own work schedule and train each other? What's wrong with that?

Clay Mathile, CEO of IAMS Pet Foods, rose through the ranks of the company and thus gained a special empathy for employees. And like Mike Conway, he, too, felt underutilized when he worked for other companies.

Mathile told me:

I never had a good work experience in my entire life until 1970, when I came to work for IAMS. And quite frankly, it's because Paul Iams just let me have freedom. He would give me challenges. I never had a good work experience because I never had a company that trusted me. I never worked for anyone who believed that my work was worthwhile, that my ideas were worthy of consideration.

When I started out with IAMS, I was driving a truck, making sales calls, and producing the product in the plant. And when we built our first plant, I started out as supervisor. So I've sort of gone elbow to elbow with most of these people. And they've seen me in different environments and roles, and I'm a real guy. I'm not some concept. I'm not some guy who walked out of Harvard Business School that happened to waltz in here on some kind of deal. I've been around, and I think most people realize that what I tell them is the truth, as I see it. And I'm willing to tell them I've made a mistake if that happens. . . . I think they relate to me.

Will Potter, chairman of Preston Corporation, was CEO of Preston Trucking when the company underwent its transformation to a participatory environment in the early 1980s. His personal philosophy of leadership is a major reason why Preston has so far succeeded in its quest to transform itself. Potter believes: "People come to work wanting, desperately wanting, to do the best job they can. People want to have a certain degree of freedom, and they want to be able to learn how they can do the job better. If they can learn something just a little bit more that will help them do a better job, then that becomes very motivating for them."

He adds: "I can't motivate anybody. The only thing that I can do is create an environment whereby people will motivate themselves, an environment where they can say, 'Gee, I have an idea here, how we can save time, or we could make it easier, and have the ability to be able to carry that out, to try it.' You can't beat people over the head. You can't force it."

Another reason why Potter has been so successful in leading his organization through the process of transformation is that he has adopted a partnership approach to working with the Teamsters union. As a result, what might have been a formidable adversary and a major obstacle to participation has become a solid ally.

Potter describes his attitude toward the Teamsters:

I can remember, and it was maybe six years ago—it was 2 o'clock in the morning, it was before the vote was about to come up on the contract, and some of my associates—I was meeting with one of the shifts—said, "Will, what should we do about the union?" I said, "Look, let me tell you something. We are always going to have a union in this company because the union keeps me honest." . . . I look at the union as a partner. The only thing I ask is that you become actively involved in the union so that you will have strong responsible leadership.

THE PROBLEM OF "UNCONTROLLED ENTHUSIASM"

Robert Levering, writing in *A Great Place to Work*, reports: "Employees talk about a 'people orientation' and a sense of community (sometimes called 'family') at especially good workplaces." These "especially good workplaces" are often, not coincidentally, organizations with a high level of employee participation. For the two go hand in hand: Companies that are committed to putting people first, that strive to create a feeling of community and caring, are the most likely to build loyalty and the full commitment that loyalty inspires.

Derryl Cox uses the term *family* in describing the atmosphere at America West: "The thing that I really like about this company is that it is not only a partnership, but it is a family feeling that you have when you work for this company. I mean, top management—Mr. Beauvais and Mr. Conway—both are tremendously affected by what the people at America West feel, especially their group of CSRs, since we're in the passengers' eye on a daily basis in all the different areas. They are very in tune with what we feel and think."

Jack Kahl, CEO of Manco, where employee involvement is also high, thinks of his entire organization as a family and told me that this "family feeling" is even expressed in the design of Manco's headquarters building: "We had the opportunity to build two years ago our first new building, so you could put your dreams into a real design. I saw this building as a park outside and as a family room inside. I didn't even see it as a whole house. I saw the entire building in my mind as a family room, and I wanted the spirit of what goes on in a family room of a house, which is a combination of warmth and discipline inside of this building. You've got to have rules, but you've got to have that warmth."

In such organizations as America West, Steelcase, Preston, and Manco, where a culture of caring exists, where a family feeling prevails, employees exhibit a noticeably different attitude and style of behavior. There is a unity of purpose linking such organizations and their employees. In walking through the front door, it doesn't take long to sense that the company and its work force are in sync, that they are thriving together as fully participating partners.

Ruth Thomson captures this feeling of unity, and comments on how different she feels at America West than she felt at other places where she had worked:

> I feel so different. On those other jobs, I would get tired of just doing the same thing all the time. Sure, landscaping was fun, and I was outside. Waitressing was great—the money was great, and I really liked working with people. But I never had some place where I had fun, where I could change it, where I could take 5 or 10 days off at a time as part of my regular schedule—or where, if I wanted to just sit for a week, I could. On a personal level, I feel like we have a voice in the company and that they care about what happens to us outside of work.

She adds: "I don't go to work and come home, and that's the end of it. The company is a part of my life. I have never had a job like this before, and I have been in the workforce for about 20 years, in all different kinds of jobs, in different states, different companies, and I have never felt like this before."

Mike Conway remarks: "People from companies in other industries come to look at our operation and ask: 'How do you get all that enthusiasm from your employees?' It's not that complicated. First, you've got to care, and then you've got to demonstrate that you care by your actions, because there is a natural skepticism that's there. It's just not that complicated, but you've got to be committed to caring."

That means you can't forget about caring when the company grows large, says Conway:

> There is a tendency as you get bigger to use that as an excuse— "Well, I don't have time to do that anymore," or "We used to do that, but we are bigger now; we just can't have anybody walking in to see anybody." In actuality, the bigger you are, usually the more successful you are, and you should have more time and resources available to the employees who got you there.
>
> What we really need to continue to instill in people is that now that we are bigger and more successful, we should have *more* time and *more* resources to apply to individual "people is-

sues." That is something we need to continue to harp on. You need to be able to spend more time with people and apply greater resources to assist them. If you are not willing to do that, then what do growth and success mean? What does it mean if it is not going to be applied to the people you asked to get you there?

Conway does admit that the enthusiasm engendered by his approach has created a unique "problem" for the company:

> We still have a tendency of too many people, because of their enthusiasm, wanting to do everything themselves. The biggest problem that we have is sort of one that many people would like to have. It's the problem associated with uncontrolled enthusiasm—of getting people to think before they move.
>
> I think we can be safer out on the ramp, although our record is as good as anyone's and better than most. People will see an airplane coming in, and they will want to get the blocks under there a little too quickly before the light goes off. It's that enthusiasm. Taking all that enthusiasm that comes with having a piece of the rock, if you will, and making the mental action precede the motor skill—we could do a better job there. But that's a nice problem to have.

After the declaration of bankruptcy in 1991, Conway was clearly counting on the enthusiasm of the AWA employee owners as a primary support to pull the company through its crisis. And he recognized AWA's need to reciprocate by maintaining its commitment to them. Conway stated: "America West must deal fairly with its employees and must be perceived as doing so by the public."

The saga of America West may have become airline legend—or airline history— after the publication of this book. Its commitment to its people and the founding values of the company may have pulled it through the crisis of 1991. Or it may have succumbed to the "permanent whitewater" that courses through the global economy in general and the airline industry in particular. Whatever the outcome, the AWA model of the fully participating partner will stand as a shining example for those organizations truly committed to employee empowerment.

Chapter Four

The Innovation
Imperative

In 1982, Patricia Gallup and David Hall invested $8,000 of their own money to launch PC Connection, Inc., a mail-order business that offers a broad range of software and accessories for IBM personal computers. In 1984, the company added a division, MacConnection, to provide similar products and services for users of Apple's Macintosh computers.

Based in the tiny hamlet of Marlow, New Hampshire, PC Connection boasted sales of $233,000 in its first year of business. By 1990, its annual revenues had grown to more than $100 million and its staff had swelled to some 250 employees. In a 1989 poll by a leading personal computer magazine, PC Connection captured the top customer service rating among computer mail-order companies— and outpolled the next four contenders combined.

The odds against winning in the crowded, cutthroat mail-order industry are overwhelming. But PC Connection has thrived in spite of the odds, thanks in part to an innovative, unorthodox approach to doing business. I interviewed and corresponded with cofounder Patricia Gallup to learn more about what led to the stunning success of her company. In keeping with the spirit of PC Connection, she was generous in providing information:

When my partner, David Hall, and I started the company, we asked ourselves, "How do *we* want to be treated when we buy mail order?" We had both had bad experiences making mail-order purchases, and we knew we could come up with better ways to conduct a business of this type.

A car stereo David had purchased through the mail once failed, and David called the company he purchased it from for help. They informed him he'd have to send it back to the manufacturer—who was located in Japan. They did not have anyone in their company who could or would assist him. In other words, he had received a low price *in exchange* for service and support.

This experience is what led us to establish the following as one of our goals: to offer software and peripherals at discounted prices, along with superior service and support. Since we started the company, unless a customer indicates that they prefer to go directly to the manufacturer, we'll always be there to help—and we never add on any surcharges.

David and I had both experienced ordering by mail and having our credit cards charged weeks prior to the items being shipped by the vendor. This, of course, gave them use of our money until they received enough orders to make it worthwhile to place *their* orders and get a low, large-quantity price. These experiences led us to establish two fairly revolution-ary policies for a company in the mail-order industry. We decided we would not charge the customer's credit card until we actually shipped their order, and we decided we would keep all products we advertised in stock.

MacConnection, our division supporting Apple MacIntosh computers, was the first company to offer a true money-back guarantee. There are others who offered to take returns, but you had to read the fine print. Most often, refunds were available only on unopened software. Our guarantee states that customers may purchase, open, use, and *return* the products, regardless of the reason for dissatisfaction. MacConnection's $3 overnight shipping was a big step and something that has really been beneficial to our customers.

Our goal is to always be looking for better and more efficient ways of providing products and information about products out to our customers and to the public. Even though you have that as a goal and you have your systems set up, you always need to monitor them, and refine them, and see if you can do it even more efficiently.

We do a lot of research. We really talk to and really listen to all of our contacts in the industry—our competitors, our vendors, our customers. We continually ask, "What's going to really make us stand out?" and "What's going to really help people or be a service they'd never expect?" You put that together with doing your homework on what's going on in the industry, and it leads to creative ideas and new types of services that haven't been offered before.

Some of my understanding of this comes from my work experiences before we started the company. When I was in school studying anthropol-ogy, I was intrigued by the process of learning and innovation and by what it was that inspired people to learn new ways of doing things. My research technique was to imitate the processes that primitive people themselves went through in learning how to accomplish particular tasks. This was not only enlightening but necessary. Many aboriginal methods were poorly documented, if documented at all, in the historic record.

It all started when I developed an interest in lithic technology and began to work with a group of graduate students in archaeology. In the lab, we would actually make stone tools, use them, and then study the wear patterns. This would help us determine how tools we found in the field had been used by prehistoric people, as we would compare the wear patterns on them to the wear patterns on those we'd made and used in the lab. This research led me down a path of exploration into the advancement of technology and how people learn to develop and use tools and methods that help them work more efficiently.

In the computer industry, you have to look at things like demographics and the changing population, and what effect that might have on your customer base. You need to always be thinking about what the customer may want in the future. We realize many people are going to want products and information at their fingertips, and they are going to want it fast. It can't be stressed enough how important it is to concentrate on and really know your industry.

We measure our success by the number of positive letters we get from our customers, not by how much money can be made. We get many letters each week, and they are almost always supportive—even the ones on the foam peanuts.

We had received a few letters, and generally they were positive, but they would say, "It's too bad you use those foam peanuts. Have you thought of using something else?" or "I am going to have to start looking for another source if you don't stop using them." People wanted to continue to order products from us, and they liked our service, but they objected to us using foam peanuts. I figured if so many people had taken the time to write us about their concerns, there must be many more who had been *thinking* along those same lines, but hadn't written. So we stopped using the foam and started using a tissue made from 100 percent recycled magazines instead.

Many people now have a lot of money invested in computer equipment, but I don't think they are being as productive as they could be. It's not just our job, but really our responsibility, to now make sure that people are able to be as productive as possible with their equipment.

Early on, we began by rewriting many of the installation instructions supplied by the manufacturers of the products. We still found that people had questions, so we started offering the toll-free technical support. People can call and get technical support on any one of the products we carry regardless of whether they've purchased it from us. Unless they need to return a product, it doesn't matter where they bought it. We'll always help.

Then we took that a step further and said, "There's a better way to do this than one-on-one support after the sale," meaning after someone is having a problem with an installation. That's where we came up with the idea for including the videotape instructions. We started our own video production studio. We call it PCTV; it's a separate division.

From installation videos came the notion that there was a better way of providing information to potential customers who were considering the purchase of computer equipment. With PCTV's satellite uplink capabilities, we are now developing programs for broadcast that will help them with their purchasing decisions, as well as encourage better use of the equipment they now have.

That's just one example. David and I have always believed that the success of the company is due to the fact that we have been willing to put ourselves in the shoes of both customer and vendor. We now see many of our employees doing this, and it pleases us greatly.

I feel we've created an environment of innovation by giving the members of our management team the freedom to explore, experiment, and make their own discoveries on how to best accomplish the goals they've set for their departments.

Patricia Gallup is understandably upbeat about the success of her business. But her company's suppliers are equally enthusiastic. I asked Elliott Levine, vice president of Merisel, a New Jersey–based supplier to PC Connection, for an informed outsider's view of the mail-order giant in the tiny town of Marlow. He told me: "I think PC Connection was the one company that almost single-handedly brought mail order and all its negative connotations out of the Dark Ages. Whenever you mention PC Connection, they're considered one of the premier support companies, in addition to distribution companies, in the industry. They've really changed the way the entire industry looks at mail order."

The stunning success of PC Connection can be explained largely by its determination and by its proven ability to produce continuous innovations in every aspect of the business. Perhaps more important, PCC has succeeded by ignoring the conventional industry wisdom that low price is the only "innovation" that attracts customers to mail order.

It is obvious from talking to Patricia Gallup that the real impetus behind PCC's success is the company's commitment to *putting customers first* in an industry that assumes people will put up with anything to get a low price. In many cases, PCC is *not* the lowest price competitor. But by catering to customers instead of pursuing the industry's "one right way," PCC has climbed to the top of the heap, while many of its cost-conscious competitors have gone bankrupt.

A review of the growing laundry list of PCC's innovations shows a clear commitment to satisfying its customers. PCC was the first company in the industry to dispense free telephone advice to callers. And the calls are fielded, not by inexperienced salesclerks, but by technical consultants who go through extensive company training programs before they are put on the phones.

When phone support seemed inadequate to handle some customer queries, PCC took the bold step of constructing a multi-million-dollar production studio to develop instructional videos for inclusion (free of charge, of course) with hard-to-install equipment.

As a standard service, MacConnection, PC Connection's division for the Apple Macintosh, offers overnight shipping anywhere in the continental United States for just $3 (in most areas of the country, if the order is placed as late as 3:15 A.M., the package arrives the same day). Furthermore, the company often offers overnight replacement of defective products. A new package is often shipped "as soon as we're notified a customer has received a defective item," according to Patricia Gallup, who adds: "In many cases, we don't wait for the defective item to be returned to us before we send a replacement out."

PCC makes a point of keeping all of its advertised products in stock. But if for some reason a particular product is out of stock, the customer invoice is written at the current price—unless the new shipment arrives at PCC with a lower price tag. In that case, the customer is refunded the difference.

To make sure that customers—all customers—receive the highest level of service, PCC maintains a noncommission sales force. That way, the customer who is buying a diskette case gets the same attention as the customer who is buying a printer.

To improve its distribution system—another way of serving the customer—PCC makes use of state-of-the-art bar coding and an electronic data exchange system. This allows PCC to track the location of any item in the distribution system at any given moment. Use of such methods is rare among mail-order firms; once again, PCC is far ahead of its competitors.

Patricia Gallup has clearly developed a highly effective formula for generating continuous innovation. She offers this advice to those who wish to follow in PCC's innovative footsteps: "Learn to truly listen to your customers. Find out what they really want, and don't assume anything. Give them what they expect—and more."

CULTIVATING INNOVATION: THE IMPORTANCE OF CLIMATE

With technological, geographic, and political barriers to business competition crumbling, there is now an enormously expanded buyer's market. In this environment, only companies that court customers by constantly developing product and service innovations can hope to win their favor—and their dollars.

Alvin Toffler believes that all companies are now faced with what he calls the "innovation imperative." He declares: "No existing market share is safe today, no product life indefinite. Not only in computers and clothing, but in everything from insurance policies to medical care to travel packages, competition tears away niches and whole chunks of established business with the weapon of innovation. Companies shrivel and die unless they can create an endless stream of new products."

PC Connection has certainly mastered the art of creating an "endless stream" of innovations. And as Patricia Gallup points out in the opening tale of this chapter, it has managed to do so by creating an *environment of innovation*, giving employees free rein to experiment with new ideas as long as these mesh with the overall goals of the organization.

Creating a hospitable climate is critical if innovation is to blossom within the organization. It's true that innovation can spring up in the most controlled environments, just as flowers can force their way through the cracks in a sidewalk. But for innovation to *thrive*, for it to be continuous and consistent, the organizational climate must encourage and nurture it.

Innovation is the product of *knowledge* (of customer needs, of market trends, of competitors' offerings, of distributors' concerns, of changing technologies) and *empowerment*, the combination of autonomy and responsibility. The climate in which innovation is most likely to flourish is one in which employees are encouraged to accumulate knowledge continually, as they are at PC Connection. It is a climate in which open communication is the norm, in which employees have easy and complete access to information. And it is an environment in which all employees are empowered to act on their accumulated wisdom in order to generate continuous innovation.

Ricardo Semler, Semco's president, has found that innovation thrives in such a climate.

Semco S/A: "Technological Innovation Nucleus"

Ricardo Semler has developed within Semco a climate extraordinarily conducive to innovation by preaching—and practicing— the virtues of democracy, profit distribution, and information sharing. Employees work in autonomous, self-managed teams, with plenty of responsibility for decisions involving production processes, schedules, even production quantities. It's a working environment designed to stimulate the creativity for which Semco is known. Even so, Semler has formed a separate group, dubbed NIT, within Semco to make sure that eager employees are not stymied by the organization in their quest to innovate. Semler explains:

> We have a group which in Portuguese is called NIT; I don't know how it would translate, but it means "technological innovation nucleus." In this area which we call NIT, we move people who we feel have a tremendous potential for developing creative products, technology of any sort, but who we feel are being encumbered by the organization. These are normally the people who, over time, leave the organization so that they can start their own business and have the freedom which they've always wanted. So we said, "Don't leave." And we move them out of the organization and into NIT.
>
> What happens there? (1) They do not have a boss; they are not subordinate to anyone. (2) They can have no subordinates; they can't hire anybody. (3) They set their own salaries. (4) They do whatever they want. And (5) They are evaluated once a year to see whether their contribution is important enough to keep them there. It's as simple as that.
>
> The people who have been in that area for 2½ years have created seven new joint ventures, three new companies, and 18 new product lines.
>
> They make a hell of a lot of money. They make much more money than if they had gone into business on their own. They develop their creativity in any direction they want, and if they can make money with it, we are happy, because we make most of it and they make a part of it. And the part of it that they make, which is anywhere between 10 percent and 20 percent, can make them a millionaire over time.

Innovating in Infertile Soil: The Saga of the GE Compressor

By creating an internal climate for innovation in which employees are given complete autonomy and a generous share in the fruits of their innovative labor, Semco has developed a hothouse of innovation.

By contrast, let's examine what happens when the climate for innovation is unfavorable. Innovation cannot be carried out successfully in an organizational context structured, however subtly or unintentionally, to sabotage innovation. That's what General

Electric discovered when it set out to build a new compressor for its line of refrigerators and ended up with a financial nightmare rather than an innovative success.

In the fall of 1981, GE's appliance division in Louisville, Kentucky, hired a consultant to review its refrigerator business. His recommendation: Go abroad to buy a better compressor for the refrigerators, or build a new one at home. The company opted for the latter.

The following spring, a team assembled to design a new compressor settled on a rotary design. By the fall of 1983, funding was authorized for a $120 million factory in which the new compressors would be built. A year later, senior executives found test data on the new compressor acceptable and authorized production, which began in the spring of 1986.

In the summer of 1987, the first compressor failure was reported by a Philadelphia customer. This was followed by a host of similar failures, and in December 1987 General Electric dropped the rotary compressor and started replacing the defective units with purchased compressors, mostly foreign made. By the summer of 1988, investigators figured out the cause of the problem: The excessive wear of two powdered-metal parts ultimately prevented cold air from entering the refrigerator. The end result: In 1988, GE took a $450 million pretax charge for fixing the compressor.

What happened? Numerous problems and warning signs were ignored or overlooked along the way, but essentially the failure resulted from two related factors: poor communication and lack of partnership.

The engineers involved in the project were inexperienced in designing compressors. Nonetheless, they refused the help of experienced consultants, including a retired GE engineer, who could have cautioned that the compressor would probably break down under heat.

Managers were eager to cut costs, so they pushed for accelerated testing, curtailing essential field tests that would have disclosed the problem, and rushed into production. Furthermore, they ignored the warning signs that *did* appear early on. Several low-level salaried technicians who carried out the preproduction testing suspected the compressor might be defective, and told their superiors that some of the tested units showed signs of excessive wear. But the information was never communicated up the chain of command.

Ultimately, the project failed because the people involved worked from separate agendas instead of sharing a single vision. While the attempt at innovation was sincere, the climate for innovation was highly unfavorable. Knowledge was suppressed, the free flow of information was curtailed, and empowerment was replaced by struggles between the managers who sought to push the project forward at all costs and the employees in the trenches who cautioned against doing so. Instead of operating as a living, interdependent system, the project team adopted to the command-and-control structure of an old story organization.

General Electric has been initiating many successful attempts at innovation. After years of representing old story thinking, CEO Jack Welch has become an outspoken advocate of information sharing and full employee participation. This thwarted attempt demonstrates how deeply embedded old story approaches are even in an organization committed to change. It also demonstrates the importance of creating a partnership environment when attempts are made to produce a major innovation.

Cultivating Pockets of Innovation: Hewlett-Packard

The extent of PCC's commitment to innovation is relatively rare. General Electric represents a more common phenomenon—an old story organization that is struggling to transform itself into an innovator, sometimes succeeding and, as with the beleaguered compressor, sometimes failing.

It's not that PCC never fails. In fact, the company's encouragement of "fast failures" and its ability to change course rapidly are what enable it to produce an ongoing stream of innovations. This positive approach to failure stems from PCC's solid commitment to the new story innovation imperative. GE, by contrast, is in process, moving from the old story to the new. As a result, its expressed commitment to innovation is sometimes contradicted by old story systems and attitudes that thwart innovation.

Many large companies find themselves in GE's position, struggling to develop or maintain a culture of innovation in the face of lingering old story attitudes and behaviors. One way in which some of these companies tackle the problem is by creating autonomous "pockets of innovation" within the larger organization, miniclimates in which innovation can be cultivated and spread throughout the organization.

Chuck House, a Hewlett-Packard director of corporate engineering, has spent much of his career promoting the cause of innovation within his company. House has long been known as a maverick at HP. He's a team player, but he's not afraid to bend the rules if it's clear that the "coach" has made the wrong decision. For example, when coach (and cofounder) David Packard ordered him to stop working on a high-quality, large-screen video monitor years ago, he listened politely—then went back to designing the new product. The monitor achieved record sales, and in 1982 senior management awarded Chuck House a medal for "extraordinary contempt and defiance beyond the normal call of engineering duty."

Over the years, House has developed "pockets of innovation" throughout Hewlett-Packard, taking demoralized, unproductive groups and turning them into crackerjack innovators. He is adept at creating the proper climate for innovation.

Here's an example: In 1974, House accepted a temporary post as research manager for HP's demoralized New Ventures group in the Colorado Springs division. The group hadn't produced a worthwhile innovation in years, and its most promising and productive members had long since left for greener pastures.

House arrived in Colorado to a depressing scene. The New Ventures group was isolated from other HP divisions working on similar projects; there was minimal sharing of information. The group hadn't a clue about what the competition was up to. It was carrying out little research of any kind. And the attitude of its members was one of collective despair.

Chuck House, starting from scratch, succeeded in completely overhauling the group within three years. He devoted the first year exclusively to accumulating knowledge. His engineers spent their time reading journals, attending trade shows and conferences. House made it mandatory for every engineer to spend at least a week working somewhere else within the company and another week at a customer location, in order to gather valuable information and insights.

Gradually, armed with its newfound wisdom, the formerly demoralized group began generating dozens of ideas for product innovations and became actively involved with customers and with other HP groups. During this time, Chuck House shielded the group from senior managers, making sure that its members were given the autonomy and empowerment they needed to follow through on their innovative ideas.

Less than three years after House took on the research manager position, the New Ventures group, formerly derided within HP as the "dregs of the organization," received Innovation of the Year honors from *Electronics* magazine. The honored innovation was later inducted into the Computer Design Hall of Fame.

The turnaround at Colorado Springs is typical of Chuck House's work in spearheading innovative efforts at Hewlett-Packard. I asked him what happens to a team after he moves on to his next assignment. He told me:

> Most of the time, it develops a life of its own. Almost always one of two things happens: Either it disbands before I leave—in other words, we ran this experiment and decided the experiment didn't make sense and stopped the experiment; or it becomes robust enough that you can say that it's worth having for the company, in which case you get a more orthodox manager to run it.
>
> You either stay long enough so that it's clear it's a failure and you shoot it, or you stay long enough that it's successful and everybody's excited and profiting. The question then is how to keep that momentum. With a team that has been successful, it's pretty hard to knock the excitement out. It doesn't have to have me around at all, which is nice.

PARTNERSHIP BREEDS INNOVATION

It is clear that innovation blossoms in a favorable climate. When employees are given free access to information, when they are allowed and encouraged to enter into partnerships and learn with others inside and outside the organization, innovative ideas multiply. A company's most important innovations often spring from such partnerships—with other employees; with customers, suppliers, distributors; even with the community in which the organization operates.

Innovation and Partnership at PC Connection

PC Connection generates many of its innovative ideas by partnering with its customers, listening to them, encouraging their
feedback, and always trying to find new ways of satisfying them.
Positive responses from customers prompted PCC to strive for
ever faster delivery times and ultimately to institute its optional
overnight service. It developed telephone support and instructional videocassettes in response to obvious customer needs. Its
decision to replace foam peanuts in packing cartons with environmentally friendly tissue is another example of an innovation sug-
gested by customers.

Elliott Levine of Merisel comments on PCC's partnership approach to winning customers: "What they do, rather than buying
market share with their dollars, is they focus their attention on
what they can do to add value to sell their products. That's the
way they're growing their business." By listening closely to customers, by encouraging their feedback and suggestions, PC Connection is ensured of a continual stream of ideas, which it translates into service innovations.

In addition to partnering with customers, PC Connection partners with suppliers. Unlike many companies that ignore, minimize, or even abuse their suppliers, PCC regards them as vital
partners.

This approach to suppliers is an innovation in itself, and it
leads to other possibilities for innovation. By taking into consideration the needs of its suppliers, PC Connection has generated
important innovations that have benefited both members of the
partnership.

One of the most interesting of these innovations is PC Connection's policy of paying many of its suppliers on a "one day net"
basis—something unheard of in the mail-order industry (and rare
in any industry). By partnering with its vendors, by catering to
their needs, says Patricia Gallup, PC Connection reaps benefits as
well. She explains: "Just like with our customers, we try to give
them more than they would expect. Because we are so prompt in
our payments to the vendors, we are always first in their minds,
and that's really a good place to be. If the vendors are having
supply problems for some reason, and they have limited quan-

tities of products to ship, they have to choose who will get them. If we are in the forefront of their minds, they will think of us first."

Partnership with its employees drives many of PCC's innovations and helps explain why it is consistently innovative. Charles Hampden-Turner points out: "There is no escaping the underlying sense that the product or service can be no better, no more sensitive, subtle, aesthetic, congruent, or intelligent than are the relationships and the communication among those who create the product." Unless employees feel a sense of partnership with one another and with the organization for which they work, a high level of service and product quality cannot be sustained over time—nor can a high level of innovation.

PCC's partnership with its employees has led to another one of its most interesting innovations: building housing for them. Recently, the company purchased a 90-acre tract in housing-scarce Marlow and subdivided it into 10 building lots. PCC has been building homes for its employees on these lots.

According to Patricia Gallup:

We had been approached by a number of our employees during the boom in the real estate industry in the 1980s. We have many people who are just starting out, young people just getting married and starting their families, and getting into a position where they are considering buying their first home.

There just weren't any houses or building lots available for them in Marlow or in the surrounding towns. There were large parcels of land available, but they needed to be subdivided. Planning a subdivision requires a lot of specialized knowledge and administrative work.

We were approached by a number of employees who said, "We would like to get a group of people together to buy some land and subdivide it. Has the company thought about ever doing something like that? Or helping a group of us do something like that?" I certainly am not a developer. But we have in-house legal counsel, and we have a CPA on staff, and I decided we had the administrative capabilities to do something like that. I did see a piece of property that went on the market, that was on what I call a main road, which in Marlow means it is paved. It was fairly flat, nice land, and so I thought, "Maybe this is the time to do something."

So we did end up purchasing the property, and we subdivided it into 10 lots. They are anywhere between 7 and 15 acres in size. It's not a typical development. Each lot is quite large, and it's very wooded and nice. So far we have built four houses, and our plan was to sell them at cost to employees. Within weeks of completion there were contracts on all four.

Patricia Gallup recognizes that for PC Connection to sustain growth, it must help to ensure the sustainable growth of Marlow, the town in which it resides. The growth of the company must be reconciled with responsibility to the community, if both are to survive and thrive in the long run.

Innovation has sprung from PCC's partnership with the community of Marlow. The company's commitment is reflected in its dedication to preserving the integrity of the historic old town. PCC set up headquarters early on in an old Marlow mill, which it restored. Now it is investing $5 million in a new corporate headquarters nearby. It plans to make the 120,000-square-foot building as unobtrusive as possible. The site is well off the road, and landscaping will screen it from public view. PCC is striving to make the building blend in with the town's architecture.

Perhaps the most striking example of innovation growing from partnership with the community is PCC's purchase and restoration of the Christmas Trees Inn, a building that dates back to 1833. PCC purchased the inn in 1984 and restored it for use as a corporate training center. The company plans to offer training to the public, the community, customers, and employees.

PC Connection hired the workers who did the restoration. Patricia Gallup recalls:

We started out by restoring the mill that we occupy in the center of town. At the time that we started, it was at the end of the recession in the late 1970s and early 1980s. There were a lot of people in the construction industry out of work. We decided that we would be our own general contractor and hire a few people, and have our own construction crew on staff.

We hired a young man in town who had been a general contractor. He hired a crew and made all the structural changes on the Inn. When the structural modifications were complete, he went on to other projects. Someone who he had hired then took over the finish work and the actual restoration of the Inn. We set up our own milling and planing operation on site to reproduce all the specialized Victorian trim that was needed. Basically we brought the building back to the way it looked at the turn of the century.

Elliott Levine has witnessed the restoration firsthand, and according to him it is a sight to behold:

This is an enormous old inn on the Ashuelot River. When they say they were renovating it, that can mean anything from scraping the paint and repainting it to gutting it and reproducing virtually everything in there, preserving the architecture, with new fixtures and so forth. That's exactly what they have done. Personally, I have never seen a renovation of a building or an old home like this in my life—the quality in the workmanship of everything from the stairway to the wallpaper. They reproduced an old tin ceiling that of course was dented and rusted. They had someone reproduce the chandeliers, reproduce the banisters. It is one of the most beautiful buildings I have ever seen.

Preston Trucking: Partnering to Survive

Preston Trucking is another company that generates innovations through partnership. It was the innovative idea of partnership itself that rescued the company from the threat of demise in the late 1970s. By changing the nature of its relationship with its unions from one of adversaries to one of partners, Preston management breathed new life into its ailing organization.

Preston is now thriving because it has made a solid commitment to providing the highest quality of service in its industry. It maintains a close partnership with all of its customers. To underscore the seriousness of its commitment, Preston has a manager of customer partnerships.

Partnership is at the heart of Preston's product and service innovations. Customers play an integral role in the process within Preston that defines and measures service improvements and generates feedback. Preston and its customers work closely together in generating innovations. For example, Preston teamed up with Air Products and Chemicals of Tamaqua, Pennsylvania, to produce a video on proper techniques for handling cylinders. Preston partnered with J. C. Penney to develop a specialized computer scanning procedure to improve control of J. C. Penney's freight inventory. And Preston got its inspiration for building a first-class video facility from researching the procedure that J. C. Penney already had in operation.

Preston goes to great lengths to ensure a free flow of innovation-generating ideas. It cofounded a Quality Round Table whose members meet regularly to swap ideas. It has established a Quality College at which customers and noncustomers learn from one another's experiences. Customers are urged to visit Preston and observe its operations; during these visits, suggestions on how to improve customer satisfaction are actively encouraged. Preston's devotion to partnering with customers has enabled it to thrive in an industry whose membership has been declining dramatically.

Manco, Inc.: Joint Innovation

Manco, Inc., our featured story in Chapter 6, systematically studies innovative organizations to discover the reasons for their success. Manco is adept at transforming what it learns from its research into innovations of its own.

For example, CEO Jack Kahl says that he learned "grassroots research" from Wal-Mart, one of Manco's top customers. He explains that Wal-Mart holds a sales meeting each Saturday morning, during which employees discuss their ideas for innovations that the Wal-Mart stores can implement. Says Kahl: "Every single good idea that comes up in a given week at Wal-Mart that is really extraordinary sees its way through the district managers, regional managers, and gets a voice on Saturday morning. This allows it to be tested the following week and literally run across all the stores two weeks later."

Kahl copied this method: "So we developed a communication system in here that listens as good as theirs and began to use Wal-Mart as a role model for communication techniques—that's been the finest company for us to learn from."

Manco is an aggressively innovative organization. And like PC Connection and Preston Trucking, it generates many of its innovations through partnerships with other companies, including such customers as Wal-Mart.

Jack Kahl tells of a Manco innovation that resulted from a partnership with Federal Express:

> I met Fred Smith [CEO of Federal Express] at a marketing conference seminar. We showed him what we do with our Care-Mail line [of packaging materials]. We said, "Fred, there ought to be a way that we can share this and tie our two companies together."
>
> This is up onstage after hearing him talk, and he said, "Let me see the ad." So we showed him our cookie box ad, and we said, "Cookies are the number one most often mailed item from the American home; chocolate chip cookies are number one." And we said it would be great to be able to put on the box a suggestion that they Fed Ex them to get them there fresh and fast, and to put their logo on there.
>
> Well, he thought that was a good idea, and six months later, after they got through all the legal hoops, they came back to us. And now on every one of the Manco cookie boxes that's in Wal-Mart, Kmart, Walgreen's, and we're in every Army/Navy PX in the world today—if you want to mail cookies, you buy a Manco wax-lined cookie box with our bubble wrap. Wrap those cookies up in bubble wrap, and if you care to, just dial the 800 number that's got the Federal Express logo on it on our box. So we tied two great names together, the Federal Express name and Care-Mail.

Partnership with Wal-Mart led to the development of Manco's highly profitable CareMail line—including the cookie boxes. Kahl explains how this came about:

> After having sold to Wal-Mart for about eight years and having gotten to know the people very well, we got a call from their stationery buyer, Bob Thomas, who we were selling a few rolls of tape to—carton sealing tape. Bob told us to come down there. We sat down with him, and he said, "Jack, our grassroots research through our Saturday morning meetings has told us that people want padded envelopes, boxes, and mailing supplies in the store. We want you to do it. If you do it, we think you guys know how to package and you will do an excellent job. If you don't do it, you stand a good chance that whoever does the job is going to get the whole business, including your tape."

So, based on that kind of information, we came back to Cleveland [Manco headquarters], we talked about it, and we had a brainstorming session. We went home, and one of the fellows that was at that meeting, on the way home he came up with the name CareMail. He called me back and said, "Jack, I think I have the name for what we want to call this whole category."

When he came in and coined that name CareMail, it just created an explosion of excitement in our company. We shared that name with the people at Wal-Mart. Within a span of three months, we sourced the products, we sized out the industry, and we said that we wanted to be Hallmark at Wal-Mart pricing. We wanted to be the best in the way we greeted people, at a price that was Wal-Mart value-priced. In 90 days, we sourced, put together, and packaged a line of over 30 products, which we delivered to Wal-Mart that Christmas, for the Christmas selling season of 1986.

From that point on, we fine-tuned it, we color-coded the packaging, all from feedback that came from Wal-Mart store managers up through their grassroots research. We designed special racking to make more products sell in a more attractive design center. Today we have 5 feet of CareMail in every Wal-Mart store in America, as well as being the leader with over 70 percent market share in hardware stores, home centers, drugstores, food stores, and other mass-market merchandisers, including Kmart.

Company-to-company partnerships provide a visible sign of the interdependency that is developing as corporations move from a machine to an ecosystem model of business. The paradox of competing through cooperating is well illustrated in the midsummer announcement, in 1991, that archrivals IBM and Apple Computer planned a jointly owned venture to produce operating software compatible with the equipment of both companies.

INNOVATION AND THE LEARNING ORGANIZATION

Manco, PC Connection, Preston Trucking and other innovative organizations are constantly learning—from their customers; from their competitors; from their employees, suppliers, and distributors; and from others that are in any way connected with their businesses. The innovative organization is a learning organization, a giant laboratory of learning in which the gathering of information and the acquisition of knowledge are ongoing, integral parts of every employee's job.

PC Connection is clearly an organization in which learning is a central task for all employees. It is in constant contact with customers, suppliers, and other outsiders, gathering information about market trends, customer needs, and the activities of its competitors. To keep its finger on the pulse of its industry, PC Connection regularly monitors hundreds of mail-order catalogs, looking for innovations, trying to identify emerging trends.

Patricia Gallup, a firm believer in the connection between education and innovation, offers this advice to companies that want to become more innovative: "Do your homework. Research what the trends are in our society and how people's needs and expectations are changing. Think about your industry and what impact these changes could have on your business, or better yet, what influence your business could have on people's changing needs and expectations."

Even the advertisements of PC Connection are educational. According to *INC.* magazine, one microcomputer publication ranked PC Connection as its best-read advertiser, well ahead of "glossy, big-name spreads from Lotus Development, Ashton-Tate, NEC, and Toshiba." That's because the PCC ads are filled, not with hype, but with information. For example, one early double-page PCC ad carried the headline "If one more person asks me a question about multifunction boards, I will write an ad" and went on at length to explain the technical details of the product. The idea for the ad grew out of the experience of PCC telephone staffers.

A New Way of Thinking

Innovation requires a way of thinking that focuses on anticipating the future. William Wiggenhorn, senior vice president of Motorola, comments on the kind of thinking that is needed to anticipate and satisfy customer needs:

> In the middle 80s, we said customer satisfaction meant meeting the expectations of the customer. And then we changed it and said that it meant exceeding the expectations of the customer. Now we are saying it means anticipating the needs of the cus-

tomer, and once recognized, responding most quickly to those needs.

So once you deal with this whole anticipation area, then you say, "All right, what are the new skills I have to have to be able to anticipate what customers are going to need, so when they recognize the need, I can give it to them in perfect condition quicker than anyone else?" . . . You are beginning to look at the whole issue of intuition and creativity, paradigm shifts, etc. more than you have in the past.

The ForeSight Group of Sweden, a consulting firm with a stellar record for implanting the seeds of innovation in European and American companies, advises its clients: "Manage your mindset and behavior for innovation. You must learn new ways of behaving because the innovative—by definition—is unpredictable, ambiguous, and uncertain."

PC Connection's success is due in large part to the fact that its thinking is extraordinarily flexible, that it is always ready to adjust to the ambiguity and uncertainty of the new story world. Patricia Gallup comments: "I think that everyone in our company is accustomed to being flexible, being able to change and change quickly because of new technologies. We've always been in a dynamic environment; if something were to not work out, and we said, 'OK, we have to change direction—we have to stop doing this and try some other way,' our people are so flexible that this happens easily."

In the old story world of business, corporate strategy was set by executives on high. But a 10-year, 5-year, or even 1-year corporate plan, however polished, has less meaning and still less effectiveness in a world that reinvents itself daily. In this new world, explains Andy Grove, CEO of Intel, "people formulate strategy with their fingertips. Day in and day out they respond to things, by virtue of the products they promote, the price concessions they make, the distribution channels they choose." Old story strategic planning is inappropriate in this fast-changing environment; what is required is *strategic thinking* on the part of every employee. Employee-led planning processes that focus on the company's ability to execute strategy quickly and flexibly will be the norm in the new story. Clearly, executives will still be involved in the planning process, engaging in dialogue with employees to ensure that strategies, and the processes used to implement them, are in sync with the company's overall mission and objectives. But rather than dictating strategy, executives will work in partnership with employees, who will play an instrumental, hands-on role in the strategic planning process.

In the new story organization, there is little room for the typical employee of the old story firm, who "went through the motions" of a clearly defined job. For such an employee, "thinking" involved no more than rote memorization of facts and figures, patterns and processes. Even predicting the future merely required extrapolating from the past.

But no forecast can accommodate the rapid and unpredictable changes that are taking place. And rote memorization of facts plays less of a role in a world in which little is fixed.

The control and manipulation of data and objects that passed for learning in the machinelike culture of the old story organization have been replaced by a type of learning that focuses on fluid relationships and processes. This, in turn, demands a kind of thinking that emphasizes intuition, creativity, and anticipation—*proactive* thinking rather than the decidedly *reactive* thinking of the old story. Being proactive requires an ability to think systemically, to understand and anticipate the impact of individual actions on the organization as a whole. It is not merely a question of increasing emotional intensity or heightening the level of activity in order to "beat the competition" or "exceed our quotas."

There is obviously a place in the organization for old story expertise, with its focus on precision, analysis, and accuracy, but it can no longer take center stage. It is useful in developing a precisely engineered computer, for example, but it cannot by itself address the more important question of what kind of computer to build or whether to build one at all.

New story thinking focuses on intuition, creativity, and anticipation, on combining processes and reconciling opposites. It is more demanding than the manipulation of facts that characterized old story thinking. But despite its difficulties, this new style of thinking can be cultivated everywhere in the organization, as PC Connection vividly demonstrates.

We see evidence of new story thinking throughout PCC's operations. Patricia Gallup calls it "Yankee ingenuity." By whatever name, such thinking involves a commitment to constant experimentation with new ways of approaching problems and processes.

PCC is a master at reconciling opposites. Many of its key innovations reconcile low cost with superior service and support, though the conventional wisdom of the mail-order industry holds that poor service and support are the price customers pay in exchange for low cost. But PC Connection has ignored the conventional wisdom and found many ways of combining low cost (though not necessarily the lowest cost) with superior service and support.

For example, PC Connection was able to reconcile speedy delivery with low cost by thinking differently about the challenge and partnering with Airborne to develop its $3 overnight delivery service. Patricia Gallup explains:

> We started out believing that anything ordered from us should arrive in two days. At that time I think our slogan was: "Two days from our house to your house." We had such positive feedback from our customers that we began to realize this was an important issue for people. That's when we started looking into it further and saying: "What can we do? Let's do more."
>
> Our ideal was to have a single carrier who would bill us a dollar a pound to ship anywhere in the world. We came up with the slogan: "A buck a pound, the world around." It's one of those things that our people could really identify with.
>
> We talked to all the major carriers and ended up testing five. We gave them each a two-week trial period to see how they would do guaranteeing that products would arrive the next day. We tested UPS, Federal Express, Emery, Purolator, and Airborne. We chose Airborne because of their exceptional performance and incomparable pricing. While they didn't deliver for "a buck a pound, the world around," they were closer than anyone else. The slogan kept people excited for the duration of the negotiations.

PC Connection helped Airborne by suggesting ways of reducing costs. For example, PCC packs cartons into curved containers that conform to the inside of a cargo carrier. The containers can be moved from the warehouse to Airborne's planes without additional handling.

Patricia Gallup says that PC Connection could not have developed the $3 overnight service if it hadn't been for the new story thinking exhibited by Airborne. She told me: "We did choose Airborne because they are also an innovative company, and they really pay attention to their customers and are willing to try new things. We could identify with them as a company because of that. Sometimes you ask your vendors about doing something out of the ordinary and they'll instantly say, 'Well, that's not the way it's done. No one has done it that way before.' I don't think companies can be successful anymore if they feel or think that way."

FORMALIZING INNOVATION

A high degree of flexibility and informality is needed to generate opportunities for the serendipitous encounters and spontaneous discoveries that lead to innovation. On the other hand, as Sun Microsystems discovered, if a company is too flexible and informal, there is no way for it to learn how to innovate *as an organization*.

Through most of the 80s, Sun Microsystems was a high-flying Silicon Valley start-up. Formed in 1982, it was known for hiring the best, brightest, most aggressive, and most independent engineers and executives. This talented crew generated plenty of innovations for Sun during its first few years in business. But by the spring of 1989, the organization had gotten out of control. Sun reported a $20 million loss for its fourth fiscal quarter. Key executives defected, and many employees followed them out the door.

Much of the trouble at Sun could be traced to its addiction to independence. A telling company slogan from the early years, when Sun's star was rising, was "To ask is to seek denial."

The company had another slogan, "Bidding to win." Technical groups would compete with one another for top projects. Internal competition was intense. "It reinforced in the culture a real aggressive attitude," said Jim Moore, a management consultant who has worked with Sun. "Even though they would miss their promised date, it would lead them to beat the rest of the industry." But the strategy doomed large projects that required various groups within the company to cooperate with one another to achieve a mutual goal.

Scott McNealy, Sun's chairman and cofounder, managed to get the company back on track by simplifying its confused product line (another legacy of independent innovation) and introducing more coordination and control. "We've learned a lot," says Edward J. Zander, Sun's vice president of marketing. "You can't have 10,000 people going off doing what they want. Now we try to keep innovation within well-defined frameworks."

Flexibility must be supported by structure if innovation is to thrive. Paradoxically, the new story organization requires both a high degree of informality, to generate innovation, and a high degree of formality, to coordinate individual efforts and "institutionalize" lessons learned from various experiments.

Keith Pavitt suggests that "[w]hen firms generate innovation, or when they adopt innovations generated by others, . . . there is, at minimum, the *opportunity* for learning. In other words, there are two separable outcomes of innovation processes, the innovation itself and the learning about the innovation and innovative process. With successive innovations comes an increased ability to innovate and manage innovation."

If innovation is to become an organization's way of life, the informality of the innovative process must be reconciled with the formality needed to institutionalize the process. The idea is to "consolidate" the lessons learned through an innovative experiment and then to apply and refine them during the next innovative experiment. In this way, the organization can learn—*as an organization*—about the process of innovating, although the details of the various experiments may vary widely.

Sun Microsystems failed to learn about the innovative process. Its hyperindependent style prevented employees from learning from one another and ensured that each individual or group launching an innovation was essentially reinventing the wheel. As a result, successive innovations brought, not an increased ability to manage innovation, but lost learning and general disorder.

The process of formalizing innovation is one way in which the mechanical style of the old story is reconciled with the more fluid functioning of the new. The new story paradigm of flexibility and continuous change does not *replace* the old story model of fixity and predictability, but rather *subsumes* it.

The struggle to create a significant innovation in the midst of a massive organization, and to transfer the lessons learned to other parts of the organization, is well captured in the story of Jim Stryker at Ingersoll-Rand.

Formalizing Innovation at Ingersoll-Rand

Ingersoll-Rand is a company that has its roots in the old story but is experimenting with new story ideas. Like most businesses, Ingersoll-Rand was feeling the pinch of global competition in the 1980s. Its Power Tool division was facing a host of new competitors that were turning out products at an accelerating pace. At the same time, the division's product development cycle was steadily *increasing*; on average, it took three years to design and develop a new tool.

In late 1987, Dick Poore, sales vice president for the Power Tool division, decided that a new approach was in order. He asked Jim Stryker to find a way to compress the product development cycle. Under the code name Operation Lightning, Stryker developed a team charged with turning out a new air grinder in one year—one quarter the usual development time.

Stryker (dubbed "the Strykeforce" by coworkers) describes how he approached the process:

> Basically, we started with the premise that we have been developing products for 75 years, and some of them we have done exceptionally well. Some of them have been less than exceptional in terms of market acceptance. Let's use our own experience and our own culture to evaluate what we did well and what we could have done better. So what we effectively did was create a development process, based upon our own experiences, which would allow us to start taking time out of the process.

One of the first challenges was to develop the proper mindset for innovation. Says Stryker:

> Everything we did to go from four years to one year was a series of paradigms we had to change, just in the way we did things.

If you have good people and your people are smart and your people want to win—if you work on that basis, then you have got to go back and ask why it took you four years and you came out as ho-hum compared to a real winner—it has got to be in the way you went about it or the way you organized to get it done.

If you make that assumption, then it says that you have got to scrap your organization structure. You have got to scrap your approach, challenge everything, and then reassemble the structure to tackle the task differently. In fact, it becomes real easy for me when I go into another organization, because more often than not I find how they are just like we used to be, and that they are seeking innovations in old ways without setting in place innovative approaches.

The traditional approach to product development at Ingersoll-Rand involved passing products "over the wall" from one department to another—from marketing to engineering to manufacturing and, finally, to sales. The process was riddled with problems along the way, including poor communication, turf fights, and plenty of finger pointing.

So Stryker scrapped the usual approach, eliminated the barriers between functions and set up a multifunctional team to develop the product simultaneously rather than in sequence. The team consisted of both insiders, from engineering, manufacturing, purchasing, sales, and marketing, and outsiders, including customers and distributors.

Creating this hub of innovation in the midst of the organization was difficult, Stryker told me: "The real challenge is: How do you create this team within an organization without causing mass confusion and raising interpersonal issues?"

Stryker handled the interpersonal issues by teaching team members to trust one another and embrace a single vision: "The more we pushed the team members to trust each other, to understand what their objective was and that everybody's objective on the team was the same, the less dissension we got among the team members."

Another challenge was to keep senior management out of the picture, so that the team would be able to work autonomously. It wasn't easy, Stryker told me: "It was very difficult. There was this inherent desire that, one, I need to know every week what you are doing, and two, I need to be told what you are doing so that I can put my managerial insight into it. If you do that, . . . the team then doesn't make any decisions. The team then says, 'Look, I have got to ask the mysterious management, whoever that mysterious management is, to find out if that's what they want us to do or not.' And that just eats up time and eliminates the innovation."

To make a long story short, after plenty of false starts, lots of heated arguments, significant compromise, a bit of luck, and a budget infusion, the new air grinder, dubbed Cyclone, was put on sale in June 1989. The new tool sold briskly from the start, and even garnered an award from the Industrial Designers Society of America. Now a number of other Ingersoll-Rand teams have embraced the Strykeforce process.

Looking back, Stryker reflects that once it became clear that the team was going to succeed, the larger organization rallied around it:

> Part of its [the team's] survival was the fact that, like a lot of other things, people want to be part of a winning team. When it became clearer and clearer, as we moved through the process, that this was going to be a winning effort, the organization finally started to understand what we were trying to do. So what has evolved has been a number of small teams being set up to deal with our long-range future development. We currently have five plus teams working on different projects within our own division.

Those teams have benefited from the experience gained during Operation Lightning, says Stryker:

> The Cyclone model was the first of a series of products, and it's kind of like the old two plus two equals five. We did super with the first series, and when we came out with the second series, it just enhanced the first series even more.
>
> The other models were developed within the cross-functional team, using primarily the same team members. The key element here is that if you cut time out of it, you also cut corners, so a lot of what we did in the second series was how to innovate in terms of cost and manufacturing processes.

The Strykeforce process has expanded outside the Power Tool division. Stryker has helped several of Ingersoll-Rand's domestic businesses to adopt the methodology of Operation Lightning.

Now that Ingersoll-Rand has successfully launched several innovative projects, it has become more accustomed to change and innovation as a way of life, according to Jim Stryker: "The whole concept of accepting change and organizationally being willing to challenge what one is doing is not totally accepted all the way down in the organization, but it is certainly substantially into the engineering group and into the manufacturing and engineering people's mindset."

Ingersoll-Rand has not only embraced the Operation Lightning process on the domestic front; it has even carried the process to its overseas businesses. Jim Stryker is enthusiastic about the company's latest adventure:

> The most exciting thing to me is that we have put our development process into the United Kingdom. Since the process must deal with organizational culture, you must break paradigms. It's exciting to see us be able to get the UK team and the whole organization in our UK facility to buy in on what we are trying to get accomplished.

Jim Stryker's experience in developing the Cyclone grinder makes him confident that innovators can be found anywhere. Looking back at Operation Lightning, he recalls:

> Quite frankly, every day there was somebody that came up with some bright idea. It really got exciting. An air grinder in a manufacturing environment is as close to a commodity product as you can get. So the degree of innovation that we were able to drive in that project, overall, was absolutely flabbergasting because we started with a product that everyone perceived as a commodity.

Stryker advises others to look at every product as a potential source of innovation and to see in every employee a potential innovator:

If you limit yourself to including on the team only "innovative thinkers," then I think you have condemned your process transferability. . . . In the normal organization, you may have one or two or three [stereotypically] innovative thinkers. And then what do you do? You can't just staff an organization with just innovative people. . . . I think the concept of staffing your team with a leader who can convey that vision to the team and push the team to create within itself innovative solutions is probably the way you can do it. You can find leaders in your organization. They don't have to be totally innovative, but I think the leadership is what drives the vision.

The ForeSight Group and Intrapreneurship

Sven Atterhed, cofounder of the ForeSight Group (mentioned earlier), agrees that it is critical to foster a spirit of innovation within the entire company rather than rely on a handful of "creative types" to carry out innovation. He told me:

> There have always been people who have done new things in companies, often against the prevailing corporate culture. They had to have a lot of strength to do that because they worked against the corporate culture. Those kinds of people have been written up by you and by Tom Peters, Gifford Pinchot, and others—Art Fry at 3M, Chuck House at Hewlett-Packard, etc. They may have spent 80 percent of their energy fighting the corporate culture, fighting the system, fighting the prevailing roles, and so on. The 20 percent left over that they have been able to use for the project has been enough to push the project through.
>
> But those kinds of people are very, very rare. If you are a company, you may have to wait for many years to get one. Now our idea is to systematically approach this, and we know that we have a system which can get you a number of these people, and utilizing "normal people." It's never going to be easy, but there are people that you find in any company.

ForeSight has developed an effective program for finding them. Ray Smith, CEO of Bell Atlantic, is enthusiastic about the results of the ForeSight Intrapreneurship Program, introduced in

1988. Dubbed the "Champion" program, it drew 300 entrepreneurial employees out into the open, where they received extensive coaching and training from ForeSight over a period of six to eight months.

Under the Champion program, employees develop proposals for projects. If the proposals are accepted, the intrapreneurs are given seed money to implement them. As an incentive, they are offered the option of taking a 10 percent pay cut in return for 5 percent of the profits produced by the project after commercial introduction.

There are now 23 active projects in the Champion pipeline at Bell Atlantic. At least one, THINX, a software program, has already met with rave reviews in the marketplace.

According to Smith,

> Champion has now become an actual revenue source in our strategic planning process. That's the ultimate testimony of importance in a corporation—a business plan with dollars of investment and targeted returns. In five years, we expect annual revenues of over $100 million from Champion projects. My question when I first saw the 1995 projection was, "Is this hope or smoke?" I was told that the figure was conservatively stated.

(For a review of the ForeSight method for teaching companies their process of innovation, see the Learning Tale in Chapter 10.)

"THE STRONGEST WILL SURVIVE"

Patricia Gallup reflects on her company's efforts to remain flexible and innovative:

> It's part of our company culture and philosophy that in order to be successful and in order to survive in our industry, we really do have to be innovative.
>
> As an anthropologist, I have a real appreciation for the process of evolution. Knowing how things evolve culturally and in nature gives you a better understanding of how people evolve, and how your company evolves. It's the whole natural selection process at work. Survival of the fittest, I guess. We try to keep the company healthy because we know that the strongest will survive.

In fact, it is the notion of "survival of the *fit*" that makes PC Connection such a resounding success. Because the company is well suited to the environment in which it operates, because it partners with internal and external stakeholders so as to achieve maximum speed, flexibility, and responsiveness, it is far more likely to thrive in a world of constant change and intense competition.

When I asked Patricia Gallup to explain PCC's remarkable record of innovation, she told me: "It's just what we like to do. Our interest is in being creative and in making life more pleasant for the person whose path crosses ours. We're not just interested in the bottom line."

She added: "If you really like what you are doing, success comes naturally because you are dedicated to learning about, and keeping up with, what's going on in your industry. This is extremely important in computers and high tech. When it comes to being successful you really need to have a true love of what you are doing and feel that it's important."

Chapter Five

Smart Teams: Self-Management in Action

Ricardo Semler, introduced in Chapter 1, assumed the leadership of Semco S/A in 1980, when it was on the brink of bankruptcy. Now Semco, which manufactures equipment for the marine and food processing industries, is one of Brazil's most profitable and most admired organizations.

I spoke with Ricardo Semler recently about his personal philosophy of business and about Semco's transformation into a team-based organization. He shared the following insights with me:

I have always had a penchant for travel. Since I took over the company, which was about 10 or 11 years ago, and specifically in the last 7 or 8 years, I do one long trip per year—between a minimum of 45 and a maximum of some 80 days. When I travel, I never call the office and the office can never find me either. It is a way that I have found to discover how much we need the organization, how much the organization needs us, and how we build all of our hierarchies around these mutual needs.

For example, last year, during October and November, I visited Syria, Iraq, Iran, Azerbaijan, and Kurdistan. The year before, I retraced Marco Polo's route through Iran, Afghanistan, the Himalayas, Mongolia, etc. The year before that, I camped through Rwanda and southern Africa. The year before that, I went through the magnetic North Pole on a dog sled.

So I keep myself busy besides the company. But the great point of all that is not only that I enjoy doing this but that the company, in the meantime, has grown nine times. Now you are probably thinking that I should travel a little bit more and it will grow even more. But it really has to do with how the company is organized and the fact that it really does not need me.

But I do contribute to it; I have to because there are systems in place so the company can fire me if they want.

When I came back from this trip, this thing with Marco Polo and retracing his route—when I got back and I was about to go to my office, they said, "Your office is not here anymore." So I said, "Well, where *is* my office?" I was on the first floor, last one on the right. They had reduced my office down to one third of what it used to be, and until today I have not found the Persian carpet that used to be under my sofa.

What does that mean? That means people have such respect for competence that they no longer need closed offices and Persian rugs and lots of secretaries, and they don't have to park that close to the door. It is not as relevant as it used to be.

People find that they no longer need some of the spaces that they had created for themselves within the organization that were based on hoarding information, and therefore power. Power within the organization will have to come from the additional value that they are able to provide.

The hierarchy tends to disappear when people have the same basis of information. Now we publish our balance sheet and all of our financials and all of our numbers monthly on the bulletin board, which means everybody knows how much we are making, what the payroll is, what raw material contributes, what strategies we have, what price increases we need.

We have one of the few plants in the world where everybody on the shop floor has flexible time. All of the associates on the assembly line come and go at whatever time they want, and they control that time schedule on their own.

When we first started this, people said, "Well, if the guy can come anytime that he wants in the morning, and he is on an assembly line, what happens if the guy next door does not come?" And we said, "He knows that too."

We start from a few basic assumptions. First of all, we only hire responsible adults. We are hiring people who have a long series of responsibilities in their homes, with their families. We don't believe that we are hiring a person and that he will come to receive his pay and that he will do his most not to work. We don't believe that, so we say, "He will solve that problem one way or the other."

When we started this system, our board of directors said, "OK, but let's set up a committee to monitor this. A committee is going to meet biweekly in the beginning and then weekly and so forth until this system is in place, and it will list all the areas that were stopped because of lack of people, and it will control it, and it will discuss it."

That committee has never met. Why? Because on the first day, the guy turned around to the other guy and said, "What time are you coming in tomorrow?" because he knew that if he didn't come in and the other guy didn't come, the assembly line would stop. So we've never really had that problem. We are starting from the assumption that people will not abuse; people are not out there to steal from you.

It is very common for me to call somebody and say, "I need to talk to this guy. Where is he?" And they tell me, "He is in Germany." And I say, "What in the hell is he doing in Germany?" And I'm told, "Oh, he has been there for two months." We are supposing that if he went off to Germany for two months, he left something in shape while he was gone.

The guy we call a partner, a person generally known as a division general manager, has marketing, finance, human resources, production, sales, etc. all under him. All of the people who report to him have 15, 20, 35 people reporting to them, and that is all the layers of management. So when the partner meets every Monday morning with these 10, 12, 14 people who have leadership positions, he's just met with everybody who decides something in terms of leadership.

At that meeting they talk about everything—about prices, about salaries, about strategies—you name it, they talk about it. They *decide* also. They don't refer back to corporate, which in any case only has 14 people. Two or 3 travel as much as I do. So it is no use consulting corporate; you won't find anybody.

When we started this whole process, we had 11, then we had 8, then we had 6 layers of management. Today we have three layers altogether.

Actually, they're not "layers." What we use is the image of concentric circles. We are really trying to symbolize the idea that there is a lot of interaction that goes on in a circle form because it moves throughout the organization, and decisions move that way. This is much different from the idea that decisions are made by someone above and the commands come downward. The concentric circles help to diminish the idea of a vertical hierarchy.

The circle in the center has the counselors. The next larger circle is the partners who are heads of the eight divisions. And the biggest circle is everybody else, the associates and coordinators.

We chose the word *counselor* for the five people in the smallest circle because we were looking to impress upon people the idea that those at the very top of the organization have to have the capacity to relate their experience, their ideas as catalysts, and not as commanders of anything. So we see them a little bit as coaches, a little bit as simple catalysts.

The managers at Semco are insecure because if they do revert to a traditional command-and-control style, they might find that their people will not necessarily follow them. People know that they do not depend on that one manager to survive, and so they can resist the command and control, knowing that their chance of being fired is very, very slim because we have committees which have to be consulted before anybody is fired.

We had a recent example where everybody wanted a change in the layout of the office. So the manager went out and hired a consulting firm, and they redid the layout of the floor.

It was beautiful. But the moment he started to put it into place, all the people on the floor stopped. And they said, "Hey, hold on. We're living in this thing, and according to the company philosophy, we want to talk about it." The manager was absolutely shocked because it simply hadn't occurred to him that they wanted to be part of it.

It was no big deal. They sat down and looked at the whole layout. They took over a week to study it, and all the associates commented on what they wanted. Then they put into place almost precisely the layout that had already been done, but now everybody was happy about it.

We are democratic about our leadership. We are all careful, in the world in general, about choosing our political leaders. But in our companies we don't mind appointing people for life. That's how most businesses are run—you take somebody you like, and you say this guy is going to be a great manager, and you appoint him. And that's the system.

So we said, "Well, let's be a little bit more democratic about that and find out whether the people who work for this guy think the same thing we do." We started a questionnaire, which is a 55-multiple-question form and which is filled in anonymously by all the people who work with a given manager. They fill in this thing twice a year. They tell us how much they respect him and if they think he is competent, and how he handles the money, and how he handles a whole bunch of things. They get a copy, and he gets a copy.

And then he sits down with these guys, again 15 people maybe, and says, "Well, I don't know who said what, but I know that 72 percent of you people think that I am not careful with money." So he's got something to talk about, and we know what he's got to talk about because everybody has a copy.

Over the years, the only way that he can remain in the company, and of course even think of a chance of promotion, is if this whole process proves that he is a competent guy.

When we need to promote somebody or when we are hiring somebody from outside, we go through the same process: Anybody who is a candidate for a promotion or a candidate for a leadership position has to be interviewed and approved by all his future subordinates as well as his future boss. This process takes longer, at least a couple of weeks longer, than it would to do it the other way. But one thing is for sure: The day the guy starts on Monday morning, everybody knows him, everybody knows all about him, everybody is an accomplice of his selection and his promotion. We don't have to worry about it anymore; there are a whole lot of people worrying about it, because it was their decision.

Our managers find, over time, that it is a tremendous relief to know that the organization could go on very well without them and that every six months people are still saying they need them. Before, you didn't know whether you needed them or not. Now you know that they want you, because they are telling you every six months. Of course, a few people are told that they are not wanted anymore, and that's obviously a problem for those people. But for the organization as a whole, it has a systemic function.

People can take the company in any direction they want, and the only people who have promotion possibilities within the company are people who are making leadership decisions every day. They are installing new product lines, increasing prices, buying machinery. This is happening all day long, and only the people who are leaders really are going to be ratified time after time within this system.

Practically no one, and it is a personal decision, stays in the same position for more than two or three years. We try to motivate people to move their areas completely from time to time so they do not get stuck to the technical solutions, to ways of doing things in which they have become entrenched. We know, over time, that the leadership people will learn much more from trying new situations and going to new areas and working with new people.

So every two or three years our people rotate functions very drastically. We will come to someone and say, "You are a scales sales manager. How would you like to be a controller for rocket fuel propellants?" The guy might say: "I don't know anything about rocket fuel." So we say, "Well, you know about people and you know about leadership, so we'd like to try you over there." Normally, people will ask for that. They will say, "Look, I think that by the end of the year I have done what I thought I had to do in this department. Now I am ready to move on to something else."

We have to be careful to give people a chance to make a lot of money even if they are not in a leadership position, without having to go into management, which may not be one of their strengths.

So we have a lot of people in the company who make more than their bosses. Why? Because the guy is a software expert or he's got a specific quality which is difficult to find.

Leadership is a pretty common thing, a pretty ordinary thing as compared to understanding software or as compared to building rockets. One of our product lines is rocket fuel propellant for space shuttle systems for NASA. It is a pretty complicated thing, and it is more complicated than sitting down with 15 people and saying, "People, let's get organized." So we pay the guy more when he knows how not to blow up a space shuttle versus how to avoid having people coming in late every morning.

Besides paying well, we want to provide jobs that are self-fulfilling. We want to provide jobs where somebody is able, after a long period, to look back and say, "What I did was worthwhile. What I did was an honorable job and it was a fulfilling job."

So we said, "What can we possibly do with a receptionist under such a concept? What can we possibly do with office boys, what can we do with some secretaries under this concept?" And the answer was, "We can try living without them and see if we can move them on to something better."

At this point, the company has no secretaries. I had three secretaries, then two secretaries, and then I had one secretary. Nobody has secretaries anymore. There are no receptionists. There are no auxiliary functions of any type. There is no assistant of anything; people do their own work.

I think none of our people would complain that they are not autonomous. They would probably complain more of the loneliness of excessive autonomy, that they would like to have more of the corporate structure to talk to. But, on the other hand, they don't want to pay for it, which is what they do every time they approve the annual budget. The corporate budget has been cut down and down and down every single year.

Even though I'm the president, it has been 10 years at least since I have signed a check or a purchase order. I do not remember, in the history of my time in the company, any major decision that I alone have made. I am sure I have not made any. I have participated, and I have lobbied.

It is much like a presidential system versus a parliamentary system. I may be prime minister, but I have to lobby. I have to call people at night and say, "Hey, what do you think about that new machine?" And then sometimes I am outvoted—I am outvoted very, very frequently.

And I don't repent. There are many times when I come back and say, "Well, had it gone my way, I am sure that this would have been a great success, but no one really knows." But I have looked back on many decisions that certainly would have been flops had I insisted.

It is not exactly civil disobedience, but people will often show that they are not willing to go along with things at Semco. For example, recently we sent out a memorandum from the counselors about a specific marketing program which we thought was especially bright. Weeks later, nothing had happened with it.

So we brought it up at a meeting. We said, "We put this out weeks ago. What happened?" And they told us, "We looked at it, we discussed it with the people, and we thought it wasn't adequate, so we didn't do it." That was that. We said, "Well, OK. Let's go on to the next item."

By wholeheartedly embracing the concept of teamwork, Ricardo Semler has succeeded in transforming Semco S/A from an ailing firm on the verge of bankruptcy into a healthy, profitable organization of fully participating partners. Semco is an exemplar of the team-based new story organization, a company in which group decision making informs and guides every aspect of operations.

The spirit of teamwork permeates the organization. Work teams "run the show" at Semco—setting their own time schedules and production goals, sharing information and profits, determining how earnings will be distributed, voting on new hires, deciding who gets promoted, formulating the corporate budget, and making critical strategic decisions, such as choosing the location of new plants. Many Semco employees even set their own salaries. The fact that Ricardo Semler can, and does, leave the company for months on end with no ill effects is testimony to the effectiveness of teamwork at Semco.

Ricardo Semler is committed to keeping Semco's divisions small enough to maintain a true spirit of teamwork and partnership. Says Semler: "We want to have, in a given business unit, only as many people as can know each other, as can come to work whatever time they want, as can assume the responsibility for the productivity of the business without us having to watch."

Semler decided to limit the size of business groups over the objections of more traditional thinkers who insisted that bigger must be better. Semler recalls:

> When we started breaking up divisions every time they got to be bigger than 100 or so people, we had people say, "Oh, you can't do that, because the economies of scale would disappear." So I said, "Well, let's look at these economies of scale one by one." And you find out that a lot of them don't work the way they were originally designed to work, because a lot of the external, environmental variables are larger than your capacity to control.
>
> But even if you could control them, the second issue is: How much are you losing because you cannot count on people? How much are you losing because employees have to clock in at a certain time, because they have a segmented function, and because they retire thinking that they could have contributed much more to the organization had somebody asked them more

questions or given them more space to do so during all those years that they were there?

At Semco, there are no such bureaucratic restrictions. Functions and leadership positions are rotated regularly to prevent hardening of the corporate arteries. Semco's circular structure and "human scale" division size ensure that hierarchy is kept to a minimum, democracy flourishes, and information flows freely throughout the organization. Employees are encouraged, and amply rewarded, for contributing their best efforts to the organization. And there is no time clock to punch.

What few management positions exist at Semco are not of the old story variety. Semco managers (counselors, partners, coordinators) serve as coaches and counselors, not as cops. As Ricardo Semler points out in the chapter's opening tale, any would-be pioneer manager who attempts to impose his will by fiat soon learns that the true power of the Semco organization rests, not with the individual, but with the team.

THE NEED FOR TEAMWORK

Semco has discovered what many companies are just beginning to recognize: If we are to tap the full potential of employees—an essential requirement for competing in the 1990s—we must bring them together in teams. Ongoing innovation, the central task of the new story organization, requires constant communication, sharing of ideas, and coordination of activities, and these in turn demand close relationships among employees. Such close relationships cannot develop among employees who are working in isolated cubicles or departments; they are cultivated in the context of teams, as the story of Semco illustrates.

A team usually consists of 5 to 30 employees who work in close collaboration in order to pursue the team's objectives. Some organizations become "team-based," utilizing teams as the dominant work unit of the organization. In others, teams come together for specific projects—for example, the development of a new product—and then disband.

Teams can be cross-functional, drawing from different departments and functions within the company. They can be directed by a manager or they can be "self-managed." Regardless of which form evolves, the team is the basic holon of the partnership organization, the fundamental process of the new story of business. I use the term *process* because the team in the new story is not a fixed work unit, not a rigid entity, but rather a fluid, flexible *pattern of movement* of people and resources over time.

Teamwork is essential in the new story world in which speed, creativity, and flexibility are prerequisites for success and constant change is the context in which the organization operates. Self-managed, cross-functional teams can move swiftly, flexibly, and effectively to produce innovations. Such teams can be assembled and dismantled quickly. Team members pool their ideas and learn one another's jobs. The teams harness and amplify the creative power of the work force. When truly empowered, they can turn bored, robotized, demoralized employees into innovative, productive, fully participating partners.

The presence of empowered teams is a clear sign of an organization on the path of transformation to the new story. For true teamwork can be built only on a new story foundation of shared values, workplace democracy, and a commitment to partnership and full participation.

TEAMWORK AT VOLVO

Volvo, the Swedish automaker, is conducting a serious experiment in teamwork. In 1974 Volvo dismantled the assembly line at its facility in Kalmar, Sweden, and replaced it with a system in which cars are built by employees who work in small, decentralized teams. Now the experiment is being extended to the company's new plant in Uddevalla.

Volvo is testing to see if the assembly line has become outdated in a world in which mass markets no longer exist. The company is betting that team spirit and a return to individual craftsmanship will improve quality, increase innovation, and lead to employees taking greater pride in their work.

The Uddevalla plant, completed in 1990, makes Volvo's 740 and 940 models. At full capacity, it can employ 1,000 workers and turn out some 40,000 cars annually in one shift. In its first year of operation, it produced 16,100 cars and that number was expected to increase to 22,000 by the end of 1991.

The introduction of teamwork has not been the rousing success its proponents had hoped for in the first year. There are indications it has boosted morale and lowered absenteeism (the norm in Sweden is 20 to 30 percent). But productivity in this experiment is nowhere near Volvo's plant in Ghent, Belgium, where it takes about half the time to build a car using the assembly line approach. Lennert Ericsson, president of the Metal Workers union at the Uddevalla plant, says: "I am convinced that our way (teams) will be successful and competitive. Our next goal is to be better than Kalmar, and when we get to that, our goal will be to get to Ghent." He added that the process of breaking in a radically new system "puts big demands on people and everyone doesn't put up with that."

An M.I.T. study on the global car industry, *The Machine That Changed the World*, predicts that Japanese-style assembly line operations will prevail in auto plants. Volvo's president, Christer Zetterberg, says it's premature to judge the Uddevalla experiment, but he's prepared to modify it if productivity doesn't improve.

At the Kalmar facility, work teams produce sections of a car. At the Uddevalla plant, self-managed teams assemble complete cars, from start to finish.

Here's how the system works at Uddevalla. Employees work in assembly teams with 8 to 10 members. There is no assembly line. Cars being assembled are not moved by conveyor from worker to worker; they are assembled in a stationary position. A special device tilts the body of a car at various angles so that workers have easy access to it.

Outside suppliers deliver components to the plant's materials center. Workers at the materials center supply assembly teams with just-in-time materials through automatic carriers that move on magnetic floor tracks. A computer controls the flow of materials, but workers are able to vary their flow in accordance with variations in the working rhythms of the assembly teams.

Volvo's teams closely parallel Semco's. Volvo's assembly teams have a high degree of autonomy and responsibility. They set their own break times and vacation schedules. When a team member is absent because of illness or for some other reason, the team simply redistributes its tasks to fill in for the absentee.

Like Semco, the Volvo teams are self-managed. They participate in policy-making and are responsible for a variety of tasks—

quality control, production and construction planning, shop floor layout, developing work procedures, servicing equipment, and ordering supplies.

Uddevalla workers, like those at Semco, are paid for performance. In addition to basic wages, employees can earn bonuses for maintaining quality and productivity and for meeting weekly delivery targets.

The Uddevalla plant has no supervisors or foremen. The only "chiefs" are the managers of the six production workshops, each of which has 80 to 100 employees who are subdivided into assembly teams. The managers of the production workshops have direct contact with the leaders—called "coordinators"—of the assembly teams, who, like Semco's leaders, are chosen on a rotating basis.

To make the system work, Volvo ensures the free flow of information within the plant. It provides employees with abundant information and takes pains to ensure that they have in-depth understanding of the company's strategy, history, and traditions. Like Semco, Volvo encourages input from its employees on everything from process innovations to new product ideas.

Volvo has invested heavily in the training of its Uddevalla workers. A 16-week initiation course is only the beginning of a 16-*month* training program in which workers learn the art of auto assembly. Seminars and informal networks encourage the sharing of experiences and the cross-fertilization of ideas. Senior managers hope that the knowledge acquired at Uddevalla can be transferred to other parts of the company, so that the innovation process can be formalized throughout Volvo.

The Uddevalla plant reflects Volvo's philosophy of putting people first. Designed by Romaldo Giurgola, a renowned Italian-American architect, it is a simple, elegant, and serene structure. Its noise levels are low, its lighting is natural, its colors are soothing, and it is well ventilated.

As noted, the team structure has already boosted morale and lowered absenteeism. And the Uddevalla quality levels already match those of Volvo's top facilities. However, it is still too early to tell how the Uddevalla experiment will play out.

Both the union and management seem confident that the new system, with its emphasis on job enrichment, full participation, flexibility, and autonomy, will lead to a healthier organization.

Goran Carstedt, former president of Volvo/Sweden stated: "The more authority you give away to [employees], the more you get back in initiatives and ideas even you did not foresee."

It's interesting to note that in 1984, a full 10 years after Volvo dismantled its assembly line at Kalmar, General Motors established its *Group of 99*. This cross-section of managers, staff, and UAW members collectively traveled 2 million miles to study new ways of building small cars. One of their conclusions was that employees performed best when they were a part of the decision-making process.

CINCINNATI MILACRON: TEAMING UP TO MEET THE COMPETITION

Another testimony to the power of teamwork comes from Cincinnati Milacron, a leading U.S. manufacturer of plastics machinery. In the early 1980s, when the U.S. market for plastics machinery was growing by roughly 10 percent a year, Japanese-made equipment began to flow into the U.S. marketplace. But because of the healthy industry growth rate, most American manufacturers of plastics machinery were not concerned.

By 1985, however, foreign competition had captured half of the U.S. market. Two thirds of the 15 U.S. manufacturers of plastics machinery were forced out of business by their international competitors during the 1980s. Cincinnati Milacron is one of just five companies that survived the decade. And it did so by embracing teamwork.

By 1983, workers at an Ohio plant of Cincinnati Milacron realized that to save the plant, and their jobs, from foreign competition, they would have to make drastic changes in their way of doing business, and specifically in their way of developing products.

Product development at Cincinnati Milacron conformed to the standard old story method that Ingersoll-Rand had practiced. In the course of the development cycle, products were passed, sequentially, from one department to another.

Like Jim Stryker at Ingersoll-Rand, when Harold Faig was assigned to manage the development of an improved machine, he organized a cross-functional team to develop the machine simultaneously rather than in sequence. The team consisted of nine employees from marketing, engineering, manufacturing, purchasing, and inventory. The machine was an injection molder, and because of team leader Faig's nine-month deadline, the operation was dubbed Project 270.

The team members began by talking to customers, researching the competition, and analyzing what the market needed and Cincinnati Milacron lacked. The information they gathered was sobering. Customers complained of slow delivery times and told them that Cincinnati Milacron's competitors offered superior *and* less expensive machines.

Faig concluded that if the team was to develop a competitive product, it would have to cut the usual two-year development time by more than half and to slash development costs by 40 percent. Furthermore, the team would have to produce a machine that was faster and offered more options than earlier Cincinnati Milacron models.

To meet the team's ambitious goals, Faig searched for ways to streamline bureaucracy and improve efficiency. He arranged to have the team report directly to the vice president of plastics machinery, thus minimizing hierarchy and ensuring autonomy. He held team meetings just once a week, urging that decisions be made when and where problems occurred, not at after-the-fact meetings. He abandoned the company's system of competitive bidding and forged a strong partnership with a few key suppliers.

To ensure the worldwide competitiveness of the new machine, Faig led his team in challenging a cherished company tradition, replacing the English system with the metric system in the measurement of machine parts. This change, essential for competition in a world market in which metric was the standard, was instituted despite vocal objections from old story bosses.

Harold Faig and the Project 270 team introduced Vista, the new injection molder, on schedule and on budget. In its first year on the market, Vista outsold Cincinnati Milacron's previous model by more than two to one.

Perhaps the best testimony to the success of Project 270 came from Japan, where the threat to Cincinnati Milacron's position had emerged: Toyota recently contracted to buy three of the newest and largest Vista models for its U.S. auto plants.

THE EMERGENCE OF THE SMART TEAM

The word *team* is used loosely in many corporations. The team designation is often attached indiscriminately to any group of employees who are herded together under the same project or work within the same department.

But just because a group carries the label does not mean that it functions as a team. Although business leaders preach the value of "teamwork," the cross-functional, autonomous teams that we see in the stories of Semco, Volvo, and Cincinnati Milacron are a relatively new, and still relatively rare, phenomenon.

What passed for a "team" in the old story organization bears little resemblance to the teams of Semco and other new story firms. The old story team was a microcosm of the machine-oriented organization that spawned it: rigid, top-down, rife with petty politics, stifled by bureaucracy and hierarchy, dependent on the larger organization to determine its membership, structure, goals, and leadership.

The new story team, by contrast, is an organic, living system characterized by partnership rather than power struggles. Unlike the old story team, it is managed from within. While *interdependent with* the organization in which it is embedded, it is not *dependent on* the organization to determine its goals, select its leadership, or choose its members. The new story team functions as an autonomous entity, with an inherent group intelligence of its own; it is a "smart" team.

The differences between the mechanical old story team and the smart team are captured in physicist Fritjof Capra's discussion of the differences between machines and living organisms:

> The first obvious difference between machines and organisms is the fact that machines are constructed, whereas organisms grow. This fundamental difference means that the understanding of organisms must be process-oriented. . . . Whereas the activities of a machine are determined by its structure, the relation is reversed in organisms—organic structure is determined by processes.
>
> Machines are constructed by assembling a well-defined number of parts in a precise and preestablished way. Organisms, on the other hand, show a high degree of internal flexibility and plasticity. . . . Although the organism as a whole exhibits well-

defined regularities and behavior patterns, the relationships between its parts are not rigidly determined.

Semco illustrates the organic nature of the smart team. Teams "grow" naturally at Semco; they are not assembled, or dismantled, on command. The structure and membership of the individual team are determined by the requirements of the task at hand, and the size of the team is self-regulated, determined by the team's internal needs to accomplish its task and by the desire of team members to maximize their share in company profits. And unlike mechanical teams, the smart teams at Semco have no preset patterns, rigid memberships, or fixed relationships. Functions and positions are rotated regularly, and employees move freely and frequently among teams.

PRINCIPLES OF THE SMART TEAM

Because the new story smart team is a living system, it adheres to the "organic laws" that underlie all living systems and determine their structures and processes. The smart team, like other organisms, is:

- *Self-Managing.* It is not commanded from above. It functions in harmony with the organization, and it may receive help from the organization/holarchy, but it makes its own decisions and organizes according to its own needs.

- *Self-Renewing.* It continues to function after its structure or membership changes. It has an inherent integrity.

- *Self-Transcending.* It reaches out into the environment and links up with individuals, teams, or organizations to exchange ideas and resources and achieve shared goals. In other words, it learns.

Self-Managing

To function effectively as vehicles of innovation, teams must be self-managed, for two reasons. First, rapid response, a crucial prerequisite for ongoing innovation, is impossible if every team decision requires outside approval. Second, no one has a better understanding of how to manage a process or improve a product than the person closest to it.

At Semco, self-management is everywhere in evidence. Semco's smart teams have a high degree of autonomy and a high degree of authority to determine the nature and structure of their work. There are no manuals to tell employees what to do, no dress codes, no company rules about travel expenses, no padlocked storerooms. Company information, including proprietary financial information, is widely shared with all team members.

Hand in glove with the principle of self-management is the concept of self-organization. Like other living systems, the smart team organizes itself, not according to commands from above, but organically, according to its own needs.

Fritjof Capra writes: "Self-organizing systems . . . tend to establish their size according to internal principles of organization, independent of environmental influences. This does not mean that living systems are isolated from their environment; on the contrary, they interact with it continually, but this interaction does not determine their organization."

The self-managing team operates in the same way. It knows when to form, how many and which members to recruit, what size is optimal, and even when to disband. Although interdependent with the larger holarchy, the organization in which it operates, its structure and functioning are not dependent on that organization. A smart team may form in response to a mission of the larger organization—for example, Operation Lightning at Ingersoll-Rand or Team Taurus at Ford—but its structure and internal dynamics are self-determined.

Ricardo Semler recounts an incident that illustrates how the principle of self-organization is demonstrated at Semco:

We were looking at a situation where one of our eight business units in particular is going to be very strongly hit by the recession that is coming here in Brazil in the next couple of months. We are expecting a 30–40 percent decrease in business in that unit, which makes dishwashers.

So we went ahead, as we always do, putting together a contingency plan, which included layoffs. As we always do, we discussed the actual layoff plan with the shop floor workers, with the shop floor committee representatives, etc., etc. And at one point they said, "Hey, hold on a minute. Why don't we try something else? Let's sit down with all the guys in the plant, and let's see if we can come up with something else."

A week later, after six general assemblies of all the workers, about 150 people, they sat everybody together and they came at us with a program which includes a 30 percent reduction in salaries, an increase in profit sharing to 37 percent as reciprocity, a system whereby they didn't even want the cafeteria run by a third party anymore. They were going to take two or three people off the shop floor to cook. They wanted to put two guys in charge of the guards, because that was provided by an outside party. Each one wanted to clean his own area so we wouldn't have to pay cleaning companies anymore.

This went on and on and on. They put up a whole program which said, "This is exactly equivalent to the layoffs you wanted to put into place. But to do all of this, we think one of the expensive things in this company that we don't need is a general manager. So we plan to run this business pretty much ourselves."

Rather than accepting the dictates of the larger organization, as the old story team would have been forced to do, the Semco team in this example developed its own response to the impending crisis. By itself, the team came up with ways to rearrange work processes, adjust salaries, and otherwise reduce costs to meet the challenge ahead.

Self-regulation at Semco is also evidenced by the fact that team size is determined by team members, not by the organization. Ricardo Semler remarks: "We have a hell of a hard time hiring people because of the profit sharing system and the way people work within the company. They don't want more people. They might want more machinery; they might want new methods. But they don't want an assistant, they don't want a receptionist, they don't want more people, because that's more people to share the profit with."

In other words, Semco's smart teams hire only as many people as are required to meet the mutual goals of team members and the organization. The teams are in no danger of growing unnecessary layers of bureaucracy, because it is not in their collective best interests to do so; more team members means fewer profits per member. The teams also have no incentive to reduce their size unduly, since productivity and profits are likely to decline as a result. Thus, the Semco teams are internally self-regulating and act to keep their size at an optimal level.

By contrast, says Jim Stryker, one of the Ingersoll-Rand teams formed subsequent to Operation Lightning grew, not organically, but in accordance with the old story philosophy of "the bigger, the better." This mechanical determination of team size inevitably reduced the team's productivity. Stryker recalls:

> We attempted to get too many people involved in the next product development team. We tried to create a core organization that included everybody through the janitor. It tended to become more oriented toward a committee-style decision-making process, and it slowed things down.
>
> If the team has an objective of cutting time out of a process, it has got to proceed like a guerrilla force and not with a lot of infrastructure, and not a lot of baggage. That's effectively what we found when we tried to expand the team to get everybody involved.

Stryker learned from this experience that it is neither possible nor desirable for the team to attempt to please everyone.

This brings up an important point about autonomy and team decision making. A widely held idea in the corporate world equates team decision making with *consensus* decision making. In fact, however, smart teams focus, not on achieving consensus, but on what the Japanese call "harmonies of difference." They reconcile the diverse opinions of group members and integrate them into a *common solution* that, most often, was not the original position of any individual or subgroup.

All too often, old story team members avoid making decisions that might leave them vulnerable politically and pretend that everyone favors the team's agreed-upon strategy. The result is the *appearance* of a cohesive team. "Consensus" decisions amount to watered-down compromises, or the position favored by one strong-willed team member, foisted upon the group. Such decisions result from efforts to squelch all differences of opinion.

When team members have serious reservations about specific decisions or strategies, they avoid stating them publicly.

When differences are aired in the open, they usually focus on finding who is right, further polarizing opinion. Old story teams fail to acknowledge and reconcile the differing viewpoints and suggestions of individual team members. However, it is just such reconciliations of opposing values and viewpoints that are central if the team is to become "smart."

When team members are free to reconcile differences rather than hammer out a consensus that only camouflages those differences, the quality of innovation is enhanced and the frequency of innovation is increased. A diversity of viewpoints multiplies the possibilities for innovative reconciliations. For this reason, Japanese companies deliberately form teams composed of people with widely divergent characteristics and backgrounds.

Such organizations as Ingersoll-Rand and Cincinnati Milacron are discovering that self-management is a powerful strategy for speeding up processes, improving product quality, and increasing productivity. AT&T is another major bureaucracy that is discovering the power of self-managed teams.

AT&T formed highly autonomous teams of 6 to 12 employees, with responsibility for making virtually every decision about the product design and development of a new cordless phone. Its 4200 phone system debuted in the late 1980s in one year—half the usual development time. The end product was higher in quality, and lower in cost, than previous AT&T systems.

Federal Express is also discovering the power of self-managed teams. As part of a corporate restructuring in 1988, Fed Ex divided 1,000 clerical workers into autonomous teams of 5 to 10 workers. After special training, the teams were authorized to manage themselves and find ways to improve productivity.

Among other things, the self-managed teams helped reduce service problems such as billing errors and lost packages by 13 percent in 1989. One team spotted and solved a multimillion dollar billing problem. The heavier the package, the greater the price Fed Ex charges to deliver it. The problem was that revenues were being lost because of the delivery clerks' sloppy weighing of packages. A new billing system was set up to monitor the problem. In 1989 alone, that team based solution saved Fed Ex more than $2 million.

A similar example comes from Levi Strauss, which is converting production in its Roswell, New Mexico, facility from assembly lines to self-managed teams. The teams determine who does which jobs and when, and manage the production of high fashion sports jeans from start to finish. As a result, it now takes just one day, instead of six, to complete a 60-pair bundle of jeans. And the defect rate has dropped from 3.9 percent under the assembly line system to 1.9 percent under team-based production.

What is most noteworthy about the Federal Express and Levi Strauss smart teams, and others like them, is that they are made up of men and women whose intelligence was underrated or ignored in the old story. Now that they are working in a team context, their intelligence and decision-making abilities are finally being validated. Joan Arnold, who oversees training for the Levi Strauss teams, calls this a "big culture change." She continues: "Our moms and dads raised us to do what the boss says, and now the boss is asking us what we should do."

Self-Renewing

The Greek philosopher Heraclitus wrote that "a man cannot step in the same river twice." The smart team, like the river, is a process rather than a fixed entity, a pattern of movement rather than an object. Like the river, the smart team is continually renewing itself—preserving form while the constituent parts change.

Fritjof Capra writes:

Self-renewal is an essential aspect of self-organizing systems. Whereas a machine is constructed to produce a specific product or to carry out a specific task intended by its designer, an organism is primarily engaged in renewing itself; tissues and organs are replacing their cells in continuous cycles. . . . All these processes are regulated in such a way that the overall pattern of the organism is preserved, and this remarkable ability of self-maintenance persists under a variety of circumstances, including changing environmental conditions and many kinds of interference. A machine will fail if its parts do not work in the rigorously predetermined manner, but an organism will maintain its functioning in a changing environment, keeping itself in running condition and repairing itself through healing and re-generation.

We can see the self-renewal process in the smart teams of new story organizations like Semco. At Semco, members migrate in and out of the team and the leadership position of the team regularly rotates. Nevertheless, the team retains its fundamental identity.

Furthermore, despite the erratic fluctuations of the Brazilian economy, the integrity of the Semco team process—the pattern of shared values and organizational principles that constitutes the Semco team—remains intact. Semco employees tend not to be possessive about their functions, positions, or teams. Since sides change frequently, there is no opportunity for rival factions to develop and no incentive to "take sides."

Ricardo Semler explains:

> It's not always the same guy that represents a business unit. Different people come and go from [team] meetings. There are people who have always been there, but there are also new people who are coming in. The sides change all the time.
>
> So in meetings there are no yes-men, and almost no yes-men in the organization. People are very strong about their opinions, but the point is that sometimes you will have three guys against the other six and then at another meeting you will have three guys against six—but it's not the same three, it's not the same six. So people don't take criticism and strong opinions personally, because they have no idea on which side they'll be during the next meeting.

Self-Transcending

The third organic principle of the smart team is self-transcendence. Capra defines self-transcendence in living systems as "a phenomenon that expresses itself in the processes of learning, development, and evolution. Living organisms have an inherent potential for reaching out beyond themselves to create new structures and new patterns of behavior."

We see many examples of self-transcendence in our new story organizations, examples in which teams or entire organizations form partnerships with customers, suppliers, and other "outsiders." Steelcase, for example, created a design partnership to strengthen its competitive position. Preston Trucking reached out to union members and customers, creating a "new pattern of behavior" that enabled it to survive and thrive under deregulation. PC Connection teamed up with Airborne (to name one of its many partners) to develop a low-cost delivery service. Manco (whose service partnerships we'll be discussing in Chapter 6) joined forces with Federal Express and Wal-Mart to develop new products. As I pointed out in Chapter 4, many important innovations are generated by such self-transcendent partnerships, which arise naturally in the context of smart teams.

Capra notes that self-transcendence expresses itself in learning. Thus we see that our team-based new story organizations, such companies as PC Connection, Motorola, and Preston Trucking, engage in continuous learning, often in conjunction with customers or other partners, to expand their horizons, improve processes, and discover innovation possibilities.

Systems expert Peter Senge offers a useful insight into the role of dialogue in facilitating the self-transcendence of each team member:

[d]ialogue is the capacity of members of a team to suspend assumptions and enter into genuine "thinking together." To the Greeks, dia-logos meant a free flowing of meaning through a group, allowing the group to discover insights not attainable individually. Interestingly, the practice of dialogue has been preserved in many "primitive" cultures such as that of the American Indian, but it has been almost completely lost to modern society. Today the principles and practices of dialogue are being rediscovered and put into a contemporary context.

Senge contrasts *dialogue*, which involves a creative mutual exploration of issues and a suspension of individual views, with *discussion*, in which opposing views are presented and defended. The objective of dialogue is to brainstorm and to search for a synthesis of viewpoints, or an entirely new viewpoint; the objective of discussion is to arrive at consensus.

According to Senge, dialogue and discussion are complementary activities, but dialogue is more challenging and in many cases, more effective, because it allows for a deeper understanding and appreciation of individual differences—and more ideas will emerge.

That's what Jim Stryker found in developing teams at Ingersoll-Rand. He believes that including employees with diverse backgrounds on a team multiplies the possibilities for innovation. Says Stryker:

> When you have a cross-functional team, and you send the team out to look, see, hear, touch, feel, smell, and sense what the customer is doing, you tend to have the advantage of getting five different functional expertise in terms of what is going on. What I see from a marketing standpoint or a sales standpoint is something entirely different from what the manufacturing guy is going to see . . . I think one of the advantages of a multi-disciplinary team is the fact that those innovations don't necessarily always come from one source. It comes from a whole series of different perspectives.

THE CHALLENGES OF IMPLEMENTING SMART TEAMS

Teamwork is still more widespread in theory than in practice. Despite the example of such team-based organizations as Semco, Volvo, and Steelcase and such experiments as Operation Lightning at Ingersoll-Rand and Project 270 at Cincinnati Milacron, new story teams are still the exception rather than the rule in business—especially American business. At the start of the 1990s, by one estimate, less than 10 percent of the American workforce was organized into teams.

One reason for the scarcity of true teamwork, despite the pressing need for it, is that many old story CEOs, schooled in old story individualism, are reluctant to empower teams. Even CEOs who have witnessed the sometimes astonishing performance of new story teams have been reluctant to move into this unknown territory. As a result, many large corporations have ignored the challenge of developing teams or have minimized the importance of doing so.

Aside from the apprehensions of executives and potential team members, there are formidable practical barriers to the creation of smart teams, especially in the midst of large bureaucracies. Chuck House of Hewlett-Packard told me about the barriers he faced in attempting to create a spirit of teamwork in the company's software business.

I had almost always worked in instruments at HP, and we dealt with small problems, tractable problems that you could solve more or less on your home turf. You didn't have to coordinate with 900 other people.

Then, somehow, I wound up in a business that was really a big business at HP, the one of developing software for micro-processors. To get to market in a very competitive business, we wound up begging, borrowing, and stealing technology from all over HP. Fourteen or 15 different divisions had stuff that we tried to borrow.

The folklore at HP was that one of the great things about the company was that we had this fabulous technology everywhere and we shared it; all the systems were set up to share it. But the facts were otherwise. You couldn't get your hands on source code, and you couldn't get your hands on documentation. You couldn't borrow the time of people—they were really busy deal-ing with their own competitive constraints.

During the course of Operation Lightning, Jim Stryker faced formidable barriers at Ingersoll-Rand as he attempted to alter the company's "one right way" of developing products. Says Stryker:

One of the biggest walls was the concept that it was Sales's responsibility to feed the customer information to Marketing. It's Marketing's responsibility to translate that into some sort of engineering gobbledygook and throw it over the wall to Engi-neering; Engineering's to put lines on a piece of paper; and then Manufacturing's responsibility to convert that into some hard-ware.

I think one of the biggest weaknesses we had was this se-ries of organizational barriers, where organizational manhood, so to speak, was tested by your ability to specify and translate everything into hard, cold numbers and to isolate everyone from what the ultimate customer really wanted. I think one of our biggest difficulties was this inability to communicate and understand what the customer wanted.

John Hammitt, vice president of United Technologies, talks about the hurdles his company faced, and overcame, in moving toward smart teams:

Within one of our businesses, we have a complex product that for as long as anyone can remember had a cycle of at least 150 days to accomplish engineering changes for that product. The use of computing technology as a lubricant between the various steps was able to take a day or so out of the cycle, but no more. Management directives that said, "You *will* shorten the cycle," didn't have much of a result either.

It wasn't until a program focused on total quality management had been implemented, and the workforce trained in the concepts associated with it, that we saw a significant change. There were teams made up of dozens of people who represented all the parts of the organization that were involved in engineering changes. As they got together and examined what they were doing, it became evident that many sign-off and "check the checker" steps had crept into the process, all well intentioned but clearly unnecessary.

The teams grappled with this problem, and the end result was more than 50 percent reduction in elapsed time, with dozens of people in dozens of organizations acknowledging that they added little or no value to the engineering change process. Although this was painful, they all recognized that they were playing a "controlling" role rather than a value-adding role.

I suppose the insight gained here is that in spite of how effective management thought they had been over the years, in both creating this process and then trying to shorten it, it wasn't until the people who actually managed the process—lived with it, conducted it—got together and asked themselves what they did, why they did it, and how they could do it differently that we saw a major cycle reduction, from 150 days down to 30 days. What this experience also produced was a sense of confidence throughout the organization that people, given the opportunity to manage themselves and solve their own problems, could do so.

Steelcase has been working under a companywide team structure since 1988 and has had to overcome many hurdles in the process of implementing teams. Wayman Britt, a divisional employee relations manager for Steelcase, told me:

Educating the workforce takes time. We've only been at it for two years, and there has been progress. We've been able to implement teams in all departments in the machine division.

Now we are finding out that it takes a bit more than the process itself—learning problem-solving techniques—to make it work. It takes a commitment to one another, in terms of treating each other with respect and constantly seeking ways to improve the system. The system itself is new; we haven't worked out all the kinks yet. So we constantly talk about it, and have some frustrations with it.

Hal Berrier, the Steelcase production superintendent, reflects on the obstacles he's faced in attempting to help restructure his plant into self-managed teams:

From the start, I've supported participative management as the right way to go, but I worried about getting the cooperation of the employees. The whole plant is organized around teams at this point, but it's been a slow process.

There are still a lot of people who are reluctant to participate. One drawback is people's normal resistance to change. Not everybody understands and supports teamwork 100 percent. From my position, I still have the job of imparting the vision and the concept to the supervisors who work for me. I can't be successful without their support. Training has been extremely important to make people feel that they're capable of handling what we're asking them to do.

Another drawback is our piecework system. That doesn't encourage teamwork, but individual effort.

Under the piecework system, Steelcase employees receive bonuses based on their individual production levels. This makes them reluctant to participate in the team process, including team meetings that take them away from their jobs and thus lower the level of individual output on which their bonuses are based.

Wayman Britt agrees that the piecework system is an obstacle to teamwork. According to Britt:

We are looking at new ways of rewarding people now that this problem is becoming clearer. We must look at paying employees for obtaining new knowledge and for finding ways to do things better. This may involve developing new performance evaluation forms which allow for extra merit pay for the involvement and cooperation employees give to the PM [participative management] process.

CREATING A CULTURE OF TEAMWORK

In Chapter 4, I noted that for innovation to thrive, the corporate culture must welcome and encourage it. The same can be said of teamwork.

It is unlikely that an organization can effect or sustain the transition to a team-oriented culture without the full commitment and consistent support of senior management. Ricardo Semler's enthusiasm and dedication are clearly an important factor in the success of Semco's team-based efforts. Steelcase appears to be succeeding in its transition to a team-oriented culture in part because of senior management's wholehearted commitment to the team concept.

Leon Flannery, an automatic press operator in the Steelcase machine division, considers top management commitment critical to implementing teams. Says Flannery:

> Ours was the first division to implement teams. Some of the employees, including me, thought this was just another thing management comes up with that lasts for six months. But now we're all set up in work cells of 6–10. The cell manages itself, controls its own amount of production, and handles quality control. We're starting to manage our own hours, in terms of workweek, hours per day that we work, and vacations.

He adds:

> The company has to commit themselves or teams won't work, and so far they have. We've had a slowdown in business, and so they put on the back burner some of our high-cost ideas, but in the meantime we're doing things that are cheaper.

Jim Stryker believes that Operation Lightning, one of Ingersoll-Rand's initial attempts to become more team-oriented, would have failed if not for the support of senior management. Says Stryker:

> As long as you had senior management—and by senior management I mean the most senior management—behind what you were trying to accomplish, then it was doable. If the general manager was not prepared to stand up and say, "Hey, I

want this and I want it this way, and I am supporting what is going on," then the thing would have been a failure—the organization would eat the team alive.

Another challenge faced by Stryker and others who have struggled to establish teamwork in the midst of large bureaucracies is maintaining the support of senior managers while keeping them at arm's length so that the team can function autonomously. Stryker talks about how he handled this challenge:

I, as a member of senior management, had the confidence of my manager to get the job done. And therefore he tended to deal with the team through me rather than trying to go directly to the team. Effectively, what happened was that he got from me whatever was sufficient for him to understand what was going on but not adequate enough for him to jump in and try to get involved. This was critical in giving the team confidence to make its own decisions.

The Operation Lightning team would meet with management periodically, says Stryker.

When we hit a milestone, when we knew we had something, we sold management on what we were doing. . . . This was going to be a sales pitch that said, "This team knows what it is doing. We are moving ahead at as fast a pace as we can, and what we are doing is going to be successful. Thank you, sir. May we now leave?"

Stryker advises:

If you can sell managers on the fact that the team and the project are working fine, then they tend to stay away. That's what we did. I am not going to tell you that it worked all the time, but enough to give us the space we needed.

The move toward a team-based organization represents a fundamental paradigm shift. Organizing smart teams is a long, arduous process, not a quick fix that can be implemented within a few weeks. If teamwork is approached casually, as the next management fad or as a Band-Aid effort to stave off the competition, it will not be sustainable.

Formalizing the Team Process: The Critical Momentum

The development of Operation Lightning and other cross-functional teams at Ingersoll-Rand is a first step on the path toward the team-based organization. Whether or not the company will continue along that path remains to be seen. At Ingersoll-Rand, unlike Semco, the roots of teamwork are shallow. The corporate culture as a whole is still fairly well grounded in the old story processes and thinking that have guided Ingersoll-Rand for decades. If Stryker and other new story leaders should leave the company, it might lose the new learning and revert to a more individualistic style of operation.

The Ingersoll-Rand example demonstrates the difficulties faced by an old story organization that is struggling to formalize the process of teamwork. Ford Motor provides another lesson in the challenges of transforming to a team-oriented culture.

Richard Pascale believes that Team Taurus was "the prototype of Ford's transforming organizational culture." The highly effective cross-functional teamwork of the Taurus project represented a sharp break from Ford's past, a break that Pascale believes could not have been made without the transformation of Ford's leadership. "Here," Pascale argues, "was the real revolution: In the sincerity and persistence of men who recognized that *they* needed to change if Ford was going to change."

He is referring, among others, to former Ford CEO Don Petersen, who spearheaded the beginnings of transformation at Ford. During Petersen's nine years as president and then CEO, Ford boosted its U.S. market share by almost 6 percent and introduced half a dozen innovative, award winning new models, including Taurus and the Mercury Sable.

During Petersen's tenure, teamwork at Ford began to build to the critical momentum that an old story company requires in order to make the move to a team-based organization. With Petersen gone, it remains to be seen whether or not the budding transformation will continue at Ford.

There are reasons to be skeptical. Several of Ford's outside directors seemed to be relieved by Petersen's departure, and may have encouraged it. These directors appear to be old story commanders and controllers who do not welcome and are not encouraging the move toward teamwork and democracy at Ford.

Furthermore, Ford is struggling at the moment. Ford's market share in the United States and Europe has been shrinking, and the auto market as a whole is depressed. In addition, its product line is older than that of any of its four major competitors and its high-priced acquisition of Jaguar, Petersen's last major commitment as CEO, burdened it with a money-losing operation. In times of crisis, as I pointed out in Chapter 2, organizations struggling to make the transformation to the new story often revert to their old story ways, and this could surely happen at Ford.

Still, there are some hopeful signs. Two dozen new Ford models are due to arrive at U.S. showrooms by 1995. And at Ford's North American Operations, Executive Vice President Alex Trotman, who may become the company's next CEO, is an enthusiastic champion of teamwork.

Trotman is committed to breaking down the remaining barriers between Ford's functional organizations. To that end, he is bringing together, in a single team, 50 line executives from all of the company's functional groups. He is seeking to revive the thinking and approach behind Taurus and Sable and to formalize the teamwork process throughout Ford. And he has assembled a cross-functional team of 20 young designers, engineers, and product planners to develop the 1995 Mustang.

Despite the efforts to rekindle a spirit of teamwork, Ford is still a long way from Semco. Cross-functional teams at Ford are still formed by mandate, rather than autonomously, and team projects are still sporadic and infrequent.

If Ford could learn from the Semco experience, if it built a more democratic, team-based organization, an organization more committed to full participation and partnership, I believe that it would rank among the healthiest and most successful organizations in the world.

The Shift from Brawn to Brains

In Chapter 1, Ricardo Semler predicted that his company would be about the same size 20 years from now but would generate much more business. The reason, said Semler, was that Semco would rely much more heavily on the brains and creativity of employees. Smart teams would increase productivity while maintaining a steady level of equipment and overhead. A company organized around smart teams can generate leaps in productivity without adding layers of bureaucracy by harnessing the latent capacity of its workforce.

William Wiggenhorn says that Motorola is heading in the same direction—growing more profitable and productive through the increasing use of smart teams. "Empowerment of teams," says Wiggenhorn, "does not mean that managers don't manage. It's just that there will be fewer managers to run the business. If we kept up our old models of managers upon managers upon managers, we would not be able to double the business with the same size organization. With empowered teams, we should be able to."

Chapter Six

The Customer Is One of Us

Manco, Inc. is headquartered in Westlake, Ohio, a suburb of Cleveland. The $60 million company, which markets tapes, weather stripping, and mailing supplies, competes head-on with such industry heavyweights as 3M. Manco's CEO, Jack Kahl, credits his company's success to its relentless commitment to service and to its close partnerships with employees, suppliers, and customers.

Wal-Mart is one of Manco's top customers, and Jack Kahl makes no secret of the fact that Wal-Mart founder Sam Walton, his friend and mentor, taught him much of what he knows about running a business and providing exemplary service. Any conversation with Kahl is bound to be filled with references to Wal-Mart.

And to the Manco duck—Manco's corporate symbol and the heart of the organization. The duck, which was inspired by customers who mistakenly referred to one of Manco's main products as "duck tape," now provides inspiration for Manco. Referred to by Kahl as "Dale Carnegie in feathers," it appears on packaging, newsletters (including Duck Tales*), and promotional materials, and it turns up regularly at company events.*

Jack Kahl took some time out to talk with me about his relationship with Sam Walton and Wal-Mart and about the service philosophy that underlies Manco's success:

For so many years, people here heard me talking about Wal-Mart, Wal-Mart, Wal-Mart and never had a chance to visit a store because we didn't have any in Ohio. This year [1990] they opened a store in Port Clinton, Ohio, 70 miles west of here.

We had a lottery, and the winning people went up there to celebrate and help open the store in grand style, the way Wal-Mart always does for every store opening. On the morning of the opening, we had 70 people on a bus, and we also took the Manco Duckmobile, which is our van, all painted up with the corporate symbol, and headed up to Clinton.

We participated with the Wal-Mart people in the opening, did the Wal-Mart cheer, and just got into the spirit of partnership between our two companies. Then we turned our people loose to shop in the Wal-Mart store. They came out with baskets full of merchandise, and, in fact, Bill Nicholson spent over $500 and had to go back there the following weekend with a van to pick up everything he bought. We had the good fortune to have the whole event videotaped. Due to an illness, Mr. Walton wasn't able to make the opening, but he got to see the tape and really enjoyed it.

It's that kind of partnership that's at the heart of our customer service philosophy around here. Years ago, we came up with the word CARE, which stands for Customers Always Require Excellence. I didn't think of it; the eight women in what we now call the Customer Care Department decided they wanted that word to define the way they came to work every day. I call them our intensive care nurses, and I remind them: "You are the closest to the customer. You bring good news to the customer, and you're also the first person who's ever going to talk to an irate customer." So they know what we think of them and the job they're doing to serve the customer.

You can't provide service every day without having people coming in here every day who know that they're important to you, and coming to work with a good attitude. You can't do it. It's impossible to ask anybody to call a customer, to get on a phone, to go sell something for you unless that person knows he's valued in this family and trusted in this family.

If you saw the amount of information that we shared with people, you wouldn't believe it. There's only one company that I have ever seen that shares as much strategic and tactical quantitative and qualitative information with their people as we do, and it's Sam Walton and his crew.

There's no doubt in my mind why I've gone to a Wal-Mart shareholders' meeting every year for the last six years. It is unquestionably the finest one-day management seminar in the United States of America, maybe the world—to watch how that company, its width, its breadth, its enthusiasm, its knowledge all come together in the shareholders' meeting.

You know how many people go to shareholders' meetings? IBM gets 300, maybe 400. But Wal-Mart had 9,500 people in the University of Arkansas field house last June 6, in a field house that holds about 6,500. The rest had to stand.

Sam Walton, as usual, was on the stage at 6 A.M. in the morning, entertaining, bringing different associates up who had done great things and giving them recognition, asking questions, pulling vendors up onstage, generally doing a well-planned Barnum & Bailey act, and just making you feel like a million bucks.

And then, at a quarter to nine, Sam Walton gets the meeting off and running, and they do what they have to do in terms of numbers, and then they motivate the living hell out of anybody that's there.

That's what I'm talking about—about spirit. You can't provide daily service in a Wal-Mart store or a Manco company unless you really work hard internally every day to support that.

In 1977, Manco was still a very small company. We had gross sales of $4 million. In 1978, we set aside every single thing that was not up to our CARE standard. We published a book containing our mission statement. It stated who we are, what we stand for, and we gave it to each of our customers. We went into stores and did research; we talked to hundreds of store owners—hardware store owners and others—asking them questions about product lines, what they liked and didn't like. We discovered lots and lots of things that were wrong with our products in terms of packaging and product quality as well.

We hired a consultant—a man who had worked for Walt Disney for years. He taught us about the importance of sight, sound, and touch in our packaging. So we designed a "look" for our packaging—it came to be called "the Sea of Green." We got thoroughly involved in setting quality standards in packaging, and ended up with packaging that was much better than even our biggest competitor, 3M. We used better packaging materials, thicker poly bags; we put little metal grommets in the bags so that they would not be pulled off the peg and look like damaged merchandise.

One thing we did here recently that we're really proud of, we went up to Ace Hardware, and Ace was changing a lot of their packaging. They thought it was getting a little old, and they hadn't set the parameters for how they wanted to make the changes, so there was no good control.

We saw what the need was, to help them write a new set of parameters.* So immediately we brought our designer in, at our expense, and said, "Don't worry about the money; we'll get this thing done right. Let's first write the boundaries, and then we'll take a whack at designing the packaging with you."

And we not only helped them write the parameters, but we came back and we codesigned their packaging. And they fell in love with what we did, and we gave it to them. I think it cost us something like $20,000 in artist bills, which was part of the partnership that we did not charge them for.

We were the first ever Ace vendor of the year. First time they've ever done it, and among 2,000 competitors, including Stanley, Black & Decker—you name it, they chose Manco, with our $8 million of volume. And it was an extraordinary experience to be in such elite company and win.

---

*Packaging standards for manufacturers to follow in developing Ace packaging for their individual products.

One other example I can give you about our commitment to service: My dad originally worked at American Greetings, and when I was a senior in college, I did a study on greeting cards as part of a marketing thesis I did. And so I've always had a pretty good understanding of the importance of sentiment and verse and even color in a greeting card.

So about four or five or six years ago, I was looking for a way to try to communicate a message of good cheer to our customers. Instead of going out with some kind of hard-hitting information, we said, "Let's do something quarterly that just gets ourselves in front of these people with the duck, with the spirit of what we're trying to do, to say thank-you and lift their spirits a little." We decided to do it with a greeting card.

So since we're known as the green company, Manco green, we decided to send our first card on March 17, and put a little leprechaun on it. And then we celebrate freedom with our Fourth of July card. And then in November, a Thanksgiving card, which is just an apropos time of the year to say thanks. And then Christmas. We're up to 32,000 now—32,000 people will get cards from us this year. And if I know a fellow's birthday, I'll get that card on my desk and I can write a little personal note to him. And that's how it goes.

Those cards are one of the best things that we ever did in this company, a way to stay in touch with our customers and reach customers we otherwise could never say thanks to. Dynamite. You know, we're cutting our trade advertising because it is absolutely getting to be passé; it's not required. And the best form of advertising we can do is one-on-one through a greeting card saying, "Thank you for what you're doing. We appreciate you."

I can't tell you the fun we have designing the cards. You know, it's the most important product we put together here. The company has fun doing it; we get ideas from all over the company and even people around the country—even family members that come up with different ideas for the cards. And we have buyers out there who have saved those cards for four and five years and have them in their office—the whole series.

And the first thing they'll do when you walk in, they'll say, "What's the next card going to look like?" And we say, "No, we're not going to tell you." There's a mystery to it. And your whole sales call starts on such a high note of friendship and levity that no matter what else you're going to deal with that day, you've already established the rapport that most companies had only hoped to have.

Manco thrives in an industry that has witnessed an enormous shakeout over the past decade, with more companies expected to fall by the wayside in the 1990s. In the midst of this shakeout, Manco continues to grow and prosper, counting among its customers some of the nation's most successful retailers, including industry leader Wal-Mart. Manco thrives because of the strong service ethic that permeates the organization—an ethic that is maintained, according to CEO Jack Kahl, by putting employees first. Kahl asserts: "The customer does not come first. Your employees do. The quality of your service over time will directly reflect the quality of care, support, and concern you demonstrate for your own people."

Kahl understands as few executives do that service, like quality, cannot be mandated; it must be volunteered. As a result, instead of focusing on service policies and procedures, he strives to build within Manco a caring culture that will *naturally* elicit high-quality service.

Like Ricardo Semler, Mike Conway, and other new story leaders, Jack Kahl places a high level of trust in his employees (whom he refers to as "partners"). The trust factor involves, among other things, sharing information with workers—a vital prerequisite for maintaining the whirlwind pace of the retail industry, an industry in which trends seem to change daily.

Information is abundant at Manco, and posted in plain view for all to see. Kahl comments:

> In our cafeteria, we have a chart of our last three years' sales, so people can graphically see, by the month, where we've come from and how we've grown. This is for visitors as well as all our people.
>
> Next to that is a board that shows the daily sales that we are taking into the company. This includes the sales that we booked for today and the shipments that go out today. The company is a living organism, and the sales are the blood and health of the company, just like the oxygen in your blood. That board shows how well we are "pumping."

Another board, called the "efficiency board," breaks out expenses and compares the selling cost of products over time. The purpose, says Kahl, is to remind employees that "the more revenue we create and the more efficiently we operate, the better we're going to serve." (Even the financial side of the business is considered by Kahl in service terms).

He continues: "Then, to reinforce that monthly, we have a partner meeting downstairs. We have a screen so we can put up overheads, and we put up profit and loss and the balance sheet every month, and we go in depth. And I mean the whole company gets together for that."

Jack Kahl sums up the philosophy behind Manco's success as follows: "I'd have to say we share a complete, universal understanding from top to bottom in this company that the customer is king . . . and also a complete, universal understanding in this company, that took years for people to put their trust in, that the way to serve the customer is to internally take care of one another."

THE SERVICE IMPERATIVE

In the 1990s, the quality of an organization's service will be a primary determinant of its success or failure. "Service is becoming in many cases the *only* road to competitive excellence." That's the conclusion of the Strategic Planning Institute (SPI), the nonprofit organization that has been compiling the authoritative PIMS (Profit Impact of Market Strategy) database since 1972. PIMS records the experiences of more than 2,000 business units (divisions, product lines, and profit centers) in more than 200 member companies around the world.

Companies can no longer compete on the strength of their products alone—not when the world is filled with competitors that have access to cheap technology and are eager to copycat ideas. What sets organizations apart today is the relative strength of their service efforts.

In the late 1980s, the Forum Corporation of Boston conducted an eye-opening study of the reasons that customers stop doing business with companies. It's generally not because quality is too low or prices too high, the researchers discovered. In fact, among the many reasons given, the least significant were "inferior products" and "too expensive," cited by just 8.3 percent of the respondents.

What is the number one reason why customers choose to take their business elsewhere? "Poor service," according to 40 percent of the buyers in the Forum study.

The changing nature of today's products brings the service imperative into sharper focus. Charles Hampden-Turner explains: "Today even products with hard edges exist in a sea of information. We sell less a thing than a pattern of use, a scenario of satisfactions."

This shift parallels the larger paradigm shift we are describing, from a view of the organization as a mechanical entity to a conception of the company as a living, dynamic system of relationships. Under the new paradigm, products and services are no longer considered separate units; they are a part of the relationship between the company, its customers, and its employees. PC Connection, profiled in Chapter 4, provides an excellent example. PCC's product is not merely direct-mail computer supplies. What PCC offers to customers is a "scenario of satisfactions" that includes, not just software and accessories, but such value-added services as free information and education, and speedy delivery at low cost. The "hard" product is just one part of the scenario.

It is increasingly the service context that surrounds products that gives them added value and differentiates them—and their producers—from the competition.

This is particularly true of "commodities," products like Manco's that can readily be duplicated elsewhere. What *cannot* be duplicated are the relationships that go into and surround those products and to a large extent determine their success or failure.

Making the Customer "One of the Family"

In our smartest companies—such companies as Manco, Wal-Mart, PC Connection, and Preston Trucking—the relationship between the organization and the customer is strong and lasting. These companies regard customers as part of the "family." They bring customers into the heart of the organization, invite and encourage them to participate in everything from designing products to developing service measures and monitoring quality. "Let the buyer be *aware*" is the rallying cry of these new story companies.

Strong relationships with customers enable such companies as Manco to survive and thrive despite intense competition from far larger organizations. For example, 3M is one of Manco's staunchest competitors. Nevertheless, Manco continues to grow, even in the shadow of this powerhouse, by forming close partnerships with its customers. It is difficult to overestimate the competitive power of such company/customer partnerships.

SERVICE THROUGH RELATIONSHIP: SMITH, BUCKLIN & ASSOCIATES

Smith, Bucklin & Associates is another organization that excels at service through building relationships. SBA was founded in 1949 by Bill Smith and Henry Bucklin to fill a need for more professional management of trade associations. Over the years, it has met with enormous success. SBA now provides leadership and logistical support for some 165 trade associations and professional societies, including the Society of Thoracic Surgeons, The National Association of Food Equipment Manufacturers, and The Popcorn Institute.

Smith, Bucklin has grown over the years strictly by word of mouth; it does no advertising. It has gained and maintained its position as the leader in its field on the strength of its reputation as a premier service provider.

Like Patricia Gallup at PC Connection, chairman Bill Smith believes in finding out what customers need and then delivering *more*: "Our clients depend on us to help shape the ongoing vision for their industry; we know how to do that," says Smith. "But it's also the little things that keep the relationship going. We respond to phone calls from any individual member of an association. We respond to letters. We always try to give people something beyond what they asked for in their initial request."

Smith, Bucklin's mission is "to continue to be the leading company in its field by establishing the highest standards of excellence in service to its clients and, in an ever-changing environment, to seize all opportunities for growth in order to provide the most challenging and rewarding careers for its people."

Smith, Bucklin lives and breathes its mission, whose most important component can be found in the last phrase, "to provide the most challenging and rewarding careers for its people." SBA's formula is simple: The company delivers the highest level of service to its employees, who then respond in kind to its growing list of clients.

One of Smith, Bucklin's most prominent clients is the Society for Information Management (SIM), which serves as a professional organization for information systems executives and other business leaders concerned with the management of information systems. John Hammitt, 1989-90 president of SIM, comments: "I think success in serving customers comes about, not because of an organization's structure or rules, but because of the mindset and values of the people in that organization. . . . It is the selection and the advancement of the service-focused people within Smith, Bucklin that has made that organization exceptional."

Four decades ago, when Bill Smith cofounded Smith, Bucklin, he believed strongly that he could succeed only by recruiting a committed staff of fully participating partners and giving them the opportunity to grow—and he believes that as strongly today as he did then. Smith reflects: "In order to bring professionalism to associations, we need to have people who are committed to careers, to learning the ins and outs of an industry. And so we have to be committed to the careers of our people. We can't provide the kind of in-depth service we do without people committed to careers within Smith, Bucklin. Sometimes their careers are almost more important than the client."

He adds: "People just don't leave Smith, Bucklin. And I think it's because they know they're loved and appreciated. People know; you can't fool them. I think that people have to feel they are understood, they are appreciated, they are going to be treated fairly. They also have to have a feeling of security in their jobs."

Smith, Bucklin strives to engender that same feeling of security in its clients. Bill Smith told me: "I think the reason we've been so successful is consistency and a commitment to long-term relationships—long-term relationships with our clients, with our employees, and with our suppliers. Smith, Bucklin doesn't drop a client like an ad agency might. In the advertising business, when a bigger client comes along, the smaller ones sometimes get dropped. We don't do that. This may be an old-fashioned principle, but it's been successful for us."

Just how far Smith, Bucklin will go to demonstrate its commitment became evident when a long-term client ran into serious financial problems and ended up owing it more than $150,000. SBA continued to support the client, "committing some of our best people over a period of seven years," says Bill Smith. No interest was charged on the outstanding debt. With this strong support behind it, the client eventually recovered. You can imagine the loyalty that the client feels toward Smith, Bucklin.

Trust and credibility are so high between SBA and its clients
that Bill Smith runs his 550 employee business without contracts:
"We have no contracts, if you can imagine that, with our clients,"
he says.

All we have is a 90-day letter of agreement. People say, "Bill,
how in the hell can you run a company with millions of dollars
worth of commitments each year, with space and payroll and
offices in three cities?" But we do it.

And you know what keeps it all together? Service. That's the
whole thing. We can't just say, "We have a contract, now we
can relax." We can never relax, because all we've got is 90 days.
It keeps us honest; it keeps us motivated. We don't want to
have anyone obligated to maintain our services, and believe
me, from a sales standpoint, this is a very significant factor.
People say, "These people must be pretty confident they are
going to be able to deliver the goods." And we do feel confident.

We've got to be proving ourselves every single day of the
year. What you did yesterday is great, but what's going to happen today, tomorrow—that's how we'll be judged. So there is
always that sense of urgency. It is not an assumed urgency; the
clients finally find that out. You can't fool people.

DEVELOPING A CULTURE OF SERVICE

Developing a reputation such as the one Smith, Bucklin enjoys
requires a commitment to service throughout the organization
that is consistent over time. Such extraordinary commitment can
be elicited only in the context of a corporate culture that emphasizes *caring* about employees and *sharing* of the service ethic by
everyone in the organization—starting with the CEO.

Service Begins at the Top

In *The Improvement Process*, H. James Harrington writes: "A corporation takes on the personality of its top management. . . . The
process starts with top management, will progress at a rate reflecting management's demonstrated commitment, and will stop
soon after managers lose interest in the process."

In *At America's Service*, Karl Albrecht expresses similar sentiments: "A commitment to service excellence must be unequivo-

cal. It radiates from senior managers, who must eat, breathe, and sleep customer service as the nucleus of their corporate culture."

While many factors are involved in the development of a service-oriented corporate culture, one of the most basic can be found in the executive suite. To a great extent, a service culture is developed by *example*. And the example starts at the top.

Jack Kahl exudes an attitude of service. He is continually thinking about, reading about, and researching new and better ways to serve his employees and his customers. And he talks about service all the time; in my discussions with him, he couldn't *stop* talking about it.

Kahl is Manco's top cheerleader. He leads the way in celebrating the service ethic that has made his company a success. For example, I have on videotape the October 1990 ceremony, famous in Manco circles, in which he made good on his vow to jump into the duck pond in front of company headquarters if sales reached the corporate goal of $60 million. Manco squeaked past its target by some $90,000 within the last two days of fiscal 1990.

The videotape shows Jack Kahl—clad in a bright green Manco sweater, carrying a Manco bath towel, and trailed by the Westlake High School band—as he marches to the pond. At the edge of the pond, he strips down to a black bikini bathing suit, bends over to exhibit a sign reading "The $60 Million Plunge"—and dives in.

Bill Smith is far more reserved than Jack Kahl, but the two are equally committed to service and to setting a service example. Smith related his leadership philosophy to me: "You try to settle for nothing less than excellence—and the fellow that is the head of the operation has to set the pace."

He continued:

You can never ask someone to do anything that you won't do yourself. All of us have to be willing to do anything. If you have to sweep the floor before the meeting, well, you have to sweep the floor before the meeting.

I have always felt that it is very important that I'm on the firing line. That way, I find out firsthand what my men and women are going through, so I can respond to their concerns. People look toward mentors. When they see someone doing something successful, they try to emulate that person's behavior. I think it's important that the leader of the company is out there on the front lines and not just sitting holed up in an office, thinking abstractly about the business.

When senior management shows by its actions as well as its words that service is a top priority, the service attitude becomes contagious. That's what managers at the Warsaw Marriott discovered. Opened in 1989, the Warsaw Marriott was the first Western-owned hotel in Poland, whose hotels have traditionally not been known for their hospitality. It saw an opportunity to set itself apart from the pack by establishing itself as a service leader.

The Warsaw Marriott recruited 20 Polish managers, none of whom had hotel backgrounds, and flew them to Boston for training in the fundamentals of hotel management, from running a smooth room service operation to taking accurate phone messages for guests. When they returned, they became hands-on executives, setting the service tone for their staff of 1,000 by their own example. Says Dorota Kowalska, the Warsaw Marriott's director of human resources: "Seeing the executive director of food and beverage actually clear tables in the breakfast room was something our people had never experienced before."

It made a big impression. Now the staff at the Warsaw Marriott has shaken off a deeply ingrained bureaucratic style and adopted the service attitude modeled by management.

Putting Employees First

I believe that service thrives at such companies as Preston, Manco, and Smith, Bucklin because these companies treat employees as equal partners. Their employees consider themselves dedicated to service, but they do not feel *subservient*, an important distinction. The employees at Smith, Bucklin, for example, know that Bill Smith would sweep the floor as readily as anyone else in the organization.

This egalitarian attitude, this commitment to people in partnership, is the key to service excellence. It is an attitude that the actions of senior executives convey and that frequently shows up in the titles by which employees are addressed. At Manco, they are referred to as "partners"; at Preston, Wal-Mart, and Semco, as "associates."

I have noted the importance of treating employees well in order to serve the customer well. It is useful to think of the organization as a hologram. Any part of the organization, like any part of a hologram, is a microcosm of the whole. More specifically, any relationship within the organization is likely to be repeated elsewhere in the organization and in the organization's interaction with the customer. The bank teller, flight attendant, or retail clerk who provides friendly, efficient service to the customer has probably been treated with respect by others in the organization. The receptionist may be surly because his or her supervisor is overly critical.

Sam Walton, who sets the standard for service excellence in the retail industry, told me that the key to Wal-Mart's success is its positive relationship with its employees:

> It all comes down to how well you can communicate and truly be sincere in helping your associates understand what our basic philosophy is, and what our basic goals are, and involving them in our business. . . . I guess our greatest technique and our greatest accomplishment is this commitment to communicating with them in every way that we possibly can, and listening to them constantly.
>
> I think every good company has got to have that kind of aura, have a partnership relationship, really, with their employees. . . . You have got to work in their best interest. . . . You have got to put their interest first, and eventually it will come back to the company.

This perspective is in stark contrast to the attitude of some old story service providers, who deliver outstanding service at the *expense* of their employees. The latter expect their workers to put in long hours in continually stressful situations, until they leave or burn out. This old story view of people as expendable work units is a sure-fire formula for failure in the new story world of business.

Empathy: The Critical Element of the Caring Culture

By listening to its employees, treating them well, and developing a partnership relationship with them, Wal-Mart has elicited legendary customer service from its employees. Because Wal-Mart *empathizes* with its employees, they can—and do—empathize with the customer.

A study by the Forum Corporation looked at various dimensions of customer service and ranked their importance to the customer. Ranked at the top were reliability, assurance, responsiveness, and empathy.

In his book, *The Regis Touch*, marketing expert Regis McKenna tells a story about Max Poll, CEO of Barnes Hospital in St. Louis. Poll, disguised as a patient, has someone wheel him around the hospital on a gurney in order to develop a feel for what it's like to be a patient at Barnes. He says he doesn't see much except for the ceiling, but what he hears sensitizes him to the level of service the hospital provides.

No amount of training can instill empathy in employees who don't want to serve. But while empathy cannot be mandated, it *can* be developed. Employees tend to show empathy toward their customers when the people in their organizations have shown empathy toward them.

It never ceases to amaze me that companies will spend large amounts of money to enhance their customer service efforts while treating with callous disregard the employees who must deliver customer service. The title of a *Wall Street Journal* article sums up the problem nicely: "Poorly Served Employees Serve Customers Just as Poorly." The article concludes: "Service providers treat customers similarly to the way they as employees are treated by management. In many organizations, management treats employees as unvalued and unintelligent. The employees in turn convey the identical message to the customer."

It's absurd to expect superior service from people who are treated with callous disregard. To paraphrase Charles Hampden-Turner, you cannot deliver high-quality service with crushed workers.

The Power of Empathy: Bugs Burger and the Tale of the "Derelicts."   On the other hand, never underestimate the power of treating employees with dignity, respect, and empathy to elicit superior service. Al Burger, whom I interviewed for my last book, *Peak Performers*, told me a story about the power of empathy to elicit top-notch service from even the most disenfranchised employees.

Burger speaks with authority. He centered his entire organization on the idea of unexcelled customer service. Though he has since sold the company, Al Burger's Bug Killers are remembered as exemplars of superior service in the pest control business.

In 1982, the public health department and television stations in Miami, where Al Burger lived, were working together on an exposé of dirty restaurants. The city's restaurant owners were panic-stricken by the possibility of unscheduled visits from television crews and the health department. Because of his background in pest elimination (pest "control" was never good enough for him), Burger decided to help the local restaurant association meet the challenge.

First, Burger hired a sanitation company and set out to identify the restaurants that were the worst offenders. The owners of these restaurants wasted no time in blaming their employees for their sanitation problems.

Although the labor pool in the area consisted primarily of "drifters, winos, and derelicts," Al Burger, a terrific manager with an abundance of empathy, suspected that the real problem lay elsewhere—in the attitudes of the restaurant supervisors, who treated their employees with condescension and disdain. He therefore decided to launch a little experiment. In his own words:

> I decided to have a two-week project. I took a restaurant that was in bad shape and proceeded, at my own expense, to hire 10 labor pool employees to come in and work this project.
>
> The first night, the workers I'd hired walked into the establishment and I followed. The restaurant's steward, not knowing I was there, proceeded to tell my crew: "Get over in the corner—don't say anything. You're a bunch of bums, and you'll do as I say." Then I walked in and told the steward to leave; these were my paid employees, and he had no right to be addressing them that way. On second thought, I added, maybe he ought to stick around and learn something.

Burger continued:

> First, I had a little talk with the crew about what I had to accomplish. Our goal was to make the restaurant sparkle, and they were the people who were going to do it. I would be there to help, encourage, and give guidance toward the goal.
>
> During the two weeks that followed, 9 out of 10 of these workers—pulled from the same pool of "losers" that the local restauranteurs were complaining about—survived the ordeal. By the end of the experiment, the restaurant shone like a mirror. And something amazing occurred: people regained their dig-

nity and self-respect. Several of them told me this had been the happiest two weeks of their life. They thanked me for the chance I gave them to prove themselves, and said they wished it could last forever.

This seemingly miraculous transformation was accomplished simply by treating the work crew with decency and respect. By serving his employees well, Burger inspired them to turn in a first-class service performance themselves.

No Empathy, No Service: A Tale of Eastern Airlines.   Jan Carlzon, CEO of Scandinavian Airlines, uses the expression "moment of truth" to describe the encounter between the customer and the company. During each such encounter, it is vital that the service provider show empathy for the customer. Such moments of truth ultimately determine a company's service reputation, for better or—as in the case I am about to describe—for worse.

I often travel across the country and around the globe. On a long flight, I count on a hot meal from the airline. So I didn't know how to respond when, during a four-hour Eastern Airlines trip, a flight attendant approached my seat in the first-class compartment and told me that she had run out of entrées—not my preferred entrée, but *all* entrées. I had last eaten a few hours before boarding; I would be unable to eat until a few hours after I landed. I was already hungry.

Deciding to make the best of a bad situation, I plunged into my work. My seatmate, Ralph, however, received the bad news with less grace. I found it impossible to concentrate on the books spread out in front of me. Ralph was carrying on an animated monologue—actually it was more like a tirade about the rotten service of the airline. He was livid. He was going to write the president of the company. He would never fly with the airline again. He would report the names of all the flight attendants. He would sue Eastern for the price of his ticket.

After a while, realizing that Ralph was not going to stop, I decided to stretch my legs and visit the restroom. On the way, I passed the cubicle in which the flight attendants prepared meals for the passengers in the first-class compartment. The curtain was drawn. I paused, reflecting that, after all, the mix-up was probably not the attendants' fault and that my seatmate had been altogether too harsh.

So I drew back the curtain, prepared to let the attendants know that I understood their situation and that it was "just one of those things." And there they sat, the two of them—eating our entrées.

I'm not usually at a loss for words, but for a few moments I stood speechless. One of the attendants said, "Well, we've got to eat too, you know." "Yes," I shot back, "but you could have shared with us."

I was fuming, but it seemed that there was nothing I could do. Or maybe there was. I looked over at my irate seatmate and called out loudly: "Hey, Ralph! Come take a look at this."

Perhaps Eastern was filled with competent, empathic employees. It didn't matter. To me, those two attendants *were* the airline, and in that one encounter the airline failed me miserably. For Eastern Airlines, the rest is history.

The High Cost of Poor Service

I do not claim that this single encounter led to the demise of Eastern Airlines, but it is reasonable to conclude that Eastern's lack of empathy—starting in the executive suite of Frank Lorenzo—hastened its demise.

Alienating customers is something that no company can afford. According to the Technical Assistance Research Program (TARP), a nonprofit organization that has made a specialty of researching consumer complaints, the average North American company spends five times more to win a new customer than to retain an old one.

Furthermore, according to TARP, dissatisfied customers will each tell at least 9 or 10 other people about their unhappy experiences with a company, but they may not tell the offending company. Depending on the size of purchase and the industry, only 4 to 30 percent of such customers register a complaint.

Furthermore, TARP reports, 81 percent of customers with minor unresolved complaints ($5 or less) won't buy again from the organization that mistreated them; for customers with major unresolved complaints (over $100), the figure is 54 percent.

These figures demonstrate the importance of doing everything possible to retain customers. Some companies greatly underestimate the cost of lost customers, and many companies underestimate the ease with which customers can be retained even after a negative "moment of truth." TARP found that when complaints are resolved quickly, up to 95 percent of customers will buy again from the offending company. Customers, it seems, will forgive and forget as long as pains are taken to resolve their complaints. MBNA America, the credit card operation of Baltimore-based MNC Financial, retains 95 percent of its customers every year, a percentage significantly higher than the industry average of 88 percent. It owes its success to its efforts to keep customers satisfied—which include making amends when necessary.

MBNA's focus on the customer is obvious to anyone who walks into the corporate headquarters building. Woven into the carpeting at each of the four entrances is this service message: "THE CUSTOMER FIRST." And prominently posted above every one of the building's 350 doorways is this sign: "THINK OF YOURSELF AS THE CUSTOMER."

Charles Cawley, the president of MBNA's parent company, is one of the reasons for its customer focus. Cawley conducted some research and discovered that it costs MBNA $100 to acquire a new customer but that customers bring in significant profits once they join the fold. For example, he found that a 5-year customer contributes an average of $100 to MBNA's annual profits and that a 10-year customer contributes an average of $300.

It's no wonder, then, that Charles Cawley makes sure MNC does all it can to keep its long-term cardholders satisfied. To that end, it has set up a department whose 68 telephone reps call customers who want to close their accounts and encourage them to reconsider. One out of two such accounts is salvaged in this way.

The branches with the highest level of customer retention go out of their way to lavish personal attention on their customers. The customers of these branches are encouraged to voice their complaints in person instead of using the complaint hotline. Leslie Joy, manager of the branch with the top record for customer retention, makes sure that no customer closes an account without first meeting with her. That meeting often changes the customer's mind.

Astounding the Customer

Tom Peters writes: "Unfortunately, we can no longer afford to merely satisfy the customer. To win today, you have to delight and astound your customers—with products and services that *far* exceed their expectations." The business that offers not just the bare-bones basics but exceptional, *value-amplified* service, that anticipates and caters to a whole range of customer needs and desires, sets itself far above the crowd.

We saw such service in the help Ruth Thomson gave to a stranded airline passenger (Chapter 3). It shows up, too, in PC Connection's nearly fanatical drive to achieve ever higher levels of service delivery and in Manco's mailing of greeting cards, several times a year, to 32,000 customers. Many of the cards, Jack Kahl notes, are personalized: "Our people will take the time to personalize thousands of those cards. And I've seen our salespeople take a whole cardboard box full of those cards with them on an airplane. And they sit there and write personal notes on those cards, and bring the box back and give it to our mail department to mail out."

Smith, Bucklin is another organization that astounds its customers. John Hammitt, past president of SIM, says that he is amazed at Smith, Bucklin's dedication to understanding the business of information management: "One would think that they were, in fact, information systems professionals, because they work so hard to understand who we are, what we need to do, what it takes to be successful. . . . They are obsessed with understanding us and our needs as an association of executives, and then delivering against that. That has required a mastery of complex topics, issues, while developing new insights."

Such obsession with pleasing the customer is at the heart of astounding service, according to Henry Givray, a vice president of SBA who serves as executive director of SIM: "Superior customer service does not only mean being competent by serving with the mind. It also means having a passionate desire to please and support your customers by serving with the heart."

One of my favorite examples of a company that provides astounding service is Westport Transportation. This Kansas City, Missouri, airport limousine service goes out of its way to please and support its customers, and does so at a price far below that of its lower service competitors.

When first-time customers call Westport Transportation, they are asked, not just their name, address, and flight time, but also what newspaper they prefer and what beverage they want—down to the quantity of sweetener for their coffee.

Chuck and Stella Bean, the owners of Westport, maintain a database that is filled with personal information on some 5,000 customers. When a customer orders a car, the database is tapped and the driver is able to stock the customer's favorite beverage and reading matter. Stella Bean dispatches Westport's eight drivers and monitors the arrival time of incoming passengers, so that the drivers can meet them at the gate or the luggage carousel.

The price for this high level of personal attention is 35 percent *below* commercial cab rates. "We can keep our fares lower because we know we're going to get that return trip," Chuck Bean explains. "Our rate of repeat business is probably 90 percent. . . . We may not see someone again, but somewhere down the line that person's going to refer someone else to us."

Such word-of-mouth advertising has helped Westport Transportation land accounts with several large local employers, including the Federal Deposit Insurance Corporation and Hallmark Cards. Travel agents from out of town refer clients to the company.

One first-time customer was astounded—but probably not delighted—by the service he received from Westport. Chuck Bean explains: "One new customer told us he wanted a caffeine-free Diet Pepsi on ice served in a blue glass," recalls Chuck Bean. "He had a $20 bet with his secretary that we wouldn't get it right. . . . he lost the bet."

DEVELOPING SERVICE PARTNERSHIPS

Henry Givray of Smith, Bucklin comments:

> Our client organizations can view us in three ways. They can look at us as simply a vendor, a provider of services at a price. They can view us as "their" staff, an extension of their resources to support what they wish to accomplish. This is a higher order relationship.
>
> The highest order of relationship is a partnership. The client views us as a teammate, a colleague, a trusted adviser. When we achieve this partnership, it releases a tremendous amount of human potential and that results in success both for our clients and for Smith, Bucklin.

Earlier I noted that our smartest companies partner with their customers, bringing them into the operational and strategic heart of the organization. There is a growing movement toward forming such partnerships to improve the quality of service and enhance the competitive position of both the service provider and the customer. It is a movement away from simply conducting *transactions* with customers and toward building *relationships* with them.

David Ulrich, professor of executive education at the University of Michigan's School of Business, writes that "companies are now broadening their definitions of customer partnerships to include office procedures, training, even hiring. If you assume the goal of staffing, training, or any other internal process is to better respond to customer needs, then it makes sense to help the customer participate in those processes."

Furthermore, it strengthens the bond between the company and its customers. Ulrich declares: "Satisfied customers remain independent from the firm. Committed customers become interdependent with the firm through shared resources and values." Smith, Bucklin involves clients heavily in the program development process. Bill Smith comments: "We encourage the client to be as creative as possible. Our work is a team effort. People will say, for instance, 'What a wonderful program Smith, Bucklin created for our organization.' In fact, 75 percent of the program was created by the thinkers in that industry."

Manco diligently pursues partnerships with both customers and noncustomers. It strengthened its bond with Ace Hardware by helping Ace to develop a new logo and "look" for Ace packaging. It teamed up with Federal Express to encourage the use of Fed Ex to ship cookies in Manco bubble wrap. And as this chapter's opening tale makes clear, it does everything it can to partner with its leading customer, Wal-Mart.

Jack Kahl talks about how Manco prepares for a Wal-Mart meeting: "When we go down there, we spend a day in the stores doing market research. It's like playing the Super Bowl. You're getting to go down to see one of the finest, fastest-moving retail teams in the world. We go down prepared, and we go down knowing that there's a lot more to do than just see the buyers. And the buyers know that. They know the tradition of a Manco call means we come in there prepared."

This level of commitment and enthusiasm goes far beyond the traditional customer-supplier relationship. In fact, says Jack Kahl, he considers Manco to be in the "consulting business," in the business of forming partnerships rather than selling Duck brand tape.

He provides an example:

Our auditor is Arthur Andersen. They are far and away the world-class leader in their field, not only in auditing and accounting services, but in consulting. And they have put something together they call Smart Store 2000; that's in Chicago. It's about a 6,000-square-foot model of an electronic store, and they have young people there to demonstrate it. Then they have a similar model, called Logistics 2000, at the Info-Mart in Atlanta and one called The Retail Place in Dallas.

Well, we chartered a plane and took our people to see the Smart Store 2000. And once we saw it, we were amazed. I asked them: "How much of this technology is available today?" And they told me, "Every bit of what you see here is available today. It's only the ignorance of people, or the lack of money, or the inability to execute it at a certain speed, that keeps them from using it." Which means that the leading edge, the guy who gets there first, is going to be the guy that wins.

So we invited Arthur Andersen to be a partner in our booth at a trade show at McCormick Place [in Chicago], and we had a kiosk set up. And we got three top partners of Arthur Andersen—$300-an-hour consultants—to come there and contribute their time freely to meet the presidents of all the companies we would get to come in and see the model.

And we presold this thing. We invited Wal-Mart and Ace Hardware, our two top customers, to come take a look at the model. They had a private showing for Wal-Mart from 6 A.M. to 8:30. And Wal-Mart subsequently brought Arthur Andersen down to Bentonville, and they've sent another crew of people up to Chicago to see the Smart Store.

So that's the kind of partnership we have with our customers. We're not even in the business of selling tape. We're truly in a consulting business, finding other ways that we can help our customers. And they literally pay it back in spades; they help us the same way.

Overcoming the NIH Syndrome

The successes achieved by Manco, Preston, PC Connection, and other new story organizations are testimony to the power of partnership. The partnerships of these companies are in striking contrast to typical relationships of old story organizations with their customers and suppliers. Rather than adopting a partnership approach, old story organizations often regarded "outsiders" as adversaries, even when those "adversaries" shared their objectives and might even hold the key to their success.

Consider the story of the failed General Electric compressor (Chapter 4). An important factor in that failure, and in the resultant loss of hundreds of millions of dollars for GE, was the engineering team's refusal to listen to the advice of experienced consultants because it regarded them as "outsiders" (though one of them was a retired GE employee). This NIH (Not Invented Here) syndrome is a leading cause of service failures, and a strong argument for establishing close partnerships to achieve mutual service objectives.

The GE fiasco brings to mind a similar experience related to me by my father, Ed Garfield. Dad was a sales engineer for Kester Solder Company (a part of Litton Industries), providing technical advice to any customers that requested it.

During the 1950s, one of Kester's customers, a personal products manufacturer in New Jersey, had just developed one of the first pressurized shaving cream dispensers. Kester received a substantial order for solder to join the valves to the cans of foam.

For a while, orders poured in from the New Jersey company. Then they abruptly stopped and Kester received an urgent phone call from New Jersey: "Your solder is no good. Send a man here immediately."

Within two or three weeks after it shipped thousands of cans of shaving cream to supermarkets, drugstores, and department stores around the country, the personal products company was flooded with calls from warehouse and store managers across the United States. All of these managers said roughly the same thing: "Your shaving cans erupted on the shelves! The cream is getting all over our merchandise, our workers, our customers. Do something, fast!"

My father was sent to the customer's headquarters to determine what the problem was. It must have seemed to the shaving cream company as if America's stores were being buried in foam. When he walked into the conference room, where seven mechanical engineers and the customer's top managers were assembled, he was almost physically attacked.

Then came a verbal assault: "Your firm supplied us with the wrong solder," one of them yelled. "We're going to sue you," another threatened.

Fortunately, my father had trained himself to handle high-pressure situations. So he calmly began asking questions.

The first question was simply: "Could I please see the valve design?" My father knew that the customer had hired a number of engineers to help with the design. He also knew that those engineers, like the engineers who developed the GE compressor design, had little background for their project. Nevertheless, like the GE engineers, they had refused the offer of help from an experienced source—in this case, Kester.

Soon after the engineers reluctantly produced a blueprint of the valve design, the cause and solution of the problem were apparent to Dad. The vertical valve on the can was held in place only by soft solder, a material never meant to be used where strength was required. The pressure within the can loosened the solder, eventually causing the can to erupt.

The solution was to attach a flange to the neck of the can to take the strain at the bottom of the valve and to use the solder as it should have been used all along—to seal the opening around the flange.

The group assembled in the conference room balked at my father's recommendation: Recall all cans of shaving cream, and correct the valve problem. Tempers flared, arguments followed, and Dad calmly walked out the door.

A few weeks later, the company called my father again. The tone was now humble. "Could you please review your recommendation?" This time it was accepted. A new valve design was drafted, the cans were recalled and replaced, and the product and Kester's reputation were salvaged.

An episode of this kind would never have taken place in a new story, partnership organization. It is impossible to imagine Wal-Mart or Ace Hardware relating to Manco in the way the personal products company related to Kester.

Even old story organizations are beginning to recognize the need for partnership. Jack Kahl cites an example: "There's only a few companies that are really out on the leading, bleeding edge of EDI [electronic data interchange]. The one that's gone the fastest, has invested the most, and gone the furthest, in terms of retail, is

Wal-Mart. And the company that's worked with them to do the pioneering work—most of it is Procter & Gamble, which once upon a time was one of the most arrogant companies in consumer marketing and today has one of the finest reputations for great partnerships. They have, literally, 43 full-time people living in Bentonville [Wal-Mart's headquarters] who are assigned full time to the Wal-Mart account, and I think they have 30 up at Kmart." Even such industry giants as Procter & Gamble, accustomed to going it alone, are coming to understand that if they want to maintain their leadership position, they must establish a partnership approach.

SERVICE LEADERSHIP

Henry Givray: Profile in Leadership

Henry Givray describes what it means to be a service leader:

> Service leadership means more than just meeting the current needs of your client competently and efficiently. It also means stepping beyond the traditional client/provider boundaries to inspire change and fulfill the promise and the potential for the client.
>
> Service leadership also means more than knowing your client. It requires the mastery of topics, issues, and insights related to your client's experiences, goals, thinking, motivations, and needs. A service leader creates a vivid picture of what will make the client prosper not only today but tomorrow. With that picture firmly in mind, the service leader then commits himself or herself to making it happen.

Henry Givray practices what he preaches. In his role as executive director of the Society for Information Management, he has shown the style of leadership that has enabled Smith, Bucklin to maintain its reputation as the leading firm in the association management field.

As I noted earlier, SIM is the professional organization for executives concerned with managing information systems. It was founded in 1969 to "provide leadership and education in the management of information technology to meet business objectives." Its activities were originally defined as providing educational forums, peer networking opportunities, publications, and research.

Smith, Bucklin was hired in 1977 to manage SIM's affairs, and Henry Givray became SIM's executive director in the fall of 1985. Since then, he has helped lead the organization to some impressive achievements.

When Givray became the executive director of SIM, the corporate world was beginning to recognize information technology's potential for boosting productivity, creating new products and services, improving sales and marketing, and enhancing customer service. Several companies had achieved dramatic successes by using information technology to make their businesses more profitable and to strengthen their competitive positions.

Henry Givray recognized that SIM's future success hinged on its becoming an effective conduit for helping industry leaders advance this phenomenon. He understood that SIM must help bridge the traditional gap between systems professionals and the nontechnical executives in the board room. Those executives controlled the future of their organizations and needed to understand the role of technology in shaping that future.

To accomplish this, SIM would have to help its members heighten their awareness of the importance of aligning their information systems goals with corporate strategy. It would also have to provide forums for members to develop their business skills, to be better prepared to participate in the senior management teams of their companies. More broadly, SIM would have to enhance its stature in the business community and the press to generate more credible exposure of key issues as well as individual members.

Henry Givray knew that before SIM could fully realize its potential, key organizational changes would have to be made. Most importantly, volunteer leaders would have to shift from a production emphasis to a strategic focus:

> Very specifically, I felt key industry leaders had to move from conference management to program development; from publications production to information content and direction; from budgeting to financial planning; from membership processing to membership marketing.

Crucial to the success of any association is the strength of its volunteer leaders. SIM's membership includes a number of outstanding industry leaders who, together with Henry Givray, set out to lead volunteer teams through the process of transformation.

SIM published its first annual report in 1987. The same year, it instituted the Partners in Leadership Award, the only one of its kind. This prestigious award recognizes organizations and two of their corporate leaders who have aligned information technology with business strategy to produce major results. Past winners include Sara Lee, DuPont, Kmart, the Government of Singapore, and the City of Dallas.

Under the guidance of Henry Givray, SIM achieved impressive results within a short time. Annual revenue since 1985 nearly tripled, from $500,000 to $1.4 million in 1990. SIM now boasts some 3,000 members worldwide. Since 1985, corporate membership has grown 57 percent. SIM's international presence was almost nonexistent in 1985, when members represented just four countries. Now the membership of SIM represents 40 countries.

In a 1989 study of senior information executives in Fortune 500 firms, conducted by Heidrick & Struggles, SIM was mentioned most often as the number one professional organization to which the respondents belonged. It received almost three times as many mentions as were received by the organization in second place.

The growth in SIM's media coverage has also been striking. The society is mentioned in almost every issue of the premier information systems publications. And those publications regularly seek the society out for story lines and for comment and opinion from its leaders.

John Hammitt describes Henry Givray and Smith, Bucklin as "the glue" that holds SIM together ensuring that it grows and prospers. "These are people who can only measure their success through the success of those they serve," says Hammitt. "They have kept their eye on the fact that leading is creating constant transformation among SIM members. . . . They're the place from which the support for change and for growth emanates within SIM."

Service Leadership: Benchmarking Against the Best

Service leadership requires a total commitment to both the customer's current needs and the customer's vision of the future. We see such commitment in Henry Givray's approach as executive director of SIM. And we see it in the approach of our other new story exemplars. Manco, for one, is never complacent about its service role. It is constantly striving to improve its performance, by every means available. Says Jack Kahl: "We're looking for measurements that make it even harder for us to maintain a high grade, because we know that the tougher we make the standards, the better we're going to be."

Manco studies service leaders diligently in order to learn their secrets and copy their successes. One service leader that Manco watches closely is 3M, its staunchest competitor.

Says Kahl:

3M is our greatest competitor and also our greatest teacher. They're one of the best benchmark companies I've ever studied. I keep telling our people they're one of the best partners we have here. As tough as they are, they also have great respectability, they have high goals, they have high profit margins; they're the third most profitable company on Wall Street in after-tax dollars.

Their cash cow division is the one we compete against. They're actually making very little money in their technology division, because Sony and Toshiba are bringing them to their knees in fighting for the videotapes and the film. So they're making little money on a $2.3 billion division in a company that's doing around $12 billion, and they need the cash cow income stream that comes from the tape and sandpaper, which is their oldest and strongest division.

So one of the best things we have is we've chosen a very wonderful competitor, a respected, profitable one that needs the profits that come from our stream. They've got to maintain a certain profit margin out there that helps us to also build our business.

In addition to monitoring Manco's leading competitor, Kahl dutifully studies individuals who are service leaders. He believes that Sam Walton is a premier model: "Sam Walton is as good a role model as a man could have. I asked him once, 'What is it that makes you feel good, the thing you feel best about?' and he said, 'Helping. Helping raise the self-esteem of other people. Seeing people be more than they think they can be.' He's probably the greatest builder of people I have ever seen."

Kahl notes that being in league with service leaders helps Manco to maintain its own high standards: "If you sell the best and you run with the fastest pack, you're always going to either commit yourself to staying with them, or you're going to get out of the race."

> We're running faster than anybody would ever imagine a $60 million company could run because we don't see ourselves as a $60 million company. We see ourselves running with Procter & Gamble and Wal-Mart.

And Procter & Gamble, to Jack Kahl's surprise, sees itself running with Manco. Kahl points out:

> You know, we benchmark against the best in the business, but the funny part I'm finding out is they benchmark against *us*.
>
> P&G studied our whole packaging merchandising system. They've got one of our package designers that we've used for 14 years, a guy here in town. He was hired by them about five years ago, and they said, "One of the main reasons we hired you is because you showed us in your presentation a company called Manco, which has more market presence by their packaging in a store than we have, and we're P&G." And they said, "We want you to start giving us that look, so there's a family look to our products."
>
> So P&G heard about us through this guy, and then they started studying our merchandising techniques. So the big guys study the little guys, and the little guys study the big guys.

TECHNOLOGY IN THE SERVICE OF PEOPLE

Technology often plays a critical role in a company's ability to maintain service leadership. An example is the superior service provided by United Technologies' Otis Elevator division through OTISLINE.

John Hammitt, former president of SIM and vice president of United Technologies, explains: "Whereas in the past we used technology as a way of *extending* a strategy, in the case of Otis Elevator *technology became a new strategy*. George David, a few years ago, saw technology as truly allowing a way of redefining the way in which our people serve the marketplace."

Hammitt is speaking here of George David, Otis chairman and CEO, who commissioned studies that showed an inconsistent response to service calls, especially during off hours. Otis then maintained equipment in the field with the help of local people, working out of local offices, each dealing with customers somewhat independently. These offices conducted business during normal business hours. If an elevator broke down in the middle of the night, it might take hours before a mechanic arrived.

Otis had a vision of achieving "zero callbacks," of maintaining elevators so well that they would be repair-free. To realize this vision, it set out to create an information system that would allow its customers to deal with it 24 hours a day, 365 days a year.

Through the use of consolidated technologies and high-speed networks, the company came up with a solution called OTISLINE. Now any Otis Elevator customer in North America can call a toll-free telephone number, describe the problem, and be assured of a quick response—in 76 minutes, on average, for a routine service call. The calls are handled by some 2,600 field mechanics, working out of more than 350 field offices. Customers are linked to a central database containing the service record on their equipment, which the field mechanics obtain even before they arrive at a customer's building. The repair call is recorded in the OTISLINE database so that managers can anticipate future servicing needs and prevent breakdowns.

The system works so well that Index Group, a management consulting firm, has called OTISLINE "one of the folk legends of competitive systems." A notable example helps explain why: In 1987, a Los Angeles earthquake left 17 passengers trapped in Otis elevators. Most of them were freed within a half hour of the initial call to OTISLINE.

Federal Express is another company whose technology has helped make it a service leader. Fed Ex uses technology to place information in the hands of the employees who serve the customer. One reason for the company's excellent service reputation is that frontline employees have instant computer access to information about packages anywhere in the delivery cycle, enabling them to deliver top-notch service to customers who call with inquiries.

Jack Kahl, not surprisingly, has studied Federal Express. The inspiration for Manco's own tracking system came from stories he read about the Fed Ex system. He explains:

Our McFix tracking system is a thing that we've developed with a company that pays our freight bills. We learned that if we went a little bit further and pushed it a little bit, we could literally take responsibility for the product and be able to track it all the way to the customer dock.

So we went to work with that company, which is in Atlanta, and we now have, through our Customer Care Department, the ability to let a customer know where the product is en route to them. Until it's delivered to them, we feel it's our responsibility.

That idea came out of reading stories about Fred Smith and Federal Express, which has an unbelievable system by satellite for knowing where every trailer is, within half a mile. So you read something like that, and that's what spawns a lot of learning around here; we're constantly reading and taking every opportunity we can to listen, read, go to seminars.

Paradoxically, the most effective use of "impersonal technology" makes service far more personal. Computer databases, for example, allow businesses to provide individualized attention to vast numbers of customers. Stan Rapp and Tom Collins write in *Maximarketing*: "The computer's radically increased cost-effectiveness in storing, accessing, and manipulating customer files has changed the rules of the marketing game. . . . A customer database [is] the most potent new marketing force, some say, since the emergence of television."

Preston Trucking is building a database system in order to offer customers more personalized service. Will Potter comments: "Through the use of computers, we will be able to bring up the unique needs of every one of our customers, so that any associate at any of our service centers can bring up ABC Company and make sure he understands exactly what that customer's needs are."

Technology can provide customers with a higher level of service while freeing employees to spend more time with their customers. Take PepsiCo's Frito-Lay subsidiary. Frito-Lay's 20,000 salespeople make 400,000 store visits a week. When a Frito-Lay salesperson visits a store, he or she punches into a hand-held computer information about the store's sales and inventory levels. That night the information is transmitted to Frito-Lay's computer center in Plano, Texas, where it is analyzed for sales trends. The salesperson gets the analysis from Plano and is thus able to advise retailers about what to put on their shelves.

Customers love the system because it helps them to be precise about stocking. Frito-Lay's salespeople love it because it saves them a great deal of time and builds customer loyalty.

The test of whether a company is using technology wisely is how well customers are being served by it. And one measure of that is the ease with which the company's employees use the technology. A system designed to provide the customer with better and faster service had better be speedy and efficient for the employees who use it to deliver the service.

Furthermore, it had better be nonthreatening. John Hammitt recalls an unexpected problem that the introduction of the OTISLINE system created for Otis Elevator. He recalls:

> As you can imagine, the changes brought about by these new technologies were difficult for our field support force because they were no longer as independent. The priorities and results of their work were being tracked on a more consistent basis.
>
> People in the field were given the opportunity to carry portable devices that allowed them to communicate with the centralized computing system and have that system communicate with them. It was surprising—and in retrospect, enlightening—how many of those devices happened to fall down elevator shafts during the pilot phase, because many people in the field saw these as ways of simply tracking them, rather than aligning them to support the customer.
>
> It took two to three years for people to fully recognize that the devices not only enhanced their job and gave them the ability to satisfy their customer better but, in doing so, strengthened the bond between them and the local customer and, of course, strengthened Otis's position in the marketplace.

From this experience, Hammitt learned a valuable lesson about the successful introduction of new technology:

> Traditional management thinking is that change is directed from the top, beginning with changing structure and responsibility, driving changes in interpersonal relationships and processes, and that it is through those cascading changes that ultimately individual attitudes and behaviors evolve.

We now recognize that, rather than trying to direct change through structure, we must encourage change by starting with individual attitudes and behaviors. Technology plays a role only after people's attitudes, values, and relationships change. Technology then becomes the means by which they can create new, more productive processes and structure.

SERVICE WITHOUT BOUNDARIES

When I asked Bill Smith how he motivated his employees to deliver consistently superior service to clients, he told me:

I try to emphasize the philosophy that the more we give in this life, the more we receive. We may not be seeking that when we give, but that's what happens.

And that's the real basis for customer service. If you don't have that philosophy, a list of 10 things you must do to have great customer service isn't going to mean anything.

Bill Smith practices what he preaches about service, in his personal life as well as his work life. He reflects on his service contributions:

From a personal standpoint, I've wanted to make a unique contribution. Since the day I left the air force after World War II, I've been acquiring land along the shore of Lake Michigan near Saugatuck, Michigan. Some of it was quite beautiful, and other parts were quite ugly—abandoned orchards and old farms with junk piles of rubbish and old machinery.

What I have done is taken this land, which is now about 600 acres, and committed it to preservation. I've built a number of lakes and ponds. I've contoured the land. I've probably planted 30,000 trees. I grow a certain amount of corn and oats that I never harvest, because I leave it for the wildlife.

The original trees I planted in the 1940s are now 30 to 40 feet in height—magnificent evergreens and also deciduous trees. The wildlife is now abundant. There are raccoons and families of deer, and flocks of geese stop in the ponds.

Anyone can come in and hike on the trails and cross-country ski. I don't allow hunting or mechanized vehicles, but anyone who enjoys wildlife and trees and flowers can come in and enjoy the property. Hopefully, we're contributing something that future generations will be able to enjoy.

In all of the new story organizations we have studied, the service ethic naturally extends beyond the organization to embrace the community. A true service culture has no bounds. Service is more than "good business" to these new story exemplars; it is a way of life as much as a way to work.

Ricardo Semler, president of Semco, is personally involved in efforts to save the Brazilian rain forests. Preston is strengthening its environmental efforts, enforcing stricter monitoring of wastewater management systems and spending millions on renovating and replacing fuel storage tank systems. Motorola, which we'll focus on in the next chapter, is extending its internal commitment to education into the community, collaborating with local school systems and forming a volunteer corps of employees to teach and plan classes or to help translate classes into programs for industry. Digital Equipment (profiled in Chapter 8) has become an international model for promoting diversity in the workplace. The Body Shop (Chapter 9) is fully committed to environmental issues and heavily involved in such service organizations as Amnesty International.

In some new story organizations, the commitment to serving the community is a personal one, as with Bill Smith and Ricardo Semler. In others, it is an organizational commitment, often encouraged or inspired by the CEO, as with Preston. In most cases, it is a combination of the two. For example, The Body Shop's emphasis on social responsibility springs from founder Anita Roddick's personal commitment to social causes.

Both Jack Kahl and Manco are strongly committed to environmental and community efforts. The company's Green Team strives to keep Manco environmentally responsible. All of the company's packaging has already been converted to recycled board, chipboard, and, according to Kahl, "everything that we could possibly do in terms of paper, stationery, cards has already been turned around."

Manco's most significant social commitment is its contribution to Providence House, a nonprofit "crisis nursery" in Westlake, Ohio, for children who come from abusive family settings.

Jack Kahl explains how Manco got involved with Providence House:

I met a woman in 1981 named Sister Hope Greener, who loved children so much, and saw the problems of the inner city and saw child abuse that was killing her. She literally opened her door down there in the inner city and started taking in this baby and that baby. And finally the city gave her an abandoned, condemned house, and that's about the time, through a chance meeting, that I met her.

She believed in Providence. She believed that if she put the money needs in God's hands and she took care of kids, things would work out. And anybody that believes that much, you just can't let down. She taught me that sometimes you have to have this unbelievable faith that you don't even have inside yourself.

So Manco adopted her. We made her an official member of the Manco family. She needed organizational help and skill that I didn't have, and I went to my vice president of finance, and I asked Greg [Klein] if he would come down there with me at one point. And he did, and he joined her board. He's been president of the board for the last six years. [Klein admits that he is "hooked" on Providence House.]

Kahl continues:

We have many people here at Manco that have volunteered to go down and take care of the babies. It's now a very large thing. We've taken care of over 6,000 babies at Providence House, and it now has a staff of 29 salaried people, and still takes no money from the state as of this day. It operates on divine Providence and the charitable hearts of a lot of people.

Kahl, like his partner Sister Hope Greener, believes that faith is the ultimate secret of an endeavor's success. He believes that Manco has grown and prospered over the years by trusting its employees and the many companies with which it does business: "We've just forged ahead and trusted one another, and trusted the companies that we were doing business with. I don't know how to measure that trust, and I don't really want to put a rope around it. I don't ever want to totally understand it. It works, it just works."

Chapter Seven

Putting People First: Hiring, Training, and Rewarding in the Learning Organization

In the early 1980s, Motorola began a major effort to improve the quality of its products. To aid in this effort, the company developed a variety of technical training courses, only to discover that much of its workforce lacked the requisite skills in basic math and reading needed to comprehend the course materials. Thus began what was to become a major new educational thrust for Motorola throughout the 1980s. That thrust culminated in the formation of Motorola University, a corporate training organization that designs, develops, and delivers worldwide training programs to Motorola employees and offers worldwide applications consulting to key Motorola suppliers and customers.

The fact that Motorola won the coveted Malcolm Baldridge Award for Quality in 1988 did nothing to lessen its fervor to achieve ever higher levels of quality by systematically improving the quality of its workforce. William Wiggenhorn, corporate vice president for training and education and president of Motorola University, told me about Motorola's evolution toward becoming a "learning organization."

In 1980, most of the people that Motorola hired were expected to perform a specific set of tasks. We didn't ask them to do a lot of thinking. And the employee's attitude was: "I will do what you tell me to do, but it's up to management to figure out the survival game."

Today the concept of shared responsibility for continuous improvement by all employees is well understood. Our attitude surveys tell us that we're "off the charts" in regard to employees agreeing that "continuous improvement means the product, means the services, means myself." I'd say we have 90 percent acceptance and understanding of that principle worldwide, in multiple languages.

In 1980, I think very few employees could have told you what our goals and objectives were. Today most employees can tell you what our goals and what our initiatives are, what are our five-year objectives, and explain their role in achieving them. That's a huge difference in 10 years.

Now the trick is to make sure they receive the training to achieve those objectives. The burden is on the training organization to provide everything they need so they can keep up.

It was in the early 80s when we started our real thrust for quality, and our focus was on improving product quality. So we started teaching statistical process control, design of experiments, and plant experimentation. Those kinds of courses assume that the participant had a decent background in math and some awareness of basic statistics.

We were not testing at that time, but we began to get the feeling that probably 40 percent to 50 percent of the participants didn't understand what we were teaching because they really didn't have the basic foundation to deal with it. As more and more people interfaced with computer terminals, they were receiving messages on a screen rather than a verbal command. We started to pick up that people could not read what was on the screen.

At that time, which was probably 1984 or 1985, we had no idea of the size of the problem. We just realized we had a problem, and it surfaced when we made the push for quality improvement in the product area.

We had designed and delivered a number of courses by then. Many of our people had taken them and gone back to their jobs, and nothing changed. The skeptics were right: We were wasting our money.

The problem really hit home when we decided to open our new cellular manufacturing facility in 1985 in Arlington Heights, Illinois, rather than overseas. The people there were going to be empowered to do much more than they'd been responsible for in the past, things like quality control and flexible manufacturing. They were already familiar with radio technology, and we figured that with all the training we'd done to that point, they could make the switch to cellular.

So we were shocked when only 40 percent of the plant passed a test containing simple percentage problems. We were astonished to find out that much of our domestic workforce was illiterate and couldn't do simple math. We concluded that about half of our 25,000 manufacturing and support people in the United States could not meet seventh-grade reading and math levels.

We knew that we had to build learning, continuous learning, into the culture of Motorola. So we began dialogues and initiated the educational partnerships that ultimately led us to form Motorola University.

The university started out as our training center in 1980. We had a board of directors for the center, and over a period of three years, they went from being neutral on training to being very positive. They began to see good return on their investments. That board helped to sell the center within the company because the members consisted of very senior executives.

We did encounter some early resistance throughout the entire organization. For instance, at the front line, people asked, "Look, why do I need these skills? I have been here 30 or 40 years. I only have 5 or 10 more years to go. I don't want to learn these things." Number two: "Are you trying to embarrass me by showing that I can't read or I can't compute?" Another response was: "I went to a class. I learned something, but I was never required to use it back on the job. So why take me away from a job and give me a set of skills I will never be required to use?"

In the middle of the organization, we heard: "Great, another corporate program. It's going to cost money, take time, and I have neither. I am sure it's not going to help me achieve my business objectives." We had disbelievers throughout the entire organization.

We had to develop a massive communication program so that our employees understood that we weren't doing this to embarrass them. We were doing it because of a competitive threat. We didn't have a right to exist as an institution unless we could compete globally and satisfy global customer requirements.

So we spent a lot of time letting them know what the employees at our competitor organizations could do and at what cost. We delineated the difference in skills between our people and theirs.

We had older employees on video communicating to other employees that we have survived massive changes before. We used the analogy that when Motorola started, we were primarily in a tube business. Then we went to transistors. From transistors to semiconductors. And now from semiconductors to software. People who are 60 years old have made three of those transitions and they are now on the fourth, and it's time to do it again, so let's work together on it.

For me, that captures our strategy: "Let's build a common force. Let's develop and constantly upgrade that force, and have it work together worldwide." That kind of approach is historically rooted in Motorola, which was founded over 60 years ago. Many of the employees were recent immigrants. They lived in the same neighborhoods. They drank in the same bars. They ate in the same restaurants. They bowled in the same bowling alleys. They worked together for survival, and a lot of that attitude is still here. People will do things here because they actually do believe that we're going to do this together.

Today we have a full-time director of external education relations who focuses on education from kindergarten through grade 12. We have decided to target a hundred school districts in this country that ultimately feed us the majority of our workforce.

We have been bringing administrators and teachers into our laboratories and factories as interns. We are putting them in our management classes. We are working with them on curriculum development. We are trying to put together packages to excite young people to continue to study math, or one more year of science, by showing them applications.

In 1980, we would never have done that. We would have said that our responsibility is only to our employees. Well, today we believe our responsibility is to the entire "people supplier," that is, the school systems.

Ten years from now, our vision is such that there would be a federation of Motorola universities spread throughout the world. Right now, the university is fairly central as far as many of the resources go, but within 10 years we are going to see it being decentralized, so that each facility has the resources necessary to meet the learning needs of Motorolans, our suppliers, and our customers in a particular geographic area. And each university will have its own board that worries about what people need to know and the best way of helping them acquire knowledge. The universities will be joined together through a common plan and a quality audit process.

Also, I think we will have retirees who will be adjunct members of the universities. We already have many retirees from both Motorola and other firms involved, but I see that expanding.

Today 90 percent of our training is done in some type of classroom. In our literacy education, more and more of it is going to individuals—individual coaching, computer interface, tapes. We would like to move in that direction, across some of the more technical fields, product knowledge fields, even management fields.

We currently have a rolling three-year training plan for the company. Our target is to develop an individualized training plan for every employee. This year we know that over 70 percent of our employees had an individualized training plan, and we feel quite confident that in the 1990s over 90 percent will have an individualized training plan.

The university will spend a lot of time in this decade trying to figure out how to bring training to the individual at the appropriate time. We also want to know what that individual really got out of it, so that if he or she didn't get what we expected, we can address that issue.

Our goal is to provide the right training, to the right persons, at the right time, and return them to the right environment, so that the skills can be used immediately. We are a long way from that, but we are looking at methods to help us get there.

———————

Motorola is dedicated to promoting continuous learning for all of its employees in order to maintain its position as a world-class competitor in the 1990s. Early in its evolution toward becoming a "learning organization," the company received an education of its own. Motorola executives tried several piecemeal attempts at training before recognizing that a more expansive, and more compelling, method was required to achieve their ambitious quality improvement objectives.

Motorola's management had assumed that the employees who needed the training courses Motorola developed would take them; they did not. Nor did they use the self-help materials in which Motorola packaged the training. William Wiggenhorn recalls: "Training, it appeared, was not something we could deliver like milk and expect people to consume spontaneously. It was not simply a matter of instructing or giving people a chance to instruct themselves. We had to motivate people to want to learn, and that meant overcoming complacency."

One reason for the complacency was Motorola's policy of hiring workers "for life." Wiggenhorn describes the policy: "Once you have been here 10 or more years, you are part of what we call the Service Club, which means you will not be let go in an economic downturn. You can be let go for poor performance, but not because of the economy."

Unfortunately, this well-intentioned policy led to the reluctance or outright refusal of some employees to learn new skills and behaviors. To overcome this drawback, Motorola expanded the policy's definition of "poor performance" to include an unwillingness to change. Says Wiggenhorn: "We adopted a policy saying everyone had a right to retraining when technology changed. If they took it and failed, we'd find a solution for them. But if they refused, we'd fire them."

He adds:

We realize that we literally have to double the business in order to retain the same number of employees we have today, 10 years from now. But our bet is that if you say to people, "Our goal is to try and keep you as long as we are an economically sound organization," they are willing to take more chances than if we say, "We could have 10,000 people today, 5,000 people tomorrow, 8,000 people the day after."

Also, our education investment wouldn't make sense if we

just had people here in the short term. Then we would just try to hire the most highly qualified people, pay them premium, keep them here as long as they are premium, and then get rid of them. I think some other organizations tend to do that, but we don't believe in it.

Motorola's enormous financial investment in training and education is testimony to the strength of its commitment to continuous learning. When the Motorola Training and Education Center was formed in 1980, senior managers projected that an outlay of $35 million over a five-year period would be adequate to cover the company's new educational thrust. Ultimately, Motorola ended up spending $60 million *per year* on learning and another $60 million on the lost work time required for learning. Much of that money went for remedial education—seventh grade level reading and math. Motorola feels the outlay has been worth it. The company saved no less than $1.5 *billion* between 1988 and 1991 because of improvements the training has made in workforce productivity.

Studies confirm that such a strong commitment to continuous learning pays off in the long term. U.S. employers spend more than 10 percent of the initial cost of their machinery to maintain it, but less than 2 percent to maintain the skills of their employees. Yet, according to Curtis Plott, executive vice president of the American Society for Training and Development, most of the productivity growth of the U.S. labor force between 1935 and 1985 was due to employee training, not to capital spending. While U.S. employers spent 15 times as much on new plant and equipment during that time, the return in productivity provided by training was *double* the return provided by new plants and equipment. Even so, U.S. companies budget less for training than their overseas competitors. And 68 percent of the money they do spend goes to further schooling for college graduates.

In offices and factories across the United States, workers are being asked to take on new responsibilities and master new techniques. Many are ill-equipped to do so. As a result, companies are scrambling to find ways to train employees fast, effectively, and continuously. Says Jere Jacobs, assistant vice president at Pacific Telesis: "The problem is much broader than K through 12 education. It is really K through life."

Motorola is gradually coming to recognize the power of the dollars it is spending on the continuous education of its workforce. William Wiggenhorn comments:

> Since we began these efforts nine years ago, there has been a major shift among senior executives to viewing Motorola's education expenses as an investment rather than a cost. They have seen returns, and employees have too; they are picking up marketable skills.
>
> The first signal we had that the new training emphasis was going to take was in 1985, which was a very difficult fiscal year for us; 1984 had been a very good fiscal year, and 85 was a very tough year. Everybody thought that all the training budgets would probably be cut in the various business centers. And just the opposite happened. The middle managers invested more in training than ever before. As a matter of fact, it went up several million dollars. More people took training that year than ever before. And my own feeling is that more of it was applied quicker than ever before.

A primary focus of Motorola's investment in education, both technical and nontechnical, is on realizing the company's ambitious goal of achieving a six-sigma quality level by 1992. A "sigma" is one standard deviation from the mean, or arithmetic average, and a quality level of six sigma means that 99.9999998 percent of products, on average, are defect-free. This translates to just 3.4 defects per million parts.

Kim Fudge, who manages operations at Motorola's main manufacturing plant, is a strong promoter of six sigma. He explains the need for this stringent level. "Five years ago," he says, "we were using all the other popular quality control ideas that everyone else uses. We had so many defects we couldn't even measure them." Operating at three sigma—a mere 99.7 percent error-free performance—wasn't tolerable, says Fudge. "We have some large data communications systems with tens of thousands of parts," he notes. "So you can see how reckless it is to operate at three sigma."

Specifically, at the three-sigma quality level, you would expect, on average, 2,700 errors per million parts. To put that in perspective, a product with 1,200 parts would have an average of 3.2

errors and only 40 out of 1,000 products, on average, would be defect-free.

In its quest for "engineered perfection," Motorola is discovering that success requires focusing, not only on math and science, but on people. After testing workers at its Arlington Heights plant, Motorola awakened to the realization that employees struggling with math and reading skills cannot, however committed, lead the way into a high-tech future. To achieve high-quality products, the company required a high-quality workforce.

Six sigma, Motorola has learned, is less about precision than about people—about valuing employees, encouraging their involvement, and providing them with the tools and training they need in order to participate effectively in quality efforts. The organization is undergoing a paradigm shift, from viewing quality as an engineering concept to viewing it as the natural by-product of a well-trained, well-motivated, and well-rewarded workforce. This shift is evident in the literature on Motorola University, which stresses that the university's focus in the 1990s will be, not on achieving six sigma, but on providing programs and services to "elevate our *workforce* [my emphasis] to a six sigma status."

THE LEARNING ORGANIZATION

The old story organization produced standardized products for a stable and predictable mass-market environment. Learning in that environment consisted primarily of memorizing facts and mastering routine skills. The emphasis was on predictability, uniformity, and consistency—of people as well as products.

Managers supplied frontline workers with the "right" approaches to work processes and provided the "correct" answers to predictable problems that arose on the production line. Learning simply involved absorbing the past and repeating it in the present. The function of the front line was not *to think* (this was severely frowned on), but *to respond* on cue, like Pavlov's dogs, to directives from above.

A learning system of this kind is effective only in an environment that is stable and predictable. No such stability or predictability exists today. Organizations that wish to thrive in the economic environment of the 1990s must dramatically shift the focus of their training and educational efforts, rethinking the very concept of learning.

This is not to say that the old story paradigm of learning must be discarded completely. Employees must still engage in routine, mechanical training to master specific tasks—for example, maintaining machinery. But such training must now be subsumed in a higher order of learning that emphasizes thinking and experimenting, responding *proactively* to an ever-changing environment rather than *reacting* to a predictable one.

This shift calls for an entirely new direction for training, one that emphasizes creative thinking rather than simple memorization. Instead of absorbing the "right answers" to predictable questions, the function of employees in the new story organization is to ask the right questions, to define, test, and refine new ideas continually. This, in turn, calls for a shift from an emphasis on individual learning to an emphasis on learning as a group, on engaging in "dialogue" (see Chapter 5) and continuous interaction with others inside and outside the organization.

Individual learning, no matter how effective, does not guarantee organizational learning. It is not uncommon for the organization as a whole to falter while many individuals in the organization are learning well and continually (recall the Sun Microsystems example in Chapter 4). If the organization is to learn *as a whole*, if it is to harness and multiply the knowledge of individual employees for its benefit, the focus of training and education takes place best in teams, the basic holon of the new story organization.

Although Motorola is striving to develop an individualized training program for each of its employees, its emphasis is clearly on learning *as an organization*. William Wiggenhorn notes:

> We are piloting a program on institutional learning that was designed at Boston University and acquired by the American Society for Training and Development. It's to try and reinforce *institutional learning* rather than simply individual learning.
>
> We are just beginning the pilot, but we are already discovering how to learn as a team, number one; number two, how to hook up a team with other teams who are looking at the same issues; three, how to relay that learning to areas of the business outside of your own individual work area. Finally, we are learning to use different methodologies to get the same information

across to different teams—for example, using games or different technologies. But again, the focus is on whole groups learning rather than just individuals.

Wiggenhorn notes that team learning represents a major shift in direction for Motorola: "Our history is one of individual contributors, not teams. So training has to emphasize team building and downplay the Lone Ranger culture we valued in the 1950s and 1960s."

The focus of training and education in the team-based learning organization is on building relationships and developing processes rather than memorizing facts and learning set procedures. Mastering specific tasks is of secondary concern to the learning organization; what is crucial to it is developing the teamwork and creative thinking skills (i.e., the *process*) for identifying the tasks to be pursued and approaches to pursuing them.

Motorola is coming to understand that, paradoxically, the key to solving practical problems is to focus on relationships rather than technical skills. William Wiggenhorn comments: "The key benefit of the whole education process is to develop a worldwide network of Motorola associates, and establish personal relationships between them."

He continues:

If you look at the early 80s, we talked to each other through fax and telex, and they are fairly unfriendly devices when you have never met the person. It is usually, "Hey, you made a mistake." Or, "I need this information by tomorrow." We don't spend a lot of time asking anything about the person.

Through our training, we are establishing a kind of networking. People now know each other, or they know the country the person is from or the business the person is from. We will still continue to use technology for communication, but we want to do it on a person-to-person basis rather than an it-to-it basis.

We developed 14 case studies internally that showed when people knew the person at the other end of that fax machine, if there was some type of interface they'd had that was positive, they would do anything to satisfy the requirements. In one case, a person drove across the Alps during the night to make sure that a part got there. Whereas before, he would have just said, "I never got the fax, I am positive." We had 13 other cases like that, where people just went way out of the ordinary business requirements because they knew the person at the other end.

This focus on relationship building represents a profound shift from the old story approach to learning. That approach focused on ingesting known facts and spitting them out. It ignored the relationships and processes by which the facts would be utilized and translated into effective action. Motorola's emphasis on building relationships is more in keeping with the way in which living organisms learn and grow—not in isolation but by "engaging the environment" and developing a fit with it.

One of the ways in which Motorola helps its employees to engage the environment is by sending employees at all levels of the organization around the globe to make firsthand observations of new business practices and techniques. William Wiggenhorn reflects:

> In the early 80s, the only people who traveled outside the United States were primarily senior managers. So they had a personal view of what was going on. Today teams of all kinds—middle managers, front line, etc.—go to other parts of the world to see how things are done. Then we have them come back to their homesite and explain it to others.
>
> Part of the reward is: one, being able to do that traveling; number two, being able to see how other people do something that they thought was impossible; number three, coming back as the teachers to their own associates. . . . It's not the boss coming back and telling them; it is really their peers coming back and sharing the knowledge with them. I see us doing more of that in the 90s.

What is so powerful about Motorola's new practice is the message it communicates about the solid partnership of all employees. This is not just a nice gesture, but a sound business decision, since Motorola's frontline workers will be instrumental in implementing the lessons they learn by "engaging the environment." Motorola's more democratic approach is essential to the organization that hopes to learn as an organization.

Democracy is a necessity for the learning organization, and at the same time an educated workforce reinforces a democratic workplace. Alvin Toffler explains:

In a continual cycle of learning, unlearning, and relearning, workers need to master new techniques, adapt to new organizational forms, and come up with new ideas.

Workplace democracy, like political democracy, does not thrive when the population is ignorant. By contrast, the more educated a population, the more democracy it seems to demand. With advanced technology spreading, unskilled and poorly educated workers are being squeezed out of their jobs in cutting-edge companies. This leaves behind a more educated group, which cannot be managed in the traditional authoritarian, don't-ask-me-any-questions fashion. In fact, asking questions, challenging assumptions are becoming part of everyone's job.

Continuous Learning at Levi Strauss

Levi Strauss & Co. is another organization that has dedicated itself to continuous learning as a way to remain competitive in an uncertain future. Sue Thompson, its director of Human Resource Development, notes: "The importance of training has grown significantly, and the recognition of the need for training is staggering. What we're finding is that as we give more and more training, it uncovers more need for other training. As so much changes in the workplace, employees now have need for a multitude of skills."

Like Motorola, Levi Strauss has shifted its training emphasis from individuals to groups. Sue Thompson reflects:

In the past, employees operated as individual contributors, but people are now working, in many cases, as groups or work teams. We are clearly seeing that in our home office, and even in our production facilities. Work groups are forming naturally. We are seeing the move to self-managing work teams, which is requiring us to relook at our pay system, for one, and secondly, to provide extensive training on how to work together and how to collaborate and solve problems. The changes are astounding, and the need for training associated with those changes is extensive.

In order to ensure that the organization truly learns as a result of corporate training, Levi Strauss integrates what is done on the job with what is taught in the classroom. Says Sue Thompson:

> Our goal and strategy are to try and make sure that the training is much more integrated into the way departments actually function. We do some team training, and then we work with the group in real time to try and help them integrate those concepts into the workplace.
>
> What we have found is that to just ship people off to a classroom and provide training for them, and then let them go back to their work environment and not provide any follow-up support, is not a cost-effective strategy. Consequently, what we now call the human resource development organization has two arms. One arm develops and administers training programs. The other is an internal consulting group. The role of the consultants is to work with managers and their work groups, to integrate the skills learned in a training session into their work environment and use their skills on the job.
>
> The HRD group is heavily involved now in working with managers and their work teams to help them better understand what the vision of the company is, what the department manager's vision is for his or her organization, and to help employees take a look at their own desired future for the company and for their department—how they need to be as a group, and what kinds of changes they need to make as a group to help them get there.
>
> Our strategy for the next five years is to make sure that every employee in the company has some fairly significant, extensive, and powerful experience in understanding the Aspiration Statement [see Chapter 2] and learning the skills needed to implement it, to provide training and consulting support to help them make that a reality in the workplace.

Like Preston Trucking and other new story organizations, Levi Strauss recognizes that the person doing the job is in the best position to understand the job and to know what skills he or she needs in order to keep pace with the competition. As a result, the company is shifting the responsibility for training from the organization to individual employees.

Sue Thompson notes:

> With increasing use of technology as new data processing systems are implemented, jobs are changing significantly. We are trying to encourage employees to take responsibility for their own training and development, to contract with their managers or supervisors, and then to be aggressive in making sure that they are developing skills that will prepare them for the future.
>
> In some cases, we don't know what those skills are. We know that jobs are changing significantly. We are encouraging employees to become more computer literate, and to network with colleagues and scan the environment, and just to stay on top of changes that are happening in the way we do business. We are trying to staff up the training and development organization so that we can be one step ahead of the training needs as they unfold.

Leadership and the Learning Organization

William Wiggenhorn believes that committed leadership is essential to a company undergoing the transformation to a learning organization. Says Wiggenhorn: "There has to be a senior executive who is going to be around for a while. To me, that means five or more years. Someone who believes that education and training will help him or her make this a better institution in new products, new market possibilities, or what have you. If that person does not exist, then I think it is a losing ballgame."

In every company that is striving to become a learning organization, we see at the top of the company a leader who is committed to developing a culture of continuous learning. When Robert Galvin was Motorola's CEO, he spearheaded the effort that culminated in the establishment of Motorola University, an effort that continues to be promoted by Motorola's present CEO, George Fisher. Will Potter, chairman of Preston Corporation, set the tone for learning when he radically restructured the company so that employees, the union, and customers could learn together how to survive in a deregulated environment. Ricardo Semler was responsible for establishing Semco's self-managed teams, which learn together and virtually run the company. Patricia Gallup has created an environment at PC Connection that allows employees and customers to learn from each other. And it took the strong commitment of Frank Merlotti to revamp Steelcase into a team-based organization that fosters continuous learning across functions.

Another organization committed to learning is Manco, and CEO Jack Kahl is the main reason. Kahl is passionately committed to studying individuals, customers, competitors, and successful organizations of any kind, always searching for ways to improve his own organization. And he urges Manco employees to do the same. He has succeeded in creating a corporate culture that not only invites, but almost demands, continuous learning.

Kahl does all he can to reinforce the concept of continuous learning at Manco. He sees that information about the company is shared freely, and in lavish detail, with all employees. Eager new sales recruits are taken along on sales calls to major customers, so they can learn the ropes as quickly as possible. And the company offers a Spirit Award—its highest honor—to employees who demonstrate a high level of curiosity.

Even Manco's physical design was created with an eye toward education. Much of the action is in the center of the organization, so there is easy access to fast-changing information. "To learn anything, you go right to the center of this company," says Kahl.

The walls at Manco are lined with the thoughts of philosophers—some of them famous, some of them Manco employees. Each executive chooses a quotation for a sign that hangs above his or her office door. Kahl's quotation, borrowed from Socrates, reads: "One thing I know, and that is that I know nothing."

In fact, the quote is misleading. It is meant to remind Kahl, not that he knows nothing, but that there is always more to learn. And learning is what Jack Kahl does best.

Kahl soaks up inspiration and knowledge from customers, especially from Wal-Mart, Manco's top customer. And he studies successful competitors, such as giant 3M. Kahl focuses on "learning from the best" as a way to become the best. "The best" from whom he has learned include such individuals as Walt Disney and Sam Walton and such organizations as Disney and Wal-Mart.

Walt Disney was a major inspiration. Through an art book, Kahl learned of his emphasis on color. That triggered the idea of having a designer create the distinctive Sea of Green packaging that unifies all Manco products. (In Chapter 6, I noted that the packaging is so outstanding that Procter & Gamble hired a designer to bring the same unifying look to its products.)

Kahl hired a former Disney executive to teach Manco about color and animation. That teaching, combined with customers' mistaken references to "duck tape," was the inspiration for the Manco duck, Kahl's alter ego. Not surprisingly, the duck is an educator, sharing what Manco has learned with customers, suppliers, and employees, in *Duck Tales*. The newsletter relays information about retailing and philosophizes about business in general. And in such communiqués as "Duck Calls," Kahl dispenses advice to the sales force.

Jack Kahl and the employees of Manco follow a disciplined process of gathering and synthesizing ideas and then—most important—*applying* them to improve the quality of his company's service. Says Kahl: "Service to me is just a theory in a book. Business is people. I get angry around here at times, when I say, 'Stop talking theory. Case studies are wonderful, but you've got to bring it out of theory and turn it into something that's going to help our customers.'"

To make sure that learning is translated into new organizational behavior, Kahl holds forums at "Manco University," a corporate conference room in which a variety of courses are offered and ideas about the business and the industry are vigorously debated every Thursday evening. Senior executives meet in the afternoon; the rest of the company has an open invitation to join in the Thursday evening debate.

Kahl, speaking through the Manco Duck in a recent issue of *Duck Tales*, emphasizes the importance of leadership in developing a culture of learning: "We've recommitted our organization to a major investment in time and money to improve the educational level of all Manco partners. One of the most difficult obstacles to cultural change in any organization is the reluctance of senior managers to admit that they don't know everything."

Kahl advises senior managers to "face this reality by committing themselves to being reeducated and by serving as an example to the Manco partners they work with." He adds: "No one in our organization needs educational cheerleaders exhorting the players to engage in lifelong learning. We need our leaders to model the learning behavior they supposedly want everyone else in the organization to live by."

"The essence of real leadership," Kahl writes, is "to allow your people to see your need and desire for learning. Your actions speak more than your words. Today's leaders must be students of change first before they become teachers of change to others."

Leadership Training. In addition to starting with a committed leader at the top, the company striving to transform itself into a learning organization must offer leadership training to others within the company.

Many companies spend large amounts of money to develop effective technical training programs, then fail to provide the training in leadership and interpersonal skills needed to ensure that what is learned in the technical programs can be applied and spread throughout the organization.

Perry Pascarella reported on a study of training patterns in which more than 1,000 managers and quality improvement professionals were surveyed. The study determined that 80 percent of outside training expenditures were applied to technical training and the installation of new management systems. Less than 20 percent of such expenditures were applied to the development of leadership skills.

However, when the participants in this study were asked to identify the blocks to service quality improvement, the ratio was almost exactly reversed. According to their responses, 80 percent of service quality problems were related to management leadership, support, and involvement and just 20 percent were related to technical skills.

Pascarella concludes: "We have found repeatedly that there are fundamental skills, in the leadership and interpersonal areas, that consistently make or break the effort to improve productivity, performance, service, and quality. Through the process of elimination, the problem eventually comes home to a leadership issue. Introducing new systems and technologies when people don't have the fundamental [leadership and interpersonal] skills is a prescription for disaster."

The importance of leadership skills in transferring learning throughout the organization is underscored in the following story about a major bank that sought to increase its asset base by bringing in new deposits. The bank's management theorized, logically enough, that training frontline workers was the key to success in this endeavor. After all, potential customers often base their decisions to deal with a bank on their interactions with the tellers.

So management tested its theory in 18 branches, giving intensive customer service training to tellers and other frontline personnel in half of the branches and no customer service training in the other branches. Sure enough, deposits rose significantly in seven of the branches that had been given the training. But they also rose in six that had not.

After carefully considering the results, management concluded that the increase in deposits was not due primarily to frontline training. Rather, it was due mainly to the high quality of leadership exhibited in the successful branches. Most of the customer service supervisors in the 13 winning branches, it turned out, had superior leadership and interpersonal skills.

HIRING IN THE LEARNING ORGANIZATION

It is axiomatic that organizations committed to continuous learning must hire employees who are able and willing to learn. As the experience of Motorola demonstrates, it is not always possible to hire well-educated employees, particularly in an era of labor shortages. But it *is* possible—and essential—to recruit workers who have the potential and willingness to learn, in partnership with the organization.

Companies committed to learning and growing take great pains to hire the right people. In many new story organizations, the interviewing process is a lengthy one; 5 to 10 interviews, even for entry-level workers, is not uncommon. Those who will be working for and with new employees take an active part in the interviewing process. Such participation is especially important in the learning organization, which emphasizes teamwork and close collaboration.

At Levi Strauss, job candidates are interviewed by a broad range of people both inside and outside the company, according to Sue Thompson. "It used to be that the hiring manager and the recruiter would see the person," she says. "And now, in many departments, the person has to go through six to nine interviews, in some cases with clients or with users or with people who would be peers, to make sure that everyone feels good about the way this person will fit into the organization, and the skills and competencies that he or she brings."

Contrast this deliberate, careful, time-consuming approach to recruiting workers with the haphazard, "quick and dirty" techniques characteristic of old story organizations. According to Robert Half, a well-known recruiter, most hiring decisions are made within the first 15 minutes of an interview, based on first impressions. Such impressions may be useful intuitions, says Half, but they are far from sufficient:

> The "judging" aspect of hiring is only one of the tools of an effective hiring strategy. . . . hiring is not simply a matter of interviewing a number of candidates and deciding which of them is the best qualified. Hiring is a complex process, of which interviewing candidates is only one aspect. . . . analyzing the job requirements, using the best recruiting sources, screening effectively, preparing properly for the interview, being diligent in your reference checking—these are considerations too. . . . The majority of hiring mistakes made each day could be prevented if the people responsible for the hiring simply did a more effective job of determining exactly what they were looking for before they started to look.

The Importance of Fit

New story organizations, dedicated to continuous learning, have a firm idea of what they are seeking when a job candidate walks in the door. They go out of their way to ensure a good "fit" between a candidate's skills, background, and aspirations and the company's philosophy, values, and workplace environment.

To ensure an appropriate match, America West Airlines conducts group interviews to see how job candidates interact with other people—a crucial consideration for a company that emphasizes extensive cross-utilization of workers. According to Rod Cox, senior director of recruitment training at AWA: "We want to find people, generally, who are very participative—not wallflowers but also not those who need to dominate every situation. This is not a good company to come into if you are really heavy into 'prima donna-ism'; it just isn't going to be rewarded."

Levi Strauss also looks for fit, according to Sue Thompson. "By 'fit,' two things come to mind," she says. "First, people's values are consistent with the Aspirations Statement; and second, their personal style exhibits flexibility to adapt to the massive changes we are experiencing in the workplace."

In their efforts to make only suitable hires, some companies seem to discourage candidates. "We want people to back out before they ever see a guest if there is any doubt that they will like this kind of work," explains Deede Sharp, manager of educational programs development at Disney World. Joe Lee, president of General Mills Restaurants, echoes this theme: "We try to interview people who will share with us the goals that we have. We are right up front about what kind of place we want to run." And Rod Cox comments that America West is very specific with job candidates about what working for the company will be like: "It is not like we expect them to get inside the company and then discover what the corporate culture is about. We try to mirror that corporate culture from the earliest contacts with the company all the way into it."

As organizations become more team-oriented, teams are becoming increasingly involved in hiring decisions, sometimes taking over the hiring process completely. For example, teams now have full responsibility for recruiting new members at Semco.

Team hiring makes good sense, since those already on a team are in the best position to know what qualifications a particular project demands and what interpersonal styles would mesh well with the present members of the team. Daryl Lev, a vice president who introduced the idea of team hiring at Com Systems, says that before the group hiring system was put in place, new employees were "in the image of their supervisor." He added that people may or may not have gotten along with each other before—now they're more likely to.

The Importance of Attitude

When analyzing prospective new hires, the learning organization searches for a history of success, in an attempt to separate peak performers from their less successful colleagues. But it also searches for positive attitudes toward failure. Says Sue Thompson: "I look for people who have learned from their experience, because learning is the key to the new organization. I look for people who are able to talk about their setbacks and failures and who have been able to learn from them as well."

In an era that demands ongoing innovation and continuous learning, it is critical to assess the attitudes of job candidates toward the failures that are an inevitable by-product of constant experimentation. Peak performers will stand out not only because of their impressive results in previous jobs but also because their ability to correct course when they're on the wrong path and their willingness to admit and learn from mistakes.

Managers of new story organizations agree that attitudes and approaches to work far outweigh technical skills. AWA learned the hard way that, by itself, technical expertise has little bearing on performance. Says Rod Cox:

> Let me talk about something that didn't work out well. This is where we had a real hiring crunch. We were expanding enormously fast, and we had to get a lot of people in place very rapidly. At the same time, a small American carrier was acquired by another airline, and a lot of people were put out of work, particularly those that had flight attendant, reservations and customer service backgrounds. Well, this seemed like a gold mine for us. So we went rather heavily into taking, if I might say now, maybe the easy way out in reaching the numbers we needed.
>
> We made a mistake. We assumed that the commonality of what we wanted and what they had was the airline experience. That shouldn't have been the commonality. It was something different and had nothing to do with airlines at all. The key is: How does one approach work? Does one have a belligerent relationship or a nonbelligerent relationship with the employer? Is it a team concept, or is it "them against us," "management against nonmanagement," and so forth? Those are really the questions we should have been asking.
>
> What we did instead was to say, "These are airline people. They will be easy to train; they will be easy to handle; they will be quickly productive." Frankly, we inherited a bunch of problems. Many of those people are not with us at this time. We had three to four times the problems with that particular group than we have had with any other group.

Sue Thompson of Levi Strauss agrees that success in hiring depends far more on personal skills than on technical skills. She told me:

The hiring errors that we've made have been with people who come in with great technical expertise but don't have the interpersonal skills or interpersonal flexibility to meld or to use that expertise as part of a team. On the other hand, we've taken more risks with people who, on paper, are not as technically qualified for the job. We've taken a risk on them and put them on jobs that they may not have been fully qualified for. And in almost every case that I can think of, they've been very successful.

DEVELOPING REWARD SYSTEMS

Motivation and Rewards

One of the greatest limitations of the capitalist system has been its exclusivity. While employees contribute to the profits of a firm, those profits have traditionally been distributed to the people who have made a financial investment in the firm and to a small number of top managers.

This approach undermines an organization's ability to learn and grow as an organization. When employees are not given a share in the fruits of their labors, they have less incentive to engage in continuous learning and innovation. By hoarding profits, investors and top managers unwittingly stem the flow of profits.

Alex Mironoff captures the shortsightedness of this stingy approach to sharing the fruits of capitalism. He writes:

At the root of freedom lies the concept of ownership or . . . control. If we believe that a certain outcome will benefit us directly or indirectly, we will put more of our energies into achieving it. Traditional ownership, including boards of directors, executive politburos, departmental mafias, and similar power blocs, tend to subvert that energy. Instead of fostering a sense of ownership and control throughout the organization, such bodies succeed in blocking any sense of ownership, interest, or participation in organizational goals at lower levels.

Mironoff continues:

The board wants a high return on equity (ROE)—the higher the better. Do the board members stop to think that if the clerk behind the counter also wanted a high ROE, she might freely choose to do the kinds of things that would help achieve it? No.

Usually, the board is plotting to keep the clerk's pay raise at an absolute minimum so that the ROE target can be hit.

Research supports Mironoff's analysis. A study conducted by the Public Agenda Foundation found that almost two thirds of workers would like to see a close connection between performance and pay. More than 70 percent of the respondents felt that their work had deteriorated because there was no connection between the two. And in a recent national poll of thousands of workers, only 22 percent said yes in answer to this question: "If you were to improve service quality and productivity, do you believe you would be rewarded accordingly?" Some 75 percent of the respondents reported that because of their exclusion from rewards, they deliberately withheld extra effort on the job.

Since the link between pay and performance should be obvious, the only surprising thing about these findings is that they *are* surprising to many managers. Yet instead of rewarding performance, management searches in vain for ways to increase productivity, often turning to the Japanese in quest of some ancient (or modern) Eastern wisdom that would transform the workforce. But as Robert Reich points out:

> There is no art to Japanese management. There is no mystery about how to meet the Japanese challenge. While there is much about the Japanese company that we would find abhorrent if transplanted here, there is also much that we can learn from the Japanese about the effective organization of production. Put most simply, we can learn that people are motivated to be productive not because they are well manipulated but because they have a direct stake in future productivity.

Unfortunately, most businesses prefer to focus on Japanese results and to gloss over an important factor in those results: Japanese reward systems that are more equitable than those of most American corporations. For example, it is not uncommon for the CEO of a U.S. corporation to earn as much as 100 times the salary of the average worker—a difference that shocks most Japanese executives. It is naive to think that the typical employee will be motivated to learn new skills and increase productivity in the face of such an enormous gap in pay.

To add insult to injury, it is generally the "average workers" in American firms who bear the brunt of layoffs, while well-compensated executives are shielded from business downturns or hostile takeovers by bonus guarantees and golden parachutes. (One of the most glaring and best publicized injustices of this kind came some years ago, when GM announced on the same day the layoff of thousands of workers and the award of executive bonuses.) We don't need an organizational psychologist to explain the impact of such discrepancies on worker performance.

Pay for Performance

Ricardo Semler comments that Semco values knowledge as much as position:

> Like anyone else, we value leadership, but it's not the only thing we value. In marine pumps, for example, we have an applications engineer who can look at the layout of a ship and then focus on one particular pump and say, "That pump will fail if you take this thing north of the Arctic Circle." He makes a lot more money than the person who manages his unit. We can change the manager, but this guy knows what kind of pump will work in the Arctic, and that's worth more. Associates often make higher salaries than coordinators and partners [more senior employees], and they can increase their status and compensation without entering the "management" line.

In the old story world, salaries were rigidly tied to position in the corporate hierarchy. With the exception of salespeople, it was unthinkable for workers to earn more than their bosses.

The concept of pay for performance is understandably jolting to managers comfortable under the old story system that tied salaries to seniority and staff size rather than measurable contribution. But it can be a boon to the underrewarded frontline employee and to the productive manager.

When the National Science Foundation reviewed 300 studies of productivity, pay, and job satisfaction, it found compelling evidence that pay based on performance yields higher motivation, productivity, and job satisfaction. One of the studies examined

400 companies and found that going from "no measure of work" to a "work measurement and performance feedback situation" increased productivity an average of 43 percent. Using a combination of performance, feedback, and incentives increased productivity an average of 63.8 percent.

Such findings come as no surprise to our smartest companies, which recognize that their own pay-for-performance systems are an important factor in employee motivation. America West has had such a system in place since its founding, sharing 15 percent of pretax profits, paid quarterly, with all employees. Preston Trucking shares its profits with nonunion employees.

Levi Strauss instituted a pay-for-performance system in 1989. Steelcase has had one for decades, with profit and productivity bonuses averaging 60 percent of employees' base pay. Steelcase CEO Frank Merlotti vouches for the system's positive impact on worker productivity: "People talk about the bonus all the time. They look at things we do in terms of 'What impact is that going to have on the bonus?'"

While Merlotti is convinced of the power of regular bonus distributions to improve efficiency, he and our other new story leaders will quickly point out that too much emphasis on bonuses can inhibit the company from achieving long-term objectives. Focusing on bonuses discourages workers from taking the risks required to achieve ongoing innovation, since risk-taking might jeopardize short-term results, on which most bonuses are based. Such "pot of gold" fixations undermine innovation and limit the company's ability to act fast and flexibly in response to marketplace opportunities.

Profit Sharing.   Profit sharing is probably the most popular and widely used pay-for-performance system. While some managers still view profit sharing as a socialistic plot, Ricardo Semler argues that it is, or should be, at the very core of the capitalist system: "Though there is a widespread view that profit sharing is some kind of socialist infection, it seems to me that few motivational tools are more capitalist. Everyone agrees that profits should belong to those who risk their capital, that entrepreneurial behavior deserves reward, that the creation of wealth should enrich the creator. Well, depending on how you define 'capital' and 'risk,' all these truisms can apply as much to workers as to shareholders."

Semler practices what he preaches. Each of Semco's units has its own profit sharing program. The company gives 23 percent of each unit's after-tax profits to three representatives who have been elected by the workers in that unit. These representatives invest the money until the unit can meet and decide by simple majority vote what to do with it. In most units, according to Semler, that has turned out to be an equal distribution: "If a unit has 150 workers, the total is divided by 150 and handed out. It's that simple. The guy who sweeps the floor gets just as much as the division partner."

One key to making the system work, says Semler, is keeping employees informed about where the company stands:

Nothing matters more than those vital statistics—short, frank, frequent reports on how the company is doing. Complete transparency. No hocus-pocus, no hanky-panky, no simplifications.

On the contrary, all Semco employees attend classes to learn how to read and understand the numbers, and it's one of their unions that teaches the course. Every month, each employee gets a balance sheet, a profit and loss analysis, and a cash flow statement for his or her division.

Everybody knows the price of the product. Everybody knows the cost. Everybody has the monthly balance sheet that says exactly what each of them makes, how much bronze is costing us, how much overtime we paid, all of it. And the employees know that 23 percent of the after-tax profit is theirs.

Solar Press: The Evolution of a Profit Sharing System. Semco's profit sharing system has been essentially unchanged since Ricardo Semler assumed the reins of leadership. The experience of Solar Press, Inc., a direct mail printing and packaging company located in Naperville, Illinois, is more typical. Solar Press installed a profit sharing plan in 1984 and has revised the plan several times since then.

Solar Press, a family-owned business, was founded in the 1970s. When the company was young, its attitude toward bonuses was casual. It started out with fewer than 20 employees, and as long as it was making money, founder John Hudetz was perfectly happy to hand out bonus checks at the end of the month, usually for $20 to $60. Everyone got the same amount. No one knew how it was calculated, but no one complained. "It was seen as manna from heaven," notes Joe Hudetz, one of six Hudetz sons at the 375-employee company.

During the early 1980s, when sales surpassed the $2 million mark, Solar Press decided to install a more formal system of pay for performance. A bonus plan was developed for the company's 75-person mail room. Employees were assigned to specific machines and divided into work teams with four or five members. The more a team produced during a given month, the bigger the bonus for each of its members. And teams would compete for additional dollars.

The bonus plan, put in place in the spring of 1984, had an immediate effect. Packaging machines ran faster than ever, and production rates doubled in many cases.

But there were problems. Because of the pressure to produce, teams put off routine maintenance, so machines broke down more often. Employees who found more efficient ways of working hoarded the information in order to prevent others from winning their bonuses. Moreover, the plan didn't take into account unfair distributions of work assignments or the fact that some jobs demanded more work than others.

In 1985, the revenues of Solar Press grew to $18.5 million. Thanks to the bonus plan, it was cranking out record volume and making lots of money. But the pressure caused by the inequities in the plan didn't abate. "The system totally dismantled any feeling of teamwork or company-wide spirit," notes Sue Smith, the scheduling manager.

At the end of 1986, Solar Press decided to scrap the pay-for-performance system. For nine months, it went back to its original method of awarding bonuses while management tried to devise a new system. This system would have to be compatible with the employee stock plan that the company had just launched, and management wanted to be sure that it would foster teamwork and be easy to calculate and explain.

The new system rewards everyone for bottom-line results according to a clear-cut formula: Every quarter, management sets a profitability goal. If that goal is met, 25 percent of the incremental earnings go into a bonus pool, which is then divided in relation to the earnings of employees during the previous quarter.

Most of the people at Solar Press feel that, overall, the new system is a big improvement. Still, Joe Hudetz anticipates some adjustments: "You have to be willing to face up to what's wrong with a system, and I think our employees appreciate that. The greatest mistakes in history have been made by people who refused to change."

Gain Sharing.   Gain sharing is a decades-old form of pay for performance that is experiencing a revival. One reason for its renewed popularity in an era of teamwork is that gain sharing systems reward the contributions of groups rather than individuals. Under such a system, profits are allocated to various teams on the basis of their productivity levels, which are measured by means of more or less complex formulas.

Scanlon plans are probably the oldest and most familiar form of gain sharing plan. They typically distribute 75 percent of a company's profits to employees and 25 percent to the company. They use complicated mechanisms and procedures to determine how employees will participate and how productivity improvements will relate to bonuses. One of the well-known firms that uses a Scanlon plan is Herman Miller, the furniture manufacturer.

Although the gain sharing concept has been growing in popularity, relatively few gain sharing plans are in operation. One reason for this is that extensive coordination and communication are required to secure agreement on the details of such plans and to work out what everyone perceives as equitable formulas for computing each team's share of potential profits. Another reason is that the emphasis of such plans on team performance, while encouraging greater collaboration among employees, can also demotivate some employees who have been accustomed to a direct correlation between their individual efforts and their share in company rewards.

Internal Venturing.   A novel way to share the wealth is called "internal venturing." According to Rosabeth Moss Kanter of the Harvard Business School, "The notion of running a piece of a large corporation as if it were an independent business is one of 'the hottest old ideas refurbished in American industry.'" The internal venture takes the idea of pay-for-performance to its limit, with participants acting as entrepreneurs whose returns depend on the success of their products and services in the marketplace.

Most internal venture systems pay participants a base salary plus bonuses that depend on the level of their financial commitment to the venture. But there is no set formula for rewarding the participants in such a system. For example, William Stritzler, the executive responsible for overseeing venture development at AT&T, offers internal venture participants compensation options that range from keeping their base salary intact to putting some of it at risk in the hope of earning a payout of up to eight times their investment. By 1987, several AT&T employees had received payouts just below this maximum.

Internal venture systems appeal powerfully to employees who long for more independence. AT&T's internal venture program was popular from the start—in fact, *before* the start. Ideas for new ventures came to Stritzler and his staff even before the program was formally announced; based on what they had heard through the grapevine, 300 potential entrepreneurs brought ideas to Stritzler. The program has funded first- to fifth-line supervisors. Fifth-line supervisors, roughly equivalent to department heads, fall just below the officer ranks. In principle, AT&T is willing to offer the program to nonmanagers too.

Equity Sharing

Equity sharing programs give employees a piece of the business, not just a piece of the profits. Probably the most common system for sharing equity is the employee stock ownership plan (ESOP). By the end of 1989, there were 10,200 ESOPs, an increase of 50 percent since the mid-1980s. New ESOPs have been forming at the rate of 800 to 1,000 per year.

Employee Stock Ownership Plans (ESOPs). In an article in *America West* magazine, Steve Salerno captured the philosophy behind ESOPs by quoting Mark Twain: "Any man worth his salt would fight to defend his home—but only a fool would fight to defend his boarding house." The motivational power of the ESOP is obvious: Employees with an ownership stake in a company will have a proprietary interest in nourishing its growth.

Under an ESOP arrangement, employees borrow money from financial institutions in order to buy stock in their company. It's a standard loan arrangement: The lender holds the stock as collateral, gradually releasing it as the loan is repaid.

When employees leave the company, they receive their individual stock distributions, which can be substantial. At Quad/

Graphics, a Wisconsin printing firm, employee shares in a five-year-old ESOP had a market value of more than $250,000 *per employee*.

ESOPs vary widely, but most of them have the following characteristics: They give employees significant equity in the company (though usually not a majority of the stock). They give employees a direct say in the company's operations, through such devices as employee input groups and voting rights. They give employees full financial and operating information on the company. In addition, ESOPs often give authority to make policy and operational changes even to employees at the front lines.

Manco has a standard leveraged ESOP. Money was borrowed from a bank, and the ESOP purchased 30 percent of the company from Jack Kahl. At the end of a 10-year period, in 1995, the employees will fully own 30 percent of the company.

The substantial motivational power of ESOPs is indisputable. Studies by Oakland's National Center for Employee Ownership found that firms with solid ESOPs enjoy gains in productivity and employee loyalty that are as much as 17 percent higher than the gains of the competition. "The research is clear," says Raul Rothblatt, a staffer at the center. "Companies with plans that combine ownership with true day-to-day worker participation grow at a much faster rate than their industry."

Companies that make the switch to ESOPs often realize dramatic increases in profitability in a short time. At Avis, pretax profits soared from $14.8 million to $41 million in the first year following the introduction of an ESOP. And the value of Avis stock—and employee holdings—tripled.

The surge in productivity following the introduction of an ESOP is due in part to substantially lower absenteeism and turnover rates. Also, companies that implement ESOPs usually experience a significant reduction in shrinkage, since most employees think twice about pilfering their own profits.

Alternative Approaches to Equity Sharing.   While ESOPs are the most common form of equity sharing, there are many other forms. Captive Aire Systems, for example, gave its employees an equity share in its production facilities, real estate, and office buildings rather than in the company itself. In this way, management chose to give employees an ownership stake without surrendering much control. At the same time, employees have an incentive to achieve higher productivity levels that will increase the value of properties critical to the success of the company.

While the Captive Aire Systems equity sharing plan fell one step short of an ESOP, the equity sharing plan of Light & Power Productions, Inc. went one step beyond. The founders of this events management and audio visual service in Scotia, New York, arranged at the outset for an eventual employee takeover. Before Charles Hanley and George Schubert started their company in 1977, they signed a binding agreement called the Plan of '88. The agreement stipulated that on October 1, 1988, Hanley and Schubert would offer Light & Power's employees the option of buying the entire company. "We wanted a dedicated cadre of employees who would think long term," says Hanley of the agreement. "So we decided not just to hire employees, but to put them in business."

The Plan of '88 offered Light & Power employees the chance of taking over the company in a leveraged buyout, with Hanley and Schubert playing the role of bankers. The agreement was binding just for the founders; employees had the option of buying, but they weren't required to buy.

As a selling price, Hanley and Schubert settled on two times retained earnings, with a $300,000 lid on retained earnings; they wanted the price to be realistic for an employee buyout. As a way for employees to accumulate funds for the buyout, they set up a liberal profit sharing and pension plan with a five-year vesting period. In addition, they agreed to allow employees to pay 50 percent of the purchase price, plus interest, in installments out of Light & Power's earnings during the first seven years after the takeover.

The motivational power of the Plan of '88 was as strong as the founders of Light & Power hoped it would be when they drafted it. In the 11 years that the company was in business prior to the takeover, only one employee quit. And in 1980, when operating expenses spiraled out of control, the employees unanimously recommended that they all take a 10 percent pay cut. The Plan of '88, combined with the company's profit sharing and pension program, has made for a very loyal group, according to Hanley.

What happened to the founders? When they were interviewed for a May 1988 article in *Inc.*, they said they would wait and see whether or not the company would offer them jobs after the buyout. "Whether we take them depends on how good their offer is," said Hanley. "If we take their offer, then we have the chance to buy in, to be owners too."

The leveraged buyout went through as planned in 1988, and the firm is still going strong. Chuck Hanley continues to work at Light & Power, as a sales consultant. George Schubert stayed with the company for two years after the LBO, as art director; he is now working as a free-lance artist. Eleven employees bought into the Plan of '88 when it was drafted; now 16 employees participate in company ownership.

CREATING EFFECTIVE REWARD SYSTEMS

Not all rewards are created equal. Alas, organizations too often demonstrate an uncanny ability to set up reward structures guaranteed to produce the opposite of their intended effect. Here are a few guidelines for creating effective reward systems.

Reward Generously

New story organizations that want their employees to learn and grow along with them reward them generously, often far more generously than their old story competitors. Whether the salaries of these organizations are lower or higher is not the primary point. The point is that they offer a superior *package* of rewards that includes not just salary but bonuses, ownership potential, and employee benefits.

Salaries at America West Airlines, for example, are not the highest in its industry, but this is more than compensated for by its stock ownership plan, such generous benefits as round-the-clock child care, and ample opportunities for career development. The same is true at Steelcase, whose piecework bonuses, flextime, and other people-oriented benefits add up to a generous overall compensation package even though its salaries are somewhat lower than the industry average.

Many cost-conscious companies wince at the thought of spending precious dollars on generous reward systems, which they fear will adversely impact the bottom line. But paradoxically, such systems can strengthen a company's profit picture. The formula is simple, according to Joe Lee, president of General Mills Restaurants: "You attract and hire people better than the norm, pay them better than the norm, and they perform better than the norm—they produce better meals and service, and more than the extra money that's needed to pay them, enough to produce a better return for investors."

For companies in which salaries are the primary reward, one way to ensure that these are high enough to be motivating is to allow employees to set their own salaries. At Semco, most employees (except for union workers, who negotiate collective contracts) do just that, according to Ricardo Semler:

> Once or twice a year, we order salary market surveys and pass them out. We say to people, "Figure out where you stand on this thing. You know what you do; you know what everyone else in the company makes; you know what your friends in other companies make; you know what you need; you know what's fair. Come back on Monday, and tell us what to pay you.
> . . . with half a dozen exceptions, our people have always named salaries we could live with.

Reward Everyone

In all of my travels, I have yet to hear a hotel bellhop tell me that the Employee of the Month selection motivated him or her to higher levels of productivity. Even when employees collectively make such selections, which is certainly better than having them made by management, few workers are motivated by the possibility of being the one person out of dozens, or hundreds, who will win.

Not surprisingly, given our individualistic culture, rewards in the workplace are all too frequently restricted to a handful of "winners," leaving the bulk of employees feeling like losers. Reserving rewards for a select few is probably the single greatest mistake that companies make in developing reward systems—particularly in an era that demands teamwork and the full contribution of every employee.

When a company singles out one or a few individuals for substantial awards, it generates resentment among those left out of the winnings—or even out of the running. The sales superstar may be motivated by the Hawaii vacation, but those left behind at the office are probably less enthusiastic. And when perks and bonuses are reserved for management only, the underrewarded masses get the message and adjust their efforts accordingly. A few winners selected with unclear and unfair criteria (as perceived by employees) in a context that's minimally rewarding won't work. If these conditions are reversed, such special awards can be useful adjuncts to a comprehensive package of rewards.

As many employees as possible should be included in reward systems—management and nonmanagement workers, line and staff. All-inclusive reward systems need not be prohibitively expensive. The money that would have paid for the executives' trip to Hawaii could be distributed more evenly among the workforce, with a greater overall impact on productivity.

Don't be afraid to experiment with multiple reward systems. Emphasizing team efforts, for example, does not mean that individual efforts must be ignored. Rather, it is a question of achieving an equitable integration of the two. Once all team members are rewarded, they can then vote on rewards for outstanding individual contributions if they so choose.

Rewards need not be lavish to be effective. Levi Strauss doles out "You're Great" coupons that entitle recipients to $25 in cash or gifts. The coupons have been "extremely popular" motivators, according to Sue Thompson.

Even sincere and timely thank-yous are appreciated by workers accustomed to receiving little feedback and acknowledgment outside of mandatory performance reviews. At Levi Strauss & Co., handwritten notes and other forms of recognition and nominal rewards from executives to workers thoughout the company are commonplace. Says Thompson:

We have made aggressive strides in the last several years to provide many more recognition vehicles for managers and employees to give their peers, and have concentrated extensively in this area. In Leadership Week, specifically, we have lots of little toys and gifts and stickers and art supplies and so on, so that people can draw a card or thank-you note, or do a little something in some way to acknowledge those colleagues who have helped with their learning experience. And what we are seeing is that the focus on saying thank-you and on recognizing people when they have done things that they particularly appreciate has increased dramatically. Many of our key managers have had note cards drafted up. I've got one in front of me here, for example, from Bob Haas, CEO. At the top it says, "I heard

"Keep up the good work, whatever it is, whoever you are."

Drawing by Stevenson; © 1988 The New Yorker Magazine, Inc.

something nice about you," and then it is just a blank note card in which he included a note. This is not unusual here; it is becoming the norm.

Don't Just Keep Upping the Ante

Many salespeople have told me that the most obvious consequence of reaching or exceeding their quotas is to have their targets elevated, or their territories cut, in the following year. Many times I have watched executives award plaques, money, and other forms of recognition to peak performers, only to follow their congratulatory remarks with a speech about "the reality of next year" and the higher goals that management hopes to achieve.

This game of "up the ante" is usually played with the intent of motivating workers to ever higher levels of achievement. In fact, it often does just the opposite. It is demotivating to praise employees in one breath and in the next to disqualify their achievements by admonishing them to "do better next year." This is a tacit demeaning of the honorees' accomplishments, and it always changes the tone of the meeting at which such awards are presented.

It's OK to "up the ante" if (1) there's honest input from salespeople about what they think can realistically be accomplished next year; (2) there is continuous learning so that people can work smarter, not just harder (after building up to a six- or seven-day work week, "harder" just isn't possible); and (3) there's a network of information sharing or system of coaching through which sales skills can be refined. Such collaboration will be far more effective if salespeople are not competing with one another for scarce and valued resources.

Reward for Specialized Skills

When climbing the corporate ladder was the only way to gain prestige and win salary increases, most employees aspired to management positions—including many who would have been happier and more productive developing their specialized skills in nonmanagement roles. Many reluctant engineers or scientists have been wooed into the ranks of management when in fact they would have preferred continuing to grow as engineers or scientists. (Many of their subordinates would have preferred this as well.)

But there's nothing sacrosanct about management, no rule that says a company cannot assign prestige and rewards in ways other than the traditional prize of a management job. I noted earlier that Semco employees with specialized knowledge are often paid more than their supervisors. This practice, or some variation of it, is being adopted by a growing number of organizations to enhance organizational learning rather than risk losing knowledge when specialists move on to management positions.

AT&T is experimenting with a new approach in this vein, according to Senior Vice President Harold Burlingame: "We are starting to have broader bands for people. Instead of getting a $10,000 raise and moving on, they can earn much more within a job as they grow in it and grow their business."

A way of rewarding workers in new story organizations with flattened hierarchies is to give them horizontal, rather than vertical, promotions. William Wiggenhorn notes that Motorola has changed its attitude toward lateral promotions: "We have slowly changed the attitude that promotion is necessarily up the ladder; it can also be across the organization. A lateral move is much more accepted than before."

Five years ago, after a career spent primarily in human resources, Anne Pol left a senior human resources position at Pitney Bowes to manage a Pitney Bowes plant that makes parts for mailing machines. She knew that she was a candidate for the company's highest positions, but she also knew that she needed to learn firsthand about operations to have a shot at one of its top jobs.

After managing the plant, Pol came back to the top personnel job and a position on Pitney Bowes's 11-person corporate management committee, but only on condition that she could go back to operations later. After a while she did, taking on the position of vice president for manufacturing operations in the mailing systems group. Pol concludes: "It's very obvious that lateral moves are necessary if you want to progress up the corporate ladder." A different challenge exists in the new story organization, in which there is no ladder to climb. In these organizations, lateral moves—job rotations and new opportunities within one's own area of expertise (e.g., Chuck House at Hewlett-Packard)—are the norm for "advancement."

Create a Rewarding Environment

While it is generally true that what gets rewarded gets done, there is one caveat: For any given reward system to have a significant impact on performance, it must be embedded in a culture and a working environment that is rewarding as a whole. Isolated reinforcement of specific behaviors will have far less motivational impact in a company that is unfair in its distribution of rewards, unclear about its mission, or humiliating in its work relationships and policies than in a company that is perceived as being fair, has a clearly defined and ennobling mission, and puts people first.

This is why pay-for-performance systems often falter. Contrary to popular belief, people are not automatically motivated to greater productivity, higher levels of service, or improved quality by generous pay, hefty sales commissions, and fat profit sharing bonuses. Examples abound of well-paid managers and employees who are chronically demotivated. It is not uncommon for sales-people to leave a company in which they are earning lucrative commissions. Despite their high income, it turns out, they never felt that the organization truly valued them. Employees also leave because they're weary of working for a company whose products, services, or values may be suspect. Conversely, Olympic athletes, who are among the most highly motivated people I've studied over the years, receive no pay. These athletes, along with dedi-cated community volunteers and others committed to intense personal missions, work extremely hard, most often in anonym-ity. Most Olympians have very little chance to win a medal, and the volunteers often receive no recognition at all. But they feel richly rewarded.

By encouraging employees to innovate, liberating their creative capacities, treating them as fully participating partners, paying them well, promoting a spirit of trust and teamwork among them, and accommodating their family needs as well as their business objectives, new story firms are creating the most powerful mo-tivator of all: a rich and rewarding working environment.

Chapter Eight

Embracing Employee Diversity

Harold Epps manages the Digital Equipment Corporation plant in Boston that manufactures computer keyboards. Since 1981, when Epps came to the plant, its workforce has become increasingly diverse, reflecting the growing diversity of the Boston population. So varied is the workforce that some of the plant's announcements are printed in English, Chinese, French, Spanish, Portuguese, Vietnamese, and Haitian Creole.

Epps took some time out of his hectic schedule to tell me about Digital's approach to managing diversity and about the challenges he faces in overseeing 350 people who originate from 44 countries and speak 19 languages:

I came to this plant in 1981 as the purchasing manager. I set a goal for myself that I wanted to be plant manager. I let some people know that was my ambition, and so the next logical step was materials manager. Then, about three years later, I became manager for both materials operations and production operations.

One of the expectations for anyone who wanted to be plant manager was that he or she had to be involved with the community. That comes naturally to me; I've been involved in many organizations and on boards and so forth. So when the opening for plant manager came up in January 1987, I was a candidate for the job, and got it

Over the past 10 years, the level of diversity in this plant has increased as the city of Boston has changed. One of the advantages of this diversity is that you get to draw on a larger pool of people, with many different perspectives.

I was born in North Carolina. I am going to bring some of that experience with me; I have a particular view of the world. We've got people in this plant who were born in France, Germany, Italy, Spain, Canada, Puerto Rico, you name it. They have different views and perspectives, different sets of experiences. And this gives us a larger set of potential solutions to a given issue. When you have a positive attitude and a willingness to value diversity, then as a manager you can benefit from all of those different perspectives.

It's important not to sweep differences under the rug. That's why we have awareness sessions at the plant, and we have activities that reflect upon the positive contributions of various ethnic groups. We don't cover them all, but we do celebrate a good number of days that are important to specific heritage groups. We celebrate during Chinese New Year, during Black History Month, we celebrate Jewish holidays, Irish and Catholic holidays—it doesn't matter. Ethnic groups are encouraged to be proud of, to display, and to communicate what their culture has done for society in general.

Every group of difference has the right to come together and be supported and support one another. There is a senior minority leadership forum, and underneath that umbrella there are about a half dozen different support groups—gay and lesbian, black Americans, Asians, Vietnamese, American Indian. Quite often the corporation will help at a minimal level in funding support groups.

We also have people who have been incarcerated before, known ex-felons who have done time. We give people another chance in life. We have no negative stories, only positive stories from that experience and the opportunities that have been provided.

We have something called *core groups*, where people from diverse backgrounds come together and talk about their differences, but also about how people are more alike than they are different. And it gets people in touch with what their own inner prejudices may be. They learn how to look at things objectively and not to look at a person and stereotype them based upon what their eyes see.

I remember one of the most difficult times for me was when I was in a "value diversity" workshop and we were asked to break out into groups. Black men were asked to break out, black women were asked to break out; so were white men and white women. Two things stood out for me: The white people said, "we don't see ourselves as white. We see ourselves as Irish, French, German, Canadian, whatever." And black women came back and said the black men treated them with disrespect because of their gender. The women saw us more as white men than they saw us as supporting and nourishing their needs. Now, that helped me understand that no matter how much you may view yourself in one perspective, other people may not view you the same way.

We offer a two-day course on "Working in a Diverse Workforce" to help people deal with issues of differences but also of sameness. Ultimately we all want the same things. We all want to be recognized for our work. We want to take care of our families, we want to grow and develop, and we want to be rewarded and recognized for that. We all come from a different place. We tell people, "Appreciate yourself. Also appreciate that some people are alike and some people are different from you."

One of the most difficult scenarios the company and the plant have dealt with recently has been AIDS. I would say that has been the most challenging issue, in my experience, for the company. We had an employee who was homosexual who was diagnosed as having AIDS. Now that's when it got tough. That's when the biases, when the fears, came out. The corporation's position on that is the person has an illness like any other, and as long as the medical profession diagnosed that person as capable of work, that person can work and there won't be any gloves or facial masks or any of that stuff in the workplace.

We brought in a couple of people from the medical profession to help educate us on how to deal with the fear, the paranoia, the anxiety. We provided a great deal of time for employees who, in turn, wanted to be educated.

Gender is a major issue when you talk about diversity. For generations and decades, white men in America were raised to consider themselves superior to women. And I think that notion has not been fully relinquished to this day. Men were better educated, got to deal in the family business at an early age, got to shadow Dad from age six, while the women in the family stayed home.

Men need to be able to treat women equally and women must believe they will be heard, will be listened to. People have to recognize that leadership comes in a lot of different packages.

I think there is somewhat of a stereotype of what a leader looks like, and I think we have got to get beyond that. A leader does not have to be an excellent orator. A leader does not always have to be up in front of the band as the drum major. You can lead from the background. You can lead in a quiet fashion. You can lead by example. Quite often, our historical picture of leaders is "Do as I say, not as I do." Well, I think the leader of today's and tomorrow's world is the one who is the role model. The words we use are: "You got to talk the talk, but you also have to walk the walk."

I think when you work in a diverse workplace—say you are a man—if you are going to be successful, you are forced to act differently than if you worked just around men. When you work in a diverse workforce, I think it is incumbent upon the person who is going to achieve success to change the way they work, to modify the way they communicate.

We have a team-based participatory management system to reinforce that we will embrace, reward, and recognize involvement and leadership. We have a recognition program that gives financial rewards on a quarterly basis to people who are exhibiting the characteristics that we espouse in our long-range plan and our mission statement. And we are about to go into a program called "Power Sharing" for all management and supervisors to have people learn how to take power and then to share. It's all part of a continuing program of moving the power and the responsibility to the people who do the work.

We have an employee assistance program that provides managers and all employees the right to have further conversations with a confidential consultant about things that are getting in their way, either personally or professionally.

One of the things that I have been able to experience in my 16 years with the company is how people are much more respectful of other groups. For instance, people used to come up and tell me a lot of jokes about other ethnic groups. I would turn around and tell them, "If you tell me that joke, you're probably telling someone else a joke about me when I am not here. So I would appreciate it if you wouldn't say those things because they are not funny to me." That doesn't happen so often now.

Many more people respect the issue of gender diversity now. Many more men are capable of working for a woman than they were 15 years ago. And many more people are capable of working for people of difference than they were 15 years ago.

I think that in spite of all the diversity, I still see another 30 to 50 years before there is any major percentage change in demographics at the higher levels of institutions. In the Fortune 1000, the CEO is in his late 50s, early 60s. His staff is in their mid-40s to mid-50s. And 85 percent to 95 percent of that group are white men, so 10 years out it's going to be the same group of people.

It's apparent that if you're going to work here, diversity is part of the environment and the atmosphere. We preach "teamness," working together for excellence, valuing diversity, the notion that we can continue to achieve a higher level of success.

It's a foregone conclusion that because of the diversity of Boston, that will be the representation in our workplace. There's no alternative. This is just the way we are. It's like a person who is born into a family of money— he doesn't have to go around weighing it all the time, not like the person who hit the lottery last week. It's that attitude around the issue of diversity, "That's us, that's the way it is."

Senior managers at Digital Equipment recognized earlier than many of their peers that embracing diversity is the wave of the future in the American workplace—and they were smart enough to do something about it. Through such programs as "Working in a Diverse Workforce" and through management efforts such as those of Harold Epps, the company has made a solid commitment to training all employees to understand and deal with the diversity that surrounds them. Instead of ignoring or hiding their differences, Digital employees are encouraged to acknowledge them, celebrate them—and wrestle openly with the inevitable conflicts they generate.

THE DIVERSITY IMPERATIVE

Although Digital serves as an exceptional role model for companies struggling with the issue of diversity, its diverse workforce is by no means an exception. We must all grow accustomed to difference, if for no other reason than that our labor force is becoming increasingly diverse. In 1987, the Hudson Institute published *Workforce 2000: Work and Workers for the 21st Century*, a landmark study funded by the U.S. Department of Labor. The study projected that 25 million people would join the American workforce between 1987 and 2000. Of the new entrants, only 15 percent would be white males, almost 61 percent would be women, and 29 percent would be minorities (minority women were counted twice).

Diversity studies such as those of the Hudson Institute tend to focus on differences in gender, culture, and ethnic background, but the definition of "diversity" also includes a variety of other differences—for example, the differences between young and old workers, between abled and disabled workers, and between straight and gay workers. All of these groups can contribute to the workforce. Unless we learn to understand and draw on the diverse talents of our rapidly changing labor pool, unless we actively cultivate the leadership of women and minorities, we will be hard pressed as a nation to remain competitive in the coming decades.

The seeds of a crisis are already present. A 1990 study conducted jointly by the Hudson Institute and Towers Perrin shows that corporations are facing shortages of technical, professional,

and secretarial workers and are experiencing high turnover because of "skills gaps." Some 70 percent of all the companies in the
study reported difficulties in recruiting scientists and technical
workers. Of the consumer products companies, 89 percent reported difficulties in finding workers with technical training,
while nearly as large a percentage of health care companies could
not find enough scientists.

As reasons for these difficulties, the study cites a lack of "leading edge" recruitment and training strategies and scarcity of progressive "support structures" for women and minority workers,
such as day-care centers and mentor programs. The problem will
be compounded by the fact that we are entering an era of labor
shortages.

It's not just demographic changes in the workplace but demographic changes in the marketplace that are compelling us to
learn more about one another. Minority markets in the United
States now buy more than any of the countries with which we
trade. Blacks, Asians, and Hispanics had a combined spending
power of $424 billion in 1990, and their spending power is pro-
jected to reach $650 billion by the year 2000. Older Americans
now control more than 50 percent of all discretionary income and
spend more than $800 billion annually. It stands to reason that the
workforce and its leadership must reflect the diversity of the markets they serve if they are to serve those markets well.

Business in a Multicultural World

Global competition, like domestic demographics, is exerting a significant pressure on us to learn about unfamiliar cultures. Lewis
Griggs, a San Francisco-based film maker and diversity consultant, told me that he was rudely awakened to the need for understanding different cultures when his own lack of such understanding stymied a potential business deal:

> I was involved in the start-up of a genetic engineering com-
> pany, in the course of which I had a meeting with some Japa-
> nese pharmaceutical executives and became amazed at my own
> ineptitude because of the cultural differences. In other words, I
> discovered that it didn't matter what degree I had [an M.B.A.
> from Stanford] or how skilled I was in business negotiations in
> this country or in a certain cultural style of business protocol

and etiquette effectiveness. All of it became totally irrelevant when my naiveté about cultural differences became the reason that this meeting could go nowhere, that no trust could be established. . . .

What happened to me was really a shock of recognition that if this was true for me, it obviously was true for a lot of Americans, and indeed was therefore one of the main reasons for our trade deficit and our lack of competitiveness and our lack of ability to perform at a peak level internationally.

While ignorance of our foreign neighbors is troublesome, far more dangerous, says Griggs, is ignorance of our domestic neighbors:

Only 10 percent of us do business with foreigners, but 100 percent of us do business with Americans who are different from ourselves, Americans who are of Asian descent or African-Americans or Hispanics or Arabs or whatever. . . . We all have cultural differences right here at home, the ignorance of which gets us into as much trouble as it does overseas.

Gary Weaver would agree. Weaver is a professor of intercultural communications at American University who conducts workshops on diversity. He notes that cultural differences can cause small disagreements to escalate into major confrontations, and cites an example: When a manager from the dominant U.S. culture saw two Arab-American employees arguing, he figured he had better stay out of it. But the employees *expected* a third-party intermediary, or *wasta* in Arabic, and without one the argument escalated.

The employees' expectation was based on the Koran and on Bedouin tradition, says Weaver. While Americans are likely to take an individualistic, win-lose approach to arguments and to emphasize privacy, Arab-Americans tend to value a win-win result that maintains the harmony of the group but often requires mediation. In such exchanges, their aim, Weaver believes, is not to decide "who's rational and who's irrational" but to understand both perspectives and become comfortable with them.

Albert Yu, vice president and general manager of Intel Corporation's Microproducts Group, echoes Weaver's theme:

One of the things I've been involved with in training classes we do, is to say: This is the norm from their background, so make sure you understand that, you accept that. When an Israeli is jumping up and down, it doesn't mean he's really mad; he's really trying to make sure that we discuss all the issues. Or a Japanese sits there and doesn't say anything; it doesn't mean he agrees with you. He just may be too polite to tell you you're full of crap. So by knowing these things, if somebody's quiet, you can ask him a question: "What do you think about this?" Now typically when you ask a question like that, the Japanese will speak up and say, "Well, I really don't feel comfortable with it." But if you don't provoke the question, he may not volunteer that he feels uncomfortable. . . . A lot of classes that we do are basically trying to get people to understand each other.

The Faces of Diversity

Perhaps the most frequently discussed aspect of diversity is gender differences—not surprisingly, considering that women constitute more than 50 percent of the workforce, while the male viewpoint has overwhelmingly dominated the corporate scene. Theoretical arguments about nature versus nurture aside, the observers of both genders I interviewed agreed that men and women bring different styles and perspectives to work.

For example, Nancy Kaltreider, a professor of clinical psychiatry at the University of California at San Francisco, believes there's a big difference in male and female styles in the workplace:

I think women have a way of listening, of gathering information, of encouraging consensus as a part of their style, and less of a need to be seen as powerful leaders. I have found that women will encourage discussion of emotion-laden aspects of the work more.

Women tend to humanize and to be aware of personal issues that are occurring in people's lives outside of the work situation, and women may be self-revealing in ways that tend to make the environment a little more relaxed. When women meet together on a work-focused activity, there is often an integration of meaningful personal events outside the office. For example, the first few minutes are more likely to involve discussion of the recent graduation of a child, death of a parent, etc. than the recent 49ers game. This acknowledgment seems to bring more unity to both lives. It is not uncommon for someone to bring light refreshments as a symbolic celebration of a work or personal event. Women nurture each other better.

Price Cobbs, a University of California psychiatrist and a corporate consultant on diversity issues, agrees: "Women are not as afraid to get into the personal aspects of themselves as they relate to work. I find many men just beginning to be even remotely comfortable tapping the personal parts of their lives. They just want to stay with name, rank, serial number, and let me tell you what I do and how well I've done it."

Diversity—whether in the form of gender, culture, ethnicity, or some other attribute—has broad implications for how work is viewed, organized, and approached. Harold Epps of Digital Equipment has observed that diversity forces traditional managers to address a wider range of issues than they would in a homogeneous environment:

Women and people of color force white men to expand the way they approach particular issues. For instance, I've got a 3½-year-old. My wife works. The agreement is: I will drop her off at preschool, and my wife will pick her up. Many of the people I work with are older than I, and most of their wives don't work. It's very common in staff meetings for the men to say, "We've got a problem here, and let's call this meeting at 7:30 A.M." The women in the room will say, "Nope, can't do that. We have to drop our kids off in the morning. Let's do the meeting over lunch." I see that occur quite often, and that goes back to the issue of balance.

Sometimes it's something that is as important as, if not more important than, "Can we get this meeting done another time?"—for example, forcing the system to look at absenteeism. We have been having a problem with that. We found out that it's because in this part of the country there is a shortage of day-care providers. We've gotten involved in helping solve that in order to improve productivity and attendance. It is generally people of difference and women that bring these issues to the table, like taking care of their parents. Quite often when somebody gets sick in the family, it's the women who are expected to stay home with them. They are the people who bring it to the table to discuss as a business issue, because it is getting in the way of their performance.

Without an understanding and appreciation of the needs, backgrounds, and unique contributions of diverse groups, communication is difficult and misunderstandings are inevitable—even with the best of intentions, as John Lynch, corporate manager of equal opportunity at Hewlett-Packard, points out: "As an example, one that comes to mind would be with some Asians. I say *some* because it really depends on the individual—but with some of our Asian engineers, it may be counter to their culture and their upbringing to stand out and be visible or to raise issues regarding their project or their environment, even to take a strong leadership role in an area which is fairly new to them."

A word of caution: It is tempting to reduce diversity to convenient categories in order to understand and manage it. But as John Lynch points out, it is dangerous to pigeonhole individuals. People are defined, not merely by what makes them "diverse," but by a broad range of personal characteristics.

Even the much-maligned white males are far from homogeneous, as Lewis Griggs reminds us: "Remember, white males aren't all the same either. . . . I'm an Anglo male, not white Polish, not Jewish; I'm midwestern, not eastern, not southern, not Californian. I'm privately educated. I'm a marketing type. I'm married; I'm heterosexual; I've got two kids, a Volvo wagon, and a golden retriever." The point is, we are as diverse as we are numerous; each of us can be considered a segment of one.

DIVERSITY AND THE ECOCORPORATION

The ecocorporation of the new story, no less than the Brazilian rain forest, requires diversity in order to thrive. Variety is not only the spice of life but, increasingly, the source of business success. Attempting to level our differences or to limit the expression of diverse viewpoints endangers our businesses just as surely as reducing variety endangers an ecosystem. Elisabet Sahtouris writes:

> The greater the variety, . . . the more stable the ecosystem is as a whole. . . . This variety principle holds also for the gene pool of any species. We have learned by hard experience, for example, that our practice of "perfecting" our food crops and domestic

animals by breeding out their genetic variety, while breeding in the features we like, leaves them weak and subject to devastating diseases. When we reduce variety by breeding a particular strain or even cloning a single individual, by replacing natural ecosystems with monocultures on bulldozed land, we risk creating a highly unstable and vulnerable artificial ecosystem.

"The human mania for making monocultures is apparent in our social behavior as well as in our agriculture," she continues,

because we simply have not recognized the vital importance of natural variety or diversity in any natural system. No such system or body could function if some of its species or organs had the power to make the other organs over in their own image. Imagine just a single such circumstance—imagine your heart trying to persuade or bully your liver into being just like it. Its success would clearly be a disaster for the body as a whole. Do we *really* want the Russians or the Americans or whoever is not like us to become just like us? Nature makes it abundantly clear that the secret of success is mutually consistent and cooperative variety.

"Cooperative variety" is particularly important in the new story corporation, which depends on continuous innovation for its survival. Harvard Professor John Kotter notes:

People who have studied decision-making processes have often observed that diversity and interdependence are essential ingredients in fostering original ideas. If there is only one person involved in a decision-making situation (no interdependence), or if the group of individuals involved all think pretty much the same way (no diversity), the breadth of information brought to bear on a problem is almost always narrow in scope. When a number of people are involved and when they have different perspectives, more information gets into the process often because more conflict develops. Conflict forces people to stop and think and look for ways to resolve it.

By ignoring, suppressing, or eliminating diversity, we unwittingly stem the flow of innovation, the lifeblood of the new story organization.

Despite the crucial connection between diversity and innovation, we have for the most part ignored the vital lessons in variety that nature attempts to teach, according to Sahtouris: "Diversity is crucial to nature, yet we humans seem desperately eager to eliminate it, in nature and in one another. This is one of the greatest mistakes we are making. We reduce complex ecosystems to one-crop 'economies,' and we do everything in our power to persuade or force others to adopt our languages, our customs, our social structures, instead of respecting theirs."

Equal Opportunity to Be a White Male.   As the vertical hierarchies of the old story corporation give way to the fluid structures of the new, as managers and employees come to understand their interdependence in a competitive world, rigid, destructive displays of "leadership" become obsolete.

But while the command-and-control style of the old story monoculture is falling by the wayside, its effects linger in the workplace. The approaches of today's top corporate managers—still overwhelmingly white males—cannot help being skewed in the direction of old story perceptions of "reality" and male-oriented approaches to problem solving.

Even enlightened leaders who sincerely desire to increase diversity in the senior-management ranks often fall back on standards familiar to them in determining qualifications for such positions. In the present transition phase, we are, as Lewis Griggs puts it, giving all employees "equal opportunity to be an Anglo male" and gauging their competence—and their potential for advancement—on their ability to be one. Griggs ponders the implications of this narrow view of what it means to be competent:

> If that were done to me, that would mean that when I go into the National Organization for Women, when I try to work at Johnson Publishing in Chicago, which publishes *Ebony*, I have to not only face the "glass ceiling" that comes from natural ethnocentrism on their part, but I'd be expected to try to meet the norms of the female culture or the black culture before my competence is truly respected. So I'd have to work 150 percent to 200 percent in order to be perceived as equal, and I can't do it ultimately—I can't be perceived of as a black male no matter how hard I try, nor as a female. And that is what we Anglo males expect people to do in our workplace all too often.

The pressure on all employees to conform to the norms of the white male monoculture is sometimes overt, more often subtle. An article in a mainstream business magazine, for example, asks in apparent exasperation, "What do women want?" It notes that a vast majority of women have lobbied aggressively for special treatment—and are getting it. The article cites promising statistics on child care, flexible scheduling, and unpaid parental leave.

But the implicit assumption that day care, parental leave, and flexibility constitute "special treatment" applies only in a culture that views child care as solely the province of women and relegates all activities requiring "flexibility" to them as well. Such views bolster the position of white males and justify continuing to lock women out of leadership roles—implications that the article conveniently ignores. (Its author, a woman, apparently missed the irony of her argument—or feared for her job.)

Labeling as "special treatment" anything that addresses the needs of those outside the dominant group is one tried-and-true way to maintain the status quo. Another is stereotyping. Walter Lippmann introduced the term *stereotype* over 50 years ago to describe the rigid and standardized way in which people see the members of groups that are different from their own. Everyone is familiar with stereotypes, and most of us have probably been victimized by stereotyping at some time or other. Stereotyping helps explain why minorities and women are often guided toward staff jobs rather than technical and line positions, which are often reserved for those on the "fast track."

Stereotypes are insidious. They defy reality checks, since "reality" can easily be interpreted to fit them. Thus, a little girl who proves to be a strong pitcher on a softball team is said to "throw like a boy," and if she becomes a shrewd businesswoman, it is because she "thinks like a man." The white male manager who pounds his fist on the table during a meeting is regarded as "tough"; the black male manager who does the same is "confrontational."

Women and minorities are also kept from power by subconscious expectations of failure. The folks at Pizza Hut call this "deskilling," which they define as a "subtle but pernicious psychological process through which members of underdog groups lose confidence in themselves and their ability, in response to on-going negative or neutral feedback."

When, and if, the "underdogs" stumble the number and importance of their mistakes are exaggerated. They are presumed incompetent until proven otherwise—a burden that often proves to be a self-fulfilling prophecy.

In some cases, women and minorities are thrust into crazymaking situations so that they lose no matter how they perform. Any behavior on their part is deemed inappropriate; they're damned if they do and damned if they don't. If black men assert themselves, they are chastised for being militant; if they do not, they are derided as lazy. Women are told that they are too compliant or too aggressive to be effective managers.

Of course, the attitudes and beliefs that elevate one group at the expense of others weren't invented by the corporation, which, after all, is a microcosm of the larger society. Long before people enter the workforce, the culture conditions them to accept certain roles and reject other roles.

For example, women have traditionally been programmed to act in a service capacity. Professor Nancy Kaltreider speaks from personal experience:

> I've found that there are role assumptions which are really on both sides, and you just sort of subtly pick it up. If there is a committee meeting in which there are coffee and doughnuts served, I'm very likely to find myself picking up afterwards. No one asked me to do that, but the men all left the room with our stuff all over the table. And there's part of me that remains very uncomfortable about the idea that anyone should have to pick up after me, so I will find myself moving into that role. As there are now more women in the committee meetings, I find we often end up just sort of spontaneously going around clearing up all the trash before we leave afterwards. So there is something about the idea of serving and being served that even with very powerful women still seems to be built into the system.

Coping Styles of the "Underdogs."   Women and minorities respond in a variety of ways to the demands and restrictions imposed by the white male monoculture and reinforced by societal norms. A few forge ahead and succeed on their own terms, usually through a combination of dogged determination, fierce self-confidence, and enormous talent. More often, they choose from a number of coping strategies designed for survival in, or escape from, a hostile environment.

One of these strategies is to hide, to assume a low profile, to be nonassertive and nonthreatening, to opt for a "safe," if unchallenging, position. Another is to drop out, to leave corporate life altogether. A growing number of women and minorities are doing just that, leaving sometimes lucrative positions and forming their own companies in order to find the challenges—and earn the rewards—that their talents justify. A third strategy, and perhaps the most common, is to assimilate.

The theory behind assimilation is captured in an age-old saw: "If you can't beat 'em, join 'em." If you cannot be yourself and succeed in the workplace, goes the thinking, you must invent a new, artificial self.

By assimilating, those who are outside the dominant culture hope to win the favor of its leaders—and thereby to share in their power. And so a minority vice president endures an ethnic joke to prove himself a "good sport" or a female executive adopts a macho style to show that she is "one of the boys."

In attempting to secure one of the few top slots that the white male majority allots to them, women and minorities often find themselves in de facto competition with other members of their own gender, race, or culture. Thus they land in the curious position of supporting the very group that strives to keep them down while deserting the group with which they most strongly identify.

This is just one lamentable aspect of assimilation, which at best is a shaky strategy for "success." Psychiatrist Michelle Clark identifies the reason: "The mistake that a lot of people in this situation make is taking the position of assimilation: 'It's not a problem; look at me, I'm making it.' But in reality, you're making it only until someone else who *really* is in control says, 'OK, it's time for you to stop making it' or 'You can only make it this far.' And this is the proverbial glass ceiling that everybody's talking about." In other words, assimilation affords the illusion, but not the reality, of power and control.

But there's a more fundamental drawback of assimilation: It robs people of their basic identity as human beings. Even those who "win" by assimilating ultimately lose, for after all it is only the artificial self who got the promotion, only the manufactured person who secured the vice presidency. As Judy Grahn, a cultural historian who focuses on gay and lesbian issues, puts it: "I think anytime we try to live as if there's one unified way of being, and everyone must fit into that, then none of us has home base."

Without a home base, without a solid sense of ourselves, we cannot draw on the unique talents that would make us truly valuable to the corporation. Michelle Hunt, vice president of People at Herman Miller, reflects on the dilemma: "I think women for a long time, particularly in management, were told to play the game the way the man plays it, and that's the way to get ahead. The problem with that is then you are not adding value. If I'm attempting to think like a man, then what am I bringing to the party?"

It's not just corporate productivity but human fulfillment that is at stake. Assimilation systematically erodes self-esteem as surely as water wears down granite. The tragic consequence of assimilation is that it destroys a piece of our selves.

The damage can be obvious and severe, but more often it is subtle and may go unnoticed or provoke only a dim sense of loss. Price Cobbs relates an example:

> I was talking not terribly long ago with a black engineer who was in a car pool, and the other members of the car pool were white. He said that on the days that he drove, he had to be conscious that he would get to his car and turn it from the soul station to a classical music station. And you say, "Well, gee, he's copping out." Well, maybe he is, maybe he isn't. But in the world that he lived in he felt, "Well, that may be a little bit too heavy for them; they may stereotype me if I'm listening to soul music." It may have been his baggage, but I venture to say that there was some reality. . . . Every time he would mention it and every time I would think of it, I would think, "Gee, what's he losing by not being able just to be himself?"—whether he was a white guy from Appalachia and was playing country music or whether he had a different ethnic background and that was the station he listened to. What was it that he might be losing because he would get up and make certain that he turned to another station?

Everyone, including members of the dominant culture, ultimately loses when diversity is not acknowledged and embraced.

Michelle Clark explains why: "We all suffer by not embracing diversity. When people don't feel appreciated, the suffering can be anything from personal stress to lack of productivity. It can also be the loss of useful input into whatever the business entity is. People will hold back if they feel they are not appreciated. So you're losing time, you're losing energy, you're losing creativity, and in the worst scenario, when the situation becomes abusive, then you're actually paying a cost to an injured employee." The bottom line is this: If you discount me and my background, why should I care about your business?

Leadership in the Ecocorporation

Global competition, changing demographics, and marketplace dynamics all support a shift to a more comprehensive style of leadership, in which the contributions of women and minorities enhance and enrich the contributions of the traditional white male majority.

As I pointed out in Chapter 1, it is too early to discern the shape and impact of this new story leadership. Of one thing we can be sure: The diverse leadership of the new story world will have an orientation far different from that of the old story world.

For one thing, the presence of more women in the ranks of upper management will probably bring a more cooperative style to leadership in the new story organization. In the view of Jean Settlemyre, former executive of AMI, a major hospital corporation, "Women tend to favor cooperation over conflict and, indeed, behave, sometimes even unconsciously, in ways that minimize conflict and discord. That sometimes can be negative because it allows things to remain covert that need to be made overt, but if they are encouraged to identify what are sources of conflict, they are much more willing, I think, to speak up about it than to tolerate the discomfort."

What Charles Hampden-Turner calls the "people-oriented" style of women, including their cooperative tendencies, has important implications for a new story world in which teams must work closely together: "In the information society, as the manager's role shifts to that of the teacher, mentor, and nurturer of human potential, there is even more reason for corporations to take advantage of women's managerial abilities, because these people-oriented traits are the ones women are socialized to possess."

Nancy Kaltreider points out that, contrary to the popular stereotype, women have always been team players. She told me:

> I think the idea of affiliation and working toward a common goal is basically what teamwork is all about, and that it doesn't matter whether or not you played a team sport. You've played a team sport if you were around a family. I've often said that I grew up reading the *Ladies' Home Journal* and the colleague with whom I was competitive grew up reading *The Wall Street Journal*, but I believe we both came to the same understanding of what it takes to run a business and that "teamness" is an attitude. It is not whether or not you have played football or baseball; it is whether or not your intention is to bring people together toward a collective outcome.

Cultural and ethnic minorities will also bring a new perspective to leadership in the 1990s and beyond. For example, Albert Yu of Intel describes the benefits of the Israeli style of relating in the workplace: "We have a major design center and manufacturing site in Israel. We have a lot of people here from Israel working in this country. And they contribute something quite dramatic. They tend to challenge a lot, tend to want to push for difference of opinion. They're even more vocal, and they consider a problem doesn't get really 'bottomed out' until you argue a lot and make sure all the angles are discussed. Then you're ready for a conclusion."

As the population continues to age, corporations will increasingly tap the growing pool of older workers, and this will broaden the scope of new story leadership as well. Joe Lee, president of the General Mills Restaurants, which actively recruits older workers, is enthusiastic about their leadership contributions: "We have tended to include older workers in all positions including management . . . for years. Right now, at the store level, you'll find a lot of older people who are supplementing retirement incomes or just deciding that they got bored with retirement and they want to do some part-time work. This has been really good for us because it's sort of like having grandfather and grandmother in the restaurant for the teenagers. It adds a stability in the store that influences the younger people."

Eleanor Hill, director of training for the division, agrees: "[Older workers] bring a maturity to the workplace that is so helpful to the younger workers who come in here; they are wonderful role models for younger workers. They really are a tremendous resource."

The point is not that the new story leadership of women and minorities will replace white male management. It is a question, not of replacement, but of enhancement. Diversity in the upper echelon of the corporation will add a new dimension to management, broaden its horizons, and liberate the old story monoculture from the contraints of a rigid command-and-control style.

THE NEW STORY: EMBRACING DIVERSITY

While valuing diversity is a noble idea in theory, it is a tall order in practice. Even those who are wholeheartedly committed to the concept quickly discover how difficult it is to translate that commitment into action. King-Ming Young, manager of the Professional Development Group of Corporate Education for Hewlett-Packard's Managing Diversity program, puts the challenge in perspective: "Even though in principle diversity is good and, of course, we should have unity through diversity, how many languages should you be tolerating in the workplace? It gets pretty tricky."

She adds:

We don't purport to say that having people from different backgrounds only provides benefits; we acknowledge that diversity creates some potential problems, like communication, like greater potential for misunderstanding, like the fact that initially it may take more time to manage people and to establish consensus. But all these problems can be potential benefits as well, and so managing diversity really means being able to maximize these potential benefits and minimize some of the potential problems.

There are as many approaches to managing diversity as there are companies attempting to do so. Through its Managing Diversity program, Hewlett-Packard strives to help employees understand how their behavior is shaped by their sociocultural conditioning. John Young, CEO of Hewlett-Packard, explains: "We challenge managers to think about the issues involved if they're managing employees who come from a culture in which a proverb states 'The nail that sticks out will be hammered down.' Compare that to the managers' own culture that says, 'The squeaky wheel gets the grease.'" The point, says Young, "is to get them to acknowledge that their culture isn't the center of the universe. This helps with managing diversity, and it helps with global thinking."

Xerox developed what it calls a Balanced Workforce Strategy for ensuring female and minority representation at all corporate levels. The strategy involves assigning strict short-term and long-term numerical goals for diversity and making managers accountable for achieving them. The plan is championed by the top ranks and has succeeded in steadily increasing the number of women and minority leaders at Xerox.

Motorola has tackled diversity on four fronts. It instituted diversity training, set up a "work and family" task force to cope with such issues as child care and elder care, formed another task force to examine the feasibility of job sharing and flexible scheduling, and established a committee to figure out ways in which Motorola could work with schools to help educate future workers.

Avon realized in the mid-1980s that it wasn't making the most of its markets or its employees. Now the president of each Avon division maintains a five-year strategic plan that links diversity to the company's business goals. Avon developed a training program to educate managers about their biases and to teach them how to manage a diverse workforce. And Hicks B. Waldron, Avon chief executive, chairs a committee that relays the concerns and ideas of women and minorities to top management. Furthermore, fast-track Avon middle managers are sent for business training to the School of Management at Morehouse College, a predominantly black insititution in Atlanta, rather than to Harvard or Stanford.

The result of all these efforts is above-average levels of women and minorities in upper-management positions—not to mention bouquets from *Black Enterprise* magazine, which dubbed Avon one of the best places for blacks to work in America.

The more than 8 million Americans with disabilities who want to work but do not, according to a 1985 Harris survey, are a vast and largely untapped labor pool. Pizza Hut is one company that is aggressively recruiting and successfully retaining disabled workers. Through its Jobs Plus program, it is providing physically and developmentally disabled individuals with jobs at its restaurants and on its delivery units.

Jobs Plus coordinates services with state departments of rehabilitation. It provides a mentor program that offers job training for selected employees and their job coaches, placement assistance and ongoing support, job assignments tailored to each employee's abilities, a nationwide evaluation system, and a strong commitment by Pizza Hut to the success of the individual employee and the overall program.

To make the Jobs Plus program work, Pizza Hut managers were trained in procedures for dealing with employees who had special needs. The training focuses on changing attitudes toward disabled job applicants and on developing strategies to place disabled workers in jobs that match their skills and de-emphasize their disabilities. Managers were also called on to figure out ways to modify or redesign tasks to fit the skills of disabled employees.

Among the challenges posed by the program was convincing skeptical social service agencies that Pizza Hut would treat disabled employees in the same way as it treated other employees with regard to hours, compensation, wages, performance reviews, and expectations and that it would integrate disabled employees into the work teams at each of its restaurants. One testimony to the success of the company's efforts is the high retention rate of its disabled employees, which stood at 72 percent in 1990.

Marriott Corporation is also busy developing this largely untapped employee gold mine. Although the hotel company experiences a 10 percent annual turnover rate among workers in general, turnover among employees with disabilities is only 8 percent.

To help the mentally disabled adjust to working life, Marriott developed a program that teaches basic social and job-readiness skills. The company also pairs disabled employees with Marriott managers who serve as coaches. "Companies have a great need to include all the talented people they can find," says Kathleen Alexander, Marriott's vice president of personnel services. "So we want to use personnel policies not to discriminate but to attract and retain."

The First Step: Breaking the Taboo on Talk

The first step for any company that sincerely desires to value diversity is to make it safe for employees to talk about differences. Whereas it was taboo to talk about differences in the era of affirmative action, workers are now being challenged to bring their biases and fears out into the open. The idea is that to value diversity, you must first acknowledge differences and come face-to-face with the anxieties they create.

This will take some getting used to, after more than two decades of denying differences and confusing "sameness" with equality. The difference between the two approaches is aptly conveyed in Lewis Griggs' "Valuing Diversity" materials:

> Valuing diversity is a state that reflects a point of view, an attitude, a purpose, and actions that are essentially different from EEO or affirmative action. Valuing diversity looks at the multicultural workforce from a positive perspective rather than a defensive position. Where EEO has had to battle against racism and prejudice, valuing diversity moves towards reaping the benefits that differences bring. In defending against prejudice, EEO work has had to deny differences because being different traditionally has been seen as a mark of inferiority. Equal rights necessarily came to mean we are all the same. Valuing diversity views people as having equal rights while being different. Valuing diversity encourages the open discussion of, sensitivity to, and understanding of, differences, be they differences of gender, race, ethnicity, class, age, physical ability, sexual orientation, or other life experience.

Diversity training programs encourage discussions that would make the 70s-era affirmative action officer cringe. For example, King-Ming Young of Hewlett-Packard told me:

> We ask people, "What are the accents that are most difficult and most annoying for you?" And then we talk about being aware of what impact this accent has on you. It's the first test because then you have to really stop yourself if you think, if you unconsciously say, "Gosh, this person is so pushy," or "This person is lacking in intelligence," or "This person does not give me all the details that I need"—and therefore make the assumption that this person is holding something back. Then you have to really

reexamine what kinds of conclusions you are drawing from the interaction. So we go through that kind of training, and people have told me they find it very helpful.

While corporations are encouraging employees to speak up, the point of "valuing diversity" strategies is not to discover differences for their own sake. Lewis Griggs elaborates: "What we are looking at here is a process whereby we reveal differences or uncover them and try to identify the *differences that make a difference,* that is, those unique aspects, characteristics, talents, gifts that can be brought to life and contributed to the common good."

In fact, assuming differences that *aren't* relevant is just as pointless as assuming that we're all alike. Price Cobbs gives an example: "I can think of talking with a guy who was doing career development with black managers. He was telling me about his career work with black managers. So then I said, 'Give me some of the issues that black managers have that differ from those of white managers.' He said, 'Well, I'm not so certain they have issues that differ.' I said, 'Then why are you conducting career development specifically with black managers?'"

The Mosaic versus the Melting Pot

The move toward the open expression of diversity in the workplace is paralleled by a social movement toward the retention of ethnic roots. This movement is what Philip Harris and Robert Moran refer to as the "new ethnicity," a renewed awareness and pride of cultural heritage and accomplishments, which, they write, "has been especially evident among the native Indians and black Americans in the United States during the last half of this century."

They continue: "As society becomes more pluralistic, and cultures become more 'open,' people become more aware of both dissimilarities and similarities between themselves and others. They also demand the freedom to be themselves, regardless of cultural context. Minorities of all types seek acceptance and tolerance, rather than discrimination and prejudice. Becoming more culturally sensitive fosters a living environment in which internal dignity, as well as equality of treatment, can coexist."

As diverse groups begin to celebrate their heritage, the traditional notion of America as a melting pot is gradually giving way to a more accurate image of the country as a cultural mosaic. "[I don't want to be] forced to become part of some mush that is 'everybody's culture,'" says James Zogby of the Arab-American Institute. "Instead, we should be able to look at the American mosaic and recognize the chip we place. And recognize the marvelous contribution that everyone's made to it."

This more accurate image has won acceptance both in society at large and in the corporation, a microcosm of that society. Dr. R. Roosevelt Thomas, Jr., executive director of the American Institute for Managing Diversity at Morehouse College in Atlanta, flatly states: "Gone are the days of 'abandoning ethnic differences at the company door.' The workplace is no longer the melting pot, since most people aren't willing to be melted down, not even for eight hours a day."

But the fact that ethnic groups are discovering their roots and celebrating their unique heritage does not mean that we are losing a sense of common culture. In fact, as changing demographics produce a more and more varied workforce, our diversity paradoxically becomes our common bond. As Harris and Moran point out: "A sense of one's separateness, one's uniqueness, one's ethnic or racial background, need not hamper an individual from becoming a multicultural cosmopolitan. Rather, it may enhance the contribution of a new infusion of diversity toward a *common culture.*"

Step Two: Awareness Training

In preparation for a seminar on diversity, Bob Abramms, a consultant with ODT, Inc. in Amherst, Massachusetts, mailed orientation packages to about 200 executives of a large oil company. The packages included a reprint of "Black Managers: The Dream Deferred," a *Harvard Business Review* article describing the black corporate experience. Without reading the article, dozens of the company's white middle managers sent it to the one black manager in the group, thinking, with some goodwill, Abramms notes, "Oh, this will interest Tom." At the seminar, Abramms scolded them: "You're the ones that need to read it," he said. "Tom *knows* what it's like." The chastened executives laughed sheepishly, according to Abramms. "You begin to see the absurdity of it, and to realize that the best we'll ever be is recovering sexists and recovering racists."

Such displays of myopia help explain why senior executives can tell me with straight faces that there is no discrimination in their companies, while the minority vice presidents of these companies consult me on the sly about how to deal with the prejudice that officially doesn't exist. However, I won't be the first to cast stones. I'm also awakening to my own biases, and my own "recovery" is an ongoing struggle.

Awareness is the key to recovery. That is why firms that deal successfully with diversity invariably utilize exercises designed to help people bring their biases into conscious awareness—the first step on the road to eliminating them.

Michelle Clark zeroes in on one reason why we cling tenaciously to our biases: "What limits the information about the other people? It's the historical, traditional stereotypes and myths and fantasies, by and large antiquated and useless, that are associated with these groups. But we hold onto them because we don't have enough experiences not to."

Lacking meaningful contact with diverse groups, we interpret their members' words and actions on the basis of our stereotypical notions. Often we do not even realize that our interpretations are biased, that we are in fact employing stereotypes. The only way to ascertain whether or not our perceptions are indeed "facts" is to put them under the microscope—to identify, dissect, and analyze them.

Before we can alter our biases, we must identify and acknowledge them. We must recognize that we value eye contact, or linear thinking, or an aggressive or low-key style, and *why* we do so. We must note our responses to body language and conversational style, our reactions to people of different color or gender or physical capabilities. We must consider when and where we learned these responses, and whether or not they are appropriate or useful. The point is not to judge or condemn our reactions and perceptions but to understand them, to bring them into the light so that they can be examined and, if necessary, modified.

Biases are by no means limited to skewed male perceptions of women or minority groups. "When you have a group of people who are different sitting around a conference table, prejudice kicks in," warns diversity consultant Lennie Copeland. "People also have difficulty working with different styles. They're not just cross-cultural or across racial lines, but even creative people versus more technical people."

One effective way to bring unconscious biases into awareness is through training exercises. Corporations and diversity consultants have developed a wide variety of innovative exercises for getting people to see things in a different light. The purpose of these exercises is much like that of the Psychology 101 professor when she shows the class a drawing that is seen as either an old crone or a beautiful young woman, depending on the viewer's perception.

To identify unconscious assumptions and make biases apparent, a trainer might ask the members of a class to complete a sentence such as "A woman manager is . . ." or "Blacks are . . ." Then the members conduct a brainstorming session, identifying all the attributes and behaviors that they automatically associate with a given group.

Lennie Copeland uses an exercise dubbed "Mentoring Mark or Mentoring Mary" to help employees uncover subtle expectations based on gender differences. In this exercise, participants are divided into two groups. One group is given the following information: The company has hired Mary, a 21-year-old college graduate who possesses a designated set of attributes. The group's members are asked to describe how they would mentor her. The other group is given the same information, but the name of the new hire is changed to Mark. The group's members are asked to describe how they would mentor him. (Variations on this exercise might focus on *minority* or *disabled* persons.)

Afterward, the two groups compare notes. "Much to everybody's surprise," says Lennie Copeland, "the mentoring the white male gets is different from the mentoring the Hispanic, the woman, or the disabled person gets. The assumption is that he's going to go further. He's told to go to Harvard Business School and then come back. She may go into a staff position rather than line management. He will be targeted into areas in which his talent will be obvious. In a really bad case, she ends up in the secretarial pool."

Copeland points out that people don't realize what they're doing in the mentoring exercises until they're done. That's when they see that they've positioned Mark to move ahead and cautioned Mary not to make waves.

At US West, the Denver-based telecommunications company, trainers place such labels as "CEO," "Joker," or "Passive" on the foreheads of participants. Although the participants don't know what labels they're wearing, they nevertheless respond to other participants in a manner appropriate to those labels. Says Lucila Altamirano, manager of leadership development, "You begin to see that once you label persons a certain way, they begin to act that way. It's amazing how quickly people in those exercises can figure out how they're being perceived."

While classroom training is effective, there is perhaps no better way for the majority group to learn to value diversity than to put themselves in the shoes of a minority group. Senior executives of Honeywell did just that, spending a week at Johnson Publishing in Chicago (the publisher of *Ebony* magazine). The executives came back, in the words of Lewis Griggs, "absolutely floored." He told me: "This is my culture; I grew up in Minneapolis–St. Paul [where Honeywell is headquartered]. These are midwestern white males—honest, open, ethical in a midwestern way, competent, hardworking, religious, believing that we're all the same, progressive in a way. And they came back from there saying, 'My God, if that's what it feels like for anyone to work in Honeywell who isn't like us, we're changing this place tomorrow.'"

Diversity and Individuality

Price Cobbs cautions: "Many times we talk about 'minority' as if all minorities are the same. That's just not so. In California, the African-American minority, the Hispanic minority, the Asian minority can be very complex, can be very different. Even how they view themselves as a minority, if in fact they do, can be very, very different."

Critics contend that there's danger in attempts to reduce diverse groups to neat, easy categories, that talking about "what women are like" or "what to expect from Hispanic workers" only deepens stereotypes.

This danger is illustrated by a training film in valuing diversity, which in one scene showed a Native American woman being congratulated in front of her peers for her work in an electronics plant and in the next scene, after her boss learned that Native Americans do not want to be singled out for praise, showed her being offered a congratulatory letter, a copy of which would be put in her personnel file.

This conclusion got an angry reaction from a Native American viewer. "She said, 'I don't know what tribe that woman is from, maybe Navajo, but I'm Cherokee and I want public praise as much as the next person,'" according to Bob Abramms, who told the story.

The critics have a valid point; done improperly, diversity training can promote the stereotypical thinking it is meant to eliminate. But ignoring differences is equally problematic. King-Ming Young of Hewlett-Packard warns: "People are basically individuals, and so, with this kind of individual orientation, there is a greater tendency for people to just sort of look at someone as an individual and not necessarily as a product of the race or culture or gender. And again, that's a double-edged sword. Because people deny the impact of cultural, gender, and racial background, the tendency is for someone to assume that the other person is more like me, which is sometimes as dangerous as stereotyping someone. Human beings are very similar, but the problems arise because of diversity, not similarities."

The key is to strike a balance between embracing the uniqueness of individuals and understanding the diverse backgrounds that employees bring to the organization. Price Cobbs puts the issue in perspective: "I remember my daughter talking with me once about something called a 'ghetto mentality,' and out of my sense of liberalism and humanitarianism I said, 'Don't you talk like that.' Subsequently, events have proven that she probably was very accurate. She was talking about a certain kind of class orientation, race orientation, living in public housing, being around few role models who were working. . . . There clearly are individual differences within a culture, but I could not even begin remotely to understand those individual differences until I at least understood those groups of kids she was talking about, the commonality in their upbringing. . . . There are common psychological ways of viewing the world and mastering that world. If we don't understand a culture, I think we can't remotely be able to understand the people who are part of that culture."

The point is, ignoring the cultural differences that help shape people's individuality is as dangerous as denying their individuality. It's not a question of either-or, but of both-and. The more we focus on cultural factors, which is positive, the more we must also be aware of individual differences.

Retaining and Promoting Diversity

Obviously, it will require much more than consciousness raising to integrate women and minorities into the organization in meaningful numbers. Awareness training is just one part of a strategy that must focus on training and promoting diverse groups of employees in addition to acknowledging differences. This raises a number of questions, according to Lewis Griggs:

> Is my method of training an Anglo male style, and do these diverse groups of people maybe need a different style of training in order to learn most quickly now? I probably should be able to train in different ways so as not to waste my training dollars.
>
> And once they're trained, are they then promoted? Do we know how to promote them, do we know how to notice if they're doing well, or are we only looking for assertiveness or brashness or verbal skill?
>
> And then are they going to stay? Retention is one of the biggest problems with people who are different from the norm, because they get so uncomfortable, as I might in Johnson Publishing or NOW, not to mention in Brazil or Tokyo.
>
> So they leave, and there we are back at the beginning again. So the actual dollars we are already spending because of our failure to retain in our rerecruiting and our retraining, and the actual dollars we are already spending on EEO complaints, suits, discrimination and harassment cases, should be enough of a financial drain to convince us that "valuing diversity" training would pay for itself quickly.

While many firms have taken aggressive strides in recruiting women and minorities, many of them have not followed through with the actions and organizational changes required to ensure that such employees stay. According to the joint study of the Hudson Institute and Towers Perrin, while 42 percent of companies engage in minority recruiting, only 12 percent train minorities for supervisory positions. Furthermore, only 11 percent have minority support groups and only 10 percent have mentor programs. And while 81 percent of the surveyed firms have formal policies banning sexual harassment, management training for women exists at only 32 percent of them and just 8 percent have created support and mentor groups for women.

Coaching.   One way to increase the retention rate of diverse groups is to provide them with plenty of opportunities to demonstrate competence. High-visibility presentations and assignments are ideal vehicles for this purpose, especially when they are provided in the context of ongoing coaching, in an environment that sincerely values diversity.

Coaching is an effective way of preparing women and minorities to enter the ranks of upper management. Peters and Austin describe how it works: "Coaching is the process of enabling others to act, of building on their strengths. . . . To coach is to facilitate, which literally means 'to make easy'—not less demanding, or less interesting or less intense, but less discouraging, less bound up with excessive controls. . . . Coaching is face-to-face leadership that pulls together people. . . . encourages them to step up to responsibility and continued achievement, and treats them as full-scale partners and contributors." Coaching is far different from mentoring, an old story strategy that in fact *devalued* diversity, as Marilyn Loden and Judy Rosener point out in *Workforce America*:

> Historically, within homogeneous institutions, mentoring has been the dominant group's method of informal succession planning. As such, those in power routinely selected others of similar core identity, shared insider information with them about unstated rules and norms, provided one-on-one counseling, and, generally, helped select individuals to move ahead. Like some traditional father/son relationships, mentoring helped to preserve the established order by concentrating organizational power in the hands of the dominant group. While this process of "natural selection" went on in virtually every institution in America, it was seldom discussed or challenged.

Coaching, by contrast, is overt, not covert. It is *inclusive*, not exclusive, not meant to propel some employees forward at the expense of others. Unlike mentoring, coaching does not presume that unwritten rules and insider information must be passed along to a chosen few. Coaching implies an *open* system in which everyone has the opportunity to advance.

Joe Lee of General Mills sees coaching as a two-way exchange that helps create an environment of productivity:

> I try to operate in a way that some people call "coaching." But I try to make sure that I listen to my colleagues' points of view very well. I make sure they hear my point of view, especially if it differs from theirs. Not necessarily hear as an order, but hear and understand that I do have a point of view that is either similar or different than theirs and have a degree of openness to considering theirs. I think of myself as an environmental engineer. There should be an environment where people can walk into my office and feel comfortable saying "I don't understand" or "There's something here that I am bothered about—can you help me with it?" rather than being fearful about coming into my office with a problem.

(For more insights on coaching from three of the best, see Chapter 10 Learning Tales, Bill Walsh, Pat Riley, and Tony La Russa.)

Rewriting the Rules of the Game

Coaching, however well intended and executed, will not succeed in a climate that encourages double standards and unwritten rules. It isn't enough to guide diverse groups of employees through a system unless the system itself welcomes them. That is why any organization with a sincere desire to value and retain employees of diverse backgrounds must eliminate the written and unwritten rules that have been developed solely to ensure that the dominant group remains dominant. If such rules are not eliminated, no amount of training or coaching will result in a high retention of women and minorities, who will continue to be frustrated by a system clearly designed with others in mind.

In addition to eliminating rules that exclude women and minorities, organizations must develop new rules that include them as fully participating partners. For example, the proverbial glass ceiling will never be broken until child care is addressed as a serious issue—and one that is the responsibility of men as well as women.

The joint study of the Hudson Institute and Towers Perrin revealed that just 15 percent of corporations have on-site or near-site day-care programs and that less than one third offer extended maternity leave. But there are signs of hope. IBM, a reliable barometer of future trends, recently committed $25 million to child care and elder care programs. Johnson & Johnson is building its first on-site day-care center. Retailer Dayton-Hudson is spending $8 million to help train home care providers so that its employees can hire qualified, responsible baby-sitters. And a key clause of the union contracts renegotiated by AT&T in 1989 was a comprehensive family care package that included a $5 million allocation to explore ways of providing community-based child care.

The Importance of Senior Management Commitment

In the late 1980s, there was an explosion of interest in "valuing diversity" programs. While this was a positive sign, it is naive to expect far-reaching effects from such programs in companies that remain essentially monocultures. Diversity programs, however worthwhile, will have little impact if the corporate culture does not welcome diversity. And the development of a corporate culture that welcomes diversity must be led from the top.

When Ortho Pharmaceuticals began changing its corporate culture in 1986, the effort was spearheaded by senior executives. Ortho's president and board of directors (all white males) were dissatisfied with the high turnover rates and the low representation of women and minorities in upper management. All 11 of them marched off to an outside consultant's training sessions on managing diversity. Then the newly trained executives sent all of Ortho's senior managers, middle managers, and supervisors through the training, in order to spread the word throughout the organization that Ortho valued diversity.

At McDonald's, senior executives are the first to attend the company's career development programs for management level employees. "We believe that unless the bosses understand what it is, how it works to the company's and individuals' advantage, there's not a lot of sense in taking time with the individuals just coming into the company," says Monica Boyles, former director of the McDonald's Changing Workforce program.

In Ortho, McDonald's, and other companies that are successfully integrating diverse groups of workers, top managers are firmly committed to the process. Xerox's Balanced Workforce Strategy is championed by top management. Honeywell sent senior executives to a minority firm in order to learn firsthand what it feels like to be an outsider—then set about creating a culture more inviting to minorities. Avon's chief executive heads a committee that relays the concerns of women and minorities directly to senior management.

Those who have access to senior managers can help secure their commitment to promoting diversity. A key to Digital's successful diversity strategy is that in the early 1980s newly hired Barbara Walker focused on training high potential employees in the benefits of diversity. She started with a core group of district managers, helping them to explore what differences meant to them and to understand the value of diversity. Today they are vice presidents and senior managers, with the commitment—and the clout—to help ensure that valuing diversity remains a top priority at Digital. (See "Valuing Diversity: A Five Step Approach" in Chapter 10 Learning Tales.)

Accountability

Fortune magazine examined the 1990 proxy statements of the 799 public companies on its combined lists of the 1,000 largest U.S. industrial and service companies. Of the 4,012 people listed as the highest paid officers and directors of their companies, *Fortune* spotted 19 women—less than one half of 1 percent.

Ted Payne at Xerox comments: "Workforce diversity is the latest fad. I hear everyone talking about it. I'm very suspicious of people who race around, most of them white and male, talking about managing and valuing diversity," he says. "Still, they're very much in charge, sitting at the top and telling the middle what to do to the bottom."

He adds: "You can have as many conferences as you want, but is anything of any real significance happening so far as viable jobs being filled by minorities and women? In my view you have to take someone and hold them accountable."

Companies that hope to integrate diverse groups of employees into the upper ranks of management must make managers accountable for hiring, training, and promoting diverse groups. Pizza Hut is one company that does. When Pizza Hut evaluates a manager, it considers his or her skill at managing diversity along with other attributes, such as decision-making, interpersonal, and communication skills. Pizza Hut managers have specific diversity-related responsibilities, such as developing plans to improve mix levels, recognizing and valuing different individual styles, staffing to build diversity, and managing gender and minority issues on an individual basis. And when Pizza Hut field divisions conduct their human resource planning, they must formulate specific goals for developing and promoting high potential employees from diverse groups.

Xerox sets firm goals for increasing the levels of women and minorities in upper-management positions. When the company developed its Balanced Workforce Strategy, it laid out a systematic plan for developing a pool of high potential female and minority talent. The strategy called, first, for identifying and reviewing the careers of top-level executives and then for identifying the key jobs ("pivotal jobs") that had prepared those executives to assume their positions. Xerox made sure that minorities and women were included in the pool for those jobs, so that they would be considered along with everyone else when top slots opened up. The strategy, launched in the early 1970s, has succeeded in steadily increasing the numbers of females and minorities in the ranks of top management.

Even without diversity training, holding managers accountable for increasing diversity levels can change hearts and minds. For example, Vice President Mark Suwyn of Du Pont is a mainstream corporate manager who reconsidered his thinking as a result of the strong corporate mandate to hire and promote minorities: "I came to realize how I have been making decisions based on subconscious stereotypes. . . . I tended to favor human behavior like mine: aggressive, a little bit of the football player. When I said to myself: 'Who do I need for a tough job?' . . . I tended to look for a tough white man. Now I have a greater appreciation of what blacks had to do just to get here. From that, I know they're prepared to do tough jobs."

Gauging the Success of Diversity Strategies

While the level of women and minorities in the ranks of top management is an indicator of the success of a company's diversity strategy, it must be viewed as a long-term indicator, since the number of top spots in a given company is limited. However, the strength of diversity efforts can be assessed in other, shorter term ways than waiting for the president to quit or the CEO to retire. One way is to conduct periodic, anonymous surveys of employees to determine how well efforts at integrating diverse people and styles are working.

For example, Honeywell prepared voluntary surveys to poll its employees on management practices, barriers to contribution, and information deficits. The employees were asked to respond to such statements as "My supervisor expresses confidence in me and my ability to go beyond my current level of skill and expertise." The five possible responses to this statement ranged from "often" to "never."

Honeywell then assembled the replies from each manager's subordinates and handed over the anonymous results to that manager. Some of the managers were stunned to find that they received low ratings in areas they considered their strong points.

The success of a company's diversity strategy can also be gauged by informal observations of employees to determine how well diverse groups interact. Such observations should be made by a person skilled in managing diversity and able to sense tension or strain that is not overtly expressed. A more objective method is to track the number of EEO complaints. And a quick and easy method is to take a look at employee retention. High turnover rates, especially among women and minorities, are a warning signal that actions have not yet caught up with the company rhetoric about valuing diversity.

Diversity and the Networking Organization

In earlier chapters, I have stressed the importance of fluid structures in an era that demands maximum flexibility and speed of response. Increasing levels of diversity in the workplace are another compelling reason to dismantle the vertical hierarchies of the old story and embrace networking forms of organization.

By their very nature, vertical hierarchies promote differences by separating employees into categories and demanding that they be ranked. Under such a structure, it's all too easy to fall back on stereotypical thinking in determining which employees will be up and which will be down. The more stringent the segregation, the more the self-worth of those in the lower ranks is diminished.

In a networking structure, by contrast, there is much less up or down, much more fluid movement in all directions. Thus there is little innate pressure for segregation, or for domination by one group at the expense of other groups.

The networking structure requires partnership and close relationships across the board. In such a structure, employees with diverse viewpoints can engage in creative dialogue about their differences. Such dialogue and the networking structure that encourages it are natural expressions of a more democratic organizational environment.

In the end, the collapse of the glass ceiling that has traditionally thwarted the advancement of women and minorities may well be effected as much by the networking structure as by corporate diversity strategies. Without a rigid structure that separates people by class to support it, that ceiling is destined to collapse.

THE LONG ROAD AHEAD

Moving from a monoculture to an environment in which a broad diversity of employees thrives will not be easy. We human beings are creatures of habit. We have each developed our own set of logical constructs around which we organize our private worlds and by which we make sense of our surroundings. We cling to our preconceived notions for a reason: However distorted, they comfort us. Letting go of our biases will be a slow and sometimes painful process.

Some biases will give way more easily than others. In a 1987 *Wall Street Journal* survey of 351 top executives, for example, only 1 percent said that they would hesitate to promote a female employee to the management committee level, while 66 percent said that they would hesitate to promote a gay employee to that level. These responses emphasize the need for education and heightened awareness to root out deeply held prejudices.

The challenge of valuing diversity is formidable for all of us— male or female, majority or minority. How quickly will men of all races and cultures be comfortable with female leadership throughout the organization? How soon will male leaders be enlightened enough to serve as coaches for the many women who will break through the glass ceiling over the next decade? How attentive will our companies be to the special challenges, such as day care and elder care, that they must address if diversity is to thrive among our leadership? Our answers to these and other vital leadership questions will help determine the competitive posture of American companies in the global marketplace of the 1990s.

No one knows how long it will take for the fully integrated corporation to become the norm; most expert predictions deal in decades rather than years. But one thing is certain: Significant movement toward a culture that values diversity will not be evident until organizations become diverse at the top.

There are signs of progress. John Lynch of Hewlett-Packard is optimistic: "If you look at our upper-management levels, about 11 percent are women and about 7 percent are minority. I am double-counting minority women. I think if you look at our top 200 managers, as an example, we've currently got 5 percent women and 1 percent to 2 percent minority, but that is changing quarterly. Just five years ago, both of the percentages—women and minorities—in the most senior categories were zero. But the challenge is still there—to increase those percentages."

He adds: "We also have a lot of women in our pipeline who will be moving into senior management jobs over the next 5 to 10 years, and I really find that encouraging. With the pipeline full like that, there will be a certain percentage that will be assuming these leadership roles, and I really think that with the critical mass improving and with the pipeline improving, what has been called 'the glass ceiling' is slowly going away."

Nancy Kaltreider agrees that different styles cannot be freely exercised and minority groups cannot be truly valued without diversity in the upper ranks:

I think the percentage of diversity is an extremely important issue. When the percentage is quite low, women tend to act like men, and when they get in management roles, they adapt in ways that are sometimes ludicrous, an exaggeration of the male macho-driven style. Whereas I've seen, as more women have come into medicine, that there is a gradual shift, with women who are leading committees or in positions of substantial responsibility being much more open and flexible, and kind of laughing at themselves, and just clearly bringing their own style to that without having to hide it.

She adds:

We serve a large Hispanic population. To an extent even greater than blacks, the Hispanics have not been represented in the professional classes. Many of the service workers at the hospital are Hispanic, and that always seems fairly natural to people, and has led to a certain pattern of expectation and perception about what their motivation, intelligence, or whatever was. When we began, by actively recruiting, to have a substantial number of Hispanics in the medical school class and eventually on the house staff, I think that was the first time people began to recognize their own innate biases and to challenge them. So I think that someone has to be perceived as a peer to really help you think through what level of bias you may be bringing to the work environment.

Avon offers another model of hope. The cosmetics giant encourages employees to organize into black, Hispanic, and Asian networks by granting them official recognition and providing a senior manager to act as coach. These networks provide management with feedback on problems that concern these minorities and help new employees adjust.

Avon once had a women's network, but it disbanded years ago. The reason? With women holding 79 percent of management positions at Avon, it simply became unnecessary.

But this doesn't mean that the challenge is over for Avon or for any other company that is dealing with issues of diversity. It takes a long time for attitudes to change, and it takes a longer time for language to catch up. As Price Cobbs told me: "We don't have the language and imagery of difference. We have really been afraid.

You and I grew up in a world where goodness was color blindness."

We live in a transitional period in which well-meaning people continue to reflect the biases of the old story in their language. For example, the mission statement of Kings Super Markets, a New Jersey firm admired for embracing diversity, goes on at length about the need to acknowledge women—and ends up by calling for "brotherhood." And an article in *Fortune* magazine declares, with obvious good intentions, that it is easier for a woman to become president of the United States than chair*man* of IBM.

This is not merely a question of semantics. Language structures consciousness, and until our language reflects diversity rather than focusing on the white male monoculture, our behavior will remain rooted in old story stereotypes.

In addition to the language barrier, there remain the ongoing challenges posed by differences themselves. Differences do not cease to be problematic just because we have acknowledged them.

An important issue that has been buried in discussions of gender diversity is the inevitable sexual implications of having people work together in an era that demands ever closer work relationships. It is naive to think that we can leave our sexuality at the front door of the corporation. As people work more closely together in environments that encourage close partnerships, the word *sex* must be allowed to reenter the workplace vocabulary so that this issue can be addressed alongside other issues of diversity.

DIVERSITY AND SOCIAL CHANGE

While the road to valuing diversity is long and challenging, broad cultural trends will help ease the journey. As we travel and mix, as we encounter diversity in our lives outside the corporation, we will become more comfortable with diversity at work. Elisabet Sahtouris writes:

> More and more people in peacetime swell transportation systems as they are sent to work and live in one another's countries or as they choose to go there on holiday. They learn one another's ways, sharing more and more ideas. Cultures are mixed

within political borders; cultures are shared through networks of local and foreign communication; ever larger numbers of people become literate and learn what is happening in their world. Even people who never set foot in another country can eat and use the whole world's products and know the whole world's ways of life in full sound and color. . . . the old separations of distance, language, and culture are bridged as the human technologies of transport and communications bind humanity inevitably into a single worldwide body.

Where diversity is concerned, we Americans have an edge over many of our global competitors. Japan and many European nations lack experience in egalitarian dealings with people of different races, religions, and cultures. The countries of Europe are still largely homogeneous. Japan is even more so.

But learning to live with diversity has been a matter of survival for Americans. After all, our nation, whether viewed as melting pot or mosaic, was built by diverse groups of immigrants. Thus we have a headstart in the diversity game that will serve us in good stead in the coming decades. The global era demands that cultures relate at the macro level. Our experience in relating to other cultures as a society will help us accommodate diversity at the micro level of the organization—another imperative of the new story.

"DIVERSITY WILL MAKE US WHOLE"

Smart companies have been fostering diversity for years, in preparing for competition in an increasingly multicultural business world. For many managers, valuing diversity is above all a pragmatic strategy for sustaining growth in an era of labor shortages: "It's about creating an environment where everybody can be successful," says Alan Zimmerle, corporate director for EEO/affirmative action at Digital Equipment. "It's about creating an environment 10 years from now, when, if we're competing for engineers, and a lot of them are Asian, or a lot of them are black women, Digital will be their company of choice."

Albert Yu of Intel regards valuing diversity as a practical strategy that will yield big dividends in an era that demands continuous innovation: "I think that we have the most diverse, the best talent from each of the ethnic backgrounds. This probably puts us in a better position than, say, a purely German company, a purely Japanese company, a purely Israeli company. I think we have the best brains from all these diverse groups, and I think that we are a very innovative company as a result."

Kevin Sullivan, human resources director of Apple Computer, also recognizes the economic advantages of valuing diversity. Prior to joining Apple, Sullivan worked at Digital Equipment— where he noted that over 40 percent of the salespeople were women and minorities. "When white male managers understand that 40 percent of their sales force is responsible for about a billion and a half dollars in orders," he observes, "it becomes an obvious bottom-line goal to keep them happy, motivated, and productive!"

It is not surprising that managers of computer firms are particularly enthusiastic in their praise of diversity. Innovation is the lifeblood of these firms, so it may be easier for them than for firms in other industries to recognize the value of diversity in generating innovation.

But it's not just innovation that is at stake. While valuing differences is undoubtedly a good business strategy, there is far more to embracing diversity than economic self-interest. Here we must distinguish between managing and valuing diversity. *Managing* diversity implies a behavioral approach to reducing bigotry and bias in the workplace, in the interest of increasing productivity. *Valuing* diversity—the real goal of the new story organization— implies something far more powerful.

What is missing in most discussions of diversity is an awareness of the deeper value inherent in diversity, an understanding that diversity will, in the words of political analyst Mark Satin, "expand our mental horizons, enrich our interpersonal lives, make us whole." Embracing diversity will not just help the bottom line; it will also enable us to fulfill our potential, activate our creativity, liberate our talents, enrich our teams, and make our organizations more fully human.

Diversity challenges us to move beyond the limitations imposed by our traditional roles. As Harold Epps points out: "Managers are quite often forced by issues of diversity to become better managers. Quite often, white men tell me this. I don't know how much white men give one another and how much they depend on one another for direct, real-time, honest feedback. Other people require it more. So managers who are not quite used to giving real, objective feedback are challenged [by diversity] to do that. Diversity stretches and liberates traditional managers." This expansion of our capacities is a key characteristic of the new story organization.

Liberating the White Male

If there is one group that is likely to resist efforts to value diversity, it is the traditional white male managers who fear that embracing diversity means a loss of power for them. But this fear is misguided. In fact, what white male managers stand to lose by welcoming diversity is not true power but only the negative, dysfunctional power of command and control that victimized them along with everybody else in the old story corporation.

Valuing diversity does not mean that I win and you lose; this either-or viewpoint is a symptom of old story thinking. As Price Cobbs sees it:

> If I'm intellectually curious, everything is additive; I don't feel I have to lose anything by learning more about you. We have to help white men tap their own diversity, or they will presume that those of us who are different are coming up with some new ways, some additive ways, to compete that they don't have, and they're going to dig their heels in. I see people, particularly the mid-level white male managers, who are resistant to the concept [of diversity]—and not so ideologically resistant, but resistant to the concept because they see you as now coming up with things that they don't have.

Not only do white males have nothing to lose by valuing diversity; they have much to gain. For behind the veneer of power, the typical old story white male has little real sense of himself, little authentic understanding of his unique potential. His talent, too, has remained largely untapped, stifled by the same forces that constrained women and minorities. Who knows what unique contributions he might make if he could discard the role of commander and controller and assume his rightful place as a fully participating partner? I saw such contributions being made on *Apollo 11*, and we see them every day in organizations whose new story orientation allows white males to be people too—such organizations as Digital, Herman Miller, and Smith, Bucklin Associates.

As author Sally Helgesen points out in *The Female Advantage*: "Men are going to have to learn to become more multifaceted in their identity, less identified solely with their position on the job, but taking their identity also from their family life and their life in their community." For most of the men I know, that would be a welcome relief.

THE ERA OF THE GLOBAL CITIZEN

Learning to value diversity is critical to survival and success in the 1990s and beyond—critical for individuals, corporations, and entire nations. The diversity of the corporation is largely a reflection of the diversity of the global society in which it nests. The corporation is a training ground that will prepare us to assume our roles in the world community of the 21st century.

Managers like Harold Epps are leading the way, teaching us what it means to accommodate and value diversity and modeling for us the behavior of the global citizens we must all become. Because of the profound influence of the corporation on global society, the vision such managers provide extends far beyond the walls of their organizations. In Chapter 9, we'll consider the tremendous influence that an organization can have on society when it embraces the role of global citizen.

Chapter Nine

The Three E's: Ethics, Education, and the Environment

In 1976, at the age of 34, Anita Roddick launched The Body Shop in Brighton, East Sussex, England, after her husband, Gordon, announced his desire to spend two years traveling in South America. Her interim way to make a living has blossomed into an international success story.

The Body Shop was founded on five principles:

1. *To sell cosmetics with a minimum of hype and packaging.*
2. *To promote health rather than glamour, reality rather than the dubious promise of instant rejuvenation.*
3. *To use naturally based, close-to-source ingredients wherever possible.*
4. *Not to test ingredients or final products on animals.*
5. *To respect the environment.*

By the time Gordon returned from his travels, The Body Shop was well on its way to becoming a thriving concern. By the end of fiscal 1990, its pretax profits had climbed to an estimated $23 million on sales of $141 million. Today there are over 600 Body Shops in 39 countries—from the Arctic to Australia, from Sweden to Singapore—and the number is steadily growing. The Body Shop employs over 1,600 people in its own shops and offices, and its franchisees employ about 3,500 people. It went public in April 1984.

The Body Shop is not only a phenomenal economic success but also an international symbol of corporate social responsibility. Known worldwide for its activist involvement in social causes, it has joined with such organizations as Greenpeace, Friends of the Earth, and Survival International to wage campaigns that have ranged from saving the whales to rescuing the rain forests. When she is not campaigning, Anita Roddick travels the world in search of new products and processes for The Body Shop. In the course of her travels, she lives with and observes women who use the same ingredients and methods to care for their skin and hair that generations of women used before them. During 1989, for example, she visited Mexico, southern India, Turkey, Oman, Nepal, Costa Rica, Niger, and Brazil.

Anita Roddick spoke with me about her travels, her business philosophy, and her views on the issue of corporate social responsibility:

I was in Saudi Arabia a few months ago, and I saw how they really did their trading—in these wonderful little lockup shops called "souks." Just three walls and a gate that goes up and down. So I said to our Saudi Arabian franchisees: "Let's do it that way. Let's put our 6 or 10 best perfumes into the souks." You have to learn from the market that you're in, rather than imposing the way you do things.

I just came back from Brazil, where we've been trading. After I attended the Union of Indian Nations conference in Altamira in 1989, I became passionately committed to the idea of helping the Indians in Brazil preserve their way of life and protect the rain forest. One obvious solution was to identify product ingredients in the rain forest that could be gathered on a sustainable basis by Indians and rubber tappers.

The Body Shop raised 220,000 [British] pounds at its international franchisees meeting. The money has been used to fund research and to address the immediate needs of the threatened Indian tribes like the Kayapo and the Yanomami. I was in one Kayapo village—a settlement of about 20 or 30 huts for about 250 people. The whole Indian tribe was sitting around in the middle of the compound, and we were trading. We've been teaching them how to extract the oils from the Brazil nuts, which is part of their gathering ritual. We actually managed to get 5 kilos of oil, and we think we can take 20 tons a year. It's very simple Third World technology.

And then we trade. We say: "What do you want?" It might be medical equipment or cooking pots. So we do an exchange. We're not screwing up their culture. They are hunters and gatherers. Trade, we believe, gives people the ability to choose their destiny when they meet the pressures of the West, and helps them utilize their resources to the benefit of their own social, cultural, and material needs.

And so maybe someday they'll say: "OK, we have enough now. Come back in 10 years." What we do is give them the patent rights—something the big multinationals would never do—so they will continue to benefit. The onus is on us to prevent the chaos a market economy would wreak on the traditions of the rain forest. The exchange of knowledge for goods has to be carried out in the traditional manner, with respect and friendship.

The Body Shop has an anthropology department and employs ethnobotanists. We don't have a marketing department, but we've turned conventional marketing on its head by linking products with social causes. That means the products become emissaries for political messages.

We do not market our products as if they were the body and blood of Jesus Christ. What we do take seriously is our product development, the ingredients we use, how we source them, and then how we educate our customers about our choices. And so our customers or our investors are able to make informed decisions about whether or not they want to do business with us. Customers crave knowledge; they want honest information. They want to feel an affinity not only with the products but with the company.

And this is why so many people want to work at The Body Shop and why no one leaves. It's our values—our goals, our causes are every bit as valuable to us as our products and profits. What moves the spirit is not a moisture cream. Our employees don't dream of soap when they go home. It's all the noble purposes we've all decided to put our energies into. For example, our group in Finland just won the major environmental award for the work they did on the animal campaign, against animal testing in the cosmetics industry. A group in Hong Kong has been working with refugees. These people humanize the company with their actions—the time they spend on other things besides trading.

All members of our staff can take off a day a month—we encourage it—to take on a project of their choice. Every Body Shop in England and around the world does community action. They do it on company time. Each department and each shop makes its choice. The shops are arenas of education for social and environmental issues. We're not an authority. We are here to attract attention, by the window posters or the leaflets we print or the videos we make. Our resources plus the audience of millions passing by on the pavement and through the shops have forced a change in consciousness among our customers. Consciousness raising is part of what we do.

Besides that, we have a training school which takes about 4,500 of our staff people over the year. There are about 45 courses that cover everything from managing motivation to the science of cosmetics, to AIDS in our society. This means we would ask AIDS sufferers to come and talk to us.

A wonderful idea came out of one of these courses. London has about 3,000 young homeless people living under bridges. We've begun working with a charity called Shelter that tried to find homes for these kids. We said: "We will train them. We'll train them back into jobs." Most of them hadn't had jobs before, so now we have in each of our shops a team of people who are mothers, fathers, protectors to one of the homeless. And they go through an intense training course. If they don't measure up, they don't go into the shops. But every one has measured up! So every one of our shops in London has these homeless kids who are now bona fide, valued members of our staff.

We also have what we call the "buddy system." Any staff member can exchange jobs with any other staff member around the world. Let's say they want to exchange jobs with someone in Melbourne. Or say they want three months to go traveling. They're guaranteed a job when they get back. Or if they want to work in the Education Department and do school visits, they can do that. That sort of migratory role is very much encouraged by us.

What I've learned here is that people become motivated when you guide them to the source of their own power. When some anonymous member of the staff, after three weeks of cleaning out orphanages in Romania, or holding AIDS babies, or campaigning for human rights, looks you dead in the eye and says: "This is the real me," take heed. She is dreaming of noble purposes, not moisture cream.

Democracy is not a spectator sport. Unfortunately, too many of us are passive civic participants. The reasons are many: We think we cannot make a difference; we aren't aware of our responsibilities; or we just don't know how to act.

The citizen's job is to keep his mouth open. What we have found with our campaigns and activities is you don't wait for extraordinary opportunities for participation. You seize common occasions and you make them great.

Anita Roddick understands as few corporate leaders do the vital link between business and the society in which it is embedded. From founding a boys' town for destitute children in southern India to crusading on behalf of the Amazonian rain forests to rescuing orphanages in Romania, The Body Shop demonstrates on a daily basis its commitment to being a fully participating partner in the world community.

The company charter makes it crystal clear that The Body Shop is not just a business but also a deeply concerned global citizen. The stated purpose of the charter is to "help turn The Body Shop vision 'of making the world a better place' into reality by," among other things, "respecting fellow human beings, by not harming animals, by working to conserve our planet." The charter declares that "honesty, integrity, and caring form the foundations" of the company "and should flow through everything we do."

This is no mere rhetoric spewed forth by a corporate public relations department. The employees wrote the words themselves, according to Roddick, who told me: "Two years ago, we gave time off to every member of our staff to create The Body Shop Charter, which is our way of running the company. They had to write it themselves and put it into practice themselves. They got as much time off work as they needed, got into groups, decided what there is to do."

Anita Roddick's devotion to activist causes is matched by her concern for her employees, who are treated to the same level of caring that The Body Shop demonstrates through its social campaigns. Starting with paychecks: "We make sure our staff are the highest paid workers of any retail group," she declares. And the company offers additional benefits to its workers, such as the Child Development Center, for children aged 3 months to 5 years. "It's the most wonderful, educational center for kids," says Roddick. "I think that's going to be the norm in any place which has 300 or 400 people."

Roddick believes that the success of The Body Shop is due in part to empowering and valuing employees: "It's empowering them without being in fear of them. It also has to do with loving labor, valuing labor, rather than saying, 'Ah, the last persons in the world you reward are your labor force.' It has to do with a sense of quality, that you are all doing the same job. The job goes beyond you as an individual. . . . People don't say they work for Gordon and me—they work for The Body Shop."

The "sense of equality" that Roddick speaks of shows up in various forms. For example, all employees become shareholders after one year with the company. And the notion of a traditional vertical hierarchy simply doesn't apply. "We are very, very grass roots," says Roddick (who readily admits that her grassroots orientation and natural idealism were formed in the 60s). "Our great pals that we drink with at night could be anybody, from one of the drivers to somebody running the Education Department, or running the Liaison Department, or somebody who is in that department. There isn't that sense of 'You can only go out and talk to Anita and Gordon if you are at a certain level.'"

Anita Roddick screens carefully for franchisees. Out of the thousands of applicants who knock on her door, only a handful will eventually open up a Body Shop somewhere in the world.

Who makes the cut? "First of all, I am not looking for normal franchisees," Roddick told me. As an example, she described a couple in Portland who are "extremely devout believers that there has got to be a new way of less consumerism, and they are looking for a way of—not an agenda but a way of life which says, 'I want to work, and I don't want to leave my values when I open the door to my workplace. I want to be as I am, as a person. I want to be reflected in what I do.' So most of them are idealists."

While The Body Shop employs a large number of idealists, Anita Roddick is not one to cram social responsibility down anybody's throat. I asked her, "What if employees say it's all they can do to take care of their kids, that they don't want any part of this social concern business?" She replied:

> It's their bloody right. It's like when I set up the company—I did not set up with an environmental agenda. My husband wanted to go off traveling across South America for two years. I set up to survive. It's just that I didn't leave what I believed at home. But, by golly, the most important thing is to survive—you bloody bet that their responsibilities are at home. I have no judgment to make on anybody. The arrogance! I don't have to say, "Come on. Be responsible. Spend time on these social causes." It's ridiculous.

She added: "I know that I have got a very strong percentage of our staff that love the company because they like the environment in which they work, and the agenda beyond that is of no interest."

But Anita Roddick, with her passionate commitment, has a way of engendering interest where there was little or none before. She was blunt about the hostility of some employees when the company decided to support Amnesty International: "Now a lot of them were very angry with us for supporting Amnesty because they said it was too political, because Amnesty came out very strongly against what the British government was doing in Northern Ireland with the IRA prisoners."

Roddick made no attempt to force her decision on anyone. Instead of saying, "Well, sorry, guys, we are more enlightened on this," a strategy she knew would never work, she tried another strategy. "We brought down two torture victims to talk to our staff about what actually can happen and what the value of Amnesty has been."

The staff was convinced.

PUTTING THE CONTEXT BACK INTO BUSINESS

In 1776, Adam Smith laid out the premises of capitalism in *The Wealth of Nations*. In that landmark book, Smith set forth his now famous theory of the "invisible hand," which posited that individuals pursuing their own interest end up serving the interest of the whole:

> Every individual endeavors to employ his capital so that its produce may be of greatest value. He generally neither intends to promote the public interest, nor knows how much he is promoting it. He intends only his own security, only his own gain. And he is in this led by an invisible hand to promote an end which was no part of his intention. By pursuing his own interest he frequently promotes that of society more effectually than when he really intends to promote it.

Over time, those words have been interpreted as a blessing for businesses to pursue their own interest, with little regard for the public good. In fact, in some quarters they have been used to decry the very notion of corporate social responsibility. Many modern economists, including Nobel prize winner Milton Friedman, continue to preach with fervor that "the only business of business is to make a profit."

Speaking of corporate social responsibility, Friedman argues that it is no better than stealing from shareholders when an executive gives corporate profits to charity, spends money to reduce pollution beyond what is required by law, or "hires hard-core unemployed instead of better-qualified available workmen." He elaborates: "In each of these cases, the corporate executive would be spending someone else's money for a general social interest. Insofar as his actions in accord with his 'social responsibility' reduce returns to stockholders, he is spending their money. Insofar as his actions lower the wages of some employees, he is spending their money." The implication that the responsibility of the corporation is only to itself—that is, to its shareholders and its employees—represents old story thinking at its worst. It is the height of absurdity (not to mention arrogance) to suggest that business can be viewed as separate from the context that supports it, and thus has no responsibility to the larger community.

Mark Vermilion, manager of corporate affairs at Sun Microsystems, has a ready answer for those who regard the corporation as an entity unto itself, with no vital links and thus no responsibility to the society in which it operates:

> I would ask them to conduct their business then without use of public roads, without use of public utilities. I would ask them to conduct their business without the use of a workforce that was educated largely on public funds. I would ask them to conduct their business without the protection of the government in terms of interstate and international trade, without the protection of armed services for the protection of the country. I would basically say, "If you think you are separate from society, then really do try to conduct your business in isolation, and see how far you get."

Unfortunately, until quite recently individuals and businesses have received relatively little encouragement to act in the interests of the community and substantial encouragement to pursue self-interest at the expense of the common good. This pursuit was elevated to the level of an art form in the 1980s.

But while individual greed was spawning fortunes for the likes of Michael Milken, Ivan Boesky, and Donald Trump, the society at large was wrestling with growing poverty and illiteracy, increasing pollution and crime. The invisible hand, it seems, was nowhere in sight.

Fortunately, there are signs that the isolationist view that dominated the old story of business is beginning to crumble, as social problems are inevitably making their impact felt within the corporation. An uneducated populace does not become suddenly literate upon entering the workplace. As social and environmental problems steadily erode productivity and threaten American competitiveness, corporate executives are beginning to rethink the notion that business needs to be concerned only with shareholder profits.

Businesses are gradually waking up to the realization that social contribution, far from being a "luxury" or mere "charity," is critical to the survival of the corporate holon. We cannot speak of a "successful" organization in the midst of a decaying society/holarchy, for the organization and the society are interdependent. To survive and thrive, the new story organization must become a fully participating partner in its local, national, and global communities. The new story manager must view himself or herself as responsible for the welfare of employees, a steward of the community, and a friend of the earth.

Although this is rarely trumpeted in business, human beings have a strong natural desire for connection and an innate awareness of their interdependence. Despite the greed that marked the 80s, caring about others is as much a part of human nature as caring about ourselves.

Even Adam Smith admitted as much. James Wilson, writing in the *California Management Review*, points out that 17 years before *The Wealth of Nations* was published, Smith stated in a work entitled *The Theory of Moral Sentiments*, that no matter how selfish man may appear to be, "there are evidently some principles in his nature which interest him in the fortune of others, and render their happiness necessary to him, though he derives nothing from it except the pleasure of seeing it." Not surprisingly, this is not the Adam Smith that is taught in Economics 101.

SOCIAL RESPONSIBILITY AND THE THREE E'S

The expression "corporate social responsibility" encompasses a broad range of beliefs and behaviors. In this chapter, I will focus on what I call the "three E's" of corporate social responsibility: ethics, education, and the environment. Ethics is the foundation on which socially responsible behavior is built. The environment and education are two vital areas in which businesses are focusing their social contributions.

Our natural environment is basic to the health and survivability of individuals and institutions. It is becoming increasingly obvious that threats to the environment jeopardize our very existence.

Education is also a survival issue for businesses. Educational deficits are at the root of many social problems that inevitably affect our companies. More immediately, such deficits have become a pocketbook issue for businesses as they struggle to deal with illiteracy in the workplace and the resultant loss of productivity.

Ethics and Corporate Social Responsibility

The Body Shop operates in 39 countries. I asked Anita Roddick what common thread ran through its hundreds of individual shops in diverse cultures around the world. She replied: "It would be the values. It would be the fact that what moves the spirit is not a moisture cream. What moves employees to want to be with us, or not leave us, is the fact that there is a high moral code."

Ethics—a company's moral code—is one of those "soft" concepts that are generally relegated to Corporate Affairs or the company legal department. More often than not, it is viewed as peripheral to the company, as an issue that will be dealt with only when a flagrant abuse of ethics arises (or, sadly, often only when such an abuse becomes public knowledge).

But ethics, far from being peripheral to the company, is its very foundation. Ethics is the set of written and unwritten moral principles by which a company operates at a core level. A company's ethics determines how it treats employees, customers, and sup-

pliers; how it develops products and processes; and how it partic-
ipates in the larger community.

More generally, "ethical behavior" means doing what is right,
what brings the greatest benefit or the least harm to all of those
involved. We may argue about what is right (for example, some
contend that disinvesting in South Africa hurts those it is meant
to help) but not about the fact that doing what is right is at the
core of ethical behavior.

It is important to note that "ethical" is different from "legal."
Installing a minimum of pollution control devices, as Milton
Friedman advocates, may be legal, but it is not necessarily ethical.
A commitment to healthy progress requires a genuine sense of
responsibility for the results of our actions, not simply taking ac-
tions that will meet the minimum requirements of the law.

Levi Strauss spent a fortune to reduce the formaldehyde levels
in the finish of its Sta-Prest pants beyond the government standards, even though there was no evidence that merely adhering to
those standards would cause any harm to consumers or employees. Its reason for doing so was that it had a policy of monitoring all chemicals used by suppliers to discover any *potential* for
harm. Levi Strauss goes beyond the legal requirements to ensure
that it is "doing what is right." This is an example of ethics in
action.

Ethics is the spiritual glue that holds the organization together.
A company's ethics determines its character, its health, and, ultimately, its success. Says Robert Haas, chairman and CEO of Levi
Strauss: "A company's values—what it stands for, what its people believe in [i.e., its ethics]—are crucial to its competitive success. Indeed, values drive the business."

Not all corporate leaders are as enlightened as Robert Haas,
and not all corporations operate as ethically as Levi Strauss. To a
great extent, American business has been separated from the
value base that would humanize it. This lack of a strong ethical
foundation has sometimes allowed corporations to pursue heart-
less and destructive actions with impunity and to justify them in
the name of "good economic sense."

Because we have minimized the ethical dimension of business,
there is little open discussion of ethics in the workplace, despite
the fact that we all face ethical choices every day. In an article

entitled "The Moral Muteness of Managers," Frederick Bird and James Waters described the reluctance of managers to discuss ethical issues at work:

> Many managers exhibit a reluctance to describe their actions in moral terms even when they are acting for moral reasons. They talk as if their actions were guided exclusively by organizational interests, practicality, and economic good sense even when in practice they honor morally defined standards codified in law, professional conventions, and social mores. They characteristically defend morally defined objectives such as service to customers, effective cooperation among personnel, and utilization of their own skills and resources in terms of the long-run economic objectives of their organizations.

There is grave danger in ignoring or minimizing the ethical dimension of business, which does not go away simply because we choose not to consider it. By ignoring the moral dimension of business, we unwittingly encourage or condone ethical abuses and produce a workforce that is literally de-moralized. Instead of being hushed up, ethics must be talked about openly, brought onto center stage, as it is at Levi Strauss, The Body Shop, and other new story organizations.

The ethical stance of a company has important implications both for the community in which it operates and for its employees. Contrast Johnson & Johnson's handling of tainted bottles of Tylenol with Exxon's response to the Valdez oil spill. On the night that the first poisoned bottle of Tylenol was discovered, senior managers of Johnson & Johnson huddled in a room to discuss what action to take. They reviewed the company's mission statement and agreed that the only thing to do was to recall the entire product. The company's ethics, as embodied in its mission statement, put people's lives ahead of profits.

Contrast this ethic of concern with the behavior of Exxon executives in the wake of the Valdez oil spill. They were slow to respond, tried to minimize the damage, and pointed fingers elsewhere, never fully accepting responsibility for Exxon's role in the tragedy. Whatever its legal responsibilities, Exxon demonstrated a lack of concern, a failure to care. Such ethical failures in business (including thousands of far less visible ones) have been a major contributing factor to the serious environmental problems that we face as we enter the 1990s.

The Environment and the Ecocorporation

"Our products create pollution, noise, and waste."

You wouldn't expect a major corporation to make such a proclamation, but that's just what Volvo did recently on the cover of a brochure that acknowledges its responsibility for the "adverse environmental effects of its products and production activities." The brochure includes a policy statement that pledges Volvo to act in environmentally responsible ways in developing products and processes and in conducting environmental research.

Volvo is one of a growing number of corporations that are taking their responsibility to the environment seriously. Such corporate environmentalism is long overdue. After decades of devastation brought on by an old story mentality that put a premium on economic growth, even at the expense of serious assaults on the environment, business is finally waking up to the folly of destroying the nest in which it lives.

Each one of our business exemplars is examining its relationship to a sustainable society, but no company exemplifies the move toward environmental responsibility more clearly—and forcefully—than The Body Shop. From the start, Anita Roddick incorporated her environmental beliefs into her company—offering only biodegradable products from natural sources, recycling waste, providing refillable containers, and immersing the company in environmental causes that ranged from saving the whales to halting the destruction of the rain forests.

The Body Shop's environmentalism is by no means limited to its external campaigns. The company practices what it preaches to the outside world. An Environmental Projects Department monitors internal compliance with its environmental principles. The agenda of the department, says Anita Roddick, is "to audit everything that we do within the company, from production to manufacturing, to the way we use our resources, energy, and human resources." The Environmental Projects Department audits all of the company's departments every six months. And the auditors meet regularly with environmental groups, incorporating their suggestions into everyday company operations wherever possible. As a result of the department's efforts, paper purchasing has been centralized and paper waste dramatically reduced, recycling programs have been introduced, and water use is regularly monitored and minimized.

Anita Roddick is constantly on the lookout for ways to improve The Body Shop's already impressive record of environmental responsibility. For example, energy-hungry company cars (including Jaguars for some of the directors) were recently replaced with energy-efficient Volkswagens. Says Roddick: "I know that outside of population control, energy is the major, major dilemma within the environmental movement. So I kept on bringing up, 'How in the hell could we be deemed and awarded and patted on the back as being an environmental company if we have so many cars?'"

In addition to replacing gas-guzzling company cars, The Body Shop recently collaborated with Volvo's truck division to create aerodynamically sound delivery trucks that cut energy use nearly in half. And as an adjunct to its car campaign, it announced that it would subsidize the purchase of a bicycle for any employee who cared to ride one to work. More than 500 bikes have been purchased by staffers, and the company has built a shed to house them.

While few organizations exhibit the level of environmental responsibility that is business as usual at The Body Shop, environmental consciousness is on the rise among mainstream corporations. Public awareness of environmental dangers has helped force the issue. Such awareness has grown dramatically during the past decade, putting pressure on corporations to clean up their act.

According to a 1989 Gallup poll, 76 percent of American consumers think of themselves as environmentalists. And a 1989 survey conducted for the Michael Peters Group, which provides consulting on products and design, found that 77 percent of Americans say a company's environmental reputation affects what they buy.

"Green consumers" are demanding environmentally responsible products—and companies are responding. McDonald's, a giant producer of paper and plastic waste, has become a crusader for recycling. In the summer of 1990, discount giant Wal-Mart asked its 7,000 suppliers to start providing it with more recycled or recyclable products and began labeling them as such. Kmart and at least a dozen grocery chains quickly announced similar programs.

Oil companies, not generally in the forefront of environmentalism, are becoming increasingly involved in ecological issues. Phillips Petroleum has teamed up with the National Wildlife Federation, Ducks Unlimited, the U.S. Fish and Wildlife Service, and the wildlife departments of Texas, Oklahoma, Kansas, Colorado, and New Mexico for a major wetlands conservation project in the Playa Lakes region of those states. Chevron, Texaco, ARCO, and other oil companies have introduced cleaner gasolines. To reinforce its commitment to the environment, ARCO recently placed a former president of The Nature Conservancy on its board of directors.

Chemical companies, traditional top targets of environmentalists, are also joining the cause. Du Pont, a frequent target of criticism, has announced significant reforms. Among other things, it is phasing out its $750-million-a-year business in chlorofluorocarbons (CFCs) because they destroy the earth's critical ozone layer.

Edgar Woolard, Jr., Du Pont's chairman and CEO since April 1989, has made environmentalism a top company priority. Woolard meets at least once a month with leading environmentalists. He has established an environmental services division and set targets for the reduction of toxic emissions, spending nearly $1 billion a year on the effort. And he has made increased environmental sensitivity one criterion in determining the compensation of Du Pont managers. Woolard's ultimate goal is to achieve zero pollution in all of Du Pont's activities. He says: "I believe anything that goes out the waste pipes may well be something that can be recycled, reused, or sold."

While such statements cause some environmentalists to raise a skeptical eyebrow, others praise Woolard for seeking to change the industry attitude that some waste is an inevitable part of the production process. "That is a brand-new thought," says David Rowe of the Environmental Defense Fund. "People used to think that a certain amount of emissions was a necessary part of production. So it is a major contribution."

Even if this new kind of thinking—call it "ecothinking"— comes in advance of concrete solutions to complex problems, it is a critical step in the right direction. It sets the stage for solutions that consider the needs of the company but also include the needs of the society in which the company nests—a clear and positive departure from the old story. This kind of integrative thinking, this reconciliation of opposing needs, is basic to the new story of business—and essential if we are to create a sustainable future.

Environmentalism has also been grabbing hold in western Europe. The rise of the Green party in Germany is just one example of the growing attention that Europeans have been giving environmental concerns. In 1989, the European Community passed legislation that imposes strict standards on emissions from new power plants and requires existing power plants to meet these standards by 2003. Italy launched a $1.6 billion program to reduce sulfur gas emissions from all power plants more than 80 percent by the end of 1999. The EC has filed suit against Britain to force its compliance with EC water quality standards. And pressured by the Germans and the rising power of the Greens, the EC stunned the auto industry by imposing U.S.-style standards for pollution control on all European cars by 1993.

The trend toward greater environmental responsibility is viewed with suspicion by companies that believe it will result in prohibitive cost increases. But other companies, such as 3M, have discovered that just the opposite is true. Through Pollution Prevention Pays, a program that involves recycling solvents and replacing volatile solvents with water-based substitutes, 3M has saved well over $1 billion since 1975.

The focus on environmentalism has also spawned a host of new business opportunities. Du Pont, for example, has entered into a massive joint recycling venture with the nation's largest trash company, Waste Management, Inc. Du Pont has also formed a safety and environmental resources division to help industrial customers clean up toxic waste. The company forecasts annual revenue of $1 billion from the new business by 2000. In the spring of 1990, Varta, a German battery maker, introduced a new line of batteries without either mercury or cadmium, two toxic chemical elements that are hard to dispose of. Since then, its share of the $120 million British market has increased from 5 percent to 15 percent.

The Winter Model of Environmentalist Business Management.
One European company in the front ranks of the international
environmental movement is Ernst Winter & Sohn, a German
manufacturer of diamond tools. In 1972, Winter & Sohn officially
declared environmental protection to be one of its corporate aims.
In the late 80s, it developed a complete model for "environmentalist business management." The so-called Winter Model allows
for the systematic incorporation of environmental concerns into
every aspect of the company and provides an excellent example
for other companies to follow.

As at The Body Shop, employee education and involvement
are central features of Winter & Sohn's environmental activism.
Employees are educated about environmental issues through
seminars, lectures, articles, and even field trips. The company has
an environment manager, analogous to The Body Shop's Environmental Projects Department, who is responsible for coordinat-
ing in-house environmental activities. In addition, a committee of
representatives from various parts of the company decides on an
environmental action plan and meets periodically to audit results.
And the company elicits suggestions from the entire workforce
about environmental issues.

Winter & Sohn strives to develop environmentally benign
products and manufacturing processes. It has developed a state-
of-the-art waste disposal system that goes beyond what the law
requires. And it recycles as much material as possible.

The environmentalist model employed by Winter & Sohn extends to the company's premises, which were designed with consideration for such environmental factors as lighting, technical
equipment, and material selection. Furthermore, the company's
manufacturing plants are located only where pollution is at an
acceptable level. By deciding against heavily polluted locations,
the company tells local authorities that they should clean up their
air and tells its employees that it cares about their health.

In addition to pursuing its own environmental agenda, Winter
& Sohn actively promotes environmentalism within professional
associations in its industry. It also supports local political initiatives that promote environmentalism, and it contributes generously to environmentalist organizations. Winter & Sohn even
goes so far as to counsel employees about environmental issues in

their homes, offering advice on such things as water consumption, the use of electricity, and garden chemicals.

As a result of Winter & Sohn's leadership, and at its suggestion, several well-known European industrial companies have formed the German Environmentalist Management Society, whose acronym, BAUM, is the German word for "tree." The aim of BAUM is to spread the ideas and practices of the Winter model. It invites companies to cooperate in an international effort toward environmentalist business management. Georg Winter, CEO of Winter & Sohn, hopes to see environmentally responsible companies in other countries form organizations similar to BAUM.

25 Things Your Organization Can Do to Heal the Environment

1. Make environmentalism company policy.
2. Conduct an environmental audit of your premises (lighting, materials, etc.) to ensure that your work areas are healthy ones.
3. Buy only from environmentally responsible suppliers.
4. Recycle or reuse as much as possible.
5. Tie bonuses and promotions to environmental responsibility.
6. Train employees in environmental issues.
7. Offer counseling in employees' homes on reducing water consumption, saving energy, and other environmental issues.
8. Create an environmental department or senior position, reporting to the CEO, responsible for environmental issues.
9. Elicit employee suggestions for environmental safeguards.
10. Utilize state-of-the-art waste disposal systems.
11. Develop environmentally sound products and manufacturing processes.
12. Locate plants only in places that aren't polluted; inform local governments of your policy.
13. Promote environmentalism within your professional associations.
14. Support citizen initiatives on the environment.
15. Support environmental organizations with dollars.

16. Give employees time off to volunteer for environmental causes.
17. Eliminate paper waste by reducing memos and mailings.
18. Lower the heat.
19. Don't use tropical hardwoods in office furniture.
20. Institute telecommuting.
21. Encourage carpooling.
22. Minimize product packaging.
23. Economize on water use.
24. Write national and local governments letters pressing for environmental legislation.
25. Don't use disposable cups and plates in the office and the corporate cafeteria.

Education and the Learning Organization

A recent study by the National Assessment of Educational Progress found that only 51 percent of 17-year-olds could use fractions and decimals adequately. The same study found that students in Japan, Hong Kong, Britain, and Poland outperform their U.S. counterparts on high school chemistry and physics tests.

According to a 1988 study by the Educational Testing Service, 62 percent of American 13-year-olds spend less than one hour a week on math homework and 58 percent cannot solve simple scientific problems, such as predicting which way a plant will bend when exposed to light.

Chester Finn, Jr., a professor at Vanderbilt University, observes: "At a time when European leaders are seriously considering requiring all secondary school students to learn three languages, only 14 percent of our 11th graders can write an adequate analytic piece in English."

What does this have to do with business? In Chapter 7, William Wiggenhorn detailed the illiteracy problems that Motorola encountered. Also consider New York Life. This insurance giant sends some of its insurance forms to Ireland for processing because it cannot find enough qualified clerks in the United States.

Or consider Baldor Electric. This maker of industrial motors had installed a high-tech "flexible flow" manufacturing system at its plant in Columbus, Mississippi, and the computer-generated work orders clearly told employees *not* to weld the shafts to the rotors of some new motors. Yet some employees were doing exactly that. Chairman Roland Boreham, Jr., was puzzled: "These were good guys. Why didn't they read the damn orders?" Boreham went to the plant to investigate—and found that many of Baldor's veteran employees simply couldn't *read* the instructions.

These are by no means exceptional examples. Workforce illiteracy is becoming a critical problem, according to a study by The Conference Board, a New York–based research organization. "Illiteracy has been a softly ticking time bomb across corporate America," said Leonard Lund, education specialist of The Conference Board. "While precise data are not available, the evidence strongly suggests that the workforce skills of many youngsters are declining at a time when new jobs are becoming increasingly sophisticated."

Nearly 20 percent of the 163 large corporations that the Conference Board study surveyed reported problems in finding people who could read well enough for entry-level jobs. Almost half of these corporations said that between 15 percent and 35 percent of their workers could not handle more complex tasks, and 10 percent of the corporations said that up to half of their workers did not have the skills necessary for promotion.

These statistics have alarming implications for business in the Age of Learning, an age in which the entire organization must become an institution for continuous learning. Writing in *PowerShift*, Alvin Toffler declares: "The most important economic development of our lifetime has been the rise of a new system for creating wealth, based no longer on muscle but on mind." Toffler warns: "The rising importance of mind-work will not go away, no matter how many scare stories are published warning about the dire consequences of a 'vanishing' manufacturing base or deriding the concept of the 'information economy.' Neither will the conception of how wealth is created (through knowledge, not physical labor)."

Education, more than the environment, is an area in which companies are beginning to discover their connection with the larger society, a connection that is becoming painfully obvious, as the Motorola, New York Life, and Baldor Electric stories illustrate. David Kearns, CEO of Xerox, speaks for a growing number of corporate leaders when he declares: "I think most chief executives understand this now: Business needs to be involved, not for some social reason, but for hard economic reasons. We can't continue to sit here in this nice environment if the rest of society collapses. We have to figure out an answer."

"Figuring out an answer" is taking up a significant chunk of time in major corporations these days, as managers struggle to cope with a workforce that lacks basic skills, much less the ability to meet increasingly sophisticated job requirements.

Kearns and some other CEOs are getting directly involved. The Xerox chief and his wife "adopted" Zach Harris, a young man from inner-city Columbus, Ohio. For three years, they acted as surrogate parents, taking him on school trips and advising him on college. Eventually he went to the University of Rochester, Kearns's alma mater, and took a long-term position at Xerox.

ARCO president Robert Wycoff spent a day as principal of Manual Arts High School in south-central Los Angeles, listening to students talk about their needs and offering management advice to teachers about shared decision making. In all, over 40 local business leaders from such companies as GTE, Hughes Aircraft, and Bank of America participated in the Principal for a Day program, part of a week-long drive sponsored by the Los Angeles Educational Partnership to encourage business involvement with schools.

While some may argue that such involvement is more symbolic than substantive, it sends an important message from the top that reverberates throughout the organization. Not coincidentally, companies whose CEOs are personally involved in education are also making company-wide contributions. Xerox and ARCO, for example, are considered leaders in this area.

Corporations are responding in growing numbers and in myriad ways to the educational challenge. Some companies are adopting classes of schoolchildren or entire schools. Merrill Lynch, to name one, is paying for the higher education (college or vocational-technical training) of 250 first graders from 10 U.S. inner-city schools.

Instead of supporting the community at large, some companies are focusing on the educational needs of employees' families. Nucor has a plan that provides $1,500 a year, for four years, to help pay for the post–high school education or vocational training of its employees' children. In one recent year, 260 children of Nucor employees were attending 120 learning institutions throughout the country on Nucor scholarships.

Other companies are setting up their own schools for the children of employees. In 1987, American Bankers Insurance Group of Miami started the first of such "satellite schools" on a patch of land next to its headquarters. A kindergarten was set up in conjunction with the Dade County public school system, which provides the teachers and curriculum.

The experiment has measurably improved productivity at ABIG. Absenteeism among parents whose children were enrolled in the corporate kindergarten dropped 30 percent and turnover declined by 10 percent. The company also discovered that having a school for employees' children was an attractive recruitment factor. In 1988 the curriculum was expanded to include first grade; the following year, second grade was added.

Business-education partnerships have been growing in popularity. At least six other Florida companies, including Honeywell and The Twin Towers Hotel and Convention Center in Orlando, have established schools for the children of their employees. And the ABIG prototype is being studied by corporations all over the country.

Other innovative approaches to partnership between business and education are being tried. Coca-Cola recently experimented with a $400,000 dropout prevention program in San Antonio, focusing on two of the city's school districts and a group of 500 Hispanic high school students and seventh and eighth graders who, on the basis of their poor performance, had a 95 percent chance of dropping out. Each week the members of this group tutored kindergartners and first graders for an hour at a nearby elementary school, earning the minimum wage for the work.

The program was a resounding success, forcing the participants to polish up their basic skills and generating increased self-esteem among them. Since the start of the program, the dropout rate among the participants has plummeted to less than 5 percent. Coca-Cola has targeted an additional $1.4 million to expand the program.

Until the 1980s, businesses primarily supported colleges and vocational schools. But as a result of a growing understanding that early intervention can make a significant difference, more and more businesses have been funneling money into elementary and secondary education.

ARCO is a good example. Prior to 1980, ARCO's contributions to education went almost entirely to research at private universities. But after making an extensive investigation, the company decided to switch its focus. In 1990, 60 percent of its education budget went to educational reform for kindergarten through the 12th grade. Many companies are following ARCO's lead.

Donating computers is another way in which companies are contributing to the cause of education. Computer-based learning is not only an effective way to capture the attention of a generation of schoolchildren raised on Nintendo; it is also an effective way of imparting an understanding of computers, a key prerequisite for functioning effectively in an era of rapidly advancing technology.

Not surprisingly, Apple and IBM are the leaders in computer donations. Apple has donated over $60 million in computers and equipment to schools since 1979, and it has spent millions more each year researching the impact of technology on teaching and learning. IBM has donated $50 million in computers and training since 1979, and it plans to spend another $50 million during the next five years.

In addition to supporting schools through donations of money and equipment, corporations are offering schools their management expertise. What corporate America learned in the 1980s about organizational restructuring and participative management is being passed along to educational institutions, which are struggling with the same issues in the 1990s. IBM, Xerox, and AT&T are three leaders in this area, offering teachers, principals, and administrators the same training that they give to their own managers in such areas as teamwork, leadership, and communications.

Increasingly, corporations have been tackling educational issues through the political system. John Akers, CEO of IBM, chairs the education task force of The Business Roundtable, an organization of 200 CEOs from the largest American corporations. Akers has persuaded 165 of these CEOs to adopt a state and to work closely with its governor, legislators, and educators in passing and implementing laws requiring systemic change in the school system. And in 1989, a group of California companies that included Pacific Bell, and Lockheed successfully lobbied the state legislature for $14 million to support technology in schools.

As more corporations recognize at a core level the symbiotic relationship between an educated society and a productive workforce, such activist involvement in the future of American education is becoming a standard feature of their operations.

But it's not just the productivity of the workforce or the competitiveness of American business that is at stake; also at stake is the quality of life of the nation as a whole. An illiterate populace cannot build a society with purpose and vision, a society that promises a high quality of life to all its members. This is perhaps the most important rationale for corporate contributions to the future of education. Thomas Kean, former governor of New Jersey, puts the issue in perspective: "When you put risk capital into a school, you are not just investors with an eye to the bottom line. You are elders looking to the survival of the culture."

25 Things Your Organization Can Do to Further Education
1. Institute in-house remedial reading programs.
2. Adopt a school, offering scholarships for students who stay in school.
3. Start a scholarship fund for the children of employees.
4. Offer students internships and summer jobs.
5. Contribute computers to schools.
6. Give employees time off to serve as volunteers in schools.
7. Hold on-site computer training classes.
8. Lobby your state legislature for more money for schools.
9. Support primary and secondary education with dollars.
10. Start a dropout prevention program with a local school.
11. Open a satellite school for the children of employees.
12. Offer management support to schools.
13. Work with state legislators and educators toward school reform.
14. Sponsor science fairs or other schoolwide learning projects.
15. Encourage other companies within your industry to support educational institutions.

16. Invite teachers at local schools to visit the company in order to learn about educational needs in specific areas.
17. Serve as a coach/support person for a student in a local elementary school or high school.
18. Donate the books, equipment, etc. that local public schools need.
19. Develop an in-house basic skills program for entry-level workers.
20. Tie bonuses and promotions in part to managers' involvement in educational issues.
21. Pay for the outside schooling of employees, at local institutions or through correspondence courses.
22. Institute internal "teaching" awards for employees who excel in educating others.
23. Get the CEO involved in the local school system—as a speaker, a part-time teacher, a sponsor for a student, etc.
24. Sponsor university-level research into new educational methods.
25. Support government educational programs such as Head Start.

MODELS OF SOCIAL CONTRIBUTION

There is no single blueprint for the "socially responsible organization." The methods, motivations, and extent of corporate social contributions vary across a broad spectrum. Some companies focus squarely on environmental issues; others are known for their involvement in education. Some companies send their employees out into the community; others offer solely financial support. Most companies utilize a variety of approaches to giving. A few, such as The Body Shop, have reconciled a strong commitment to social responsibility with running a very profitable business. This reconciliation becomes the raison d'être of the enterprise.

If we think of social contribution as a continuum ranging from the traditional philanthropy practiced by such old story industrialists as Andrew Carnegie and the Mellons to the practices of such companies as The Body Shop, for which social responsibility is a central attribute, we can broadly divide organizations into four models of social contribution. The point is not to label organizations according to these models or to imply that one model is superior to another. Rather, it is to show that corporate social responsibility has evolved in a manner that roughly corresponds to the models and that parallels a gradual change from old story consciousness to new story consciousness.

Model 1: Traditional Philanthropy

The most common form of social responsibility in the old story industrial era, and a form still practiced, is traditional philanthropy—monetary contributions to social causes. Under this model, the amounts and recipients of corporate bequests are determined by the CEO or a handful of senior executives. Employees have little or no say about where the money goes, and the corporation does not attempt to track its donations to ascertain their impact. Furthermore, giving is discretionary; there is no built-in mechanism for guaranteeing continued contributions once the CEO or other philanthropically minded executive leaves the company.

A distinguishing feature of traditional philanthropy is that the company, while supporting social concerns, sees no real connection between itself and the larger community. It views society as something "out there" to which contributions are made. This can lead to major contradictions between a company's practices and its philanthropic activities—for example, the sponsorship of tennis tournaments by Virginia Slims cigarettes. Companies that see no real connection between themselves and the larger community often regard philanthropy more as a goodwill gesture or a sound public relations strategy than as a vehicle for expressing true social concern.

An extreme example of this mentality can be found in a speech in which George Weissman, CEO of Philip Morris, argued that a corporation "must consider its expenditures for corporate social responsibility as seriously as it considers expenditures for marketing, administration, and the other costs of doing business." He then asked rhetorically, "Does all that responsibility pay off?" His answer:

What I do know is what's happened to Philip Morris in the 35 years I have been with the company. We have gone from sixth place to become the largest cigarette manufacturer in the United States. . . . So while I can't tell you that being actively responsible has helped us, I sure can tell you that it hasn't hurt.

As James O'Toole points out, Weissman apparently didn't see the irony of referring to "all that responsibility" in one breath and in the next breath boasting about his company's success in producing a questionable product. This is not to say that companies engaged in traditional philanthropy necessarily exhibit such schizophrenia. However, their failure to grasp their connection with the larger society, to appreciate the true meaning of "social responsibility," can result in such glaring inconsistencies.

Model 2: Low Partnership

The Low Partnership model of contribution is another form of corporate responsibility. Under this model, the corporation sees some connection between itself and the larger community. Its social contributions extend beyond simple philanthropy to active involvement with the community. Conversely, it allows the concerns of the community (including the concerns of its employee/ citizens) to affect its internal operations.

Companies practicing the Low Partnership model of social contribution encourage their employees to volunteer for community activities. The range of involvement can vary widely. Employees may do anything from donating blood, participating in a walkathon to support a local cause, or engineering a neighborhood cleanup to taking on large-scale community projects.

For example, Aetna Life & Casualty employees staff a volunteer lawyers' project that offers free legal assistance to elderly low-income people. General Mills, Honeywell, and Shell Oil have programs that involve retirees in voluntarism in their communities. In addition to donating money and computer equipment, IBM engages in a wide range of activities that reach out into the community. Its Community Service Assignment Program allows selected employees to take paid leaves to work on community projects. It also lends employees, whose full salaries it continues to pay, to universities, colleges, and high schools with large numbers of minority or disadvantaged students, usually for a full academic year. IBM also supports community job training centers, and it teams up with universities, research groups, and government agencies to address problems by developing new computer applications.

Under the Low Partnership model, social responsibility is practiced within the company as well as outside its walls. The company applying this model might invest in child care facilities, remedial learning centers, or other facilities or programs that address the broader needs of employees. For example, among the broad range of America West's employee benefits is round-the-clock child care, which the company offers in acknowledgment of the connection between the working lives and the personal lives of its employees. And in response to its employees' request for help, PC Connection went so far as to build housing for them and to sell it to them at cost.

This model also includes policies and practices whose purpose is to ensure that the company will not benefit at the expense of its employees or society. For example, the company of one of our interviewees declined to accept a contract with a cigarette manufacturer because the contract specified that it reverse its "no smoking" policy. And Herman Miller discontinued the use of rosewood in its office furniture in response to a growing environmental concern over the depletion of tropical rain forests.

Unlike traditional philanthropy, these companies contribute funds where they will have a significant impact and track the results of the programs funded. Employees have some input into the selection of the projects funded and the community activities undertaken. Furthermore, social contribution is not dependent on who happens to be the CEO. It is built into corporate operations, via the mission statement, policy statements, and other enduring mechanisms.

Although Model 2 acknowledges the link between the corporation and society, it does so within the context of a traditional old story hierarchy. Greater employee participation may be allowed by companies employing this model, for example, but a strong vertical chain of command remains intact. What distinguishes Low Partnership from the next model, High Partnership, is the amount of learning that takes place within the organization *because of* its social contributions. In the Low Partnership model, social contribution has little, if any, impact on the day-to-day internal workings of the organization. In the next model, the information and skills gained through its contributory activities feed back as lessons for the organization as a whole.

---

25 Things Your Organization Can Do to Support Your Community

1. Organize a neighborhood cleanup project.
2. Support or start a community job training center.
3. Offer free legal assistance to needy area residents.
4. Organize a walkathon to promote a community cause.
5. Hold a blood drive on the company premises.
6. Adopt a nursing home, and support it with employee volunteers.
7. Lobby local, state, and national legislators about community issues.
8. Sponsor an AIDS Awareness Week.
9. Offer funding and volunteers to a local drug rehabilitation center.
10. Join with local banks to develop an affordable housing program.
11. Wage a community literacy campaign.
12. Sponsor an entrepreneurship program for area high school students.
13. Support a local children's hospital.
14. Train high schoolers in the community in career development and interviewing skills.
15. Support a child abuse program.
16. Sponsor a center for the homeless.
17. Donate excess inventory to local schools, churches, etc.
18. Offer employees sabbaticals for work on major community projects.
19. Invite community organizations to speak to employees about their needs.
20. Donate advertising help and/or money to nonprofit groups.
21. Get retirees involved in community volunteering.

22. Help develop a business for inmates within the local prison system.
23. Develop a hiring/training program for ex-inmates.
24. Collect clothing and food on an ongoing basis, and deliver them to needy families in the community.
25. Provide the elderly with telephone reassurance and "check-ups."

Model 3: High Partnership

The High Partnership model of social responsibility builds on the Low Partnership model. Under Model 3, organizations clearly recognize the connection between their self-interest and the interests of the larger society (including their own employee/citizens) and fundamentally change their structure and functioning as a result of that recognition. Internally, they adopt a networking structure in order to maximize the participation of all employees. They focus on teamwork, value and incorporate diversity, hire employees who exhibit new story values, and reward their employees generously. Externally, they are proactive in their support of social and environmental causes. For example, they view environmentalists as allies rather than enemies. In their internal dealings and in their dealings with customers, suppliers, the community, and other outsiders, they strive for partnership. High partnership companies realize that from the vantage point of society, the corporation *must* be one of us.

Under Model 3, as under Model 2, social concern is not discretionary but built into the business. And employees have a significant say in what social causes the company will support.

Many of the organizations we discuss in this book practice the High Partnership model of social responsibility. Levi Strauss is a good example. It is known for its social responsibility to the communities in which it operates around the world and for its dedication to partnership with its employees, embodied in its Aspirations Statement. It consistently receives high ratings both as a social contributor and as a desirable place to work.

Model 4: Ecobusiness

Companies that base themselves on the Ecobusiness model not only make social contribution a standard feature of their operations but view it as a primary reason for their existence. In these companies, social concern is woven into the very fabric of the organization. They see themselves as an integral part of the community, as holons within a larger holarchy. There is considerable consistency between the internal and external behaviors and policies of these companies. Their decisions and policies balance the interests of the holon with those of the larger holarchy.

Ecobusinesses provide high-quality products and processes that show concern for customers as much as concern for profits. They minimize environmental disruption by recycling, using recyclable materials, developing pollution-free production processes, and supporting environmental research. They promote social equality within and outside the corporation. Internally, they view and treat employees as fully participating partners within a networking organization that allows for individual growth and development. Externally, they support causes that enhance the growth and development of the community as a whole. Profits are then considered crucial to the health of the organization whose mission is social responsibility.

This central focus on social responsibility is the main characteristic that distinguishes the Ecobusiness model from the High Partnership model. This focus separates these exceptional companies from very fine companies that view social concern as a responsibility but not as the central value of the company.

The Ecobusiness model represents the truest expression of the new story of business. Not surprisingly, this model is more an ideal than a reality. The Body Shop, with its focus on employee development, its extraordinary concern for customers, and its no-holds-barred support of global social and environmental issues, is a company that comes close to realizing the potential of the Ecobusiness model.

The Spectrum of Contribution

While I have cited specific examples of companies that exemplify one or another of the four models presented above, I do not mean to suggest that any company falls squarely into one or another of these categories. For example, it is not uncommon for a company that gives away a lump sum of money with no strings attached in one area (Model 1) also to integrate contributions with voluntarism and track the effects of funding in another area (Model 2). The point of the models is not to label companies but to suggest the broad range of their possible contributions and to demonstrate how they evolve as they develop a greater awareness of their interdependence with the communities outside their walls.

TARGETED CONTRIBUTION

Sun Microsystems, in the heart of California's Silicon Valley, is generous in its financial contributions to the communities that surround it. But it is quite selective about the areas in which it makes those contributions, and it offers no apologies for excluding a broad range of causes. The company focuses its grant-giving on economics education, job training, leadership, and business enterprise development, on what CEO Scott McNeally calls "capacity building" programs, for the emerging ethnic population in the Silicon Valley.

Mark Vermilion explains:

It is a philosophical approach some people don't particularly care for because it excludes certain areas of funding. Our belief is that there are many problems in society. But it's our belief that for the time being at least we want to prioritize our giving and focus on community economic development. We are prepared to say, "Yes, we have made a choice, we can't be all things to all people, but these areas are the most critical, we think, to us and to our surrounding communities. So that is what we will concentrate on, given the resource base we have—to donate to those areas. We do, of course, support employee donations with direct matching company grants to the arts, for instance.

Vermilion elaborated on the rationale for Sun's focus on community development:

We might give a grant to a program to help kids within grades 7–12, to promote them staying in school, because if they don't stay in school, graduate, and go on to college, they will not be a contributor to the workforce, they will not be part of the economic system, the successful part of the system.

He added:

For minority communities and other communities to really participate in the economy, they have to be more than consumers. They need to understand how they can create an economic unit, create jobs, and through being successful, pay taxes and develop their own ability to create economic wealth. And so we support job training, leadership development, and entrepreneurial programs.

Sun Microsystems is not alone. More and more companies are forgoing traditional contributions in favor of putting their money —and, increasingly, their time—where they feel it will have the greatest impact. The old story approach of "throwing dollars at a program" (often out of a sense of guilt or a passion for public relations) is being replaced by an emphasis on ensuring that the dollars and days donated make a difference.

One reason for the trend toward targeted contributions is that a combination of factors, including foreign competition, restructuring, mergers and acquisitions, and declining profits, have put a squeeze on the contributions budgets of many organizations. As a result, corporate executives have been taking a hard look at where they donate their dollars and their time.

Such focused giving can make a significant difference to the community. Take General Electric. GE, which relies heavily on scientists, has been a steady contributor to science and engineering in universities over the years. In 1980, it decided to shift its emphasis to primary and secondary schools. GE helped turn around Benjamin Franklin High School, a drug-infested institution in Manhattan's Spanish Harlem. It was considered one of New York City's worst schools, and only 7 percent of its students graduated. In 1982, it became the Manhattan Center for Science and Mathematics. GE developed some of the curriculum and set up a CAD/CAM lab. It created the GE Scholars program, picking the top 20 or 30 juniors for special courses and assigning each of them a coach from the company. It brought in an SAT prep course that raised the school's average scores 170 points. Children from around the city, nearly all of them minorities, compete for admission now. The overwhelming majority of those selected for the program—96 percent of the seniors—go on to college.

Control Data: Social Contribution as Business Venture

Control Data has taken the notion of targeted contributions one step further. Well known for its long history of social involvement, CDC is equally well known for never throwing money at a problem. In fact, its focus is not on contributions at all, but rather on *building businesses as a way of contributing.* It addresses major social problems by developing moneymaking enterprises.

With this objective in mind, Control Data has established a broad range of business partnerships with the community, including such enterprises as the City Venture Corporation, which supports businesses in the inner city, and Rural Venture, Inc., which was set up to help small family farms become more efficient.

Control Data even turns internal company programs into businesses. It started the first employee assistance program in this country—then began selling it to other companies. In 1990, this program covered CDC employees and 250,000 employees in 155 other firms.

CDC does not focus on "easy wins." Over the years, it has established three successful manufacturing plants in the inner city and another in the most impoverished section of Appalachia. In addition, it sent six of its manufacturing executives to help audit the Minnesota prison industries program and recommend changes. And at the request of an inmate serving a life sentence, CDC helped establish an in-prison program that allows inmates to pursue college courses and receive degrees from the University of Minnesota. It supplied funding and computer terminals to help launch the program, which quickly became self-supporting, with the inmates developing a successful telemarketing business whose profits were used to pay for tuition and books.

As a result of this experience, CDC began marketing computer terminals to prisons throughout the United States. The terminals are being used, among other things, to deliver basic skills remediation course work and employment preparation courses.

THE MOVE TOWARD SOCIAL RESPONSIBILITY: SIGNS OF PROGRESS

Allen Hershkowitz is an expert on solid-waste disposal at the Natural Resources Defense Council. He has won many legal battles with big business. Now high-ranking executives visit him to make sure that their companies won't be added to his "hit list." As Hershkowitz puts it: "They come in here to see what they've got to cover their asses on." He adds: "My primary motivation is environmental protection. And if it costs more, so be it. If Procter & Gamble can't live with that, somebody else will. But I'll tell you, Procter & Gamble is trying hard to live with it."

Whatever their motivations, a growing number of companies are making social contribution an integral part of their business operations. One telling statistic: All but 7 of the 305 Fortune 500 and Service 500 companies that responded to a 1990 *Fortune* survey of educational contributions reported that they were involved in supporting public education. Nearly a third said that they contributed between $100,000 and $500,000 annually to public schools, and 18 percent said that they contributed $1 million or more annually. Furthermore, 70 percent of the top executives of these companies reported that they were actively involved in their companies' educational contributions.

As American corporations become more involved in social and environmental issues, organizations are springing up to recognize and encourage their efforts. Each year the Council on Economic Priorities hands out awards to "honor an exemplary program which . . . serves as a model [of social responsibility] for other corporations to emulate." In 1990, the award recipients included AT&T, which was selected because of its environmental stewardship in the form of a program to end all use of CFCs by 1994 and probably earlier; Cummins Engine Company, which was recognized for giving 5 percent of its average domestic pretax profits to charity and for encouraging employee input into its grant making; and US West, which was honored for its strides in supporting workforce diversity by sponsoring employee support groups. (The CEP also bestows honorable—and *dishonorable*—

mentions. In 1990, Exxon was a "winner" in the latter category, for being unprepared to meet one of the worst environmental disasters in U.S. history.)

In 1989, Norman Lear founded the Business Enterprise Trust in order to "identify and promote acts of social responsibility." The Business Enterprise Awards, bestowed by the trust, are meant to recognize socially responsible businesses, and thereby to increase awareness and inspire others. "I believe in the creative power of good examples," says Lear.

Perhaps the brightest sign of progress is the small but growing number of start-up companies that are devoted exclusively to the pursuit of environmental and social concerns. Stephen Garey & Associates and Working Assets Money Fund are two notable examples. Garey's company is perhaps the first U.S. ad agency to be devoted exclusively to the promotion of environmental health. It will take on as a client "any firm whose product, service, and method of manufacturing brings no harm" to the planet.

Working Assets, led by Frank Tsai, is one of the country's most successful money market funds. Its mission, says Tsai, is to "promote the use of financially sound products and services consistent with a commitment to peace, maintaining a healthy environment, social justice, and other concerns." He adds: "Although you learn in business school that a corporation's main objective is to maximize shareholder wealth, we feel that's not the only objective; it must also make a contribution to the community."

All the major vendors of Working Assets are screened in the same way as potential investments are screened. First, they are checked for creditworthiness. Once they pass that financial screening, they are screened in five key areas: (1) Are they involved in South Africa? (2) Are they involved with nuclear power? (3) What percentage of their total revenues comes from defense contracts? (4) How do they treat their employees? and (5) What are they doing to the environment?

As Working Assets continues to grow, the company faces new challenges, according to Tsai: "We're still exploring, we're still learning, and we're still making mistakes. One thing that we're considering for next year is to have what has been called a 'social audit' done on ourselves to identify some of the weaknesses we might have."

It is important to note that even companies thoroughly dedicated to social responsibility, such as Working Assests, are not perfect. No company can claim to be flawless, no matter how ethical or responsible it is. Despite its strong commitment to ethics, Johnson & Johnson maintains its testing on animals, a fact that would cause many socially responsible investors to eliminate it from consideration. Levi Strauss, for all its exemplary social contributions, lays off U.S. workers in favor of cheaper foreign labor in order to be "competitive." Both of these companies raise troubling questions about reconciling profits with social concerns.

Another company praised for its environmental concern is Wal-Mart. Yet an awareness of living systems must take into account *all* of the environment, including the community in which one operates. Having become the largest retailer in the country, Wal-Mart often looks like (and some say, acts like) Goliath to the small retailers in the small towns where it builds its stores.

One study cited in *The Wall Street Journal* found that competition from Wal-Mart caused sales of specialty retailers in 15 Iowa towns to drop 12.1 percent in a three-year period. More than 80 percent of Wal-Mart's sales can come at the expense of other local businesses that struggle to compete with Wal-Mart's low discount prices and wide selection. The resentment can be strong: "I'd have liked to engage the National Guard to fire five rounds of a 105 millimeter Howitzer through their front door," says druggist Mons Langhus of Anamosa, Iowa.

Wal-Mart contends that its arrival creates a retail hub that attracts business from outside the community and helps to "plug retail leakage" from the community. The retail giant makes no bones about the fact that it's very difficult to compete with them on price. One solution: Local retailers are beginning to learn to compete more effectively by cooperating and networking with one another.

Few would consider Johnson & Johnson, Levi Strauss, or Wal-Mart to be socially irresponsible, despite their flaws. These anecdotes point out the complexity of evolving systems. There is no need to disqualify the efforts of transforming organizations just because they are "imperfect" in certain areas. There are no simple or permanent solutions to complex questions of ethics and social responsibility. The point is not to search for perfection—even if we could define it—but to highlight examples of commitment to social responsibility that others can build on.

Nor are there final solutions in an ever-changing world. For example, what was deemed environmentally responsible behavior in 1950 would be considered irresponsible today, in light of our vastly increased knowledge. In a living, changing system, the corporation must continually learn and correct course—reevaluating its practices, examining alternatives, and developing new temporary solutions.

To complicate the discussion further, there is often widespread disagreement about what constitutes an acceptable solution to a social or environmental problem. For example, while some environmentalists congratulate Du Pont for deciding to halt the production of CFCs by the year 2000, others have called for an end to CFC production well before 2000 to prevent an increase in skin cancer rates.

Du Pont executives point out that most of the existing cooling equipment uses CFC refrigerants and that none of the proposed replacements will work without substantial modifications to that equipment. "There is $135 billion in air-conditioning and refrigeration equipment in the United States alone," according to Bruce Karrh, vice president for safety, health, and environmental affairs at Du Pont. " One reason we can't immediately stop making CFCs is that the equipment manufacturers have to make new equipment to use the new products. We think it would be irresponsible if we arbitrarily stopped." Which side is right?

Stephen Garey, for one, wants the corporation bashing to stop: "Abe Lincoln once said, 'You don't help the wage earner by bringing down the wage payer.' One of the things that I would like to see stopped is the pointing of blame at the corporations. I would like to see this end as soon as possible. We're all responsible, we're all involved, we're all on a learning curve. No one could have known the impact that our industrial society was to have, although some saw it—some farsighted, visionary individuals. Still, as we were going along, the benefits of it overwhelmed the environmental impact."

Even Allen Hershkowitz of the NRDC is no purist: "Hey, civilization has its costs. We're trying to reduce them, but we can't eliminate them."

The Importance of Being Earnest: Does Motivation Matter?

Some wonder whether companies are getting the religion of social responsibility out of fear of adverse public relations and more stringent government regulations rather than out of a genuine concern for the welfare of society and the environment. Others wonder whether social and environmental responsibility have become just another way to make a fast buck.

Does motivation matter, so long as a company is pursuing a sound social agenda? The answer is yes or no—depending on whom you ask.

One manifestation of "social responsibility" that is raising eyebrows in some quarters is "cause-related marketing," a marketing strategy in which a company contributes to a cause when customers buy its products. American Express introduced the idea with its program to contribute one cent to the restoration of the Statue of Liberty for each use of its charge cards.

Advocates say that everybody wins with cause-related marketing. The marketer gets exposure for its product, while the non-profit partner gains visibility and funding. But critics are fearful that cause-related marketing will ultimately hurt nonprofit partners by tying funding to marketing benefits and that it will skew support in favor of established, noncontroversial causes whose results can easily be tracked—which are not necessarily the most worthy causes.

Mark Vermilion of Sun Microsystems sees another problem with social-responsibility-as-marketing-strategy. He believes that when the going gets tough, corporate social contributions will fall by the wayside: "I think motivation matters a lot. If someone is motivated for the wrong reasons, if a company engages in sort of puff community relations, puff pieces, or puff grants, or something that doesn't have the right motivations behind it, and if it is only done for publicity, when times do get tough, those programs will dry up fast. They will just go away very, very quickly. They have no depth to them."

Working Assets founder Frank Tsai has a different point of view. Tsai suggests that motivation may not matter in the long run, because companies start to behave responsibly, *for whatever reason*, they raise the public's awareness of social issues and create an expectation among the public that they will continue to behave responsibly.

Tsai says he doesn't care what executives' motives are, as long as they do the right thing. He concedes: "People do the right thing for the wrong reasons. To me, it doesn't make any difference why they are doing it. I can't judge somebody else's motivations, so it doesn't matter. We look at the behavior of investment candidates, and if their behavior is what we think and we call 'socially responsible,' then we are going to identify them as a socially responsible company. To me, it doesn't make any difference; I can't judge motivation."

What *is* important, Tsai believes, is for the public to demand social responsibility: "I think the community has to expect [socially responsible behavior] from its businesses. We do a fair amount of letter writing to our companies, and even if we don't invest in them, we still send them a letter saying, 'This is why we are not investing in you. If you change your behavior in this certain way, we will reconsider our decision.' And I think more people have to take that step. We will never have the shareholder strength to force a company to do it. But I think the force of public image will help do it."

DO PROFITS AND SOCIAL RESPONSIBILITY MIX?

Levi Strauss patriarch Walter Haas, Jr., gave a speech in 1990 to introduce 40 owners of small businesses in Emeryville, California, to the idea of philanthropy. He told his audience: "Some people argue that doing what's right is somehow contrary to doing what's good for business. I find this view both puzzling and wrong. In my own company, we have learned over and over again that when we do what we believe is proper, the company gains. I don't know how to translate that value into a number that appears on a financial statement, but I do know that we wouldn't want to be in business and we would not be the leader in our industry if we did not enjoy this kind of relationship with our people."

And Frank Tsai, of Working Assets, points out: "There's no indicator that says you cannot earn equal or better returns on making social investments. Our gross yields are comparable to anybody in money market funds. We wanted to show individuals

"Safety? Of course we're committed to safety—we're committed to safety and any other damn thing that sells cars."

Drawing used with permission of William Hamilton.

and institutions that you can promote social change and still make a decent return."

The Body Shop is certainly living proof that a company thoroughly committed to social responsibility can also be a financial success. As Anita Roddick puts it: "We are walking with our talk. And still doing OK financially." To say that The Body Shop is "doing OK financially" is a gross understatement. For more than 10 of the 15 years that it has been in business, its sales have grown an average of 50 percent a year. In London financial circles, The Body Shop stock is referred to as the "shares that defy gravity."

It is not that profits are unimportant to Levi Strauss, Working Assets, The Body Shop, and other socially concerned companies; it's just that they are not the central priority. Says Anita Roddick: "Profits are an integral part [of the business], but you do something more, beyond your own accumulation of material wealth.

You do something more which spiritually enhances you or edu-
cates you."

Paradoxically, companies that focus on values instead of profits
often end up enhancing their profit picture as a result. U.C.L.A.
business professor Bill Ouchi observes that "among the fastest-
growing, most profitable major American firms . . . profits are
regarded not as an end in itself nor as the method of keeping
score in the competitive process. Rather, profits are the reward to
the firm as it continues to provide true value to its customers, to
help its employees to grow, and to behave responsibly as a corporate citizen." Maybe Adam Smith had it backward. There is reason to suggest that companies ensure their own interest by promoting the public interest, rather than the opposite.

In addition to generating monetary rewards, social investments
generate less obvious returns. The socially responsible actions of
Levi Strauss generate a high level of goodwill. "During our most
difficult crisis, when we were closing plants, we had to close one
in Arkansas," says Martha Montag-Brown, a former director of
community affairs at Levi. "We were a major employer, and it
was going to have a big impact on the community. We anticipated
negative press. Instead, the paper read: 'Arkadelphia Loses Best
Friend.' Every agency in the community offered help and set up
services in the plant."

While the effect of such goodwill is hard to quantify, it unquestionably contributes to the firm's financial stability by winning the
loyalty of suppliers, retailers, and employees—not to mention the
all-important customers, who are becoming increasingly sophisticated shoppers. A 1989 poll conducted by Opinion Research Corporation shows that a company's reputation often determines
which products 89 percent of adults will buy—and which they
will not buy. Not long after the Valdez oil spill, 41 percent of
Americans were angry enough to say that they would seriously
consider boycotting Exxon. And public pressure forced H. J.
Heinz, which sells Starkist tuna, to stop buying tuna harvested in
drift nets that also capture dolphins, which drown in their attempts to escape.

Social responsibility also profits companies by enabling them to
recruit a high quality labor force. Georg Winter writes about the
disenchantment of young workers with corporations' lack of environmental concern: "[A] lot of young people are asking themselves quite seriously what is the point in diligence and hard

work. To pollute waste waters even more and to add yet more pollution to the beaches? Why, they wonder, should they get to work on time every morning just to help create more refuse and add more pollution to the community's drinking supplies? Why, they wonder, should they produce high quality work just to generate profits for a factory whose inadequately filtered flue gases are polluting the environment and ruining people's health?" Companies that exhibit socially responsible behavior, that don't require employees to sell their souls in exchange for their paychecks, are rewarded by attracting a more dedicated, loyal, high quality workforce.

Patricia Gallup, CEO of PC Connection, believes that the company's social involvement has helped it attract high-caliber employees in an area where unemployment is virtually nil: "The publicity we received in areas such as recycling, historic research, and employee benefits encouraged people to apply to the company. People look at what we are doing and say, 'This is the type of company that I really would like to be involved with.'" And Anita Roddick believes that The Body Shop's activist involvement and commitment to values generate the incredible loyalty of her staff, who she flatly states, "will not leave us to work anywhere else."

There is yet another powerful way in which companies benefit from social responsibility. It has to do, not with the bottom line, but with the enrichment of the human spirit.

Levi Strauss's Community Involvement Teams consist of employees who volunteer their time to review the needs of the local community, then develop and implement projects to meet those needs. The payoff is not just to the communities that are helped, according to Bob Dunn, the company's vice president for community affairs: "I have seen people whose lives have been transformed. There is much talk about the need 'out there.' We don't focus enough on what people get by doing this work—how it satisfies their need to apply their skills for a useful purpose." In short, giving helps the donor as well as the recipient.

REWRITING THE BOOK ON BUSINESS

Charles Hampden-Turner writes: "Corporations have great power, and where that power is humanized, lasting and significant changes can occur to the very fabric of our society." As we approach the new millennium, as we come face-to-face with the negative consequences of our old story ways, we can, by a shift in our thinking and a will to change, embrace a new story of business, one that will contribute to the health of the global community instead of profiting at its expense.

Business as a collective body represents the most influential institution in the world. Like it or not, the values adopted by the corporation of the 1990s will, to a great extent, determine the quality of life on the planet as we enter the next millennium. As Mark Vermilion of Sun Microsystems sees it: "It is with business where the hope lies for any kind of change. Government can mandate, the nonprofit sector can intervene and in some cases advocate and in some cases confront—but it will need to be business that changes things, because it is the economic engine of society."

A small but vocal minority of new story leaders are charting a new course for the corporation. Leaders like Anita Roddick and companies like The Body Shop are showing the way to an enlightened partnership between business and society, a partnership in which economic, environmental, and social ends merge rather than compete. Such a partnership mutually optimizes the needs of all stakeholders—employees, customers, suppliers, the community, and the environment, as well as shareholders.

Roddick believes that by the year 2000 The Body Shop model of corporate social responsibility will be adopted on a wide scale: "I think it's going to be the norm. I would think you will have businesses where the bottom line is absolutely where it should be, at the bottom. . . . I think there are going to be far more socially responsible products and responsible services which are going to be demanded from the marketplace."

Roddick is optimistic about the possibilities inherent in the new vision of business as a fully participating partnership: "Business does not have to be drudgery. It doesn't have to be the science of making money. It is something that people—employees, customers, suppliers, franchisees—can genuinely feel great about, but only on one condition: The company must never let itself become anything other than a human enterprise. I think you can trade ethically; be committed to social responsibility, global responsibility; and empower your employees without being afraid of them. I think you can rewrite the book on business."

Chapter Ten

Learning Tales

Throughout this book, we have presented tales of organizations that are struggling, each from its own vantage point, to make sense of the changes that are transforming the corporation. The following pages contain additional tales from people I have interviewed, leaders who are struggling to define the shape of the new story organization. (The exception is Goran Carstedt, whom I learned about in a discussion with Charles Hampden-Turner of the London Business School.)

The tale of Goran Carstedt shows the fully participating partner in action. Sven Atterhed shares the ForeSight Group's formula for teaching corporations how to develop a culture of innovation. Bill Walsh, Tony LaRussa, and Pat Riley, all peak-performing coaches, speak to the importance of leadership in developing teamwork. Sue Thompson and Jenny Crowe-Innes of Levi Strauss discuss, from their own experience, how to engage in "downsizing" while putting people first. Barbara Walker explains how Digital Equipment is teaching its employees to value workforce diversity.

Finally, in "Crazy Horse Monument," we present an inspiring tale about a group of individuals whose vision spans generations. It is a tale that captures, better than any other I know, what it means to be motivated by a mission. And it provides us with the long-term perspective we must all adopt if we, our corporations, and our planet are to survive and thrive in the 1990s and beyond.

Global Diversity: The Tale of Goran Carstedt*

Goran Carstedt, the son of a Swedish Ford dealer, joined Volvo in 1974 after earning a doctorate in business. He soon became vice president in charge of corporate planning, a position that he found too abstract for his taste. Later he joined Volvo's French car division as a roving consultant, and within a matter of months he took over as its general manager, a job more in keeping with his hands-on management style.

When Carstedt arrived in France, Volvo's car division was in a sad state. In 1978, plans had been made to increase its annual sales from 10,000 cars to 20,000. Instead, they *fell* to 8,000 and by 1982 had inched back to 10,000. The situation looked even bleaker in light of the fact that imports were capturing a progressively larger share of a growing French market. In 1982, Volvo's market share stood at just 0.5 percent.

Since Volvo worldwide was going gangbusters at this time and even its French truck division was prospering, it seemed that only major rationalizations could justify the poor performance of the French car division. And Goran Carstedt got plenty of those when he arrived.

He was told that few French motorists realized that Volvo was available in France (this was true but beside the point); that Volvo models were too old, too heavy, too stodgy and the 760 model was too expensive; that too much performance had been sacrificed to safety; that the importer interfered too much and helped too little; that deliveries were slow, promised new models late; etc., etc.

But the rationalizations covered up the real problem: Volvo France was the victim of a highly negative story circulating

---

*Adapted from Charles Hampden-Turner, *Two Versions of Capitalism*, Corporate Culture for Competitive Edge: A User's Guide.

throughout the car division, a story repeated so often that it had come to be accepted as truth. Scandinavians, according to the myth, were practical and passionless, preoccupied with safety and keeping warm, whereas the French were hot-blooded Latins. Volvo's cars were viewed as cold and cerebral, lacking in style, with no flair for romance. The passionate French, Carstedt was assured, would never buy such unromantic vehicles.

Carstedt had Volvo's Italian sales figures in his briefcase to show that hot-blooded Latins could indeed be sold "cerebral" Volvos in large numbers, but he was smart enough to know that facts were not the issue. The issue was that the Volvo dealers in France had been sold on the prevailing myth.

Carstedt's only option was to help the dealers reinterpret the Volvo story for the French audience. Carstedt believed that the French had a skewed view of Volvo cars and of the culture in which they originated, and he was determined to change that view. He did this by taking French Volvo dealers back home with him to observe the Swedish culture firsthand.

As Carstedt sees it, Sweden is at the juncture of two major world trends. "We are a very individualistic nation, and yet we've been social democrats almost continuously since the war," he says. "We've had to combine the initiative and commitment of the individual with the ethic of social concern for the welfare of others. From the convergence of these two streams has emerged our paramount concern with building safe cars."

By the time the French Volvo dealers returned from their visit to Sweden, they had a very different view of the Volvo story. They now viewed the Volvos as superior cars produced by small groups of dedicated craftspeople who managed themselves and signed each car they made. Volvo no longer conjured up images of cold-blooded engineers working through the bleak Nordic winter to develop new safety devices for cars that were already too conservative. Instead, they saw it as a forward-thinking company that combined individualism with social responsibility, expressed in a commitment to safety and reliability. They were now proud to be part of the company, and this newfound pride translated into newfound sales. With few new product introductions and despite a 20 percent decline in the size of the French market, annual Volvo sales in France climbed from an anemic 10,800 to a robust 21,000 between 1982 and 1986. Only the creative leadership that Goran Carstedt displayed by reconciling two widely separated cultures could have led to this happy ending of the Volvo story in France.

Imagine what Goran Carstedt would have done if he had been a typical old story manager faced with the same situation. He would probably have laid down the law, cajoling dealers to "get their act together." He might have fired a few of the lowest volume dealers in an attempt to "shake up the troops." He might have beefed up promotional efforts, emphasizing the same points that had been made all along with lackluster results. Maybe he would have brought in an executive from the French truck division to show the car division "how to run a business."

None of these actions would have had any bearing on the *real* reason for Volvo's sagging sales: the negative image of Volvo and Scandinavia that Volvo's French dealers had firmly fixed in their minds. Imagine an old story manager responding in a positive, attentive way to the idea that poor performance was due to something as "soft" as a myth.

Fortunately, Goran Carstedt is not an old story manager. In dealing with Volvo France, he exhibited the facilitative style of management that characterizes the new story leader, the fully participating partner. Instead of attempting to command and control the French Volvo dealers, he helped them develop a spirit of partnership with their parent company in Sweden. The rest was relatively easy. Once the dealers visited Sweden and observed Volvo's operations firsthand, they didn't have to be admonished to "sell harder." They communicated their newfound pride to prospective customers. Increased sales were the result. And Goran Carstedt later went on to become CEO of Volvo/Sweden.

The ForeSight Group: Teaching Companies How to Innovate

For the past 12 years, the ForeSight Group of Sweden has been working with companies all over the world, teaching the skills of entrepreneurship and innovation to employees who voluntarily choose to participate in its intensive training program. These intrapreneurs (a term coined by the group's friend, author Gifford Pinchot) then serve as role models for other employees, thus enhancing the learning and innovation of their organizations.

Sven Atterhed, partner and co-founder of the ForeSight Group, described for me the five steps of the yearlong ForeSight Group training program:

We introduce intrapreneuring through a five-step process. Number one is to secure top management commitment and to have a top management group agree on the direction of innovation. You have to have a vision for the company built in from the start.

Number two, we work on corporate culture. This involves working with top managers on strategic issues in an entrepreneurial way. We teach them how to experiment and how to approach new things with an entrepreneurial mindset. For example, some Japanese companies like Komatsu, Canon, and Honda use a very entrepreneurial approach. They set a vision, and they start experimenting. This is what we work with top managers to do. They then understand what intrapreneurs have to go through and are more able to support them.

The third step is to encourage intrapreneurs to emerge through self-selection. One of the fundamental things about entrepreneurs and intrapreneurs is that they all self-select. Nobody told Henry Ford to start doing what he did. I think this is very typical of the new knowledge worker also, in large companies. You can't really command people anymore and help them achieve their best. It's not really instructions that are needed, but self-selected people who work within a given vision which they embrace.

So we ask people to come to an information meeting. It's a very simple invitation: Come and listen to a message about what it is to be an intrapreneur. The top management group, or representatives, will be on hand at this meeting. We'll have the president explaining why the company needs to innovate and why they need people to implement new ideas. Out of perhaps 1,500 employees invited in a division, maybe 70 or 80 will come.

The next step is to ask these people to take part in an interview where they have an opportunity to ask relevant questions and where we can find out what they have done in their lives. For instance, we ask them to name three situations when things worked very well and three situations that didn't work out well. This is to assess the peak performance potential.

We have maybe 100 other questions to ask. Mainly, we are looking for people with an action orientation, vision, and people who are ready to self-select. Also, they have to be able to work well with others.

We tell these self-selected potential intrapreneurs that it is going to be tough work, very hard work, and then they tell us if they are still interested. If they are, we give them training and coaching over a period of about a year. It's mainly coaching, and it is all "action learning." They work with their own projects, and they know it's all real work, not case studies.

The objective is to have them develop a business plan and a first customer, so the project is set up like a real commercial proposition. Having a first customer makes a great deal of difference, compared to just a plan on paper.

The training is intended to have people grow while they work on their project, to get them to develop certain entrepreneurial skills, skills that can be taught. They work from a very fuzzy idea to a business plan, which is the language in which managers communicate.

The essence of what we teach is for them to forget about traditional planning, which is very much based on having answers to everything before you are ready to begin a project. That's impossible if you are going to do something new—it takes too much time. Entrepreneurs don't approach things that way. They go fast. Time compression is the name of the game. They set up a vision, and then they start to do a number of experiments. Every experiment will lead to some learning, more action, and time gain.

The training of intrapreneurs takes place over nine months, and we meet every six to eight weeks. We work in concentric circles. We start out at the beginning covering all subjects, and then we go more and more in depth. We have about 20 people and maybe 10 projects in each group. The focus of the work is on contacting customers, experimenting with ideas, and working with very limited resources (what we call "creative frugality").

They are learning to operate as intrapreneurs in a company environment.

Although these intrapreneurs are working in companies with major resources, their own resources are deliberately limited, because then they have to use their brains. Often what happens is that a small company will capture market share from a larger company. And they don't do it with money; they do it with brains, action, and learning. They innovate—that's what we try to teach in the training.

We have found that innovative people are everywhere. You just have to provide the climate and the space for them, and soon they'll sprout up. In a way, what we are trying to do is help companies move from a bureaucratic culture to an entrepreneurial culture. We create role models by developing intrapreneurs. If you were sitting next to somebody who suddenly starts to perform great things, you would say, "Well, I can do that too." This is one of the keys to the intrapreneurial training: Get more and more people to join in as the work goes on. We help companies to become learning organizations."

Bill Walsh and the
San Francisco 49ers

If anyone understands what it takes to build and coach a winning team, it's Bill Walsh, former coach of the San Francisco 49ers. During his tenure in San Francisco, Walsh led the Niners to three Super Bowl Championships.

I asked Bill Walsh to share his views on teamwork and the role of the coach:

The very fundamental of success is the standard of performance. You don't necessarily concern yourself with the opposition, whether you are in awe of them or you have a lack of appreciation for them. It's your own standard of performance [that is important]. And that takes years to develop. Each year, it can get better, more refined, the problem areas more isolated. So that standard should cut through the misfortune and miscalculations that occur.

We had open communication, open exchange. Everyone participated. People could step forward and express themselves without being questioned later about the stupidity of their decision. You could be wrong and not be castigated. If you had an idea, and it was off the wall, we just kept going.

Now in that atmosphere, people had to understand that their own egos would be damaged a little bit when we didn't absorb and accept everything they had to offer. But in an open forum, open exchange, people are not second-guessing each other. Whenever a player would have an idea, I would stop and give it serious consideration because often the players were correct.

It's absolutely critical that you account for every individual, that the athlete is not treated like an object, which has become typical behavior of the media and of the coach and of the fan. The athlete is not an object; he's not number 14, or 15, or 82. He's a human being, and you have to understand the person's need to be appreciated, identified, and acknowledged. And you have to account for each individual in the way of a professional ethic—be evenhanded, fair, and then allow for everyone's dignity and self-respect.

The insightful coach and a coach with experiences (positive and negative or disappointing) will finally come to the realization that there has to be room for individual style, individual qualities, and obviously, individual attributes. And you must recognize that there are different levels of learning, different learning capacities, different learning readinesses, different backgrounds.

We have a veteran group and a younger group. We have veterans who have been together on this team 5, 8, 10 years, and their families are very close. We have different economic levels. One player is very affluent and drives up in his Mercedes and another comes up in his Datsun. So we account for that. We have different religious and political beliefs, and when we get on the subject, they can become very severe. We have different ethnic groups; we have black and white and other. Most people will feel more comfortable within their own group; some won't. But this is not a platform for any ideology, any religious convictions, any racial or ethnic beliefs. The bottom line here is that this team wins, and we find a way to do it.

I say to players, "Find a way to appreciate something about that guy next to you. What does he bring to you in a positive sense? Find something redeeming about him. You don't necessarily have to like his social set or his lifestyle—but what, in this locker room, can you find that is positive about him?"

The difference between an average player and a great player is your willingness to sacrifice for your teammates. And your expectations of their performance, your determination not to let them down, and your assuming and trusting that they feel the same way about you, that they will compete and sacrifice for you. So often we've seen, unfortunately in warfare, that men in small groups fight best, and they're not necessarily fighting for a flag, for a country, but for each other. And that's how they sustain themselves. It's much the same in football.

As a coach, you have to have an ethic in which you, regardless of sentimentality and feelings, must expect yourself to do what you should for the team and make the decisions related to the best interests of everybody. This was most difficult for me in the case of Joe Montana when I had to substitute him on occasion. But in those instances, the bottom line flashed through my mind: "Now look, this is my job; this is my role." My own personal ethic means that I have to live that role and not excuse myself from the responsibilities of it.

It's the job of the coach to continually remind everyone that each player is an extension of his teammates. If Jerry Rice catches a pass, it's because Fred Quinlan sacrificed by blocking for him. If Roger Craig makes five yards, it's because Randy Cross was sacrificing for him. So each player's an extension of the other. When that kind of environment or atmosphere exists, then you're beginning to develop what it takes to be a sustained, continued winner.

Tony La Russa and the Oakland A's: Take Nothing for Granted

For five years, Tony La Russa has managed the Oakland A's, guiding one of the most successful teams in major league baseball into three World Series and a world championship. Tony La Russa shared with me some of the most important management lessons he's learned along the way:

My feeling every year is that I start from zero with the club, as far as respect level is concerned. My attitude is that I have to earn it from them.

So how do you earn it? You earn by your commitment, by the fact that you are coming to the park every day in spring training with a program for that day, a program that you have put several hours into. That gets the players' attention. They say: "He's trying."

So I try to earn their respect by commitment and a certain amount of knowledge. If you tell them, "Hey, fellas, our offense works best if we do it this way," or "We are getting sluggish in this department," and you point out the reasons, they will tend to listen.

Now, after 11 or 12 years, because I have been around for a while and won some, I might have a player's attention at first. But you have to do something that maintains it, that keeps his attention.

For instance, if a hitting coach was a great hitter, he's got the instant attention of the players. But if, over a period of time, he's not giving them something of substance, something that can help them, something that they see as real quality, he's going to lose them. They are not impressed with a person out here for very long unless he's delivering something of substance.

One of the aspects of coaching that I really concern myself with is keeping the message fresh. When I first joined the A's, the team had obviously never heard me talk about certain things before. Now I run the real risk that when I bring up a subject, whatever it is—whether it's about bunt defense or the overall mission for the club, the players can say: "I've heard Tony talk about this before," and they might lose interest. So you are always looking to keep the message fresh.

In 1989, the year we won the championship, I talked a lot about mission. It had interest for me because it was fresh, and it was fresh to the team. More important, it had substance, and I used the idea of the A's having a mission to motivate the team.

The biggest mistakes I have made in managing over the years have happened because of taking things for granted. In 1990, I took for granted that our club knew we were playing for history. There is a popular misconception that motivation shouldn't be a problem if you've already gotten to the World Series, and we had.

But the fact is that our club was not properly motivated for the 1990 World Series [in which the A's lost to the Cincinnati Reds].

There's another thing you can't take for granted. If a guy is playing in the major leagues, and he's making a million dollars, or two million, or three, you might assume he's got to be playing his heart out. After all, it's the major leagues, and he's making all that money.

Unfortunately, one of the real dangers of recent developments in major league baseball is the reality that you can perform at much less than your excellence level and still make a very, very good living.

That personally affronts me. I would probably hold that against the guy—if I kept seeing him just getting by. And yeah, I think that ends up upsetting your team. I try to get rid of people like that. Nobody gets to take anything for granted on this team.

Pat Riley and the
Los Angeles Lakers

Pat Riley experienced his first professional basketball championship as a player on the Los Angeles Lakers in 1972. Later, as assistant coach of the Lakers, Riley helped spur the team on to another victory. As head coach, Pat Riley subsequently led the Lakers to four more NBA championships before leaving the team in 1990. He is now head coach of the New York Knicks.

Riley shared with me his philosophy of coaching and leadership:

My father was a coach, and I had 14 other coaches in my life, so I've always felt that *coaching* was a word that was synonymous with trust, integrity, dignity, and wisdom, and that coaches were people you could count on, talk to, and be counseled by.

I think that every coach or every leader has to create, or try to create, the best possible environment in which talent can flourish.

I mean, that is your product when it comes right down to the bottom line—regardless of your offensive strategy, or defensive strategy, or your overall philosophy. It comes down to those players being able to make that philosophy work.

I think that with basketball there has to be one voice, and I think that's very important. My voice was the voice that I wanted them to hear and get used to, but it wasn't the kind of voice that was closed. If there was something that was perplexing to them that I would say, or try to teach, then I would be the first one to read that body language. I would open it up to discussion, and if it was something that was strongly felt by the group as the wrong direction, then I would change immediately. I would never, ever force upon a group of players something they didn't believe in. And I never, I never felt averse to making those changes if I felt they were in the best interests of the team.

On the other hand, I have found that the players that I have coached in the 80s—and the greatest players in the history of the game: Kareem Abdul-Jabbar, Ervin "Magic" Johnson—demanded discipline. They demanded structure. They didn't want it easy. They didn't want you to lay back and allow them to slide.

Ervin would use his God-given skills, his greatness athletically, but more important, his attitude in really wanting, sincerely, other players on the team to get out of the game everything they wanted. And he accomplished that and he was happy for other players' success. And when other players were successful, Ervin would get everything he wanted because that's how the whole operation works.

There are only a handful of people like that in each sport, and those of us who've had the opportunity to play with them or coach them or be around them really feel that we were blessed, because they become your greatest allies. Ervin Johnson was my greatest ally as a coach, as was Kareem, because I knew I never had to worry about those two players. They would do whatever they could do to help me facilitate or motivate or to get those other guys on the same wavelength. Their attitudes are special. They know that the only way they can win and get all of the things they want out of the game is to use their talent to help the other players. When that becomes a common thread that goes through the team and you get everybody trying to help everybody else become better—well, you have a hell of a basketball team.

Levi Strauss & Co.: How to Manage "Downsizing"

If an organization is to remain cohesive, if it is to learn and grow as an organization, how it handles layoffs is as important as how it hires. Employees learn a great deal about the values of an organization by observing how it dismisses employees. If the employees left behind are fearful for their jobs, by virtue of seeing a badly mismanaged layoff, they will probably not be committed to the continuous learning that improves the organization, but only to learning that makes them more marketable.

The way Levi Strauss handled its need to "downsize" in the mid-1980s serves as an example to other companies. Sue Thompson, director of Human Resource Development at Levi Strauss, and Levi's director of Employee Relations, Jenny Crowe-Innes, described their approach to me.

How do you lay off over 5,000 people at 17 manufacturing and distribution facilities and do it in keeping with a company ethic that says fair treatment of employees is a top priority? That's what Levi Strauss was faced with in 1984. There was a definite downturn in the jeans market in the early 1980s, and we had to come to terms with a word nobody likes: *downsizing*.

We handled it pretty much the same way in each location. Several executives flew to a plant three days before a closing was to be announced. Workers were told the news of the plant closing, and then they split up into discussion groups to air their concerns. Individual counseling was also made available on the spot.

The layoff package, which was described to employees that day, included 90 days of notice pay plus a week of severance pay for each year of employment, three months of health benefits beyond the 90-day notice period required, any unused vacation pay. In addition, we offered job counseling and priority on jobs available at other Levi plants. And that included some relocation assistance too. Most of the laid off workers chose to stay in their communities rather than relocate, but I do know that of the 155 people laid off at the Denison, Texas, plant who went through job retraining, 126 got new jobs.

Our focus was primarily on those people who were going. We did a significant amount of outplacement counseling. We provided a recruiter to help them write résumés and practice interviewing skills. We conducted workshops to help people get clearer ideas about their jobs and career ambitions and goals.

What we did not do well was deal with the feelings of those people who were not laid off, and particularly dealing with the feelings of those in departments where the layoff was most significant. I think we've learned from those mistakes.

Subsequently, we recognized that a layoff is a very, very painful experience for everyone, not just those leaving, and that the feelings of those left behind are critical as well. Our employee assistance group is now intimately involved in any potential layoffs—working with managers, helping the managers understand their own emotional reaction to the layoff and coaching them through it, and also working with the managers to help them deal with the feelings—the fear and anger and concerns—of those employees who will be left behind. We do one-on-one counseling, workshops, and we are involved in a variety of activities to help managers and employees to get through that time.

A company should do as much as possible with the employees who are laid off. This can mean helping them either get the skills they need, or retraining them, or assisting them in making a transition to another employment situation. You almost cannot do enough. Typically employees who have been laid off are in a state of shock. Counseling, advice, résumé assistance, and whatever you can possibly do, in the long run, will reap the most benefits.

Another thing that we have learned from our early layoff is the importance of communication. At the time of the decision to lay off, we now develop a complete communication plan that includes memos to employees affected by the layoff, and memos to employees who are left behind and communications to the public. We are trying to do a much better job of keeping the employees informed and trying to minimize the morale effect at the time of layoff. You just can't communicate too much.

Don't underestimate the time required for the integration of the emotional impact for employees and managers. Both those staying and those going will have very strong feelings, and it takes time to help work through those feelings. To allow them that time is a key factor.

Valuing Diversity:
A Five-Step Approach

Barbara Walker is vice president, Human Resources and Human Relations, University of Cincinnati. When I spoke with her she was the manager of international diversity at Digital Equipment Corporation. Her mission is to "help develop strategies which would make valuing differences a worldwide value." She shared with me Digital's five-step approach for educating employees to value workforce diversity:

When someone asks what valuing diversity is about, we say there are five pieces involved in the work. The first is learning to strip away one's stereotypes. I don't care whether you are talking about people, or ideas, or organizations. Our first task in the personal development work we call "valuing differences" is to understand what a stereotype is, understand the process of facing one's own stereotypes, and then start trying to strip them away, whatever that means for you.

We are talking about *all* differences. We draw on the board a cycle of differences that puts at the top race, gender, sexual orientation, AIDS, physical ability and disability, and then we continue on down the board with cultural differences, language differences, geographical differences, learning styles, and so forth.

People begin very directly, very straightforwardly, looking at the stereotypes. Every core group begins with an examination of these questions: "Blacks are . . . ? Whites are . . . ? Women are . . . ? Men are . . . ? Hispanics are . . . ? Black women are . . . ? White men are . . . ?" If you put 100 people in the room, you can get 100 different answers to the questions.

We have a theory that I have pushed at Digital, and it seems to be working—that is, that in this country race and gender can be used as metaphors for all other differences. In this country, the primary metaphor differences are race and gender. The theory is that, given how this country was built, given the dream, given the issues of black and white, race issues are part of everybody's psyche one way or another. It's there. If we could get people to deal with race and gender, they might be able to open up their way of thinking about all the other differences. That's the theory.

So people will begin by looking directly at their stereotypes and having conversations, and in some cases confrontations, about whether a particularly held belief is a stereotype or not. It's in those discussions and confrontations that I think people do a lot of refining of their views.

The second step, or piece of the work, is learning how to listen and flow with the differences in the assumptions of others. Even if we had a magic wand and could get rid of every stereotype that we have, we would all still be left with different assumptions, different values, different ways of seeing the world. We don't take enough time to explore what those are. I personally work to keep stereotypes in one category and assumptions in another category. Sometimes people get it all mixed together, and then I don't think they know which one they are dealing with.

Let's say you and I are putting a course together, or putting a plan together, or putting a product together, and you think it should be done in Z way, and I think it should be done in A way. In other words, we absolutely disagree. Learning to value difference means to me that I will slow down and listen to you. I don't agree with you, and that's clear; but I am not going to automatically count you out or rule you out.

I will say to myself, because I am empowered by differences, "Well, Charles, he's a sensible person. He's got X experience, his experiences are different from mine. There must be something in there. So let me go for it." And then, as I value differences and value my own ideas at the same time, I say, "Now listen, Charles, let me tell you where I am coming from. I don't see how you can approach it that way, because my experience teaches me blah, blah, blah." And slowly, through that process of not being afraid of each other just because we disagree with one another, one of us may come to some other idea, totally different from each of our ideas. So this dialogue brings about synergy and creativity.

The third piece of the work is proactively, deliberately going out of one's way to build authentic and significant relationships with people one regards as different. People in core groups, people who are really trying to learn how to value differences, must build relationships with people they regard as different, and build the relationship *with those differences*. We are saying that part of the work in building that relationship is keeping the differences in mind.

The fourth piece of the work, which is the largest piece, I think, is learning how to deepen or enhance one's sense of empowerment by *talking* about differences, especially talking about the ways in which we feel victimized by differences.

The fifth piece of the work is done when one has already done some small part of the other four pieces of work. Then one perhaps can feel empowered enough to try to identify and explore the differences among groups of people. But I hesitate to encourage people to do that fifth step until they have at least learned what a stereotype is, until they have at least been through some part of a process of examining assumptions, until they have at least one black friend, or Asian friend or friend of the opposite gender—until they feel a little bit empowered. Otherwise, people will use the fifth piece of the work to legitimize the very stereotypes that they began with: "All Asians are technical, all women are . . ." They will take one experience, and broaden it, and make it the whole of their experience.

The point of all this work is to get people to understand and acknowledge differences and, most importantly, to *respect* those differences. And then to understand that each individual is unique.

So, to recap, the major challenge in learning to value difference is helping people get comfortable with difference; that's number one. Then it's helping people become empowered by difference, empowered enough to deal with difference. And finally, it's helping people learn how to work together interdependently and synergistically so that they can be productive.

That's how the work started back in the early 80s, and it has worked very well, which means that we ended up with more minority men and women as plant managers. Those are the plum positions at Digital. They are in some of the other leadership positions also.

We've been so successful that some parts of the company believe the work is done, when we know that that's probably one of the most dangerous places you can be. A lot of people will say, "We did that five years ago, and we did well," and then not continue to work at it. But you can succeed in 1981, or 1982, and in 1990 it feels like you are failing. What we are learning, those of us who are paying attention, is that you have to do this work over and over and over again.

Crazy Horse Monument: A Mission for Many Generations

As the sun sinks low in the South Dakota sky, temporarily turning the Black Hills to gold, floodlights illuminate the four presidential heads of the Mount Rushmore National Memorial. Seventeen miles down the road, floodlights illuminate a stone carving 10 times larger than Rushmore. This is the Crazy Horse Memorial, a statue in progess begun in 1948, a monument to the great Sioux leader and to the Native American people who still call the Black Hills their own.

The stone carving of Crazy Horse on his steed stands 563 feet tall—8 feet taller than the Washington Monument. When completed, it will be 641 feet long and will be the backdrop for a small museum dedicated to the American Indian. The monument is so massive that a 10-story office building could fit into the opening under Crazy Horse's arm and all four' faces of Mount Rushmore could fit inside his head. His outstretched arm will be 263 feet long; his pointing finger will be 37½ feet long; and his hand will be 33 feet thick. The head of his horse will rise 219 feet tall from the base of the mountain. The completed Crazy Horse Memorial will be the biggest sculpture in the world.

The man who pursued the impossible dream that is now unfolding in the Black Hills was the late sculptor Korczak Ziolkowski. His story, and the story of those who are continuing to realize his vision, illustrate the seemingly unlimited human creativity that is available when the power of mission is unleashed.

The Dakota Indians, better known as the Sioux, came to the Black Hills more than a century ago. They were widely admired for their achievements —physically, mentally, and morally. They were admired for their bravery in battle and for their horsemanship; one American general described them as "the best light cavalry in the world."

The Sioux loved and venerated the Black Hills. They lived peacefully in the wilderness of South Dakota until 1874, when an expedition under General George Custer discovered gold in the Black Hills. Soon white prospectors, miners, and desperadoes despoiled the area and disrupted the lives of the Sioux.

The Sioux rose up to defend their sacred mountains, and the Black Hills became a bloody battleground. Eventually, they found that they were no match for the invaders' weapons and sheer numbers. They lost their beloved Black Hills to the white man.

Crazy Horse, a leader in resisting the incursion of the white man into Sioux territory, is remembered principally for his role in the Battle of the Little Big Horn, fought in 1876, in which the Sioux overwhelmed General Custer's regiment. Crazy Horse was considered an "Indian's Indian," a brave warrior and a brilliant leader. A year after his victory over General Custer, he was bayoneted in the back by an American soldier at Fort Robinson, Nebraska, where he had gone under a flag of truce.

An American soldier who fought against Crazy Horse said: "[He] was one of the great soldiers of his day and generation. As the grave of Custer marked the high-water mark of Sioux supremacy in the trans-Mississippi region, so the grave of Crazy Horse marked the ebb."

Crazy Horse died on September 6, 1877, at age 34. On September 6, 1908, 21 years later, Korczak Ziolkowski was born in Boston. Korczak (pronounced "Corjock") was orphaned at age one. He fled from his brutal guardian at age 16 and set out on his own. Eventually, he became a prominent sculptor.

In 1939, Korczak's marble sculpture of Ignace Paderewski, the great Polish pianist and statesman, won first prize in sculpture by popular vote at the New York World's Fair. Later that year, Korczak received a letter from Henry Standing Bear, an old Sioux chief who lived on South Dakota's Pine Ridge Indian Reservation. In the letter, Standing Bear asked Korczak whether he would be interested in carving a memorial to Crazy Horse in the Black Hills.

In 1941, Korczak came to South Dakota to meet with Standing Bear and discuss the project. Shortly thereafter, the United States entered World War II and Korczak enlisted as an army volunteer. While in Europe, he spent a great deal of time considering Standing Bear's request, finally deciding to take on the challenge if the Indians would benefit from it. According to his widow, Ruth Ziolkowski, he was determined that the Crazy Horse project would not be a tourist gimmick, but a memorial to benefit the Indian people, culturally and educationally.

I asked Ruth what convinced Korzcak that he should take on a challenge so great that the word *formidable* doesn't even begin to describe it. She told me, "I think one thing that convinced him that he really wanted to do this was the one line in Chief Standing Bear's letter that said, 'Will you carve us a mountain so the white men will know the red men had great heroes too?' He often said that there was a strong parallel between the Native Americans and the Polish people as far as their history is concerned. . . . Maybe that's part of the reason why he said yes to the Indians."

After his discharge from the army, Korczak set out for South Dakota, arriving in the Black Hills on May 3, 1947, with $174 in his pocket. The rest of his life savings had gone to purchase the rights to a 6,000-foot mountain that he and Standing Bear had chosen as the site of the Crazy Horse Memorial. Korczak dubbed the towering block of granite Thunderhead Mountain because of the ominous cloud formations overhead. After selecting the site, Korczak established the Crazy Horse Memorial Foundation, with the ultimate goal of building a university, a museum, and a medical training center for the Indians of North America.

Korczak soon learned that many whites in the Black Hills area did not look upon Indians favorably—to put it mildly. He recalled: "My biggest surprise out here was how they hated Indians with a purple passion. I had no idea. If I hadn't seen it with my own eyes, I wouldn't have believed it. I'm not an 'Indian lover.' I'm just a storyteller in stone, and the story of the American Indian is a truly epic tale that needs telling. If you are going to live today for the future, you have to have an understanding of the past."

And so the telling of the epic tale began. The carving was officially dedicated on June 3, 1948. Chief Standing Bear touched off a dynamite charge that blasted the first 10 tons of rock off Thunderhead Mountain. Four hundred Indians took part in the ceremony. Among them were five of the nine remaining survivors of the Battle of the Little Big Horn.

Ruth Ross was one of the many student volunteers who came to the Black Hills to work on Korczak's project. She had first met Korczak when she was a teenager in West Hartford, Connecticut, where she volunteered to help him with another project, a 13½-foot likeness of Noah Webster. The two were married on Thanksgiving Day in 1950. He was 42; she was 24. Korczak and Ruth had 10 children—five boys and five girls. All of them were born in Crazy Horse, South Dakota.

In the early years of the project, Korczak worked alone, dynamiting and removing thousands of tons of rock to create a rough profile of Crazy Horse. But the work was painfully slow, and it was almost impossible to discern the progress that was being made.

Korczak and Ruth then decided that he would paint the outline of the sculpture on Thunderhead Mountain, so that the results would be visible from below. This undertaking took up the entire summer of 1951. Korczak used 176 gallons of paint to create the outline, each line of which had to be at least 6 feet wide.

Over the long, difficult years, Korczak refused any assistance from the U.S. government, twice turning down offers of $10 million in federal aid. In answer to official queries, he said: "I have copies of 365 treaties the government made with the Indians and then violated. Am I to believe you would keep this one?" Among other things, Korczak was concerned that the government would never finish the job. He knew that Gutzon Borglum, the chief sculptor of Mount Rushmore, had experienced great difficulties as a result of working with federal funds. And he noted that work on Mount Rushmore had stopped when Borglum died; Borglum's last scale model for Mount Rushmore shows that he intended to carve the four full busts down to the waist.

In 1978, after spending 30 years blasting and carving on Thunderhead Mountain, Korczak realized that he was not going to live long enough to see the finished monument, much less to build a university for the Indians—one of his primary goals. As a token gesture, he started a scholarship program with $250 of his own money, planting the seed that he hoped would grow into a healthy fund.

Korczak Ziolkowski died on October 20, 1982. He was buried at the foot of his sculpture. His last words were: "You must keep building; Crazy Horse must be finished. But you must do it slowly so you do it right." To assure that the remaining work was done right, he had prepared three lengthy volumes of notes and instructions, detailing how it was to be carried out.

Now Ruth, the Ziolkowski family, and a host of others are carrying on the work that Korczak began in 1948. Today 7 of the 10 Ziolkowski children are working on Crazy Horse full time. Says Ruth: "They are here because they want to be. Every one of them has gone out and seen something else in the world and decided, 'Gee, Crazy Horse wasn't so bad after all. I really think that I would like to be there.'"

For Ruth Ziolkowski, Crazy Horse is far more than a project; it is her life. "I grew up with this," she says. "I was 13 when I met Korczak, and I am 64 now. I have lived with it all my life, and it's just as much a part of my life as it was of Korczak's.

"I am very fortunate. I look at so many people that I know who hate Monday morning and are just looking forward to Friday afternoon for the weekend, and I think how lucky I am. I love getting up every day of the week and I'm tickled to death that I am here to do it.

"There's nothing any different about me than there is about anyone else except that I am fortunate enough to have found something to do with my life that I want to spend the rest of my life doing, and I thoroughly enjoy it.

"I think that you have to find something in life, or something in life has to come to you, that you thoroughly enjoy, that you want to do, and that you keep working on. You don't necessarily start as the president of the company, if that's your object in life. You start, and you work, and just so long as you can look at yourself every day in the mirror, and you're proud of what you are and what you've done, and you know that you have done the best you can do, you can always go on and grow."

When I commented that the carving of the Crazy Horse Memorial appeared to be a superhuman feat, Ruth disagreed. "If somebody threw this whole thing at you, the way it is now, and you never had anything to do with it, it no doubt would be impossible. If you grow with it a step at a time, and a day at a time, anything is possible."

She added: "Korczak was a great believer that you could do anything in this world that you wanted to do, if you wanted to badly enough and you were willing to work hard enough. But he said first your pride has to be intact."

According to Ruth, Korczak hoped that the Crazy Horse Memorial would help restore the pride wrested from the Indians by the white man: "He said we white people did such a great job of trying to take the Native Americans' pride away from them that if this memorial and this mountain carving would give them back some sense of their pride, then that in itself would be one goal. And the fact that this is 8 feet taller than the Washington Monument is not lost on a lot of the Native Americans who come in here."

During his lifetime, Korczak single-handedly raised and spent more than $5 million on Crazy Horse. Since his death, the financial contributions of others have enabled Ruth and her crews to keep the dream alive. And an admission fee to the memorial and the museum, already operating, helps defray some of the massive costs of the project.

In addition to monetary gifts, contributions have come in other forms. For example, eight lighting companies spent two years putting together funds to light the mountain at night. Says Ruth: "It is absolutely gorgeous. That was done through the efforts of one man in Rapid City. He decided it should be done. If Rushmore could be lighted, Crazy Horse should be."

When I asked about the tremendous technical problems of the Crazy Horse project, Ruth shrugged. "Oh, you just take them one at a time, and they aren't really problems, they are just things that you need to learn about and that are challenges. Yesterday the whole crew was up on Rushmore while they were doing their annual facelift, as they call it up there, and checking for cracks and filling them if they found any. And [the crew] went through the archives [at the Hall of Records] to look at how they had worked on the eyes of the four different presidents. You do things one step at a time, and you learn a little bit as you go. You can't go to school to learn how to carve a mountain."

Ruth Ziolkowski thinks that by 1992, the 500th anniversary of the "discovery" of America, there will be a "rough outline" of the profile of Crazy Horse on Thunderhead Mountain. But when I asked if she knew when the monument would be completed, she

replied flatly: "No. Your guess would be just as good as mine."
She reflected: "[Korczak] often compared Crazy Horse, as far as
time was concerned, to the Sphinx and the number of people who
worked at that, compared to him working alone or with just the
family. We have nine people up there now, and to him that
would have been an army. He used to talk about the fact that
some of the old cathedrals took 600 years to build—and Crazy
Horse started out as just one man against a mountain. Look at
Rushmore—they worked on that for 14 or 16 years, depending on
how you want to figure time, and they didn't move 500,000 tons
of rock, and we've already moved 8.5 million tons, which is 17
times more. We have been at it for 42 years."

Could the Crazy Horse Memorial be considered the beginning
of the white man's apology to the Native Americans for past
wrongs? "Well," said Ruth, "it would be a good place to begin.
This is the year of reconciliation in South Dakota [1990], and I
certainly think that they need to do something about Wounded
Knee. It's the hundred-year anniversary of Wounded Knee. I
don't think you can do [just] one thing, but at least it is symbolic."

Korczak Ziolkowski's vision of the Crazy Horse Memorial was
so powerful, his enthusiasm so contagious, that he was able to
convince all around him of the possibility of his impossible
dream. Ruth recalls: "Back in 1948, when the first blast was set off
on the mountain to dedicate it, *Life* magazine was here, the *Omaha
World Herald* was, the *Des Moines Register*, the *Minneapolis Tri-
bune*—papers from all over. And to this day I can't get over the
fact that every one of them said, *"When* it is finished," not *"If."*
They didn't have a question, they didn't have a doubt. They met
Korczak, they listened to him. His sincerity and his belief came
through."

Before he began work on the world's biggest sculpture, Korczak Ziolkowski was told a story by Old Black Elk, a contemporary of Crazy Horse. The story was confirmed, through transla-
tors, by the Indian survivors of Little Big Horn who attended the
dedication ceremonies in 1948. It seems that Crazy Horse habitu-
ally wore a stone in his ear and that when asked about the stone,
the great Sioux chief always gave the same reply:

"I will return to you in the stone."

Conclusion: Giving Voice to the Vision

Like the blind men in the Hindu parable, each of our exemplar companies has a grip on a "piece of the elephant." Each company is striving to fashion a coherent whole from its piece, in order to make sense of the new story of business. Empowered employees. Innovation. Self-managing teams. The customer as one of us. Lifelong learning. Diversity. Social concern. Each company's vision is centered on one or more of these "pieces." Yet as they realize their vision, each is discovering that the piece it possesses is part of something larger.

At some point in the evolution of each company, one or more of its leaders experienced an awakening, a shift in perspective, an "Aha!" For some companies, such as The Body Shop, the shift preceded the company's founding and was basic to its birth. More frequently, the shift occurred when the company faced a serious challenge to its survival, internally or in the marketplace. For such companies as Steelcase, it was prompted by the fear that a challenge of this kind might be imminent. Although each of our interviewees describes his or her experience of the shift differently, and although each was groping in the dark, they all felt certain they were on to something strange and important. And indeed, they were. They realized the need to transform their companies from machines into living systems.

I think that a subtle and significant message of the elephant tale is that vision alone is incomplete. Like the blind men, we must "exclaim aloud." We must rely on voice as well as vision to reconcile our views and "to put the pieces together."

In business, we emphasize the importance of "visionary leadership." But vision alone, however powerful, cannot guide our organizations into the future. A vision remains in the imagination until it is communicated to others. The leadership eye searches the horizons; the leadership ear tunes to the voices of dialogue within its midst. Only when we give voice to our visions of business as a living system will they possess the power to transform our companies.

The time has come to "give voice to our visions." I am referring here not only to the voice of managers, but also to the voice of any member of the organization who is engaged in dialogue and reciprocal learning. Each speaker is at the center of the system, and the message of each voice moves outward to others in many directions at once. When taken together, these voices are telling the new story of business.

I encourage each of you to "give voice" to your vision, to share the stories of this book and those of your own organization. The shape of the new story of business will emerge more clearly as we continue the dialogue. *Second to None* is an attempt to share my "piece of the elephant" with you. I welcome the opportunity to hear about yours. Please send letters or audiotapes to: The Charles Garfield Group, 6114 LaSalle Ave. Suite 642, Oakland, CA 94611, U.S.A.

Heard in the Hallways: Action Learning in the New Story of Business

The following quotes capture key elements of the new story of business. Each set of quotes represents the chapter in which it is embedded. This section, when taken as a whole, provides a running commentary on the essential messages of the book. It is another, albeit briefer, way of learning the new story.

The quotes can be used at the core of an extensive training effort, or pondered more casually by the reader learning alone. They are especially useful as part of the dialogue and discussion of a smart team whose aim is to understand those systemic forces that help—and those that hinder—the emergence of the new story in a given company.

Hopefully, this material will help the reader to experience a shift in perspective, a breakthrough or "Aha!," similar to the shifts that awakened the exemplars in *Second to None*. It may also help reveal those organizational beliefs, policies, and structures that make it difficult to act on such awakenings. Additionally, the quotes should be a provocative prod to action when coupled with the question, "Could these comments be heard in our hallways?"

Note: The added "white space" is to encourage the reader to write comments and observations directly on these pages. There is no substitute for actively engaging this material; agreeing, disagreeing, and expanding on it from beginning to end.

CHAPTER ONE

In *Second to None*, we are focusing on a burgeoning new story of business; something deeper than a few incremental reforms. Corporate leaders around the world are turning their organizations inside out, developing a radically new notion of "How Things Work." They are moving from the notion of the company as a machine to the company as an ecosystem.

> "We kept saying we were the best. We started thinking maybe the best time to start making some changes and try something different is when you're on top rather than waiting until we are in trouble and then trying to claw our way back up. We talked about the old frog syndrome: If you throw a frog in a pot of boiling water he jumps out, but if you put a frog in a pot of cold water and heat it slowly, he'll sit there and boil to death. We didn't want to get boiled."
>
> *Frank Merlotti, Steelcase, Inc.*

> "To move toward a winning culture, we've got to create what we call a 'boundaryless' company. We no longer have time to climb over barriers between functions like engineering and marketing, or between people—hourly, salaried, management, and the like."
>
> *Jack Welch, General Electric*

> "It's not just wrong to exploit workers, it's stupid. . . . The trouble with crushing workers is that you then have to try to make high quality products with crushed people."
>
> *Charles Hampden-Turner, London Business School*

CHAPTER TWO

At the heart of the new story of business are organizations and employees thriving together as fully participating partners. Organizations that are transforming themselves, in large measure, by putting people first.

"When times get rough, the guys in the black hats gain credibility because they offer this clear, unambiguous response to any crisis: 'Cut the gooey malarkey, and get tough.'"

James O'Toole,
University of Southern California Business School

"I believe in the past many companies viewed individuals as being expendable. If you didn't have the right skill mix, you could always buy it. And I think now we're realizing that, one, you can't always do that because of demographics; there simply aren't going to be enough people with certain skills. Two, loyalty has a value. Just putting people on the street and hiring new ones is not a good way for the long haul. If you're asking people to accept change and deal with constant change, then it has to be a longer term commitment."

William Wiggenhorn, Motorola University

"People don't like to sign up for revolutions. People with power especially don't like to. That's just not big on their list. They want to perpetuate the existing systems as long as they can."

Chuck House, Hewlett-Packard

CHAPTER THREE

Men and women of the enterprise function best as fully participating partners when they have the tools, training, and autonomy that they need to participate, own a piece of the business,
and work in a climate of caring and trust.

> "We used to have a foreman or forewoman control about
> 27–30 people. The foremen are running around like
> chickens with their heads cut off all day, trying to keep
> those 27 people active, busy, supplied, talking about their
> personal problems, who did something wrong today. What
> we had to do was convince these guys that if you had five
> teams that you're responsible for—instead of 27 people—
> you may have 60–70 people. But the team members are
> doing all the running around, not you. They're solving
> their own problems. And you're sitting back and doing
> some planning, and doing what all the books always said
> the manager should do, and what not 1 out of 100 do,
> because they're always running around, putting out fires."
>
> *Frank Merlotti, Steelcase, Inc.*

> "We set up a suggestion process so that a coordinator can't
> turn it down. In other words, he can either implement it, or
> pass it on to a higher level. . . . If he says, 'Gee, I can't
> approve it because it costs too much money,' it goes up to a
> higher level, where he says, 'I can't approve it because it
> involves people outside our area.' Then it goes up to a
> higher committee in the terminal, and then as quickly as
> possible, an answer gets back to that associate who made
> the suggestion."
>
> *Will Potter, Preston Trucking*

> "It is not unusual for somebody to be in my office, for
> example, with a shoebox full of bills. We will just pay off all

of the bills. We put the employee on a program that they can handle, paying the company back over an extended period of time at a very nominal interest rate, far better than they could get at any bank."

Mike Conway, America West Airlines

CHAPTER FOUR

A value-added benefit to the company of these fully participating partners is their liberated ingenuity and creativity; the human talents necessary to produce continuous innovations in every aspect of the business.

> "In the middle 80s, we said customer satisfaction meant meeting the expectations of the customer. And then we changed it and said it meant exceeding the expectations of the customer. Now we are saying it means anticipating the needs of the customer, and once recognized, responding quickly to those needs. . . . You are beginning to look at the whole issue of intuition and creativity, paradigm shifts, etc., more than you have in the past."

> *William Wiggenhorn, Motorola University*

> "Sometimes you ask your vendors about doing something out of the ordinary and they'll instantly say, 'Well, that's not the way it's done. No one has done it that way before.' I don't think companies can be successful anymore if they feel that way or think that way."

> *Patricia Gallup, PC Connection*

> "What they do, rather than buying market share with their dollars, is they focus their attention on what they can do to add value to sell their products. That's the way they're growing their business."

> *Elliott Levine, Merisel,*
> *speaking of PC Connection*

CHAPTER FIVE

Ingenuity and creativity are best liberated in self-managing work teams. These fully informed teams are essential in the new story world in which speed, flexibility, and close relationships are prerequisites for continuous innovation.

> "The hierarchy tends to disappear when people have the same basis of information. Now we publish our balance sheet and all of our financials and all of our numbers monthly on the bulletin board, which means everybody knows how much we're making, what the payroll is, what raw material contributes, what strategies we have, what price increases we need."
>
> *Ricardo Semler, Semco*

> "As long as you had senior management—and by senior management I mean the most senior management—behind what you were trying to accomplish, then it was doable. If the general manager was not prepared to stand up and say: 'Hey, I want this and I want it this way, and I am supporting what's going on,' then the organization would eat the team alive."
>
> *Jim Stryker, Ingersoll-Rand*

> "There were teams made up of dozens of people who represented all the parts of the organization that were involved in engineering changes. As they got together and examined what they were doing, it became evident that many sign off and 'check-the-checker' steps had crept into the process, all well-intentioned, but clearly unnecessary. The teams grappled with this problem, and the end result was more than a 50 percent reduction in elapsed time, with

dozens of people acknowledging that they added little or no value to the engineering change process. Although painful, they all recognized that they were playing a 'controlling' role rather than a value-adding role."

John Hammitt, United Technologies

CHAPTER SIX

There is no impermeable boundary when it comes to welcoming customers as partners in the enterprise. Our smartest companies bring customers into the heart of the organization. They invite and encourage them to participate on teams designing products, developing service measures, and monitoring quality. Such companies see each customer as "one of us" and are connected to each in long-lasting relationships.

"Service leadership means you master the customer's way of thinking, their concepts, their needs, their requirements, what makes them tick, how they think. It means that one has to understand, and literally own, and have a clear vision of what will make the customer a success not only today, but tomorrow . . . and then go out and be committed to making it happen."

Henry Givray, Smith, Bucklin & Associates

"You can't provide service every day without having people come in here every day who know they're important to you and come to work with a good attitude. You can't do it. It's impossible to ask anybody to call a customer, to get on a phone, to go sell something for you unless that person knows he's valued in this family and trusted in this family."

Jack Kahl, Manco, Inc.

"In order to bring professionalism to associations, we need to have people who are committed to careers, to learning the ins and outs of an industry. And so we have to be committed to the careers of our people. We can't provide the kind of in-depth service we do without people committed to careers within Smith, Bucklin. Sometimes their careers are almost more important than the client."

Bill Smith, Smith, Bucklin & Associates

CHAPTER SEVEN

Customers, employees, suppliers, and even competitors are seen
as partners and potential sources of learning. Organizations that
hope to thrive in the current economic environment must dramatically shift the focus of their training, rethinking the very concept
of learning.

"We were shocked when only 40 percent of the plant
passed a test containing simple percentage problems. And
we were astonished to find out that much of our domestic
workforce was illiterate and couldn't do simple math. We
concluded that about half of our 25,000 manufacturing and
support people in the United States could not meet seventh
grade reading and math levels. We knew we had to build
learning, continuous learning, into the culture of Motorola.
So we started the dialogues and began building the
educational partnerships that ultimately led us to form
Motorola University."

William Wiggenhorn, Motorola University

"We are seeing the move to self-managing work teams,
which is requiring us to relook at our pay system, for one,
and secondly, to provide extensive training on how to work
together and how to collaborate and solve problems. The
changes are astounding, and the need for training
associated with those changes is extensive."

Sue Thompson, Levi Strauss

"The essence of real leadership is to allow your people to
see your need and desire for learning. Your actions speak
more than your words. Today's leaders must be students of
change first, before they become teachers of change to
others."

Jack Kahl, Manco, Inc.

CHAPTER EIGHT

The learning organization of the new story, no less than the Brazilian rain forest, requires diversity in order to thrive. Attempting to level differences or to limit the expression of diverse viewpoints endangers our businesses just as surely as reducing variety endangers any ecosystem.

> "I'm very suspicious of people who race around, most of them white and male, talking about managing diversity. Still, they're very much in charge, sitting at the top and telling the middle what to do to the bottom."
>
> *Ted Payne, Xerox Corporation*

> "I was born in North Carolina. I am going to bring some of that experience with me, and this is my view of the world. We've got people (at DEC) born in France, Germany, Italy, Spain, Canada, Puerto Rico, you name it. They have a different view and perspective, a different set of experiences to a degree. You get a larger perspective which will lead you to a larger set of potential solutions to a given issue."
>
> *Harold Epps, Digital Equipment Corporation*

> "I think women for a long time, particularly in management, were told to play the game the way the man plays it, and that's the way to get ahead. The problem with that is then you are not adding any value. If I'm attempting to think like a man, what am I bringing to the party?"
>
> *Michelle Hunt, Herman-Miller*

"Older workers bring a maturity to the workplace that is so helpful to the younger workers who come in here; they are wonderful role models for younger workers. They really are a tremendous resource."

Eleanor Hill, General Mills Restaurants

CHAPTER NINE

Our exemplars understand, as few companies do, the vital link between business and the diverse needs of the society in which it is embedded. Their sense of corporate social responsibility runs deep and is basic to their health and the success of their mission.

"This is why so many people want to work at The Body Shop, and why no one leaves. It's our values—our goals, our causes are every bit as valuable to us as our products and profits. What moves the spirit is not a moisture cream. Our employees don't dream of soap when they go home. It's all the noble purposes we've all decided to put our energies into."

Anita Roddick, The Body Shop

"When you put risk capital into a school, you are not just investors with an eye on the bottom line. You are elders looking to the survival of the culture."

Thomas Kean, Former Governor of New Jersey

"Some people argue that doing what's right is somehow contrary to doing what's good for business. I find this view both puzzling and wrong. In my own company, we have learned over and over again that when we do what we believe is proper, the company gains. I don't know how to translate that value into a number that appears on a financial statement, but I do know that we wouldn't want to be in business and we would not be the leader in our industry if we did not enjoy this kind of relationship with our people."

Walter Haas, Jr., Levi Strauss

CHAPTER TEN

Supporting the corporation's health and mission, giving its actions clarity and coherence, are the stories we tell each other
about the Way Things Work. Stories about why the organization—and all of business—exists, where it is trying to head and
what it is trying to become. These deeper stories shift through the
telling of innumerable smaller, more personal, stories recounted
each day on the job. More and more, these everyday stories are
revealing a "pattern that connects"; a pattern that tells a larger
story of collaboration, partnerships, and the reconciliation of diverse viewpoints. A new story of business.

"We are always going to have a union in this company
because the union keeps me honest. I look at the union as a
partner."

Will Potter, Preston Trucking

"3M is our greatest competitor and also our greatest
teacher. They're one of the best benchmark companies I've
ever studied. I keep telling our people they're one of the
best partners we have here. As tough as they are, they also
have great respectability, they have high goals, they have
high profit margins; they're the third most profitable
company on Wall Street in after-tax dollars."

Jack Kahl, Manco Inc.

"We had received a few letters, and generally they were
positive, but they would say: 'It's really too bad you use
those foam peanuts. Have you thought of using something
else?' or 'I am really going to have to start looking for
another source if you guys don't stop using them.' People
wanted to continue to order products from us, and they

liked our service, but they objected to us using the foam peanuts. I figured if so many people had taken the time to write to us, then there must be many more people thinking along the same lines. So we stopped using foam and started using a tissue made from 100 percent recycled magazines instead."

Patricia Gallup, PC Connection, Inc.

Bibliography of Recommended Readings

Albrecht, Karl. *At America's Service: How Corporations Can Revolutionize the Way They Treat Their Customers*. Homewood, IL: Dow Jones-Irwin, 1988.

Albrecht focuses on the implementation of the service management model he introduced in *Service America*. Executives are beginning to recognize that the old manufacturing model of management does not work for organizations that wish to provide superior service. The model, which Albrecht terms the "General Motors" approach to management, calls for the vast majority of workers to do little more than carry out instructions. The service management model, by contrast, gives all employees responsibility for satisfying the customer in each interaction, rather than commanding them to take orders. Albrecht shows why and how putting customers first—making their needs and problems the central concern of management—results in employee enthusiasm and commitment, as well as superior service.

Albrecht, Karl, and Ron Zemke. *Service America! Doing Business in the New Economy*. Homewood, IL: Dow Jones-Irwin, 1985.

In this well-received book, Albrecht and Zemke discuss the focus of the American corporation on the quality of service. We live in an era in which organizations must perform rather than produce, an era in which physical products are distinguished by the quality of the accompanying service. As a result, improving service has become a top priority of most organizations.

"Service management" focuses on what happens during thousands of "moments of truth"—the critical encounters between customers and organizations, from which customers form their impressions of the organization's quality and service. This book and its sequel, *At America's Service: How Corporations Can Revolutionize the Way They Treat Their Customers*, offer many useful ideas and strategies for improving relationships with customers and enhancing service quality.

Capra, Fritjof. *The Turning Point: Science, Society and the Rising Culture*. New York: Simon & Schuster, 1982.

In this fascinating volume, Capra shows how the revolution in modern physics—from the Newtonian to the Einsteinian world view—foreshadows an imminent revolution in *all* the sciences and a transformation of our world views and values. "The major problems of our time are all different facets of one and the same crisis, which is essentially a crisis in perception," Capra writes. In his view, the crisis derives from the fact that we are trying to apply the concepts of an outdated, mechanistic world view to a reality that can no longer be explained in terms of the old paradigm.

In place of our mechanical, reductionist approach to systemic problems, Capra offers us a new vision of reality. It is one that involves fundamental changes in our thoughts, perceptions, and values. The Capra book provides a fine overview of what we are calling the "new story." It will prove enlightening to those readers who want to understand the "why" of the new story in addition to the "how."

Davis, Stanley M. *Future Perfect*. Reading, MA: Addison-Wesley, 1987.

In this engrossing book, Davis argues that the limits to innovation, and to modern businesses, lie not in technology, but in a misguided managerial mind-set. Davis explains that limiting our thinking to the familiar context of the Industrial Age—the old story of business—will never allow us to fully utilize the essential raw materials of "the new economy"—time, space, and matter. He discusses the vital importance of time in the new story world; demonstrates why we need organizations without hierarchy; and highlights the growing importance of intangibles (what he calls "no-matter") in both products and services. Davis describes how successful managers think in the "future perfect tense." He emphasizes the importance of understanding and managing *process* rather than focusing on specific, isolated events as a key to success in the fast-paced future world of business.

Garfield, Charles A. *Peak Performers: The New Heroes of American Business*. New York: William Morrow, 1986.

This book reports on the results of my career-long study of high achievers, a study begun during my work on the *Apollo 11* project, which landed the first men on the moon. Included in the book is a profile of peak performers. These everyday heroes possess an identifiable set of characteristics and skills that others can learn. Specifically, peak performers are motivated to achieve results in real time by a personal mission; they possess the twin capacities of self-management and team mastery; and they have the ability to correct course and manage change. My challenge to the reader is to learn and apply the skills developed by the peak performers profiled in the book—from the frontline employee to the middle manager to the CEO in the executive suite.

Hampden-Turner, Charles. *Charting the Corporate Mind: Graphic Solutions to Business Conflicts*. New York: The Free Press, 1990.

In this challenging book, Hampden-Turner, a researcher at the London Business School, contends that an organization's success depends on its ability to reconcile seemingly opposite values and strategies. For example, companies must decide whether to pursue mass marketing or flexible production and whether to target broad or niche markets. Through interviews with managers of major corporations like Shell Oil and Apple Computer, Hampden-Turner introduces a mapping scheme—a step-by-step logic based on systems dynamics—that allows managers to reconcile and integrate opposites and thus resolve the major dilemmas that impede the success of the organization.

This book is especially useful for readers of *Second to None* who are interested in furthering their understanding of the thinking that undergirds the new story of business. Hampden-Turner is one of a rare breed of individual, a first-rate thinker who has managed to reconcile humanism and pragmatism and develop workable approaches to some of the most pressing problems facing organizations today.

Hampden-Turner, Charles. *Corporate Culture for Competitive Edge: A User's Guide*. London: The Economist Publications, 1990.

Here, Hampden-Turner tackles the elusive yet critical topic of corporate culture. The culture of an organization, says Hampden-Turner, defines behavior, motivates individuals, and determines problem-solving approaches. He notes that culture governs the way a company processes information, its internal relations, and its values. Most significantly, Hampden-Turner contends that in the world of increasingly fast-paced business and sophisticated, knowledge-based products, control and understanding of the corporate culture are key responsibilities of leaders.

Using some of the same concepts described in *Charting the Corporate Mind*, Hampden-Turner defines the role of the corporate leader in creating an environment in which opposing forces can be reconciled to create value and optimize growth. His aim is to help readers understand the culture of their organization, assess the limits of that culture, appreciate its potential, and use that potential to increase the effectiveness of the organization.

Harman, Willis, and John Hormann. *Creative Work: The Constructive Role of Business in a Transforming Society*. Indianapolis: Knowledge Systems Inc., 1990.

The authors pose the question: "What are the new ways of doing business that can provide every citizen opportunities for meaningful and fulfilling work?" In response, they describe a profound transformation of work and business that is already underway. At the heart of this transformation, they note, are the changing goals and deepening values of the vast "creative middle-band" of the workforce—men and women who are demanding that the corporation provide them with meaningful work. In addition, a growing number of employees want their companies to act as responsible planetary citizens as well as responsible employers. The authors emphasize that businesses are in a unique position to channel these newfound employee aspirations for fulfilling work and a healthier environment into a constructive transformation of the marketplace, a transformation that will also help to heal an ailing society.

Liebig, James E. *Business Ethics: Profiles in Civic Virtue.* Golden, CO: Fulcrum Publishing, 1990.

Liebig asserts that the corporation is the dominant social institution in America today and, as such, it has a great responsibility to contemporary society. When business leadership is practiced irresponsibly, Liebig states, the society suffers along with the business. By contrast, responsible business leadership benefits society as well as the corporation. Liebig presents 24 case studies of executives whose ethical, responsible leadership has had a dramatic positive impact on their companies and on the larger society in which they operate.

Loden, Marilyn, and Judy B. Rosener. *Workforce America! Managing Employee Diversity as a Vital Resource.* Homewood, IL: Business One Irwin, 1991.

Loden and Rosener note that by the year 2010, white males will account for less than 40 percent of the total American workforce, and women and people of color will fill 75 percent of the 24 million new jobs created in the United States over the next two decades. With these statistics in mind, they discuss the creation of a workplace that capitalizes on the creativity and richness that increased diversity offers.

Loden and Rosener show how to develop more productive working relationships by building bridges among diverse groups of employees. They describe the leadership skills required to manage a diverse workforce effectively and argue the importance of viewing differences as organizational assets rather than liabilities. This is a straightforward and practical guide which shows that managing diversity as a vital resource can lead to "increased creativity, innovation, and enhanced productivity—beneficial to both the organization and its employees."

O'Toole, James. *Vanguard Management: Redesigning the Corporate Future.* New York: Doubleday, 1985.

O'Toole, a business professor at the University of Southern California, believes that management is a moral undertaking and not simply a money-making endeavor. While his focus is more on ethics than on profits, he argues that no company has ever gotten into "financial hot water by taking the high road." Throughout the book, O'Toole profiles what he calls the "Vanguard Companies," successful firms that may stumble and fall along the way, but which always return to a strong set of guiding principles and ethics. Using one of our exemplars, Motorola, O'Toole makes the point that Vanguard Companies do nothing fundamentally different in bad times than in good. They may respond to a downturn by making appropriate strategic, tactical, and product changes, but they never abandon their fundamental principles. In Motorola's case, "employee participation and decision making, sharing of product gains, open and complete argument on controversial issues, and the goal of zero product defects." This is in stark contrast to the crisis management styles evidenced by many companies when they confront a serious problem.

O'Toole sees the success of the Vanguard Companies, especially in hard times, as due to: (1) balancing the legitimate claims of the corporation's constituencies—employees, customers, suppliers, dealers, shareholders, and managers; (2) consistent dedication to their guiding principles; (3) continuous learning; and (4) high aim, that is, being the very best at what they do.

Pascale, Richard Tanner. *Managing on the Edge: How the Smartest Companies Use Conflict to Stay Ahead.* New York: Simon & Schuster, 1990.

Pascale, a lecturer at the Stanford Business School, makes the observation that nothing fails like success. Companies flourish, only to lose their competitive edge through a process that is both relentless and likely invisible, according to Pascale. He discusses the limits to growth of any organization, and shows how success inevitably breeds problems of its own. With this in mind, Pascale addresses the central question: How can executives sustain organizational learning and ensure sustained vitality?

Pascale believes the answer is to cultivate and harness tension. Many executives, he notes, are uneasy with conflict, contention, and contradiction. As a result, they search for the middle ground, thinking that compromise is the answer to all problems. The result is what Pascale calls "the blahs": organizations without distinction and with little creativity. On the other hand, some organizations are so filled with contention and conflict that they lose their focus and may degenerate into chaos.

Pascale suggests that companies which thrive in the long run neither eliminate conflict nor advocate excessive chaos, but instead pursue an ongoing process of managing conflict productively. Relying on extensive interviews with business leaders and in-depth, on-site reporting at such companies as IBM, Ford, Honda, Intel, Citicorp, and General Electric, he shows how companies can use tension creatively to integrate opposing views and to sustain the organization's competitive edge. Along with Charles Hampden-Turner, Pascale is one of the most important contributors to the thinking presented in *Second to None*.

Peters, Tom. *Thriving on Chaos: A Handbook for a Management Revolution*. New York: Alfred A. Knopf, 1987.

In his latest book, which touts the need for a "revolution" in corporate management, Peters provides a great deal of practical, useful advice on such topics as delivering value to customers, providing superior service, valuing the creativity of all workers, and leadership at all levels. Peters contends that challenging everything we thought we knew about managing is a necessity if the corporation is to survive and thrive in today's chaotic, fast-paced global economy. These times demand that flexibility and "the love of change" replace our longstanding attachment to mass production and the status quo, based as they are on a relatively slow-paced, predictable environment—an environment which no longer exists. The "revolution" detailed in this useful book is part of a much larger revolution in our notion of How the World Works, a fundamental shift in paradigm that is transforming every aspect of the corporation.

Pinchot III, Gifford. *Intrapreneuring: Why You Don't Have to Leave the Corporation to Become an Entrepreneur*. New York: Harper & Row, 1985.

An insightful book about "the dreamers who do"—those em

ployees who take hands-on responsibility for creating innovation within an organization. This is a practical book filled with useful information on how to harness the entrepreneurial talents of employees who would otherwise leave the corporation.

Pinchot believes that when the CEO calls for innovation, very little happens—not because of a lack of good ideas, but because of the difficulty innovative employees encounter in trying to implement their ideas in the midst of the bureaucracy. Nevertheless, we frequently find small, independent groups of action-takers who are willing and able to circumvent the system and champion innovation. Pinchot shows how the corporation can help rather than hinder these efforts. This book is an excellent read for those who wish to understand how enterprising employees and managers can learn to innovate in the often stifling environment of modern business.

Reich, Robert E. *Tales of a New America*. New York: Times Books, 1987.

In this eloquent book, Harvard University professor Reich explains that our culture is shaped by mythology—the tales we tell each other about The Way Things Work. We take these tales as articles of faith, whether or not they are in fact true. If our politics, our economic system, and our organizations seem to be in disarray, says Reich, it is because the stories that define them no longer have validity. For example, a central tale we tell and retell in America is that of the "triumphant individual" who towers above the masses of workers (the "drones," to use Reich's term). Clinging to this outmoded story in an era that demands mutual responsibility and the full participation of all workers is dangerous.

Until we begin telling ourselves new and more appropriate tales, says Reich, we will be blind to new approaches to the problems that beset us as a society. The concept of the old and new stories of business presented in *Second to None* is furthered by Reich's work. Along with Hampden-Turner and Pascale, I highly recommend this book for those who wish to extend their understanding of some of the basic concepts presented in *Second to None*.

Sahtouris, Elisabet. *Gaia: The Human Journey from Chaos to Cosmos*. New York: Pocket Books, 1989.

A superb book that offers a basic understanding of living systems and ecosystemic thinking—central to the new story of business. Recent discoveries support a relatively new scientific viewpoint that is gaining credibility: That the planet Earth functions as a single living organism and that we, as part of the planet, are *life within life*. Sahtouris, who embraces this new planetary model, explains how we can solve many of the problems that beset our corporations and our societies by learning from nature.

The book describes, in fascinating detail, some of the critical concepts, derived from nature, which undergird the new story of business—the concept of diversity, the notion of holarchy, the relationship between competition and collaboration in nature and in business, the idea of a living network structure. Sahtouris believes that businesses must work as allies of the Earth rather than its adversaries if we are to ensure both our long-term survival and the health of the planet on which we depend for life.

Senge, Peter M. *The Fifth Discipline: The Art and Practice of the Learning Organization*. New York: Doubleday Currency, 1990.

"Learning disabilities are tragic in children, but they are fatal in organizations. Because of them, few corporations live even half as long as a person—most die before they reach the age of forty." So writes MIT's Peter Senge in this path-breaking book on building "learning organizations." Senge's learning organization manages to avoid certain crippling learning disabilities that plague other organizations. The most serious disability is the delusion of learning from experience.

Specifically, Senge argues that we can no longer understand the future by relying on the past. To do so is to find ourselves trying to resolve the same problems over and over again, despite a changed context. Like Stanley Davis, Senge stresses that managers must give up their fixation on isolated events and focus on the underlying processes that impact the organization—processes to which we are "90 percent blind."

Senge's discussion of teamwork is useful background for understanding the differences between the old and new stories of business. He discusses "the myth of teamwork" and claims that most
teams operate below the level of the lowest I.Q. in the group. The
result is "skilled incompetence" with team members growing in-
credibly efficient at keeping themselves from learning. Senge uses
physicist David Bohm's concept of "dialogue," which is central to
understanding the new story smart team.

Toffler, Alvin. *PowerShift: Knowledge, Wealth and Violence at the
Edge of the 21st Century*. New York: Bantam Books, 1990.

In this third book of the trilogy that began with *Future Shock*, Toffler turns his attention to the largely unnoticed shifts of power
that are taking place in the personal, everyday world we in-
habit—the world of retail stores and hospitals, banks and business offices. He discusses how these "powershifts" are transforming many aspects of our personal and business lives.

In a chapter entitled "Power in the Flex-Firm," Toffler argues that
many diverse and seemingly unrelated conflicts and upheavals in
business today are actually the result of a "new system for wealth
creation"—a system based on knowledge rather than physical
raw materials. Only those companies that share knowledge with
their employees can generate the ongoing innovation that is the
source of success in modern business.

Sharing knowledge with employees upsets the traditional power
structure of the organization. Toffler details the profound impact
of the knowledge revolution on corporate structure and functioning. He demonstrates why a shift in power from the executive
suite to the factory floor is inevitable, and shows how corporations that embrace "the revolution" rather than fear it are likely to
lead the way in the coming decades.

Weisbord, Marvin R. *Productive Workplaces: Organizing and Managing for Dignity, Meaning and Community*. San Francisco: Jossey-
Bass, 1987.

Weisbord asserts that to develop a productive workplace, managers must address three central issues. They are: employees'
hunger for community; the need for total involvement of all

employees; and the resolution of the inner conflicts that inhibit employees from working effectively in groups—specifically, the conflicting desires for autonomy and dependence, and for individuality and belonging. Weisbord shows how dignity and meaning are enhanced as managers address and resolve these issues, and how an increasingly productive workplace can result.

This excellent book offers a broad historical overview of the forces that shaped the American corporation during the twentieth century. It emphasizes the need for a systems approach to modern organizations, and offers insights into reconciling the needs of individuals and their companies.

Winter, Georg. *Business and the Environment*. New York: McGraw-Hill, 1988.

Until recently, any manager determined to run his or her company both profitably and with an eye to the environment was daunted by numerous complex and seemingly insoluble problems. No framework existed for dealing with these dilemmas. Winter offers such a framework. He presents a comprehensive model for "environmentalist business management."

Along with a compelling discussion of the need for the model, Winter offers an extensive list of practical suggestions for companies that want to incorporate environmental awareness into every aspect of the business, without jeopardizing profits. Winter focuses on environmental protection measures that cut costs and increase profits; outlines measures that can guard the corporation against increasingly stringent liability for environmental damage; and shows how companies can react promptly to the public's accelerating demand for "environmentally friendly" products.

A side benefit of this focus on environmental issues, says Winter, is increased employee satisfaction. Employees are gratified by the knowledge that their work is not jeopardizing the health of the environment, their own health, or that of their children and of future generations.

RECOMMENDED PERIODICALS

I recommend the following periodicals, which collectively offer a broad view of the changing story of business. Each source contains articles that capture the old and the new stories of business and the struggle of corporations attempting this transformation. A regular review of these sources will further familiarize the reader with the issues discussed in *Second to None*.

California Management Review
350 Barrows Hall
University of California
Berkeley, CA 94720
415-642-7159

Fortune
P.O. Box 60001
Tampa, FL 33660-0001
800-621-8200

Harvard Business Review
P.O. Box 52624

Boulder, CO 80322
800-274-3214

Inc.
38 Commercial Wharf
Boston, MA 02110
617-248-8000

Sloan Management Review
204 North Roche
Knoxville, IA 50138
800-876-5764

Interviewees and Their Companies

I want to recognize those men and women whose stories led me to many of the key concepts in *Second to None*. They proved to be a whirlwind of ideas, information, and actions; an innovative network in themselves. Each of them would be quick to describe their success by saying that they had lots of help. This is inevitable because in making a business or a team happen, one has no choice but to depend on others.

Our interviews combined aspects of the research interview, the clinical interview, and a conversation between colleagues. As a research interview, certain topics had to be covered. However, I was as sensitive as possible to the feelings expressed by each interviewee. As conversations between colleagues, the relationships were egalitarian and I usually felt free to respond with personal experiences of my own. The result was not simply a formal research encounter, but a relationship of some intensity and intimacy.

Our interviewees constitute a small sample of the inspired and inspiring individuals who are consciously creating healthy work environments in America and around the world; environments that support many more company stakeholders than in the past. This book is really their story, and I offer them my deepest thanks and admiration.

Sven G. Atterhed
Co-Founder
The ForeSight Group
Sweden

Guy Benjamin
Director of Sports in Society
New College of California,
San Francisco

Michelle Clark, M.D.
Senior Attending Physician/
Black Focus Unit
San Francisco General
Hospital

Price Cobbs, M.D.
President
Pacific Management Systems,
San Francisco

Mike Conway
President
America West Airlines

Derryl Cox
Customer Service
Representative
America West Airlines

Rod Cox
Senior Director of Recruitment
Training
Professional Development and
Human Resources
America West Airlines

Jenny Crowe-Innes
Director of Employment
Employee Relations and EEO
Levi Strauss

Harold T. Epps
Site Manager
Digital Equipment Corporation

Patricia Gallup
President and CEO
PC Connection, Inc.

Stephen Garey
Co-Founder and Creative
Director
Stephen Garey & Associates

Edward Garfield
Sales Engineer, Retired
Kester Solder, a part of
Litton Industries

Henry Givray
Executive Director
Society for Information
Management
Vice President
Smith, Bucklin & Associates,
Inc.

Lewis Griggs
Filmmaker and Diversity
Consultant

Andrew Grove, Ph.D.
President and CEO
INTEL Corporation

John Hammitt
Vice President
Information Systems
United Technologies

Eleanor Hill
Director of Training and
Development
General Mills Restaurants

Charles House
General Manager
Software Engineering Systems
Division
Hewlett-Packard

Michelle Hunt
Vice President for Corporate
Development
People Services
Herman-Miller

Victor Hunter
President
Hunter Business Direct

Jack Kahl
President and CEO
Manco, Inc.

Nancy Kaltreider, M.D.
Professor, Department of
Medicine
University of California at
San Francisco

Tony LaRussa
Manager
The Oakland Athletics

Joe Lee
Executive Vice President of
Finance
General Mills, Inc.

Alvin P. Lehnerd
Vice President of Product
Development
Steelcase, Inc.

Elliott Levine
Vice President of Retail Sales
Merisel

John Lynch
Corporate Manager
Diversity and Affirmative
Action
Hewlett-Packard

Clay Mathile
Chairman and CEO
The IAMS Company

Frank H. Merlotti
President and CEO
Steelcase, Inc.

Raymond E. Miles
Professor of Business
Administration
Walter A. Haas School of
Business
University of California at
Berkeley

Will Potter
Chairman
Preston Trucking

Pat Riley
Head Coach
New York Knicks

Anita Roddick
President
The Body Shop
International PLC
England

Ricardo Frank Semler
President
Semco
Brazil

Bill Smith
Chairman and CEO
Smith, Bucklin & Associates,
Inc.

Jim Stryker
Marketing Manager
Business and Industry
Development
Ingersoll-Rand

Sue Thompson
Director of Human Resource
Development
Levi Strauss

Ruth Thomson
Customer Service
Representative
America West Airlines

Frank Tsai
Management Company Board
Director
Working Assets

Mark Vermilion
Director of Corporate Affairs
Sun Microsystems, Inc.

Barbara Walker
Vice President
Human Resources and Human
Relations
University of Cincinnati
(formerly) International
Diversity Manager
Digital Equipment Corpora-
tion

Bill Walsh
Former Head Coach
San Francisco 49ers

Sam M. Walton
Chairman
Wal-Mart Stores, Inc.

A. William Wiggenhorn
President, Motorola University
Corporate V.P. of Training &
Education
Motorola, Inc.

Eugene R. Wilson
President
ARCO Foundation

King Ming Young
Manager, Professional
Development Group
Corporate Education
Hewlett-Packard

Albert Yu
Vice President
Micro Products Group
INTEL Corporation

Ruth Ziolkowski
CEO
Crazy Horse Memorial
Foundation

Acknowledgments

All books are collaborations with the author receiving the lion's share of the credit when the work is well received and a similar share of the blame when its reception is cool. A special team of fully participating partners worked diligently on *Second to None* to ensure a positive outcome. Through it all, they were scrupulously organized, ever attentive, and always eager to proceed with the project.

Cindy Spring, who the really careful readers of my recent books may recognize from previous acknowledgments. Heartfelt thanks, partner, for making *Second to None* your project as well. Many times she stayed up half the night with me discussing ideas, improving sections that needed work, and organizing tasks. Finally, we'd collapse in exhaustion, heads spinning, only to begin anew the next morning. Cindy's primary contribution was designing the structure of the chapters. She also added wisdom, first-rate editorial input, and a genuine enthusiasm for the project. Thanks for your patience and perseverance. Most of all, thank you for sharing the mission. Without you, dear wife, this book simply would not be.

Jeannine Marschner, whose superb skills as a writer were always in evidence and whose organizational and editorial skills warrant special thanks. We produced the earliest chapter drafts together when the going was rough and polished the final versions of the chapters when deadlines were near. She was a partner in all facets of the project, bringing to bear her considerable business acumen in helping to create the finished work. I can pay her no higher compliment than to say I would welcome the opportunity to work with her again.

Ellen Broda, whose commitment, intelligence, and dedication to *Second to None* manifested themselves in many months of mighty effort as researcher, interview coordinator, permissions liaison, typist, and general logistics supervisor. She spent countless hours tracking down leads for interviews, convincing very busy people to participate in the project, and then getting their best efforts in final revisions. She located dozens of secondary sources, secured the necessary publisher permissions, and, all in all, functioned as a full partner on our team.

No author could have hoped for better colleagues than the expert professionals at BUSINESS ONE IRWIN. This team of talented men and women worked endlessly to ensure that *Second to None* lived up to its title. I could not conclude the book without acknowledging them by name.

- Richard J. Borto, Publisher of BUSINESS ONE IRWIN, led a team of publishing professionals that was truly second to none.
- Jeff Krames's editorial creativity and commitment to this project made him the kind of editor that authors hope for but never expect to find. Thanks for caring so much about the book and for enthusiastically representing it to your colleagues at BUSINESS ONE IRWIN.
- Mike Desposito spearheaded the superb sales effort, making sure that *Second to None* could be found on bookstore shelves coast to coast.
- Rick Riddering, Manager of Publicity, is a breath of fresh air in the publishing industry. He contributed consistently with his many good ideas and his everpresent partnership.
- Tony Frankos put his committed staff of sales peak performers to work on the all-important campaign to make the book available to corporations and associations worldwide.
- Carol DeSelm wore many hats on this project, all of them expertly. She was responsible for trade sales, library sales, and an ambitious, results-producing advertising campaign.

- Drew Gierman, Director of Telemarketing, emerged from a detail-flooded office every night with stellar book sales that impressed all of us.

- Louis DeWinter, a consummate professional, represented *Second to None* on four continents, helping us make the book an international publishing partnership.

- Sharon Ginsberg gave new meaning to the words tenacity and enthusiasm in her successful effort to make *Second to None* a main selection of the Executive Program Book Club.

- Tim Kaage, one of the industry's most creative jacket designers, produced one of the most compelling book covers I have ever seen.

- Ray DuBois coordinated the development of BUSINESS ONE IRWIN's excellent announcement catalog as well as the direct response catalogs that introduced the book to the public.

- Jane Lightell is as expert a Project Editor as there is in the industry. Jane's versatility and thoroughness were vital in the final push to complete the project.

- Ann Cassady, Production Manager, displayed skills in the production phase and expert attention to detail that were important contributions throughout the book's evolution.

- Eugene Zucker, an exemplary and rare copy editor, made significant contributions to the book's clarity and coherence. His intelligence regarding the content was an unexpected, value-adding delight.

- Julie Thompson worked diligently with the entire staff on everything from the jacket copy to those stunning ads in *Publishers Weekly*, *The New York Times*, and elsewhere.

- Barbara Novosel handled many of the behind-the-scenes tasks so vital to a good book campaign.

I would like to express my gratitude to a few people whose assistance added significantly to the book. It is my privilege and pleasure to acknowledge their support.

Sven Atterhed, co-founder of The ForeSight Group of Sweden, one of our new story companies, for paving the way for my interviews with Anita Roddick of The Body Shop and Ricardo Semler of Semco, and for reconnecting me with Randy Root of Root Publishing. Like everyone else who meets Sven and his colleagues, Lennart Boksjo and Gustaf Delin, I must say that global business would be in far better shape if all of us underpromised and overdelivered like the ForeSighters.

Randall Root, president of Root Publishing, Inc., for his kind introductions to Jack Kahl and Manco, Inc., and Will Potter and Preston Trucking. Both interviews contributed mightily to the book and its message.

Jack Kahl, CEO of Manco, Inc., another of our new story exemplars, for arranging the interview with Sam Walton, CEO of Wal-Mart. Manco's proud partnership with Wal-Mart is a bright light in this still too adversarial age.

Henry Givray, vice president of Smith, Bucklin and Associates, and executive director of the Society for Information Management, for sharing his invaluable insights on both organizations and for obtaining the fine comments of John Hammitt, vice president, United Technologies. Thanks also to Henry's colleagues at SBA for their ongoing support, especially Bill Smith, CEO.

Bertil Norfolk, president of Humana Development, for serving as a special liaison to Volvo/Sweden and securing the specifics on the Uddevalla plant. Thanks for conducting interviews at Volvo, translating them expertly into English, and having them typed and forwarded on time.

Guy Benjamin, director of Sports in Society at New College of California in San Francisco, for his insights on sports and team structure, and for arranging the interview with Bill Walsh, former head coach of the San Francisco 49ers.

I readily acknowledge a number of intellectual debts to a few genuine explorers whose contributions to business—and to this book—are most appreciated.

Charles Hampden-Turner of the London Business School, whose work on dilemma theory and corporate culture is an example of the first-rate thinking badly needed in business today.

Richard Tanner Pascale, a lecturer in business administration at Stanford University, for his superb insights into leadership and managing contention in modern organizations.

Robert Reich, a lecturer in public policy at the John F. Kennedy School of Government, Harvard University, for his groundbreaking work on how our myths and the tales we tell about business and ourselves structure our beliefs and actions. Specifically, how the tale of the radical individualist, the Lone Pioneer, has become largely dysfunctional.

Peter Senge, director of systems thinking and organizational learning at Systems Dynamics, Massachusetts Institute of Technology, whose writing has helped us understand the learning organization.

Fritjof Capra, physicist and founder of the Elmwood Institute in Berkeley, California, for his penetrating insights into the social and economic transformation evolving today. Specifically, his analysis of self-managing systems was invaluable in our discussion of smart teams.

Elisabet Sahtouris, scientist and independent scholar, whose writings on the need for diversity in ecosystems, the role of competition and collaboration in nature, and the interdependence of holarchies were springboards to understanding living systems.

Tom Peters, management theorist, for his willingness to challenge consistently the many aspects of business orthodoxy. Most helpful was his idea that our companies must learn to thrive on chaos if they are to survive in these tumultuous times.

There can be no full accounting of my debt to the hundreds of men and women who contributed to this project since its inception. I offer my special thanks to the following:

Bernie Swain, Harry Rhoads, Jr., Fred Slowick, Jr., Tony D'Amelio, Michael Menchel, Georgene Savickas, Sheila Geoghegan, Anne Wold, Marsha Horshok, and their co-workers at the Washington Speakers Bureau, friends and colleagues all, for contributing magnificently to my speaking schedule. The engagements they secured allowed me hundreds of additional opportunities to research and speak to our smartest companies.

My colleagues at The Charles Garfield Group in Redwood City and Oakland, California, who further our organization's newest mission: to understand the values and visions of our smartest companies and their people, and to learn how their success serves as a catalyst for social and economic transformation worldwide.

A business book is no better and no worse than the values and insights communicated in the stories people share. I am deeply indebted to the innovative men and women I speak with weekly in my travels and who are teaching us the new story of business. These individuals and thousands like them around the world are crystallizing a shift from the paradigm of the machine to the paradigm of the ecosystem. Collectively, they are accelerating a move to deeper understandings of new story ideas that often float in the business community with the clarity of a murky solution. Sometimes what is needed is for an idea to be said just right, in a way that does justice to the explanatory power that is seeking expression in that idea.

In business today, there is so much of deep importance that people feel, but that has not yet been given voice in the workplace. This creates a special need for our exemplars and their peers everywhere to give voice to such ideas and feelings for the whole of a dispersed, and largely unheard, business community. Anyone who really takes the time to listen will hear their message: "Something very profound is changing out here. Something central to the way things work. Something that makes it imperative that we put people first."

Final heartfelt thanks go to two people whom I will always put first:

My mother, Sylvia Garfield, who, during the most challenging time of her life, was there to support me with love, intelligence, and enthusiasm from day one to the finish line. Mom proofread the galleys so the work was "just right," an act of loyalty and devotion to her husband and her son.

Edward Garfield, my father, to whom *Second to None* is dedicated. Dad saw only the dedication and not the final manuscript prior to his death in April 1991. Yet, after a long career in old story corporate America, he was thrilled to learn that his son's book about putting people first was dedicated to him.

Notes

Any direct quotes not cited in Notes are taken from the author's interviews.

Chapter 1

p. 9 "a constellation of concepts":

Thomas Kuhn, *The Structure of Scientific Revolutions*, cited in Jim Clemmer, *Firing on All Cylinders*, Macmillan of Canada, 1990, p. 12.

p. 11 "Tycho was the greatest":

Carl Sagan, *Cosmos*, Random House, 1980, p. 60.

p. 11 "It is no wonder":

Stanley M. Davis, *Future Perfect*, Addison-Wesley, 1987, p. 6. Reprinted by permission of Addison-Wesley Publishing Co., Inc., Reading, MA.

p. 11 "The trouble is":

Richard Tanner Pascale, *Managing on the Edge*, Simon & Schuster, 1990, p. 14.

p. 14 "We think of people's lives":

Jeremy Rifkin, *Entropy: Into the Greenhouse World*, Bantam Books, Bantam Doubleday Dell, rev. ed., 1989, p. 32.

p. 16 "During years spent":

From POWERSHIFT by Alvin Toffler, p. 204. Copyright © 1990 by Alvin Toffler and Heide Toffler. Used by permission of Bantam Books, a division of Bantam Doubleday Dell Publishing Group, Inc.

p. 17 "One worker said":

Robert Levering, *A Great Place to Work*, Random House, 1988, p. 144.

p. 17 "It's not just wrong":

Charles Hampden-Turner, "Humanistic Psychology and the Crisis of the American Economy," a keynote presentation made to the International Association of Humanistic Psychology at Mills College, Oakland, California, August 6, 1987.

p. 17   "If you are enamored":

Harold Gilliam, "The First Environmentalist," *San Francisco Chronicle* (This World), April 8, 1990, p. 19.

p. 18   "Seen from a global viewpoint":

Willis Harman and John Hormann, *Creative Work*, Knowledge Systems, 1990, p. 144.

p. 19   "Each holon, says Koestler":

Fritjof Capra, *The Turning Point*, Simon & Schuster, 1982, p. 43.

p. 19   "by coining the word 'holarchy' ":

Elisabet Sahtouris, *Gaia: The Human Journey from Chaos to Cosmos*, Simon & Schuster (Pocket Books), 1989, p. 35.

p. 22   "by the time his kids are his age":

Joe Harvey, *Rocky Mt. Institute Newsletter* 6, no. 2, Summer 1990, p. 3.

p. 23   "Already three companies":

"All Set to Bounce Back," *Fortune*, April 22, 1991, p. 282.

p. 23   "technology with a human face":

E. F. Schumacher coined the term "technology with a human face" in his landmark book, *Small Is Beautiful*, Harper & Row, 1973.

p. 25   "Bureaucracies, with all their cubbyholes":

From POWERSHIFT by Alvin Toffler, p. 177. Copyright © 1990 by Alvin Toffler and Heide Toffler. Used by permission of Bantam Books, a division of Bantam Doubleday Dell Publishing Group, Inc.

p. 26   "Despite all the slashing":

Ronald Henkoff, "Cost Cutting: How to Do It Right," *FORTUNE*, April 9, 1990, p. 43.

p. 27   "To move toward a winning culture":

Fortune, March 26, 1990, p. 30.

p. 28   "Business writer Aaron Bernstein compares":

From "Lorenzo and Eastern's Turbulent Times," a review of Bernstein's book, *Grounded: Frank Lorenzo and the Destruction of Eastern Airlines*, by John J. Nance (author of *Blind Trust*, William Morrow, 1986) in the *San Francisco Chronicle*, Review section, August 19, 1990, p. 4.

p. 29 "Frank's a confrontational":

"Workers of the Future," *Fortune*, April 22, 1991.

p. 30 "When *Fortune* surveyed the reputations":

Patricia Sellers, "Does the CEO Really Matter?" *Fortune*, April 22, 1991, p. 80.

p. 30 "But as Robert Reich so eloquently outlines":

Robert Reich, *Tales of a New America*, Random House (Vintage Books), 1988, p. 118.

p. 35 "two or more opposites were conceived":

A. Rothenberg, *The Emerging Goddess*, University of Chicago Press, 1979, p. 111.

p. 35 "In an apparent defiance of logic":

Ibid.

p. 36 "To demonstrate how opposites":

Stanley M. Davis, *Future Perfect*, Addison-Wesley, 1987, p. 85. Reprinted by permission of Addison-Wesley Publishing Co., Inc., Reading, MA.

p. 37 "Even when confronted":

Richard Tanner Pascale, *Managing on the Edge*, Simon & Schuster, 1990, p. 15.

p. 38 "While Brahe amassed facts":

Ibid., p. 15.

p. 38 "The only sure way":

Robert Levering, *100 Best Companies to Work for in America*, pp. 142–143.

Chapter 2

p. 45 "Roughly 400 of the company's":

Employee information cited in "A Glimpse of the 'Flex' Future," by Bob Cohn, *Newsweek*, August 1, 1988, and updated by Steelcase.

p. 47 "rich and confident":

David Halberstam, *The Next Century*, William Morrow, 1991, p. 33.

p. 48   "Evolutionary biologists argue":

James F. Moore, "Taking Cues from Natural Disasters," *The New York Times*, May 19, 1991, p. F11.

p. 48   "In general, the 1980s proved":

"Who May Thrive Now?" *Fortune*, April 22, 1991, p. 64.

p. 49   "I have been in this business":

Alex Taylor II, "The Odd Eclipse of a Star CEO," *Fortune*, February 11, 1991, p. 94.

p. 52   "profit will not motivate":

Jeffrey J. Hallet, *Worklife Visions*, American Society for Personnel Administration, 1987, p. 168.

p. 55   "We began to smell":

Hazel Henderson, *The Politics of the Solar Age*, Knowledge Systems, 1988, p. 174.

p. 56   "The pursuit of sustainability":

Our Common Future, World Commission on Environment and Development, 1987, p. 67.

p. 56   "A sustainable society is one":

Lester R. Brown, Christopher Flavin, and Sandra Postel, "Picturing a Sustainable Society," *The State of the World 1990*, W.W. Norton & Co., 1990.

p. 57   "The ecological investigations":

Harold Gilliam, "The First Environmentalist," *San Francisco Chronicle* (This World), April 8, 1990, p. 19.

p. 58   "Wells Fargo Bank provides":

Susan Burkhardt, "Hard-Driving Bank Leaves Many in the Dust," *San Francisco Examiner*, March 25, 1990, p. A-1.

p. 58   "They figure they can get":

Ibid.

p. 59   "to put this whole unpleasant matter":

Susan C. Faludi, "Safeway LBO Yields Vast Profits but Exacts a Heavy Human Toll," *The Wall Street Journal*, May 16, 1990, p. 1.

p. 61   "democracy in industry is not":

Philip Slater and Warren G. Bennis, "Democracy Is Inevitable," *Harvard Business Review*, September–October 1990, p. 167 (first printed in the March–April 1964 edition of *HBR*).

p. 62   "An individual without information":

"Competing on Your Learning Speed," *The ForeSight Intrapreneur*, 2nd quarter, 1990.

p. 62   "By definition, both force":

From POWERSHIFT by Alvin Toffler, p. 20. Copyright © 1990 by Alvin Toffler and Heide Toffler. Used by permission of Bantam Books, a division of Bantam Doubleday Dell Publishing Group, Inc.

p. 63   "Alvin Toffler refers to the emerging":

Ibid., p. 191; and see Chapter 16, "The Flex-Firm."

p. 63   "dynamic network model":

Raymond E. Miles, "Adapting to Technology and Competition: A New Industrial Relations System for the 21st Century," *California Management Review* 31, no. 2, Winter 1989, p. 21.

p. 63   "Miles uses the example":

Ibid.

p. 64   "Whether locating materials":

Ibid.

p. 64   "Companies simply can't prosper":

"Today's Leaders Look to Tomorrow," *Fortune*, March 26, 1990, p. 30.

p. 65   "We set goals for each group":

Gretchen Haight, "Managing Diversity," *The Conference Board Magazine* 27, no. 3, March 1990, p. 23.

p. 66   "I didn't learn much at business school":

Tom Peters, "Strategy Follows Structure: Developing Distinctive Skills," *California Management Review* 26, no. 3, Spring 1984, p. 118.

p. 68   "We can no longer assume":

Peter Vaill, *Managing as a Performing Art*, Jossey-Bass, 1989, pp. 3–14.

p. 69   "It would perform outstandingly":

From *Charting the Corporate Mind: Graphic Solutions to Business Conflicts* by Charles Hampden-Turner, p. 4. Copyright © 1990 by The Free Press, a Division of Macmillan, Inc.

p. 72 "You are not going to combine":

Ibid., p. 5.

p. 73 "The word *teamwork* was used":

John Judis, "Myth versus Man," *Business Month*, July 1990, p. 32. Reprinted with permission, *Business Month* Magazine. Copyright © 1990, by Goldhirsh Group, Inc., 38 Commercial Wharf, Boston, MA 02110.

p. 73 "They wanted us to eat":

Ibid.

p. 76 "James O'Toole describes how Atlantic Richfield":

James O'Toole, *Vanguard Management*, Berkley Books, 1987, p. xix.

p. 77 "Motorola plans ahead":

Ibid., p. xv.

p. 78 "In moving from the traditional":

Peter Senge, *The Fifth Discipline*, Doubleday, 1990, p. 290.

p. 79 "permanent white water":

Peter Vaill, *Managing as a Performing Art*, Jossey-Bass, 1989, p. 3.

p. 82 "There was no single node":

Richard Tanner Pascale, *Managing on the Edge*, Simon & Schuster, 1990, p. 125.

Chapter 3

p. 89 "Trust is a hallmark":

James O'Toole, "The Spirit of Phoenix," *Business Month*, October 1989, p. 28.

p. 90 "Another America West program":

Ibid.

p. 90 "tough on the problem":

Charles Hampden-Turner, *Corporate Culture for Competitive Edge: A Users Guide*, The Economist Publications, 1990, p. 99.

p. 96 "They never asked about our needs":

Carol J. Loomis, "Can John Akers Save IBM?" *Fortune*, July 15, 1991, p. 54.

p. 99 "The Employee Owners of America West":

Advertisement in the *Arizona Republic*, Sunday, June 30, 1991.

p. 100 "eliminating all the can'ts":

Tom Peters, "To Cut the Manual, NCR's Policies Self Destruct," *On Achieving Excellence* [newsletter] 4, no. 1, January 1989.

p. 100 "Until we're done":

"PayLess Drug Stores Unravels Reams of Policies—But Will It Ever Be Bureaucracy-Free?" Tom Peters, *On Achieving Excellence* [newsletter] 4, no. 1, January 1989.

p. 107 "children of successful executives":

Brian O'Reilly, "Why Grade-A Executives Get an F as Parents," *Fortune*, January 1, 1990, p. 36.

p. 107 "Peter Senge of M.I.T.":

Peter M. Senge, *The Fifth Discipline*, Doubleday, 1990, p. 306

p. 107 "all too common, Senge notes":

Ibid., p. 307

p. 108 "some 10 million mothers":

p. 108 "Wendy Koerner is a Steelcase product engineer":

Alan Deutschman, "Pioneers of the New Balance," *Fortune*, May 20, 1991, p. 60.

p. 108 "major competitive strategy":

Bob Rast, "Good Benefits, Good Business," Newhouse News Service, June 10, 1990, p. D3.

p. 108 "DuPont lengthened":

Ibid.

p. 110 "We want 300,000 people":

Richard Tanner Pascale, *Managing on the Edge*, Simon & Schuster, 1990, pp. 209–10.

p. 111 "David Rhodes, of the consulting firm Towers Perrin, predicts":

David Kirkpatrick, "Is Your Career on Track?" *Fortune*, July 2, 1990, p. 39.

p. 111 "In a study of eight plants, Dr. Klein found":

Total Employee Involvement [newsletter], Productivity, Inc. 2, no. 1, February 1989.

p. 113 "I did not feel too good":

"Preston Trucking Drives for Productivity," Labor-Management Cooperation Brief, U.S. Department of Labor, Bureau of Labor-Management Relations and Cooperative Programs, no. 13, February 1988.

p. 115 "Keith Dunn, a CEO who started out":

Adopted from "The Odyssey of an 'Excellent' Man" by Joshua Hyatt, *Inc.*, February 1989, p. 63.

p. 118 "a fantasy version of empowerment":

Peter Kizills, "Crazy About Empowerment?" *Training*, December 1990, p. 55.

p. 118 "How lovely to have energetic":

Ibid.

p. 121 "Employees talk about a 'people orientation'":

Robert Levering, *A Great Place to Work*, Random House, 1988, p. xxi.

p. 124 "America West must deal fairly":

Arizona Republic, June 29, 1991, p. A8.

Chapter 4

p. 130 "No existing market share":

From POWERSHIFT by Alvin Toffler, p. 213. Copyright © 1990 by Alvin Toffler and Heide Toffler. Used by permission of Bantam Books, a division of Bantam Doubleday Dell Publishing Group, Inc.

p. 132 "We have a group which we call":

Ricardo Semler, "Inverting the Pyramid: Reflections of a Leading Edge Practitioner," presentation at a joint conference by The ForeSight Group and The Economist, June 5–7, 1990.

p. 132 "Innovating in Infertile Soil":

Adopted from "GE Refrigerator Woes Illustrate the Hazards in Changing a Product," by Thomas F. O'Boyle, *The Wall Street Journal*, May 7, 1990.

p. 138 "There is no escaping":

From *Charting the Corporate Mind: Graphic Solutions to Business Conflicts* by Charles Hampden-Turner, p. 5. Copyright © 1990 by The Free Press, a Division of Macmillan, Inc.

p. 144 "flossy, big name spreads":

Robert A. Mamis, "Real Service," *Inc.*, May 1989, p. 80.

p. 144 "For example, one early double-page PCC ad":

Ibid.

p. 145 "people formulate strategy":

Ronald Henkoff, "How to Plan for 1995," *Fortune*, December 31, 1990, p. 70.

p. 148 "It reinforced in the culture":

John Markoff, "A Gunslinger's Growing Pains," *New York Times*, January 13, 1991, p. F23. Copyright 1990/91 by The New York Times Company. Reprinted by permission.

p. 149 "We've learned a lot":

Ibid.

p. 149 "when firms generate innovation":

Keith Pavitt, "What We Know about the Strategic Management of Technology," *California Management Review* 32, no. 3, Spring 1990, p. 17.

p. 155 "Champion has now become":

Rosabeth Moss Kanter, "Championing Change," *Harvard Business Review*, January–February 1991, p.128. Copyright 1991 by the President and Fellows of Harvard College; all rights reserved.

Chapter 5

p. 166 "I am convinced that our way":

Steven Prokesch, "Edges Fray on Volvo's Brave New Humanistic World," *New York Times*, July 7, 1991, p. 5F. Copyright 1990/91 by The New York Times Company. Reprinted by permission.

p. 166 "An M.I.T. study on the global car industry":

Ibid.

p. 168 "The more authority you give away":

Charles Hampden-Turner, *Corporate Culture for Competitive Edge: A Users Guide*, The Economist Publications, 1990, p. 112.

p. 168 "It's interesting to note":

Charlene Marmer Solomon, "Behind the Wheel at Saturn," *Personnel Journal*, June 1991, p. 72.

p. 168 "Cincinnati Milacron: Teaming Up to Meet the Competition":

Adapted from "The Soul of an Old Machine," by Peter Nulty, *Fortune*, May 21, 1990, p. 67.

p. 170 "The first obvious difference":

Fritjof Capra, *The Turning Point*, Simon & Schuster, 1982, p. 268.

p. 172 "Self-organizing systems":

Ibid., p. 269.

p. 175 "AT&T formed highly autonomous teams":

Brian Dumaine, How Managers Can Succeed Through Speed," *Fortune*, Feb. 13, 1989, p. 54.

p. 175 "Federal Express is also discovering":

Brian Dumaine, "Who Needs a Boss?," *Fortune*, July 7, 1990, p. 52.

p. 176 "It now takes just one day":

"The Workers of the Future," *Fortune* Special Issue, Spring 1991, p. 72.

p. 176 "Our moms and dads raised us":

Ibid.

p. 176 "Self-renewal is an essential aspect":

Fritjof Capra, *The Turning Point*, Simon & Schuster, 1982, pp. 271–72.

p. 177 "a phenomenon that expresses itself":

Ibid., p. 285.

p. 178 "dialogue is the capacity":

Peter Senge, *The Fifth Discipline*, Doubleday, 1990, p. 10.

p. 185 "the prototype of Ford's transforming":

Richard Tanner Pascale, *Managing on the Edge*, Simon & Schuster, 1990, p. 141.

p. 186 "Still, there are some hopeful signs":

Alex Taylor III, "The Odd Eclipse of a Star CEO," *Fortune*, February 11, 1991, p. 86.

Chapter 6

p. 194 "Service is becoming":

"The Strategic Management of Service Quality," *PIMSletter* 33; cited in Jim Clemmer, *Firing on All Cylinders*, Macmillan of Canada, 1990, p. 12.

p. 194 "Forum Corporation of Boston conducted an eye-opening study":

"Customer Focus Research: Executive Briefing," copyright 1988 by the Forum Corporation, Boston, MA.

p. 195 "Today even products with hard edges":

Charles Hampden-Turner, "Humanistic Psychology and the Crisis of the American Economy," a keynote presentation made to the International Association of Humanistic Psychology at Mills College, Oakland, California, August 6, 1987.

p. 198 "A corporation takes on the personality":

H. James Harrington, *The Improvement Process*, McGraw-Hill, 1987, p. 95.

p. 198 "A commitment to service excellence":

Karl Albrecht, *At America's Service*, Dow Jones-Irwin, 1988; cited in Jim Clemmer, *Firing on All Cylinders*, Macmillan of Canada, 1990, p. 105.

p. 200 "Seeing the executive director":

Patricia Sellers, "What Customers Really Want," *Fortune*, June 4, 1990, p. 58.

p. 202 "A study by the Forum Corporation":

"Customer Focus Research: Executive Briefing," copyright 1988 by the Forum Corporation, Boston, MA.

p. 202 "In his book, *The Regis Touch*":

Cited in *Healthcare Forum Journal*, May/June 1991, p. 86.

p. 202 "Service providers treat customers":

Robert Kelley, "Poorly Served Employees Serve Customers Just as Poorly," *The Wall Street Journal*, October 13, 1987, p. 15.

p. 205 "According to the Technical Assistance Research Program":

TARP statistics cited in Jim Clemmer, *Firing on All Cylinders*, Macmillan of Canada, 1990, p. 22.

p. 206 "MBNA America, the credit card operation":

Patricia Sellers, "What Customers Really Want," *Fortune*, June 4, 1990, p. 58.

p. 206 "Unfortunately, we can no longer afford":

Tom Peters, from a promotional letter; cited in Jim Clemmer, *Firing on All Cylinders*, Macmillan of Canada, 1990, p. 58.

p. 209 "companies are now broadening":

David Ulrich, "Tie the Corporate Knot: Gaining Complete Customer Commitment," *Sloan Management Review*, Summer 1989, p. 20.

p. 209 "Satisfied customers remain independent":

Ibid.

p. 218 "one of the folk legends":

Donald Lucas, "The OTISLINE 'Legend': How It Can Ensure Customer Satisfaction," *SIM Network* [newsletter], July/August 1989.

p. 219 "The computer's radically increased cost-effectiveness":

Stan Rapp and Tom Collins, *Maximarketing*, McGraw-Hill, 1984, p. 112.

Chapter 7

p. 230 "Training, it appeared":

William Wiggenhorn, "Motorola U: When Training Becomes an Education," *Harvard Business Review*, July–August 1990, p. 71.

p. 231 "U.S. employers spend more than":

John Eckhouse, "How Training Produces Profit," *San Francisco Chronicle*, March 18, 1991, p. B1.

p. 231 "Yet, according to Curtis Plott":

Ibid.

p. 231 "Much of that money went":

"Shaking the Blue Collar Blues," *Fortune*, April 22, 1991, p. 216.

p. 231 "Even so, U.S. companies budget":

Erik Calonius, "Smart Moves by Quality Champs," *Fortune* Special Issue, Spring/Summer 1991, p. 23.

p. 231 "The problem is much broader":

Nancy J. Perry, "The Workers of the Future," *Fortune* Special Issue, Spring/Summer 1991, p. 71.

p. 232 "Five years ago":

Mark Stuart Gill, "Stalking Six Sigma," *Business Month*, January 1990, p. 42.

p. 234 "We are piloting a program":

William Wiggenhorn, "Motorola U: When Training Becomes an Education," *Harvard Business Review*, July–August 1990, p. 71.

p. 235 "Our history is one of":

Ibid.

p. 237 "In a continual cycle of learning":

Alvin Toffler, *PowerShift*, Bantam Books, Bantam Doubleday Dell, 1990, p. 211.

p. 241 "We've recommitted our organization":

Manco Inc., "Duck Tales," September/October 1990.

p. 242 "The essence of real leadership":

Ibid.

p. 242 "We have found repeatedly":

Perry Pascarella, *The New Achievers*, The Free Press (Macmillan), 1984, p. 152.

p. 242 "The importance of leadership skills":

"TEI Warning: Don't Bank on Operator Training Alone," TEI newsletter, 3, no. 1, p. 7.

p. 244 "The 'judging' aspect of hiring":

Cited in Tom Peters "Group Hiring at Com Systems," *On Achieving Excellence* [newsletter], November 1988, p. 4.

p. 245 "People may or may not":

Ibid.

p. 247 "At the root of freedom":

Alex Mironoff, "De-Stalinizing the Corporation," *Training*, August 1990, p. 30.

p. 247 "The board wants a high return":

Ibid.

p. 248 "A study conducted by the Public Agenda Foundation":

H. James Harrington, *The Improvement Process*, McGraw-Hill, 1987, p. 191.

p. 248 "If you were to improve service quality":

Robert Desatnick, "Service: A CEO's Perspective," *Management Review*, October 1987, p. 41.

p. 248 "There is no art to Japanese management":

Robert Reich, *The Resurgent Liberal*, Random House, 1989, p. 83.

p. 249 "When the National Science Foundation reviewed":

Ron Zemke with Dick Schaaf, *The Service Edge*, New American Library, 1989, pp. 71–72.

p. 250 "Though there is a widespread":

Ricardo Semler, "Managing Without Managers," *Harvard Business Review*, September–October 1989, p. 76. Copyright 1989 by the President and Fellows of Harvard College; all rights reserved.

p. 251 "Nothing matters more than those vital statistics":

Ibid.

p. 251 "Solar Press, a family-owned business":

Bruce G. Posner, "If at First You Don't Succeed," *Inc.*, May 1989, p. 132.

p. 253 "You have to be willing to face":

Ibid.

p. 253 "The notion of running":

Rosabeth Moss Kanter, *When Giants Learn to Dance*, Simon & Schuster, 1989, p. 250.

p. 254 "For example, William Stritzler":

Ibid.

p. 254 "Ideas for new ventures":

Ibid.

p. 254 "By the end of 1989":

Steve Salerno, "Democracy at Work," *America West Magazine*, June 1990, p. 39.

p. 254 "Any man worth his salt":

Ibid.

p. 255 "Studies by Oakland's National Center for Employee Ownership":

Ibid.

p. 255 "The research is clear":

Ibid.

p. 255 "Captive Air Systems, for example":

Bruce G. Posner, "Owning Up," *INC.*, January 1989, p. 118.

p. 256 "We wanted a dedicated cadre":

Steven Flax, "The Ultimate Incentive," *Inc.*, May 1988, p. 147.

p. 257 "Whether we take them depends":

Ibid.

p. 258 "Once or twice a year, we order":

Ricardo Semler, "Managing Without Managers," *Harvard Business Review*, September–October 1989, p. 76. Copyright 1989 by the President and Fellows of Harvard College; all rights reserved.

p. 261 "We are starting to have broader bands":

David Kirkpatrick, "Is Your Career on Track?" *Fortune*, July 2, 1990, p. 39.

p. 262 "It's very obvious that lateral moves":

Ibid.

Chapter 8

p. 269 "'Workforce 2000: Work and Workers for the 21st Century' projected":

Beverly Geber, "Managing Diversity," *Training*, July 1990, p. 23.

p. 269 "A 1990 study conducted jointly":

Gilbert Fuchsberg, "Many Businesses Responding Too Slowly to Rapid Work Force Shifts, Study Says," *The Wall Street Journal*, July 20, 1990.

p. 270 "Minority markets in the United States":

Lennie Copeland, "Valuing Workplace Diversity," *Personnel Administrator*, November 1988, p. 38.

p. 271 "In such exchanges, their aim, Weaver believes":

Jolie Solomon, "As Cultural Diversity of Workers Grows, Experts Urge Appreciation of Differences," *The Wall Street Journal*, September 12, 1990.

p. 274 "The greater the variety":

Elisabet Sahtouris, *Gaia: The Human Journey from Chaos to Cosmos*, Simon & Schuster (Pocket Books), 1989, p. 213.

p. 275 "The human mania for making monocultures":

Ibid., p. 201.

p. 275 "People who have studied decision making":

From *Power And Influence: Beyond Formal Authority* by John P. Kotter. Copyright © 1985 by John P. Kotter. Reprinted by permission of The Free Press, a Division of Macmillan, Inc.

p. 276 "Diversity is crucial to nature":

Elisabet Sahtouris, *Gaia: The Human Journey from Chaos to Cosmos*, Simon & Schuster (Pocket Books), 1989, p. 27.

p. 280 "I think any time we try":

Mark Satin, *New Options for America*, California State University Press, 1991, p. 122.

p. 281 "In the information society":

Charles Hampden-Turner, conversation with the author, March 7, 1990, at the London Business School.

p. 284 "We challenge managers to think":

Charlene Marmer Solomon, "The Corporate Response to Workforce Diversity," *Personnel Journal*, August 1989. Copyright August 1989. Reprinted with the permission of PERSONNEL JOURNAL, Costa Mesa, California; all rights reserved.

p. 285 "To make the Jobs Plus program work":

Steve Zivolich and Richard Millard, "Jobs Plus: Pizza Hut's Corporate Initiative to Employ 3000 Workers with Disabilities," *The Journal of Staffing and Recruiting*, Spring 1990, p. 21.

p. 285 "Companies have a great need":

"The Workers of the Future," *Fortune* Special Issue, Spring 1991, p. 72.

p. 287 "the 'new ethnicity'":

From *Managing Cultural Difference*, Third Edition, by Philip R. Harris and Robert T. Moran, p. 504. Copyright © 1991 by Gulf Publishing Company, Houston, Texas. Used with permission. All rights reserved.

p. 287 "As society becomes more pluralistic"

Ibid.

p. 288 "I don't want to be forced":

Mark Satin, *New Options for America*, California State University Press, 1991, p. 122.

p. 288 "Gone are the days of 'abandoning ethnic differences'":

Presentation by Dr. R. Roosevelt Thomas, Jr., at the Food Marketing Institute Human Resources Conference, October 1, 1990, Hilton Head, South Carolina.

p. 288 "A sense of one's separateness":

From *Managing Cultural Difference*, Third Edition, by Philip R. Harris and Robert T. Moran, p. 504. Copyright © 1991 by Gulf Publishing Company, Houston, Texas. Used with permission. All rights reserved.

p. 288 "Oh, this will interest Tom":

Jolie Solomon, "As Cultural Diversity of Workers Grows, Experts Urge Appreciation of Differences," *The Wall Street Journal*, September 12, 1990.

p. 288 "You're the ones that need":

Ibid.

p. 289 "You begin to see the absurdity":

Ibid.

p. 289 "When you have a group of people":

Charlene Marmer Solomon, "The Corporate Response to Work Force Diversity," *Personnel Journal*, August 1989, p. 42. Copyright August 1989. Reprinted with the permission of *Personnel Journal*, Costa Mesa, California; all rights reserved.

p. 290 "Much to everybody's surprise":

Ibid.

p. 291 "You begin to see that once you label":

Beverly Geber, "Managing Diversity," *Training*, July 1990, pp. 26–27.

p. 292 "She said, 'I don't know what tribe'":

Jolie Solomon, "As Cultural Diversity of Workers Grows, Experts Urge Appreciation of Differences," *The Wall Street Journal*, September 12, 1990.

p. 293 "According to the joint study":

Gilbert Fuchsberg, "Many Businesses Responding Too Slowly to Rapid Work Force Shifts, Study Says," *The Wall Street Journal*, July 20, 1990.

p. 294 "Coaching is the process of enabling":

Tom Peters and Nancy Austin, *A Passion for Excellence*, Random House, 1985, pp. 325–30.

p. 294 "Historically, within homogeneous institutions":

Marilyn Loden and Judy Rosener, *Workforce America*, Business One Irwin, 1991, p. 212.

p. 296 "The joint study of the Hudson Institute and Towers Perrin revealed":

Gilbert Fuchsberg, "Many Businesses Responding Too Slowly to Rapid Work Force Shifts, Study Says," *The Wall Street Journal*, July 20, 1990.

p. 296 "But there are signs of hope":

Joel Dreyfuss, "Get Ready for the New Work Force," *Fortune*, April 23, 1990, p. 165.

p. 296 "We believe that unless":

Charlene Marmer Solomon, "The Corporate Response to Work Force Diversity," *Personnel Journal*, August 1989, p. 42. Copyright August 1989. Reprinted with the permission of *Personnel Journal*, Costa Mesa, California; all rights reserved.

p. 297 "*Fortune* magazine examined the 1990 proxy statements":

Jaclyn Fierman, "Why Women Still Don't Hit the Top," *Fortune*, July 30, 1990, p. 40.

p. 298 "Xerox sets firm goals":

Charlene Marmer Solomon, "The Corporate Response to Work Force Diversity, *Personnel Journal*, August 1989, p. 42. Copyright August 1989. Reprinted with the permission of *Personnel Journal*, Costa Mesa, California; all rights reserved.

p. 298 "I came to realize how I have been making decisions":

David Maraniss, "Firm Makes Racial Revolution from Top Down," *The Washington Post*, March 8, 1990, p. A-22. Reprinted with permission.

p. 299 "For example, Honeywell prepared":

Beverly Gerber, "Managing Diversity," *Training*, July 1990, p. 23.

p. 300 "In a 1987 *Wall Street Journal* survey":

Cynthia Crossen, "A Lingering Stigma," *The Wall Street Journal* Special Report on Executive Style, March 20, 1987.

p. 302 "Avon once had a women's network":

Joel Dreyfuss, "Get Ready for the New Work Force," *Fortune*, April 23, 1990, p. 165.

p. 303 "More and more people in peacetime":

Elisabet Sahtouris, *Gaia: The Human Journey from Chaos to Cosmos*, Simon & Schuster (Pocket Books), 1989, p. 196.

p. 304 "It's about creating an environment":

Jim Schachter, "Firms Begin to Embrace Diversity," *Los Angeles Times*, April 17, 1989, Part I, p. 1.

p. 305 "When white male managers":

Lennie Copeland, "Making the Most of Cultural Differences at the Workplace," *Personnel*, June 1988, p. 52.

p. 305 "expand our mental horizons":

Mark Satin, *New Options for America*, California State University Press, 1991, p. 122.

p. 307 "Men are going to have to learn":

"Sally Helgesen Articulates 'The Female Advantage,'" Tom Peters, *On Achieving Excellence* [newsletter], July 1990, p. 34.

Chapter 9

p. 315 "Every individual endeavors":

Adam Smith, *The Wealth of Nations*, 1776.

p. 316 "hires hard-core unemployed instead of better-qualified available workmen."

Milton Friedman, "The Social Responsibility of Business Is to Increase Its Profits," *The New York Times Magazine*, cited in James O'Toole, *Vanguard Management*, Berkley Books, 1987, p. 361.

p. 316 "In each of these cases, the corporate executive":

Ibid.

p. 317 "there are evidently some principles":

James Q. Wilson, "Adam Smith on Business Ethics," *California Management Review* 32, no. 1, Fall 1989, p. 59.

p. 319 "A company's values—what it stands for":

Robert Howard, "Values Make the Company: An Interview with Robert Haas," *Harvard Business Review*, September–October 1990, p. 133. Copyright 1990 by the President and Fellows of Harvard College; all rights reserved.

p. 320 "Many managers exhibit a reluctance to describe":

Frederick B. Bird and James A. Waters, "The Moral Muteness of Managers," *California Management Review* 32, no. 1, Fall 1989, p. 73.

p. 322 "According to a 1989 Gallup poll":

Connie Koenenn, "How 'Green Consumers' Are Changing the Marketplace," *San Francisco Chronicle*, March 26, 1990, p. B1.

p. 322 "And a 1989 survey conducted for the Michael Peters Group":

David Kirkpatrick, "Environmentalism: The New Crusade," *Fortune*, February 12, 1990, p. 44.

p. 322 "McDonald's, a giant producer":

Ibid.

p. 323 "I believe anything that goes out":

John Holusha, "Ed Woolard Walks DuPont's Tightrope," *New York Times*, October 14, 1990, p. F1. Copyright 1990/91 by The New York Times Company. Reprinted by permission.

p. 323 "That is a brand new thought":

Ibid.

p. 324 "The rise of the Green party in Germany":

Shawn Tully, "What the Greens Mean for Business," *Fortune*, October 23, 1989, p. 46.

p. 324 "But other companies, such as 3M":

David Kirkpatrick, "Environmentalism: The New Crusade," *Fortune*, February 12, 1990, p. 44.

p. 324 "In the spring of 1990, Varta":

Shawn Tully, "What the Greens Mean for Business," *Fortune*, October 23, 1989, p. 46.

p. 326 *"25 Things Your Organization Can Do to Heal the Environment"*:

This list draws heavily on the Integrated System of Environmentalist Business Management (known as the Winter Model). For a detailed review of the model, see Georg Winter, *Business and the Environment*, McGraw-Hill, 1988.

p. 327 "A recent study by the National Assessment":

Alison J. Sprout, "Do U.S. Schools Make the Grade?" *Fortune* (Special Issue), Spring 1990, p. 50.

p. 327 "According to a 1988 study by the Educational Testing Service":

Andrew Kupfer, "Turning Students On to Science" *Fortune* (Special Issue), Spring 1990, p. 82.

p. 327 "At a time when European leaders":

Alison L. Sprout, "Do U.S. Schools Make the Grade?," ibid., p. 50.

p. 328 "These were good guys":

Joel Dreyfuss, "The Three R's on the Shop Floor," ibid., p. 86.

p. 328 "Nearly 20 percent of the 163 large corporations":

"Worker Illiteracy Called a Time Bomb," *San Francisco Chronicle*, October 9, 1990, p. C4.

p. 328 "The most important economic development":

From POWERSHIFT by Alvin Toffler, p. 9. Copyright © 1990 by Alvin Toffler and Heide Toffler. Used by permission of Bantam Books, a division of Bantam Doubleday Dell Publishing Group, Inc.

p. 328 "The rising importance of mind-work":

Ibid., p. 83.

p. 329 "I think most chief executives":

"Why I Got Involved," *Fortune* (Special Issue), Spring 1990, p. 46.

p. 329 "The Xerox chief and his wife":

Ibid.

p. 329 "Arco president Robert Wycoff":

Nancy J. Perry, "Being Principal for a Day," *Fortune* (Special Issue), Spring 1990, p. 65.

p. 329 "Nucor has a plan that provides":

James E. Liebig, *Business Ethics: Profiles in Civic Virtue*, Fulcrum Publishing, 1990, p. 116.

p. 330 "The experiment has measurably improved productivity at ABIG":

Bernie Ward, "Corporations and Kindergartens," *Sky Magazine*, April 1991, p. 28.

p. 330 "Coca-Cola recently experimented":

Brian Dumaine, "Making Education Work," *Fortune* (Special Issue), Spring 1990, p. 12.

p. 331 "Arco is a good example":

Ann Kyle, "The Ultimate Capital Investment," *California Business*, July 1990, p. 36.

p. 331 "Not surprisingly, Apple and IBM":

Nancy J. Perry, "Computers Come of Age in Class," *Fortune* (Special Issue), Spring 1990, p. 72.

p. 332 "And in 1989":

Brian Dumaine, "Making Education Work," *Fortune* (Special Issue), Spring 1990, p. 12.

p. 332 "When you put risk capital":

Ann M. Morrison, "Saving Our Schools," *Fortune* (Special Issue), Spring 1990, p. 8.

p. 334 "must consider its expenditures":

James O'Toole, *Vanguard Management*, Berkley Books, 1987, p. 369.

p. 341 "Take General Electric. GE, which relies heavily":

Andrew Kupfer, "Turning Students On to Science," *Fortune* (Special Issue), Spring 1990, p. 82.

p. 342 "Control Data: Social Contributions as Business Venture":

Adopted from James E. Liebig, *Business Ethics: Profiles in Civic Virtue*, Fulcrum Publishing, 1990, pp. 44–51.

p. 343 "They come in here to see":

David Kirkpatrick, "Environmentalism: The New Crusade," *Fortune*, February 12, 1990, p. 44.

p. 343 "My primary motivation is environmental":

Ibid.

p. 343 "One telling statistic: All but 7 of the 305 Fortune 500":

Susan E. Kuhn, "How Business Helps Schools," *Fortune* (Special Issue), Spring 1990, p. 91.

p. 343 "honor an exemplary program which":

America's Corporate Conscience Awards, Press Release, March 29, 1990.

p. 345 "One study cited":

Barbara Marsh, "Merchants Mobilize to Battle Wal-Mart in a Small Community," *The Wall Street Journal*, June 5, 1991, p. 1.

p. 345 "I'd have liked to":

Ibid.

p. 346 "There is $135 billion in air-conditioning":

John Holusha, "Ed Woolard Walks DuPont's Tightrope," *New York Times*, October 14, 1990, p. F1. Copyright 1990/91 by The New York Times Company. Reprinted by permission.

p. 346 "Hey, civilization has its costs":

David Kirkpatrick, "Environmentalism: The New Crusade," *Fortune*, February 12, 1990, p. 44.

p. 348 "Some people argue that doing what's right":

Ann Kyle, "The Ultimate Capital Investment," *California Business*, July 1990, p. 36.

p. 350 "among the fastest growing, most profitable major American firms":

Alan L. Wilkins, *Developing Corporate Character*, Jossey-Bass Publishers, 1989, p. 74.

p. 350 "During our most difficult crisis":

Ann Kyle, "The Ultimate Capital Investment," *California Business*, July 1990, p. 36.

p. 350 "A 1989 poll conducted by Opinion Research":

Ibid.

p. 350 "41 percent of Americans were angry enough to say":

David Kirkpatrick, "Environmentalism: The New Crusade," *Fortune*, February 12, 1990, p. 44.

p. 350 "[A] lot of young people are asking themselves":

Georg Winter, *Business and the Environment,* McGraw-Hill, 1988, Epilogue.

p. 351 "I have seen people whose lives":

Ann Kyle, "The Ultimate Capital Investment," *California Business,* July 1990, p. 36.

p. 351 "Corporations have great power and where":

Charles Hampden-Turner, "Humanistic Psychology and the Crisis of the American Economy," a keynote presentation made to the International Association of Humanistic Psychology at Mills College, Oakland, California, August 6, 1987.

Corporate Index

A

Ace Hardware, 191, 209, 210
Aetna Life & Casualty, 335
Airborne, 147–8, 178
Air Products and Chemicals, 140
American Bankers Insurance Group of
    Miami, 330
American Express, 30
America West Airlines
    child care at, 336
    company profile, 85–88
    employee benefits at, 57, 106
    employee cross-training at, 100, 101–2
    employee participation at, 89–94, 103,
        122–24
    financial health of, 67–68
    hiring at, 244, 245, 246
    introduction, 85
    reward system at, 257
    values of, 99
    other references, 77, 250
Apple, 143, 305, 331
ARCO, 76–77, 323, 329, 331
Arthur Andersen, 210
AT&T
    child care and, 296
    internal venture program at, 254
    job benefits at, 109
    reward system at, 261
    teamwork at, 175
    training and, 331
Avis, 255
Avon, 284, 297, 302

B

Baldor Electric, 327–28
Bell Atlantic, 155
Ben & Jerry's Ice Cream, 97

Body Shop, The
    company profile, 310–12
    environmental responsibility and,
        321–22
    financial health of, 349
    introduction, 309–10
    social responsibility and, 313–15, 318,
        333, 339, 351, 352
    other references, 51, 57, 97, 222, 377

C

Captive Aire Systems, 255–56
Chrysler Corporation, 30, 31, 73–74, 81
Cincinnati Milacron, 168–69
Coca-Cola, 330
Com Systems, 245
Continental Airlines, 28, 29, 85, 89
Control Data, 342–43
Corning Glass Works, 109
Crocker Bank, 58
Cummins Engine Company, 343

D

Dayton-Hudson, 296
Digital Equipment Corporation
    employee diversity and, 367–70
    employee diversity at, 265–69, 297,
        304, 305
    introduction, 265
    other references, 222, 304, 305
Disney World, 245
Du Pont
    environment and, 49, 323, 324, 346
    family needs and, 108–9

General Index

447